Psychology for Professional Groups

Psychology for Teachers

Psychology for Professional Groups

Series Editors: Antony J. Chapman and Anthony Gale

Psychology for Professional Groups is a new series of major textbooks published with the British Psychological Society. Each is edited by a teacher with expertise in the application of psychology to professional practice and covers the key topics in the training syllabus. The editors have drawn upon a series of specially commissioned topic chapters prepared by leading psychologists and have set them within the context of their various professions. A tutor manual is available for each text and includes examination questions, practical exercises and projects, further reading and general guidance for the tutor. Each textbook shows in a fresh, original and authoritative way how psychology may be applied in a variety of professional settings, and how practitioners may improve their skills and gain a deeper understanding of themselves. There is also a general tutorial text incorporating the complete set of specialist chapters and their associated teaching materials.

Published with this book
Psychology and Management. Cary L. Cooper
Psychology for Social Workers. Martin Herbert

Subsequent titles
Psychology for Physiotherapists. E. N. Dunkin
Psychology for Occupational Therapists. Fay Fransella
Psychology and Medicine. David Griffiths
Psychology for Nurses and Health Visitors. John Hall
Psychology for Careers Counselling. Ruth Holdsworth
Psychology for Speech Therapists. Harry Purser
Psychology and People: A tutorial text. Antony J. Chapman and Anthony Gale

Psychology for Teachers

David Fontana

First published 1981 by THE BRITISH PSYCHOLOGICAL SOCIETY
and THE MACMILLAN PRESS LTD.

Distributed by The Macmillan Press Ltd, London and
Basingstoke. Associated companies and representatives
throughout the world.

ISBN 0 333 318 587 (hard cover)
ISBN 0 333 318 803 (paper cover)

Printed in Great Britain by Wheatons of Exeter

Note: throughout these texts, the masculine pronouns have
been used for succinctness and are intended to refer to both
females and males.

The conclusions drawn and opinions expressed are those of
the authors. They should not be taken to represent the
views of the publishers.

Contents

Foreword

This book is one of a series, the principal aims of which
are to illustrate how psychology can be applied in particular professional contexts, how it can improve the skills
of practitioners, and how it can increase the practitioners'
and students' understanding of themselves.

Psychology is taught to many groups of students and is
now integrated within prescribed syllabuses for an increasing number of professions. The existing texts which teachers
have been obliged to recommend are typically designed for
broad and disparate purposes, and consequently they fail to
reflect the special needs of students in professional
training. The starting point for the series was the
systematic distillation of views expressed in professional
journals by those psychologists whose teaching specialisms
relate to the applications of psychology. It soon became
apparent that many fundamental topics were common to a
number of syllabuses and courses; yet in general introductory textbooks these topics tend to be embedded amongst
much superfluous material. Therefore, from within the
British Psychological Society, we invited experienced
teachers and authorities in their field to write review
chapters on key topics. Forty-seven chapters covering 23
topics were then available for selection by the series'
Volume Editors. The Volume Editors are also psychologists
and they have had many years of involvement with their
respective professions. In preparing their books, they have
consulted formally with colleagues in those professions.
Each of their books has its own combination of the
specially-prepared chapters, set in the context of the
specific professional practice.

Because psychology is only one component of the various
training curricula, and because students generally have
limited access to learned journals and specialist texts, our
contributors to the series have restricted their use of
references, while at the same time providing short lists of
annotated readings. In addition, they have provided review
questions to help students organize their learning and
prepare for examinations. Further teaching materials, in the
form of additional references, projects, exercises and class
notes, are available in Tutor Manuals prepared for each
book. A comprehensive tutorial text ('Psychology and
People'), prepared by the Series Editors, combines in a

single volume all the key topics, together with their associated teaching materials.

It is intended that new titles will be added to the series and that existing titles will be revised in the light of changing requirements. Evaluative and constructive comments, bearing on any aspect of the series, are most welcome and should be addressed to us at the BPS in Leicester.

In devising and developing the series we have had the good fortune to benefit from the advice and support of Dr Halla Beloff, Professor Philip Levy, Mr Allan Sakne and Mr John Winckler. A great burden has been borne by Mrs Gail Sheffield, who with skill, tact and courtesy, has managed the production of the series: to her and her colleagues at the BPS headquarters and at the Macmillan Press, we express our thanks.

Antony J. Chapman
UWIST, Cardiff

Anthony Gale
University of Southampton

May 1981

Introduction
David Fontana

The purpose of this book is to acquaint the reader with
those areas of psychology of most practical value to the
teacher. It deals, therefore, not only with matters relating
directly to the classroom, but with matters pertaining to
the child's background outside school and to his own self-
perceptions and self-concepts. The teacher's task can only
be clarified if he has a knowledge of children as complete
persons rather than simply as individuals who spend the
hours from nine o'clock until four sitting in classrooms.
The child's personality, his ability to learn, his motivation, his social behaviour, his attitudes towards school,
are all formed as a consequence of a complex set of inter-
related factors which begin at birth (and even before) and
extend throughout each moment of his waking life. By the
time he has finished this book the reader should have a
clear idea of what these factors are, and of how they
influence child behaviour. He should also have a clear idea
of the part the teacher himself plays in the determination
of this behaviour, and of how the teacher can best help
children to benefit from the learning opportunities that
school has to offer.

The application of psychology to education has a long
and honoured history, and stretches back to the first
occasion when man tried to influence the behaviour of the
young. But it is only in comparatively recent years that the
association between the two subjects has been given a firmly
scientific basis. By this we mean that it is only during the
last 60 years or so that psychology has developed the
precision and methodology that allow it to make accurate
generalizations about child behaviour, and to provide the
teacher with the kind of information necessary if he is to
make objective professional decisions and judgements. Without such information, he can only fall back upon the sort of
anecdotal evidence that we often hear when people are discussing children. We hear, for example, that children are
supposed to be basically honest (or dishonest), that they
like (or do not like) firm discipline, that they have (or
have not) a sense of fair play, that they learn best in
informal (or in formal) teaching environments, that they are
influenced (or not influenced) by what they see on television and so on. One school of thought has it that

1

children's behaviour is the result of conditioning, another that they have the freedom to decide for themselves. We are told on the one hand that abilities such as intelligence are largely inherited, and on the other that they are largely the result of environmental influences. Small wonder that faced with such conflicting statements the young teacher often feels confused, and decides in the end he must make up his own mind on these and other important matters.

It would be wrong to suggest that modern psychology has final answers to all the questions that face us in education. Children (and teachers) are individuals, and often must be studied as individuals before detailed guidance on particular problems can be given. And, in any case, there are still large gaps in our knowledge that remain to be filled. Human behaviour is very complex and its measurement and assessment fraught with many difficulties. It is in fact this very complexity that gives the study of psychology much of its fascination. But psychology helps the teacher recognize the factors that influence child behaviour and learning, and assists him in developing strategies to cope with the tasks that face him in the classroom. Furthermore, it helps him examine his own general professional behaviour, and to identify areas where this behaviour may itself have contributed towards particular problems that may have arisen. As we stress repeatedly throughout the book, psychology shows us that no child's behaviour can be fully understood unless we study also the behaviour of others - teachers, parents, school friends - towards him. Each individual stands at the centre of a complex matrix of inter-related influences, each of which must be taken into account if we are to comprehend why he lives his life as he does. In the case of the child this matrix is of particular importance since he is still at an early formative stage in his development, very much dependent upon the behaviours of others towards him. When the teacher, for example, speaks critically of the child's performance in a particular subject, the child may get the impression that this indicates he lacks basic ability in it, and his future performance may deteriorate even further. If we are to help him improve his standards we must look therefore not only at the gaps in his knowledge, but at the way in which the teacher, albeit unwittingly, has been undermining his confidence in his own potential.

Psychology also helps us answer some of the questions on the origins of individual differences. Are we born different, or do we simply become different as the result of experience? Put another way, are individual differences genetically or environmentally determined? By individual differences we mean not only intelligence but such things as personality, creativity and motor skills. As we shall see, these answers are of critical importance for the teacher since they indicate some of the limits to the influence which education can have upon our lives. If individual differences are largely inherited then there is little that education can do beyond developing what is already there. If, on the other hand, these differences are mainly the result of environment, then education has enormous potential to redress and alter the consequences of early disadvantage and to help all children achieve the same high standards.

The book deals with children from an early age through into adolescence and the end of compulsory schooling, but this does not mean that the reader should pick out only those sections that apply to the ages he plans to teach or is actually teaching. For a full understanding of older children the secondary school teacher needs to know something of the formative influences that have been at work during the earlier part of their lives, while the primary school teacher needs to know something of the problems that may lie ahead of his children as they grow older if he is to play his part in helping them develop the skills and strategies necessary to cope with them. The book is designed for both serving teachers and students in training, and the emphasis throughout is upon the practicalities of the teacher's task. Thus theoretical areas of psychology that may be of interest in themselves but that have little real application for what the teacher actually does with children are avoided. A high premium is also placed upon clarity, so that the non-specialist should be able to read the book without experiencing undue difficulties in understanding any of the points raised. Finally, the book can be read as a whole or dipped into, depending upon the needs of the reader. The important thing is that it should be of some use.

The plan of the book
The plan of the book is simple. In Part I we look at the child in the home, indicating for example the importance of parent-child relationships, the influence of family size upon school performance, and the apparent links between social class and success in school. Part II then examines cognitive factors (i.e. mental factors to do with thinking, intelligence and learning) while Part III looks at affective factors (i.e. emotional factors to do with personality, attitudes and values). Part IV looks at social factors; that is, at the factors involved in the child's relationships with the teacher and with the classroom group, and at the teacher himself, at what we know about the qualities that make the successful teacher and at the ways in which we study interaction between the teacher and the class.

Each chapter outlines current knowledge in the areas concerned, and concludes (except for the last three chapters, for reasons explained on page 341) with a section which points out its relevance for the work of the teacher. In each case this section is prepared by the present writer, as is the material that forms the main part of many of the chapters. In common with the other texts in the 'Psychology for Professional Groups' series, however, certain chapters contain contributions from other authors, and where this is the case acknowledgement is made in the chapter concerned. Each chapter in the book contains suggestions for further reading, together with a list of questions and discussion points. These questions are not designed so much to test the reader's factual knowledge as to draw attention to some of the most important issues discussed in the chapter and to start him thinking creatively about them. Additional questions and suggestions for projects, plus further guidance on reading, are given in a tutor manual available to accompany this volume.

Part one

The Child in the Home

Introduction   The child's social life begins in the home. Throughout his formative years he spends more of his waking hours in and around the home than he does in school. For a five-year-old child the ratio is approximately 5:3 in favour of the home, and for an adolescent it rises to about 2:1. His closest relationships are usually formed within the home, and he also locates there most of his physical possessions and most of his leisure interests. Not surprisingly, therefore, the influence of the home is of critical importance in a child's psychological development generally, and in particular in the use he makes of his abilities, in the formation of his attitudes and opinions, and in the development of his motivation towards school and towards a future career.

In the chapter by Schaffer which follows, the author examines the most important issues associated with the child's early social development in the home. Some of the points raised are emphasized further when we discuss the general relevance of this development for the teacher at the end of the chapter, while others will be returned to in Part III when we come to personality development.

I

Social Development in Early Childhood

H. R. Schaffer

Psychologists study children for two main reasons. First, they want to find out how a helpless, naïve and totally dependent baby manages in due course to become a competent, knowledgeable adult. They are interested therefore in studying the process of development. The second reason stems from the many social problems associated with childhood. Should we protect children from viewing violence on television? Are children of mothers who go out to work more likely to become delinquent? Does hospitalization in the early years produce later difficulties? How can one mitigate the effects of divorce on children? Why do some parents become baby batterers? Increasingly the psychologist is asked to examine such problems and produce answers useful to society. It is primarily to this aspect of child psychology that we shall pay attention here.

How a child develops depends very much on the people around him. From them he learns the skills and values needed for social living, from the use of knives and forks to knowing the difference between right and wrong. Other people are always around the child, influencing him by means of example and command, and none more so at first than the members of his own family. On them depend the initial stages of his socialization.

Disadvantaged children and their families

It is, of course, only too apparent that not every family carries out its socializing task with equal effectiveness. By way of illustration, let us look at the way in which the child's intellectual development is shaped by his social environment.

At one time it was thought that intelligence is entirely determined by an individual's inborn endowment. There are few who now believe this: it seems rather that the environment in which a child is reared can have a powerful effect on his development.

The issue has been much debated in relation to the poor educational achievement of 'disadvantaged' children. These are children who come from the economically and socially most deprived sectors of the community and who so often

8

appear to be at a severe disadvantage when first starting school, because (as it has been put) 'they have learnt not to learn'. Their failure in the education system, in other words, is ascribed not so much to some genetic inferiority as to factors operating in the home, which result in an inability to make use of whatever intellectual capacities they have.

A great many schemes have been launched to counter this situation, especially in the USA. Some of the earlier efforts, designed to give children some extra training in basic cognitive skills before school entry, were clearly inadequate and produced no lasting benefits. This is partly because the schemes were too brief, partly because they came too late in the child's life, but partly also because they left untouched the home situation. Given a conflict of values about education between home and school it is highly likely that the home will always win. It is there that the child has already lived and learned for several years before ever starting school, and it is therefore significant that more recent efforts have attempted to involve the parents as well as the child or even to work solely through the parents.

There is now little doubt that parents can enhance or suppress the child's educational potential. One way in which they apparently do this is by the extent to which they foster the development of language: a function so necessary for the expression of intelligence. There are pronounced social class differences in the style of language mothers use to communicate with their children; in addition, however, it has also been shown that mothers from disadvantaged homes engage in face-to-face talking with their infants less frequently than middle-class mothers. The poorer child often lives in much noisier surroundings than the middle-class child in his quiet suburban home, but to profit from stimulation the young child must be exposed to it under the personalized conditions that only the to-and-fro reciprocity of a face-to-face situation provides. It is in this respect that many lower-class 'socially deprived children' are at a disadvantage.

Child effects on adults

Let us not now jump to the conclusion that children's development is totally a matter of what parents do to them. A child is never just a passive being that one can mould into whatever shape the adult desires. Even the youngest baby can already exert an influence on his caretakers and so help to determine how they behave towards him.

Take an obvious example: babies cry and thereby draw attention to themselves. It is a sound that can have a most compelling effect on the adult: we have all heard of the mother who can sleep through a thunderstorm, but is immediately awoken by her child's whimper in the next room. The baby, by this powerful signal, can initiate the interaction: he can thereby influence both the amount and the timing of attention which others provide.

9

Babies come into the world as individuals. Some are active and restless, others quiet and content; some are highly sensitive, others are emotionally robust and easygoing. The kind of care provided for one is therefore inappropriate for another, and any sensitive mother will therefore find herself compelled to adopt practices suitable for her individual child. A good example is provided by babies' differences in 'cuddliness'. Not all babies love being held and cuddled: some positively hate it and resist such contact by struggling and, unless released, by crying. It has been found that these 'non-cuddlers' tend to be more active and restless generally, and to be intolerant of all types of physical restraint (as seen when they are being dressed or tucked into bed). The mother is accordingly forced to treat her child in a manner that takes into account his 'peculiarity': when frightened or unwell these children cannot be comforted by being held close but have to be offered other forms of stimulation such as bottles, biscuits or soothing voices. Each mother must therefore show considerable flexibility in adjusting to the specific requirements of her child.

There is one further, and perhaps unexpected, example one can quote of the way in which parents are influenced by their children. It concerns the phenomenon of baby battering, which has attracted so much attention in recent years. It is by no means a new phenomenon; historically speaking, it is probably as old as the family itself. What is new is public concern that such a thing can happen, and this in turn has given rise to the need for research into such cases. As a result of various investigations it is now widely agreed that violence results from a combination of several factors: the presence of financial, occupational and housing problems facing the family; the parents' emotional immaturity which makes it difficult for them to deal with such problems; their social isolation from potential sources of help such as relatives and neighbours; and, finally, some characteristic of the battered child that singles him out as a likely victim.

It is the last factor that is particularly relevant to us, for it illustrates once again that the way in which parents treat their children is influenced by the children themselves. There is evidence that children most likely to be battered are 'difficult': they are more likely to be sickly, or to have been born prematurely, or to have feeding and sleeping problems. Being more difficult to rear, they make extra demands that the parents are just not able to meet. The child's condition acts on the parent's inadequacy, and so the child, unwittingly, contributes to his own fate.

Mother–child mutuality

It is apparent that children do not start life as psychological nonentities. From the beginning they already have an individuality that influences the adults around them. Thus a mother's initial task is not to create something out of nothing; it is rather to dovetail her behaviour to that of the child.

Such dovetailing takes many forms. Take our previous example of the non-cuddlers. If the mother herself has a preference for close physical contact with the baby which he then rejects, some mutual readjustment will need to take place. Fortunately, most mothers quickly adjust and find other ways of relating to the child. It is only when they are too inflexible, or interpret the baby's behaviour as rejection, that trouble can arise from a mismatch.

Mutual adjustment is the hallmark of all interpersonal behaviour; it can be found in even the earliest social interactions. The feeding situation provides a good example. Should babies be fed by demand or by a rigid, pre-determined schedule? Advice by doctors and nurses has swung fashion-wise, sometimes stressing the importance of exerting discipline from the very beginning and of not 'giving in', at other times pointing to the free and easy methods of primitive tribes as the 'natural way'. In actual fact each mother and baby, however they may start off, sooner or later work out a pattern which satisfies both partners. On the one hand, there are few mothers who can bear to listen for long to a bawling infant unable as yet to tell the time; on the other hand, one should not under-estimate the ability of even very young babies to adjust to the demands of their environment. An example is provided by an experiment, carried out many years ago, in which two groups of babies were fed during the first ten days of life according to a three-hour and four-hour schedule respectively. Within just a few days after birth each baby had already developed a peak of restlessness just before the accustomed feeding time, and this became particularly obvious when the three-hour group was shifted to a four-hour schedule and so had to wait an extra hour for their feed. In time, however, these babies too became accustomed to the new timetable and showed the restlessness peak at four-hourly intervals. We can see here a form of adaptation to social demands that must represent one of the earliest forms of learning.

Not surprisingly, the major responsibility for mutual adjustment lies initially with the adult. The degree of flexibility one can expect from very young children is limited. Yet the very fact that they are involved in social interactions from the very beginning of life means that they have the opportunity of gradually acquiring the skills necessary to become full partners in such exchanges. Observations of give-and-take games with babies at the end of the first year have made this point. Initially the baby knows only how to take: he has not learned that his behaviour is just one part of a sequence, that he needs to take turns with the other person, and that the roles of the two participants are interchangeable (one being a giver, the other a taker). Such and other rules of behaviour he will learn in time; they form the basis for much of social intercourse, and it is through social intercourse that the child acquires them in the first place.

11

Socialization is sometimes portrayed as a long drawn-out battle, as a confrontation between wilful young children and irritated parents that must at all cost be resolved in favour of the latter. Goodness knows such battles occur, yet they are far from telling us everything about the process of socialization. There is a basic mutuality between parent and child without which interaction would not be possible. The sight of the mother's face automatically elicits a smile from the baby; that produces a feeling of delight in the mother and causes her in turn to smile back and to talk or tickle or pick up, in this way calling forth further responses from the baby. A whole chain of interaction is thus started, not infrequently initiated by the baby. Mother and child learn about each other in the course of these interactions, and more often than not mutual adjustment is brought about by a kind of negotiation process in which both partners show some degree of flexibility. On the mother's part, this calls for sensitivity to the particular needs and requirements of her child, an ingredient of parenthood that we return to subsequently; on the child's part, it refers to one of the most essential aspects of social living that he must learn early on.

**me conditions that
ter development**

If we are to promote the mental health and social integration of children, it is necessary to identify the factors that further, or on the contrary hinder, such an aim. We all have our favourite theories as to why some children do not develop in what we regard as a desirable manner: not enough parental discipline, too much violence on television, the declining influence of religion, the social isolation of today's family, and so on. It is much more difficult, however, to substantiate through objective research that any one factor does play a part. Nevertheless, there are some conclusions to which we can point.

The blood-bond: myth or reality?

Is it essential, or at least desirable, that children should be brought up by their natural parents? Is a woman who conceived and bore a child by that very fact more fitted to care for this child than an unrelated individual?

This is no academic question. Children have been removed by courts of law from the foster parents with whom they had lived nearly all their lives and to whom they had formed deep attachments, in order to restore them to their biological mother from whom they may have been apart since the early days of life, and all because of the 'blood-bond'. Yet such a thing is a complete myth. There is nothing at all to suggest that firm attachments cannot grow between children and unrelated adults who have taken over the parental role. The notion that the biological mother, by virtue of being the biological mother, is uniquely capable of caring for her child is without foundation.

Were it otherwise, the whole institution of adoption would be in jeopardy. Yet there is nothing to suggest that adoptive parents are in any way inferior to natural parents. In a study by Barbara Tizard (to which we shall refer again), children who had been in care throughout their early years were followed up on leaving care. One group of children was adopted, another returned to their own families. It was found that the latter did less well than the adopted children, both in the initial stages of settling in and in their subsequent progress. The reason lay primarily in the attitudes of the two sets of parents: the adoptive gr up worked harder at being parents, possibly just because the child was not their own. There have been a good many studies which have examined the effects of adoption, and virtually all stress the high proportion of successful cases to be found. And this despite the difficulties such children may have had to face, such as problems in the pre-adoption phase and the knowledge gained later on of the fact of their adoption. Successful parenting is a matter of particular personality characteristics that need to be identified, not of 'blood'.

Fathers as parents: more myths?

Do children have to be cared for primarily by women? Is there something about females that makes them more suitable for this task than males? What part should fathers play in the child's upbringing?

The answer is simple. There is no 'should' or 'should not'. It is a matter of what each society and each family decides about the division of roles between the parents. There have in fact been marked changes over the last few decades in the extent to which fathers participate in child care. They now do so to a far greater extent than they used to, and this trend is continuing. For instance, with increasing unemployment it is no longer uncommon to find families in which a complete role reversal has taken place: mother, having found a job, goes out to work, leaving her unemployed husband in charge of home and children. Fortunately, there is no evidence to indicate that the biological make-up of men makes them unfit for this task or even necessarily inferior to women in this respect. Parenting is unisex; the reasons for the traditional division of labour (such as the need to breast-feed the child and the importance of using men's greater physical strength for hunting and tilling the fields) are no longer applicable.

Children brought up without a father are more likely to encounter difficulties than those in a complete family. There are various reasons for this. One is that in any single-parent family the remaining parent must cope with a great multiplicity of stresses - financial, occupational, or emotional - and the strain felt by him or (more often) her is very likely to have repercussions for the child too. Again, a fatherless boy has no model to imitate, and the developmental tasks of acquiring sex-appropriate behaviour may be more difficult. And, finally, the child isolated with his mother and caught up in one all-encompassing relationship does not have the same chance of learning from the beginning about some of the complexities of the social world: having two parents helps him to learn at once that not all people are alike and that he must adapt his own behaviour according to their different characteristics and different demands.

Parenthood: full-time or part-time?

Until fairly recently there was a widespread belief among parents and professional workers that children in the pre-school period required full-time mothering, and that it was the duty of mothers to stay with the child night and day, 24 hours on end. Otherwise, it was feared, children's mental health would suffer.

We can look at this situation from both the mother's and the child's point of view. As far as mothers are concerned, a crucial consideration is the recent finding of an extremely high incidence of depression among house-bound women. With no outlet such as a job, tied to the house by the presence of several dependant children, a large proportion of mothers (especially among the working class) become isolated and hence depressed. Mothers, on the other hand, who do go out to work are far less likely to suffer from depression, anxiety and feelings of low self-esteem.

As far as the children are concerned, comparisons of those with mothers at work and those with mothers at home have not found any differences between them. Far from being adversely affected, the former may even stand to gain both intellectually and socially. The intellectual effects stem from the extra stimulation and extra provision of play materials that most children in day care obtain: a point of particular significance for those from disadvantaged backgrounds. And, socially, not only is there no evidence that the child's attachment to the mother is in some way 'diluted' by a daily period of being apart, but also the child in day care has the enormous advantage of coming into contact with other children. The benefit of such experience for social development has until quite recently been overlooked; yet other children, even in the early years, can exercise a considerable socializing influence, and in addition may further the child's diversification of social behaviour. After all, the more a child is encouraged to adapt to a variety of other individuals the more his repertoires of social skills will grow.

Thus a daily period away from mother may produce good rather than harm. There is, however, one important proviso, and this concerns the quality of the substitute care which the child receives. For one thing, there is a need for consistency: a young child continually being left with different people is likely to become bewildered and upset. And for another, we have the enormous problem of illegal childminders, looking after an estimated 100,000 children in Britain. According to recent findings, the quality of care provided by such childminders is only too frequently of an unsatisfactory nature, being marked by ignorance and neglect that in some cases can be quite appalling. It is only in the officially provided facilities, such as nursery schools, that the care given by trained staff is such that the social and intellectual benefits can be felt.

Sensitive and insensitive parents

A child's development does not take place in a vacuum; it occurs because the people responsible for his care carefully and sensitively provide him with the kind of environment that will foster his growth. They do so not only by such conscious decisions as what toys to buy him for Christmas or which nursery school to send him to, but also quite unconsciously by the manner in which they relate to him.

Take the language which adults use in talking to a child. This is in many ways strikingly different from the language used to address another adult: it has a much more restricted vocabulary, a considerably simplified grammar, and a great deal of repetition. In addition, it is characterized by a slowing down in the rate of speech, a high pitch of voice, and the use of special intonation patterns. Not only mothers but most adults will quite unconsciously adopt this style when confronted by a young child. What is more, the younger the child the more marked is the simplification, repetition, slowing down and all the other characteristics listed. It is as though the adult is making allowance for the child's limited ability to absorb whatever one tells him, thereby showing sensitivity to the abilities and requirements of that particular child.

Such examples of (usually quite unconscious) sensitivity in relating to children are numerous. Watch how a mother hands her baby a rattle to grasp: how carefully she adjusts the manner and speed with which she offers the toy to the still uncertain reaching skills of the child. She shows thereby that she is able to see things from the child's point of view, that she is aware of his requirements and can respond to these appropriately. Sensitivity is an essential part of helping a child to develop. Children brought up in institutions, in which they are all treated the same and where care is never personalized, become developmentally retarded. While most adults show sensitivity to children quite naturally, some parents are unfortunately devoid of this vital part of parenting. Why this is so we still do not know for certain; it does seem, however, that parents who themselves had a deprived childhood and did not themselves experience sensitive care are more likely to show the same attitude to their own children.

Are the early years special?

There is a widespread belief that experience in childhood, and particularly so in the earliest years, has a crucial formulative influence on later personality. Thus the early years are said to be the most important, and special care therefore needs to be taken to protect the child during this period against harmful experiences that might mark him for life. Let us look at the evidence for this belief.

The influence of child-rearing practices

According to Freud, a child's development is marked by a series of phases (oral, anal, genital) during which he is especially sensitive to certain kinds of experience. During the oral phase, for example, the baby is mainly concerned with activities like sucking, chewing, swallowing and biting, and the experiences that matter to him most thus include the manner of his feeding (breast or bottle), the timing of feeding (schedule or demand), the age when he is weaned, and so on. When these experiences are congenial to the child he passes on to the next developmental phase without difficulty; when they are frustrating and stressful, however, he remains 'fixated' at this stage in the sense that, even as an adult, he continues to show characteristics such as dependence and passivity in his personality make-up that distinguish babies at the oral stage. In this way Freud's theory suggests that there are definite links between particular kinds of infantile experiences on the one hand, and adult personality characteristics on the other.

However, this theory has not been borne out. A large number of investigations have compared breast-feeding with bottle-feeding, self-demand with rigidly scheduled regimes, early with later weaning, and other aspects of the child's early experience that could be expected to produce lasting after-effects. No such effects have been found. The sum total of these investigations adds up to the conclusion that specific infant care practices do not produce unvarying traces that may unfailingly be picked up in later life. Whatever their impact at the time, there is no reason to believe that these early experiences mark the child for good or ill for the rest of his life.

And just as well! Were it otherwise we would all be at the mercy of some single event, some specific parental aberration, that we happened to have experienced at some long-distant point in our past. Freud's theory made little allowance for the ameliorating influence of later experience, yet the more we study human development the more apparent it becomes that children, given the opportunity, are able to recuperate from many an early misfortune. Let us consider some other examples that make this point.

Maternal deprivation

In 1951 a report was published by John Bowlby, a British child psychiatrist, pointing to the psychological ill-effects of being deprived of maternal care during the early years. The evidence, Bowlby believed, indicated that a child must be with his mother during the crucial period of the first two or three years if he is to develop the ability to form relationships with other people. Deprived of a relationship with a permanent mother-figure at that time, such an ability will never develop. Thus children in institutions and long-term hospitals, where they are deprived of this necessity, become 'affectionless characters': that is, they are unable ever to form a deep, emotionally meaningful relationship with another person. Having missed out on a vital experience, namely being mothered, the child is mentally crippled for life. And that experience has to happen at a particular time, namely in the first years. No amount of good mothering subsequently can remedy the situation.

There is no doubt about the tremendous influence on the practice of caring for childen that Bowlby's ideas have had. And no wonder, for so many children are thereby implicated. Many thousands of children every year are taken into the care of local authorities; many thousands are admitted to hospital. Anything that can be done to improve the lot of so many children is therefore worth considering, and there is no doubt that in the last two decades a great deal has been done in the UK. Children's institutions have become less impersonal with the introduction of family group systems; there is greater emphasis on fostering children with ordinary families and, most important, far more stress is placed on prevention and keeping children with their own parents. Similarly, the psychological care of children in hospitals has improved greatly during this period. Visiting by parents is nowhere near as restricted as it was at one time; mother-baby units make it possible for parents to stay with their children; and again the emphasis on prevention means that rather more thought is now given to the need to admit the child in the first place.

Anyone who has ever seen a young child separated from his mother and admitted, say, to a strange hospital ward, where he is looked after by strangers and may be subjected to unpleasant procedures like injections, knows the extreme distress that one then finds. It is perhaps difficult for an adult to appreciate the depth of a child's panic when he has just lost his mother: a panic that may continue for days and only be succeeded by a depressive-like picture when the child withdraws into himself from a too painful world. Parents also know only too well about the insecurity which the child shows subsequently on return home, even after quite brief absences, when he dare not let the mother out of sight. There is no doubt about these dramatic short-term effects, and for their sake alone the steps taken to humanize procedures have been well worth while.

Far more problematic, however, is the question of long-term effects: that is, the suggestion that periods of prolonged maternal deprivation in the early years impair the child's capacity to form interpersonal relationships. What evidence we have here suggests that things are not as cut and dried as Bowlby indicated, and to make this point we can do no better than to turn to the report by Barbara Tizard to which we have already referred.

Tizard examined adopted children who had spent all their early lives in institutions, with no opportunity to form any stable attachments to any adult during that period. One might have expected them to be so marked by this experience as to be incapable of forming any emotional relationship to their adoptive parents and to show all the signs of the affectionless character. Yet this proved not to be the case. Nearly all these children developed deep attachments to their adoptive parents, and this included even a child placed as late as seven years of age. They did show some deviant symptoms, such as poor concentration and over-friendliness to strangers, but there was no indication that the inevitable outcome of their earlier upbringing was the 'affectionless character'. We must conclude that children's recuperative powers should not be under-estimated: given a new environment in which they receive very much improved treatment, the outlook can be good. There is no reason to believe that they will be marked for life by earlier misfortunes, just because these occurred early on.

Birth abnormalities and social class

When misfortune takes a 'physical' form, such as some abnormality of the birth process, the outcome is again not necessarily a poor one. Once more, it all depends on the child's subsequent experience.

Take such birth complications as anoxia (the severe shortage of oxygen in the brain) or prematurity. Follow-up studies of children who arrive in the world in such a precarious condition show that, on the basis of the child's condition at birth, it is impossible to predict his subsequent development. Two children coming into the world with the identical kind of pathology may develop along quite different lines. In one case, the child's condition at birth may give rise to a hole sequence of problems that continue and even mount up throughout his life; in the other, the difficulty is surmounted and the child functions normally.

The answer to this paradox lies in the different kinds of social environment in which the children develop. Where these are favourable the effects of the initial handicap may be minimized and in due course be overcome altogether. Where they are unfavourable the deficits remain and may even be amplified. The outcome, that is, depends not so much on the adverse circumstances of the child's birth as on the way in which his family then copes with the problem. And this, it has been found, is very much related to the social class to which the family belongs.

Social class is in many respects a nebulous concept. Nevertheless, it does refer to a set of factors (concerned with education, housing, health and so forth) that usually exert a continuing influence on the child throughout his formative years, and it is therefore not surprising that social and economic status turn out to have a much stronger influence on the course of development than some specific event at birth.

Thus even organic damage, just as the other aspects of a child's early experience, cannot in and of itself account for the particular course which that child's development takes. The irreversible effects of early experience have no doubt been greatly overrated. To believe in such effects is indeed dangerous for two reasons: first, because of the suggestion that during the first few years children are so vulnerable that they are beyond help if they do encounter some unfortunate experience; second, because it leads one to conclude that the latter years of childhood are not as important as the earlier years. All the evidence indicates that neither proposition is true: the effects of early experiences are reversible if need be, and older children may be just as affected by unfortunate circumstances (though possibly different ones) as younger children.

Conclusions

A child's development always occurs in a social context. Right from the beginning he is a member of a particular society, and the hopes and beliefs and expectations of those around him will have a crucial bearing on his psychological growth.

There is still a tremendous amount to be learned about the nature of the child's development and the way that it is affected by particular features of the environment. But in the meantime we can at least make one negative statement with some very positive implications: development can never be explained in terms of single causes. Thus we have seen that isolated events, however traumatic at the time, do not preclude later influences; that the one relationship with the mother does not account for everything. For that matter, development is not simply a matter of the environment acting on the child, for the child too can act on his environment. Not surprisingly, when confronted with a specific problem such as child abuse, we invariably find that a combination of circumstances needs to be considered if one is to explain it. Simple-minded explanations of the kind, 'juvenile delinquency is due to poverty (or heredity or lack of discipline)' never do justice to such a complex process as a child's development. And, similarly, action taken to prevent or treat which focusses on only single factors is most unlikely to succeed.

Questions

1. What are the principal controversial issues that have been raised by the study of maternal deprivation?
2. In what way can a child's social experience affect his intellectual development?
3. Can and should children be studied scientifically?
4. What advice would you give to the mother of a three year old who is considering taking up employment?
5. Why are the effects of early experience not necessarily permanent? Describe the circumstances under which you do find them to be long-lasting.
6. What is known about the reasons for baby battering? What effects on the child would you expect such treatment to have?
7. Discuss the pros and cons of parent education schemes. On what principles would you organize such a scheme?
8. What is the role of the father in the family?

9. How can one mitigate the effects of social disadvantage on the young child's intellectual development?
10. The parent-child relationship is said to be 'reciprocal'. Explain what is meant and provide examples.
11. Discuss the role of language in intellectual development, and examine the suggestion that there are class differences in language use.
12. Socialization - conflict or mutual adjustment?
13. What principles ought to guide a child's adoption?
14. Should education begin during the pre-school years? Explain what you mean by 'education' and discuss the settings in which it could take place.
15. Describe some of the social skills that children generally acquire during the early years, and the conditions that foster their development.
16. Explain what is meant by 'sensitivity' in a parent, and describe the likely effects on a child of its absence.
17. In what way is a family's social class likely to affect a child's development?
18. How do relationships with other children affect development during the pre-school years?
19. What implications does our knowledge of social development in the early years have for the upbringing of handicapped children?
20. What psychological principles should be taken into account in looking after children in residential care?

Annotated reading

Booth, T. (1975) Growing up in Society. London: Methuen (Essential Psychology Series).

> A general account of the influences that determine the way in which people grow up together. It takes into account not only the contribution of psychology but of such other social sciences as sociology, anthropology and social history. Its main value lies in the way child development is seen as occurring within the social context of each particular culture.

Bowlby, J. (1965) Child Care and the Growth of Love. Harmondsworth: Penguin.

> A more widely available version of Bowlby's classic report, first published in 1951, concerning the link between maternal deprivation and mental pathology. It should be read in conjunction with Rutter's book (see below).

Clarke, A.M. and Clarke, A.D.B. (1976) Early Experience: Myth and evidence. London: Open Books.

> A collection of contributions by different authors, all concerned with the question of whether early experience exerts a disproportionate influence on later development. A wide range of research studies are reviewed, and the consensus is against seeing the early years as

in some sense more important than later stages of development.

Dunn, J. (1977) Distress and Comfort. London: Fontana/Open Books.

Discusses some of the issues that concern parents during the early stages of the child's life, with particular reference to the causes and alleviation of distress, but places these issues in the wider context of the parent-child relationship and its cultural significance.

Kempe, R.S. and Kempe, H. (1978) Child Abuse. London: Fontana/Open Books.

An account by the foremost experts on child abuse of the state of knowledge regarding all aspects of this vexed area: causation, treatment and prevention.

Lewin, R. (1975) Child Alive. London: Temple-Smith.

Various researchers summarize in brief and popularized form what we have learned about child development in recent years. Most contributions deal with young children, and the book as a whole emphasizes how psychologically sophisticated even babies already are.

Rutter, M. (1972) Maternal Deprivation Reassessed. Harmondsworth: Penguin.

A systematic review of the evidence on this controversial topic that has accumulated since Bowlby highlighted its importance. Discusses the various studies that have been carried out on the effects, both short-and long-term, of early deprivation of maternal care.

Schaffer, H.R. (1971) The Growth of Sociability. Harmondsworth: Penguin.

A description of work on the earliest stages of social development. It shows how sociability in the early years has been studied, and reviews what we have learned about the way in which a child's first social relationships are formed.

Schaffer, H.R. (1977) Mothering. London: Fontana/Open Books.

An account of what is involved in being a parent. Brings together the evidence from recent studies of the mother-child relationship, and examines different conceptions of the parent's task. Gives special emphasis to the theme of mutuality in the relationship.

Tizard, B. (1977) Adoption: A second chance. London: Open Books.

An account of an important research study on children in residential care who were subsequently adopted. Raises some crucial issues regarding the effects of early experience and the public care of young children.

Relevance to the
teacher
DAVID FONTANA

Schaffer draws our attention firmly to the fact that
although abilities such as intelligence may be in part
determined by inheritance (a theme to which we return in
more detail in chapter 6), environment also has a powerful
effect upon their development, and 'there is now little
doubt that parents can enhance or suppress the child's
educational potential'. He also stresses that each child is
an individual, and responds to other people in different
ways. Thus the child himself plays a part in determining the
attitudes of his parents towards him. He may, for example,
be a contented child who takes minor irritations in his
stride, and who responds warmly to the affectionate advances
of his parents, or he may be difficult and restless and
apparently struggle hard to avoid these advances. This
question of inherited temperament is discussed more fully in
chapter 9, but the point to be emphasized here is that not
surprisingly most parents relate more readily, from the
early weeks of life onwards, to a contented, easy child than
to a more difficult, fractious one. And inevitably they
convey something of this to the child himself.

The teacher, of course, also finds it easier to get on
with some children than with others, but if we are to
understand human relationships we must accept that each
relationship is an interactive process. It takes the interaction between two people to make a relationship, and in the
course of this interaction each may antagonize the other.
Thus in the case of parents and children we may find that
sometimes their behaviour is mutually antagonistic from the
beginning, and becomes increasingly bitter and difficult as
the years go by and the opportunities for discord and misunderstanding multiply. At their worst, of course, relationships of this kind can lead to physical abuse of the child,
and it is important that teachers of all age groups should
be alert for the signs of the bruises and cuts that provide
evidence of this distressing phenomenon. It is estimated
that some two or three children die each week as a result
of physical assault from parents or parent substitutes, and
many thousands more receive physical injuries of varying
degrees of severity. The psychological damage inflicted upon
these unfortunate children, who go in constant physical fear
within the home, is incalculable. However, when discussing
the causes of baby battering and child abuse, Schaffer
indicates that we must look closely at the child himself as
well as at the parent. There is, he tells us 'some characteristic of the battered child that singles him out as a
likely victim', and where such children are brought up in
poor economic circumstances, in adverse living conditions,
and in social isolation (which together place added strains
upon the parents) then battering becomes more likely to
occur.

None of this should be taken as an attempt to excuse
baby battering and child abuse, or to place the blame upon
the child himself. All we are indicating is that factors in
the child's own behaviour, often apparent in the early weeks
of life and long before he has had a chance to learn to

modify them, may lead to parental frustration and antagonism. This antagonism upsets the child and intensifies his
problem behaviour, which causes increased parental antagonism, which in turn further upsets the child. The vicious
circle continues until, given the deprived circumstances to
which we have already made reference, the child is put
increasingly at risk. There is some evidence to suggest that
parents who lose control and abuse the child may themselves
have been victims of a violent and loveless childhood, and
therefore may not have learnt the lessons associated with
the giving and receiving of affection. They also appear,
perhaps as a consequence of this early deprivation, to be
lacking in maturity, and therefore perhaps in the ability to
cultivate patience and understanding in their dealings with
their children.

Baby battering and child abuse are the most disturbing
examples of the handicaps placed upon some children in their
early social development, but they are by no means the only
ones of interest to the teacher. In dealing with these
Schaffer destroys a number of hitherto influential myths. He
indicates, for instance, that provided there is good substitute care, normally there appears to be no deleterious
effect upon the child if the mother goes out to work, even
in the pre-school years. He also shows us that there is
nothing magical about the blood bond. Children do equally
well with good adoptive parents as with good biological
ones, since 'successful parenting is a matter of particular
personality characteristics ... not of blood'. Nor is there
any truth in the notion that fathers cannot carry out the
functions of parenting as effectively as mothers. With
employment patterns changing there is no good psychological
reason why fathers should not stay at home and look after
the children while mothers go out to work, provided both
parties are happy and efficient in their roles.

Language and social development
Of even more direct relevance to the teacher, however, is
Schaffer's discussion of the importance of language in the
child's social development. Although much of the early
communication between parent and child takes the form of
touch, language quickly establishes itself as the principal
medium of social contact, and the child who comes from a
verbally fluent and expressive household has enormous
advantages over the child whose home is verbally impoverished. By talking to the child, by encouraging him with
verbal praise, by naming the objects with which he plays,
and simply by conversing with him even though he is unable
to understand at first all that is said, the verbally fluent
parent quickly helps the child to build up a working vocabulary. As we see in chapter 5 when language is discussed in
more detail, it is through language that the child becomes
able to indulge in complex thinking, to communicate fully
with those around him, and to express his specific likes and
dislikes. Language therefore seems essential to the

development of much of the behaviour that we identify as
intelligent and, particularly in the early years of schooling, a child may be classified by a teacher as generally
backward when in fact his main problem may be simply that
he comes from a verbally unstimulating background. Such a
child may also sometimes appear physically more aggressive
than the norm because he lacks the linguistic sophistication
to relate to people more appropriately or to express his
feelings verbally. In addition, he will seem less well-
mannered in social encounters with adults, and will be less
ready to pick up language related skills such as reading and
writing.

Clearly the onus is upon the teacher to recognize the
social and intellectual inadequacies in a child that stem
from a verbally impoverished home life. Such recognition
not only allows the teacher to be more patient with the
child's problems, but also enables him to offer the right
kind of remedial help. The difficulties faced by the verbally impoverished child are often made worse, for example,
by the fact that throughout his school career he tends to
mix primarily with children who share his verbal disadvantage. His lack of verbal skills makes it hard for
him to form close friendships with more articulate children,
and in group work within the class he often gravitates
towards others performing at the same level as himself. The
teacher should see to it, therefore, by general classroom
organization, that this kind of child is given every chance
to take part in the sort of verbal encounters likely to
improve his skills. This means encouraging him to play and
work with verbally fluent children, and to make his rightful
contribution to classroom discussion and debate. Importantly, the teacher himself should take every opportunity to
talk to the child, using appropriate language, and should be
prepared to listen patiently and encouragingly to his
replies. Too often in a busy professional life the teacher
does not allow himself sufficient time to listen in this
manner while a relatively inarticulate child tries to tell
him something. Either he well-meaningly but misguidedly
finishes the child's sentence for him, or else he conveys to
the child by impatient signals that time is too valuable to
be taken up in this way. Not surprisingly the child either
grows antagonistic towards the teacher because he feels he
cannot be bothered with him, or he gives up the effort to
communicate any but the simplest ideas. Either way, the
teacher has failed to help the child redress the balance of
early disadvantage.

Social class
In his final paragraphs, Schaffer draws our attention to the
part played by social class in a child's development. This
is a difficult topic because many teachers and student
teachers very laudably dislike attaching social labels to
children and assigning them to so-called middle- or working-
class groups (more academic labels like 'upper social and

economic status' and 'lower social and economic status' prove little more acceptable). They argue that such labelling carries undesirable judgemental implications, and that in any case the use of class-orientated terms only helps to perpetuate social inequalities. Nevertheless, there are for the teacher a number of helpful practical lessons to be learnt from the research that has gone into the effects of social class background upon educational performance. Extended discussion of these lessons belongs more properly to a text on sociology than to one on psychology, but we must emphasize that such research indicates that the poor living conditions, the economic problems, the verbally unstimulating environment, and the lack of cultural and leisure facilities experienced by many lower social and economic status families inevitably act as a powerful handicap to the educational progress of their children. Such children often have nowhere at home where they can read quietly or do home-work, are not introduced to books within the family, have limited access to play facilities, to libraries, and to other cultural amenities like museums and theatres. They also find themselves in a social environment that may place little stress upon the importance of education, which offers them little vocational guidance, and which generally finds itself at odds with the aims and value systems held by the school. In consequence, a home-school conflict may develop, with the child taught quite different standards and patterns of behaviour at home from those which are placed before him at school. Inevitably the child is inclined to resolve the situation by rejecting the things for which the school appears to stand, and by identifying more with the home and with the mores of his immediate social environment. If he fails to do so then he may find himself at sharp variance with his family and with local peer groups.

The role of the teacher when working with children from social backgrounds of this kind is a complex one. He must uphold the values of the school, yet at the same time must sympathize with the problems of the child, and must not alienate him further by attempts to turn him against the sub-culture in which he has been raised. It is the job of the teacher to demonstrate to the child that the purpose of school is to help him to tackle the tasks and difficulties that face him in life. Thus, far from simply being concerned to measure him against academic standards and find him wanting, it has direct relevance for both his current experiences and for the years that lie ahead. The purpose of schooling is to increase the range of desirable possibilities that face the child in terms of his leisure and his vocational interest and, whenever a child dismisses school as irrelevant, careful thought must be given to the way in which this purpose is being translated into concrete curricular terms. Detailed discussion of the curriculum would be out of place in the present text, but from a psychological viewpoint we must emphasize that the relationship between teacher and child is very much conditioned by what the child supposes the school is able to offer him.

Family size

One final point on social factors and their relationship
to a child's educational progress is that family size
appears to be inversely correlated with school performance.
In their extensive longitudinal study Davie and his colleagues (Davie et al, 1972) found that, irrespective of
social class, children from large families tended to do less
well in reading, number work, oral skills and creativity
than only children or children with one or two siblings.
This may well be a direct consequence of the fact that in
large families parents normally have less time to spend with
individual children, and the latter therefore receive less
verbal and other forms of stimuli within the home. Davie
also noticed that it appears usually to be the oldest child
who suffers most, presumably because he is increasingly left
to fend for himself as younger and more demanding siblings
make their appearance on the scene. Obviously teachers can
do nothing about family size, but it behoves them to be
aware of the educational disadvantage often experienced by
children with many brothers and sisters, and to see that
everything possible is done to compensate for it within the
school. Children from large families may also prove particularly prone to demand teacher attention to make up for the
lack of adult attention within the home, and the teacher who
is aware of the reasons for such demands is more likely to
respond to them with the sympathy and the patience that they
warrant.

 The discussion of family size brings us to the broader
context of the family itself and its influence upon a
child's early development and his progress in school. We
have emphasized that the relationship between parent (or
parent substitute) and child is the most important one in a
child's social growth, but there are a number of other
issues within the home that also play their part. Problems
may occur, for example, not because the child relates
unsatisfactorily to one or other parent but because the
parents relate unsatisfactorily to each other, or because
there is alcoholism or mental illness or unemployment within
the family. In the next chapter, the author provides an
introduction to the wider study of the family, and draws
attention to the important issues that we must understand if
we are to appreciate the way in which it influences the
lives of its members. As he stresses in his opening paragraph, 'some problems which were initially identified as
"belonging" to the individual adult or child are now seen,
more appropriately, as problems of the family system'.

Reference

Davie, R., Butler, N. and Goldstein, H. (1972)
From Birth to Seven. London: Longmans.

Additional reading

Davie, R., Butler, N. and Goldstein, H. (1972) From Birth to Seven. London: Longmans.
    This book details the findings of the National Child Development Survey relevant to the early years of life, and contains much illuminating data.

Davie, R. (1978). In D. Fontana (ed.), The Education of the Young Child. London: Open Books.
    This is a discussion of social development.

Mussen, P.H., Conger, J.C. and Kagan, J. (1979) Child Development and Personality (5th edn), New York: Harper & Row.
    Contains excellent chapters on social development and allied topics.

Clarke, A.M. and Clarke, A.D.B. (1976) Early Experience, Myth and Evidence. London: Open Books.
    Examines the particular place of learning and early relationships in social development.

Lee, V. (1973) Social Relationships and Language. Bletchley: Open University Press.
    A good account of the relationship between social factors and linguistic development.

Kellmer-Pringle, M. (1974) The Needs of Children. London: Hutchinson.
    This looks sympathetically at all aspects of the social and other needs of the young child.

Wedge, P. and Prosser, H. (1973) Born to Fail? London: Arrow Books.
    This book looks specifically at underprivileged children.

Parke, R.D. and Collmer, C.W. (1975) Child abuse: an interdisciplinary approach. In E. M. Hetherington (ed.), Review of Child Development Research, Volume 5. Chicago: University of Chicago Press.
    Covers the distressing phenomenon of child battering.

2

The Family
Neil Frude

Many people are professionally concerned with aspects of family life. The family is studied by anthropologists concerned with the ways in which social patterning is organized in different cultures, by sociologists concerned with the ways in which the institution of the family mediates the relationship between wider society and the individuals within it, and the psychologist. The psychologist may regard the family as a background against which to view the individual, asking perhaps how the parents influence the development of a child or how families of alcoholics may help the individual to overcome difficulties, or alternatively the family itself may be the unit of study. The family is a small group and we can observe the patterns of communication within it, the process of mutual decision making, and so forth. It is a system, with individuals as sub-units or elements within. Typically, psychologists have focussed their interests on the biological and social nature of the individual, but they are now becoming increasingly concerned not only with individuals or even 'individuals in relationships', but with the relationships themselves. This has come about partly because studies have repeatedly shown how very much the individual is affected by the social context, by special intimate relationships and in particular by those few very close relationships within, typically, the household unit. The reciprocal and interactional nature of these influences has become more and more apparent so that relationships have now become topics of interest and study in their own right.

Many other professionals are interested not so much in studying the nature of family relationships but in actually dealing with families, particularly those with problems, and the experiences of social workers, marriage counsellors, lawyers, doctors and many others have provided invaluable evidence for psychological insight and research, and at the same time identified problems with which the applied psychologist might be able to provide some help. Clinical and educational psychologists, for example, are increasingly working within the family context and some problems which were initially identified as 'belonging' to the individual adult or child are now seen, more appropriately, as problems of the 'family system'. Also, psychologists working with handicapped children, for example, have come to recognize that the powerful influence and involvement of the parents means that they can be harnessed as highly potent sources of training, and such clinicians are increasingly using these strategies to establish a far more effective educational programme than they themselves could possibly provide. But the needs of parents, and the stresses which such a high level of involvement may place upon them, are also recognized and so the psychologists may well regard themselves as involved with the problems of the family as a whole.

Family structure and dynamics

It is impossible to make any universal statement regarding the structure or composition of the family because it comes in so many shapes and sizes. It is often even very difficult to say where a family ends. There are legal and blood-ties in most families but there is no universally agreed definition of the family and for our purposes, of course, we want some definition which is based not on some legal or religiously sanctioned grouping but on a high level of interpersonal intimacy and involvement. If we cannot make universal statements there is the possibility of taking some typical or 'modal' grouping. In everyday life we often 'see in our mind's eye', when the word 'family' is mentioned, a combination of two parents living in a single household with one or more children. This picture is becoming less representative of households as they really are, however, as more and more single-parent families and childless couples are found in the community, and it also used to be the case that the 'grandparent' generation was more involved in the nuclear family's everyday life than it is now. With more and more people also living in same-sex pairings, and more young couples living together without legal or religious 'approval', there is now a greater diversity of family forms and living arrangements than ever before. Consequently there is increased interest in the life styles, needs and problems of single-parent families, homosexual couples and such unusual arrangements as communes.

Bearing in mind the non-universality of the 'two parents and children' model, we can nevertheless use this (since it still represents life styles more than any other single pattern) as the basis for a discussion about family structure and dynamics. One obvious structural property of this grouping is generational. There are different roles and expectations, duties and rights for parents and children. Another structural property is related to the sex of the family members. The 'wife' role (expectations and behaviour, assigned tasks and attitudes) is somewhat different from the 'husband' role. Boys may be treated very differently from girls in the family. These structural properties influence, for example, the power relationships within the family and the tasks which each member takes on. In recent years some aspects of this have changed. There appears to have been a move towards more equal sharing of power by husband and wife, and with more women working outside the home the 'breadwinner' function may also be shared. It appears that inside the home, too, there is more of an overlap of tasks, with more men now doing the washing up and changing the baby and more women changing electric plugs and driving the car. But task differentiation is still marked. It is still unusual to find the husband taking the major responsibility for the ironing or the wife taking a major part in car maintenance. The question concerning the origin of such differentiation is a highly controversial one, with some maintaining strongly that they reflect only a social and cultural 'norm'. Whatever the truth of this matter, it is the case that social learning and expectation do play major roles, that most tasks (some would say all) could be equally well carried out by men and women and that, in fact, there is a great overlap not only in what they could do but in what they actually do.

These 'modal' and 'positional' roles within the family represent only one level of the role structure. The individual personalities of the family members, and their particular interests and skills, also affect the division of power and the assignment of tasks. A wife may dominate the family and this can sometimes be the basis of a happy and stable family life, whereas some families are very much 'child centred' and the ill-health or handicap of one member may radically change the pattern of relationships. During the family life cycle, with children coming and then leaving, and with the later death of one or both parents, the structure will also change. Families adapt to such altered circumstances by revising their role structure and the nature of their contact with their relatives and neighbours, and sometimes they may need additional help at a practical or psychological level from one or other of the caring professions. Problems may spread, with poverty, for example, sometimes leading to marital conflict, to poor care of the children and to later problems with the health and behaviour of the youngsters themselves. Such vicious circle processes may lead to a situation in which the 'multi-problem family' emerges.

**irth and early
iteraction**

The process of birth is biological, but the importance of social variables is also apparent. The pregnant woman may anticipate the sex and looks of her baby, but initial acceptance is by no means inevitable. Premature babies, for example, may look very unlike the baby-food advertisements which may have conditioned the mother's expectations, and if the infant needs to be removed to a special unit for additional medical care then this may interfere with the process in which, by handling the baby and having him close and dependent on her, the relationship becomes mutually a very special one. Fathers are now often present at the birth and there is evidence that this helps the woman in the birth process itself and also helps the couple to feel that the baby is a part of both of them. The demands which the baby makes may not have been fully anticipated and the initial period with the infant may call for a difficult process of adaptation and adjustment, just as the first period of the couple living together calls for give and take and the setting up of new norms of interaction.

Not all babies are the same; they differ in their activity level, their crying and their patterns of sleep and wakefulness. Some are not easy to care for; they may be unresponsive and difficult to soothe. Baby-care makes great demands and the mother may be totally unprepared for the energy and level of skill required. Surveys show that many mothers find the period of early childhood highly stressful. They may be tired and feel inadequate and, at times, very angry. If they fail to understand and control the baby their treatment of him may be poor and, at times, harsh. The majority of mothers report that after having a baby them- selves they feel more able to understand why some mothers end up battering their infants. The level of medical care in pregnancy and around the time of the birth may be high, but many mothers then feel isolated with the baby, unsure about such matters as feeding, toileting and weaning. They may be unsure how to react to the baby's crying, and find it im- possible to determine what the various cries mean. In assuming that a 'mother's instinct' will aid her in these tasks we may have seriously under-estimated the extent to which, in earlier times, the informal training opportunities offered to the young girl by larger family units and the close neighbourhood community helped her in her own parent- ing. Child-care manuals may fulfil a useful function, but they only go part of the way and they are used by only a section of the mothers who need them.

The developing child

In early years interactions with parents form the major social background for the child. There is a good deal of in- formal teaching and the child learns by example. Guidance and discipline help to establish a set of internal rules, and encouragement and praise help to develop skills and intellectual abilities. Overhearing conversations between adults enables the child to learn about the structure of language and conversation and the rules of social inter- action. Watching the parents' interactions and reactions enables children to develop their own emotional repertoire and social skills, and they will experiment and consciously imitate the behaviour of their parents. The child may identify strongly with a particular parent. Games of pre- tence enable youngsters to practise complex tasks and build a repertoire of interactive styles, and in collaboration with other young children they may rehearse a number of roles. In both competitive and co-operative play social interaction patterns are devised and perfected, children learn about rule following and discover their strengths and weaknesses relative to their peers.

31

Different parents treat their children differently, and there are many styles of parenting. Some parents are warm and affectionate, others are more distant, and some are openly hostile. Some give the child a lot of freedom and exercise little control while others are very restrictive. Not surprisingly, the children of highly restrictive parents tend to be well-mannered but lack independence, the children of warm parents come to have a confident high regard for themselves, and the children of hostile parents tend to be aggressive. There are various ways in which such findings can be explained. Do the aggressive children of hostile parents, for example, behave in this way because they are reacting against pressures which their parents put on them, are they simply imitating the behaviour of the adults around them and picking up their interactive styles, or is there perhaps some hereditary biological component which makes both parents and children hostile?

Probably, as in so many cases of such overall correlations there is a combination of such factors. It is also possible, of course, that hostility originating in the children themselves causes a parental reaction. We must beware of the conclusion that children simply respond to the atmosphere of their home. They also help to create that atmosphere, and the relationship between parents' behaviour and the child's behaviour is a fully interactive one. Children are not shapeless psychological forms capable of being moulded totally in response to their social environment, but have dispositions and levels of potential of their own which they bring into the family.

Even within the same family different children are treated differently. This is related to their age and their sex, to their ordinal position (the role of 'eldest child' or 'baby of the family' may be regarded as special by the parents), to their personality, temperament, abilities and interests. A handicapped child, for example, may be heavily protected by the parents and, whatever their position, be assigned the 'youngest child' role. A child with behaviour problems may assume a 'black sheep' role and their conduct may be used by the family to explain any difficulties which they are having. The degree to which boys and girls are treated differently varies widely. In some families the toys which are provided may reinforce traditional stereotypes of sex-rules and the differential encouragement of school achievement and interest in future occupational roles may be considerable.

Children have certain psychological needs which the family context should be able to provide. They need a certain stability, they need guidance and a set of rules to follow and the feeling needs to be conveyed to them that they are 'prized' by their parents. In the traditional system with two parents there may be a certain safeguard for the constant provision of these needs by one or other of the parents and for the prevention of total lack of interest or of rejection. But if the natural family with two parents is ideal in many ways as an arrangement in which to provide for the child's development, this is not to say that the child's best intere ts cannot also be met in alternative contexts. Most children in single-parent households fare well and develop happily. For the child living apart from his natural parents adoption seems to be a better option than does fostering (though long-term fostering seems to share many of the positive features of adoption), and fostering seems to be better for the child than a continued stay in an institution. Even this context, however, can provide reasonably well for the child's needs if there is stability, a high level of staffing, high intimacy between staff and children, and the provision of high levels of verbal and other types of stimulation.

The family and stress

Just as a family is a principal source of a person's happiness and well-being, it can also be the most powerful source of stress. Research has been done to try to establish inventories of the life stresses which people experience, and in even a cursory glance through such a list it is difficult not to be struck by the extent to which the relationships within the family are bound up with personal change. Some of these events, like the birth of a handicapped child or the death of a child, happen to only a few people, but others, such as the older child leaving home, marital conflict, sexual problems, and the death of a parent happen to many or most. Stress precipitated by such life events has been shown to have a marked effect on both physical and mental health, and if illness is the result then this in turn will provide added hardship.

Few of the important things which happen to a person do not also affect their family. The family shares joy and adversity and may act as an emotional buffer, enabling the individual to cope with difficulties arising from problems with health or employment. Almost all individuals who have been married for even a short while recognize that they have acted at some time in a 'therapeutic role' towards their spouse and that their partner has acted in such a way towards them. Couples generally feel that they have been greatly helped by talking over things, by expressing their feelings, confiding their fears and anxieties and discussing possible solutions. What we know of the effective processes of psychotherapy taking place in a professional setting suggests that such informal interaction may be a powerful influence in the prevention and relief of psychological problems. One of the useful functions of the other people in the family, then, is in providing therapeutic opportunity and in alleviating stress.

It is not only particular events which cause stress. The constant presence of ill-health, handicap or marital conflict can similarly take its toll over the years. On the other hand, the stability and comfort of the family setting, and the constant presence of others seems to provide much that is beneficial. Marriage reduces the risk of alcoholism, suicide and many forms of psychological ill-health, and interviews with separated and widowed people reveal the elements which they feel they are now missing in their lives, and which in turn may help to explain why living in relative isolation tends to be associated with a greater risk of experiencing psychological problems. As well as providing the opportunity to discuss problems and providing stability, the presence of a spouse reduces loneliness. It also facilitates discussion of a variety of issues and so enables the partners to forge a consensus view of the world; it provides extra interest and social contact; the opportunity to give love and express concern; and provides constant feedback to the individual about themselves, their value and their role. Practical tasks may be shared and the person may be aware of being prized by the other. This then fosters the sense of self-worth which has been found to be very important for overall well-being.

Of course, not all marital relationships are good and some may lead to far greater problems than those of living in isolation. Certainly recent family changes and conflict seem, in many cases, to be a trigger factor leading to subsequent admission to a psychiatric hosptial. Overall, however, it seems that the emotional impact of an intimate relationship, in adult life as in childhood, is likely to involve many more gains for the individual than losses, and that people value the protection which such relationships provide and often suffer when such support ends.

Schizophrenia, depression and the family

There is a popular notion that schizophrenic illness originates in family relationships, and that certain forms of family communication, in particular, may cause an adolescent or young adult to become schizophrenic. A considerable number of studies has now been carried out to establish whether or not there is a firm evidential basis for such an assumption and, at this point, it looks as if the decided lack of positive evidence should lead us to abandon the hypothesis that such relationship problems constitute the major cause of the illness. While no strong data to support the family interaction claim have been forthcoming, however, a great deal of evidence implicating the role of genetics in schizophrenia has been found, and it now looks as if a predominantly biological explanation may eventually be given. But while there is no good evidence that family relationships are formative in schizophrenia, there is strong support for the notion that family interaction markedly influences the course of a schizophrenic illness and the pattern of relapses and remission from symptoms over the years. It seems that the emotional climate in the home and particular family crisis events often trigger renewed episodes of schizophrenic breakdown.

On the other hand, it seems that depression often has its origin in severe life events and difficulties and that the family context provides many of these. In a recent study conducted in London, Brown and Harris (1979) found that depression was more common in those women in the community who had recently experienced a severe event or difficulty. Many of the events involved loss. Women with several young children were more vulnerable than others, as were the widowed, divorced and separated. Social contact seemed to provide a protective function against the effects of severe life events, and the rate of depression was lower in those women who had a close, intimate relationship with their husbands. Women without employment outside the home were found to be more vulnerable, and the loss of a mother in childhood also seemed to have a similar effect. Brown and Harris suggest that such early loss through the death of a parent may change the way in which the person comes to view the world and attempts to cope with the problems that arise. The study provides clear evidence that family relationship factors may make a person more or less susceptible to clinical depression, and again illustrates how the contribution of family life to personal problems is two-sided. The family may be the source of much stress, but a close supportive marital relationship will enable the individual to cope with many problems without succumbing to the threat of clinical depression.

Alcoholism

Despite the fact that more and more women are now becoming alcoholics the problem is still more typical of men, and it has long been appreciated that an alcoholic husband or father is often a source of great strain and embarrassment to the other members of his family. The fact that many wives of alcoholics have personality problems has been interpreted in a variety of ways. It seems that wives of alcoholics are frequently also daughters of alcoholics, and an early formulation suggested that the wife had family-based neurotic problems and tended to marry the alcoholic to fulfil needs of her own. Recently the psychological condition of the wife has been seen more as a reaction to the stress which her husband's drinking places on her and the marriage. The husband's alcoholism means that he is likely not to be dependable, and may be inadequate in providing for the family and fulfilling many of the other aspects of his roles as husband and father. The drinking will often be associated with bitter conflict, sometimes even physical violence, and will affect his sexual responsiveness.

In such a situation the wife may react with increased independence, taking over many of the husband's responsibilities and making most of the decisions in the family. Her capability may underline the husband's inadequacy and serve to further reduce his self-respect. If the alcoholic condition improves then the wife may be reluctant to surrender her power, and it has been suggested that the considerable reorganization of roles within the family group which the alcoholic's recovery may bring about can disadvantage her

and have detrimental effects on her health. Thus our understanding of the internal dynamics of the alcoholic's family
group suggests that the shift in power and dependency which
may be indicated as a strategy for coping with the husband's
inadequacy can later militate against successful treatment
and readjustment.

There are various ways in which the wife of the alcoholic copes with his drinking, and these have been shown to
have a considerable influence on his chances of recovery.
She may belittle her husband, extract promises from him,
threaten him with leaving or divorce, or offer comfort or
support. The effects of the problem often extend beyond the
immediate family group, affecting people in the neighbourhood and friends and relatives, so that the husband's
behaviour may be a further source of embarrassment and
humiliation for the wife and children. Central to their
reaction is their view of the nature of the condition. They
may be of the opinion that the alcoholism is a disease and
that the man needs help, or they may feel that he is to
blame and hold him wholly responsible for the problem. The
'social reality' of the drinking constructed in this way by
the other family members may have an important effect on
the husband. The view that he has only himself to blame, for
instance, may lower his self-respect or may encourage him
to 'pull himself together'.

While the effects which the alcoholic observes on the
family may affect his motivation to be 'cured' or to
'reform', the coping style of the wife is of particular
importance. A wife's high level of nurturance and caretaking
is not found to be associated with sobriety and is often
counter-productive, but threats of divorce and disengagement
from the relationship are also positively related to continued drinking.

The optimal coping strategy for the wife appears to be
one in which there is continued support and an implicit
assumption that the marriage will continue, but with a
strongly communicated abhorrence of the drinking and its
effects. Any anger and rejection should be directed at the
drinking problem rather than at the person. In fact many
wives do regard the husband as a 'different man' when he is
drinking, and clearly feel that underneath the alcoholism
there is someone worthy of continued support.

The attitudes of children to their alcoholic fathers
vary greatly and they often pick up important cues from
their mother. They tend to take the same attitude towards
the problem as she does, and the adoption of an 'illness'
view may help to sustain an overall positive regard of the
father despite the embarrassment and stress which the drinking causes. While there is little to suggest that these
children have an increased frequency of serious psychiatric
conditions, there is evidence that they tend to be rated by
their teachers as 'problem children'. Their attitudes to
drinking also show great variation. Some of them later
disdain alcohol completely while many drink heavily

themselves in adulthood, and the sons of alcoholics do frequently come to have a problem of excessive drinking.

The high level of control which is often taken by the mother may be resented by the children or they may become especially close to her, feeling that they share a mutual problem concerning the father. The mother may take a specially protective attitude towards her sons and daughters or may use them as scapegoats for the major family problem. She may use their reactions and anxieties as a stick with which to beat the husband, hoping thereby to stop him drinking.

There has been relatively little research on the impact of the growing number of female alcoholics on their families. It is known that their marriages are less stable and there appears to be a variety of reasons for this. It has been found that female alcoholics are more disturbed in a number of ways than their male counterparts, and it is true that heavy drinking by women is less socially acceptable. It also seems likely that many husbands find it particularly difficult to be supportive towards their alcoholic wives.

Family conflict and violence

There is open conflict at times in most families. Sometimes the focus of disagreements is easily apparent and may centre, for example, on matters concerning money, sex or the handling of children, but at other times the row seems to reflect underlying resentments and difficulties in the relationship. Studies have been made of how arguments start, how they escalate and how they are resolved, and some research in this area has been successful in identifying patterns of conflict which seem to predict later marital breakdown. It appears that there are right ways and wrong ways to fight with the other family members. In some marriages there may be constant conflict which, however, is successfully worked through and which does not endanger the basic relationship.

Inter-generational conflict is also common. In the early years the parents have the power and may use discipline to settle matters of disagreement. Again the way in which this is done is important and it seems that parents should not use their power in such a way that the child feels rejected. The children should be made to feel that their behaviour rather than their whole personality is the target of the parents' disapproval. In the adolescent years the child's struggle for power and independence is often the focus of conflict. Adolescence is frequently a period of stress and the young people may have doubts about their status and future. It is also a time when peer-influence may conflict with that of the parents.

Marital conflict sometimes leads to physical assault and a number of wives have to receive medical attention for injuries inflicted by their husbands. Many such wives choose to return to the home after such an incident, although some seek the haven of a women's refuge. Even where there is repeated violence the wife often feels that her husband is not likely to treat her badly in the future; she may feel that drinking or stress triggered the assault, and such wives often report that the man is generally caring and responsible and that his violent outbursts are out of character. Jealousy and sexual failure or refusal are also associated with attacks on the wife, though it is also true that for some couples physical assault or restraint represents a modal response in conflict situations, and that in some marriages (and indeed in some sub-cultures) there are few inhibitions against the couple hitting one another.

Violence against children also occurs with alarming frequency in families and, as we have already seen, it is estimated that about two children die each week in England and Wales as a result of injuries inflicted by their parents. The children involved are often very young and it does not take much physical strength to seriously injure a small child or baby. Only a small proportion of the parents involved in these attacks have a known psychiatric history and, contrary to one popular image, they often provide well for the general needs of their children. Sadistic premeditated cases do occur but they are relatively rare. Generally the attack occurs when a child is crying or screaming or has committed some 'crime' in the eyes of the parent. The mother or father involved is often under considerable stress, and there are frequently severe marital difficulties. The parents involved are often also young and may have little idea of how to cope with the crying child and, as we have also seen, there is evidence that many abused children are themselves difficult to handle. They may be disturbed, overactive or unresponsive, though of course many such problems may themselves be the result of longer-term difficulties in the family.

Attempts are now being made to try to predict which children are likely to be attacked, with the hope that additional support and protection may be given. There are also a number of new approaches to the treatment of violent parents, many of which centre on general improvement of family relationships or on teaching parenting skills, but some attempt to enable the parent to suppress anger and aggression. Many people feel that there is inadequate protection given to children who have been attacked, and some argue that parents in such cases should regain custody of the child only after the authorities are completely assured that there will be no repeat of the assault, and that all adequate provisions for the child's care and development will be made by the parents. They argue that where such assurances cannot be given it should be more easy for a 'divorce' to be arranged so that the child can grow in an environment which is safer and more adequate for ensuring optimal development than is the natural family.

The effects of marital breakdown

Divorce statistics represent a very conservative estimate of marital failure and a still more conservative estimate of marital unhappiness and disharmony, but the rates are high and increasing. There are various estimates of the likely divorce rate of currently made marriages, but one in four is a frequently encountered figure. There are certain known predictors of marital breakdown. It is more frequent, for example, when the couple married at an early age, when they have few friends, when they have had relatively little education and when their life style is unconventional. The marital success or failure of their own parents also bears a direct statistical relationship to the couple's chances of breakdown.

Psychological studies have shown that certain measures of personality and social style are also predictors of failure. If the wife rates her husband as being emotionally immature, if the husband's self-image is lacking in coherence and stability, or if either of the partners are emotionally unstable, then marital breakdown is more likely than if the reverse holds. Good communication, a high level of emotional support and the constructive handling of conflict situations are, not surprisingly, features of relationships which are associated with high levels of marital happiness and low rates of breakdown. In many of these studies it is, of course, difficult to disentangle cause and effect.

The process of adjustment to a marriage may be a long and difficult one and some marriages never successfully 'take'. The highest rates of breakdown therefore occur in the first years, but many relationships are stable and satisfactory for a while and are then beset with difficulties at a later stage. Divorce is usually preceded by months or years of intense conflict and may eventually come as a relief, but the evidence suggests that generally the whole process is a very painful one for many members of the family involved, both adults and children.

Research with divorcees has revealed a high degree of stress and unhappiness which may last for a very long time. On the whole it appears that the experiences of women in the situation result in rather more disturbance than those of men, but for both sexes the status of divorce is associated with higher risk of clinical depression, alcoholism and attempted suicide. The psychological effects of a marriage breakdown may stem largely from lack of social support, the absence of an intimate relationship and a loss of self-esteem, but there are often additional pressures relating to the loss of friends, increased financial problems and the difficulties of loss of contact with the children or of having to bring them up alone. There is a high rate of remarriage among the divorced; and divorce itself, for all the apparent risks which it brings, is still often preferable to continuing in a marriage which has failed.

The 'broken home' is associated with increased aggressiveness and delinquency in children but there is apparently only a weak association with neurotic and other psychiatric problems of childhood. While the rate of conduct problems in the children of divorce is considerably higher than that for children of stable marriages, there is apparently little increase in such antisocial behaviour for children whose homes have been broken by the death of a parent. This suggests that it is the discord in the home which produces the effect rather than the mere absence of one parent. This is supported by the finding that conduct problems also occur with increased frequency in homes with continual discord even when there is no separation or divorce.

Several mechanisms have been suggested to explain the link between conflict or breakdown and delinquency. The relationship is particularly strong when it is accompanied by rejection of the child and when there is a continued atmosphere of hostility together with overt conflict. Thus such children are likely to have low self-esteem and a low opinion of the family. They may also have a model of relationships which centres on protest and conflict, and in addition they are likely to be subjected to direct stress in the home. In adult life, the children of broken homes are more likely to develop a personality disorder or neurosis and are more likely to attempt suicide. They are also less likely to have a successful marriage themselves. Such increased statistical frequencies do point to the potential aftermath of an unhappy and disrupted home background, but it should be remembered that many of the children from such families do not exhibit such problems either in childhood or in later life.

ngle-parent families

Children are raised in single-parent families when the mother has not married, when there has been a divorce or separation or when one parent has died. 'Illegitimacy' is a somewhat outmoded term and an increasing number of single women now feel that they want to rear their child on their own. Social attitudes against illegitimacy and single parenthood have softened over the years and this has encouraged more mothers to keep the baby rather than have it adopted. We have seen that the results for both the child and the adult of the death of a parent or partner may be very different from those resulting from separation or divorce, and so we might expect in a similar way that the effects of the deliberately chosen single-parenthood situation might be somewhat different from either of these. This does in fact appear to be the case. Single-parent families are increasing in number and it is now estimated that about one in nine children of school age has only one parent living with them.

Single parenthood appears to be more stressful for the remaining parent than sharing the responsibilities with a partner. Lack of emotional support and of adult company are some of the reasons for this but there are also likely to be increased financial hardships, and the homes of single parents have been shown to be overcrowded and often lack both luxuries and basic amenities. During times of parental illness there may be few additional social resources to call upon, and the single parent is less likely to be able to organize a social life for herself (about 90 per cent of single parents are women). A number of self-help organizations have now been formed to fulfil some of the special needs of the single parent.

One-parent families are viable alternatives to the more traditional nuclear family and most of the children raised in such circumstances do not appear to show any signs of disturbance or impaired development. There is, however, an increased frequency of maladjustment and problems at school, but this is slight and may reflect the economic conditions of the home rather than relationship and care factors. The child may, however, lack an adequate model of adult-adult relationships, and there has been a detailed examination of the effects which the lack of a same-sex adult model might have. It was suggested, for example, that the boy without a father might tend to be more effeminate but it has been found that most boys brought up by their mothers are as masculine as the rest. If anything, they do tend to make fewer sex-identity based assumptions about tasks and roles. We could say that they seem to be less 'sexist' than other boys. Similarly, the girl brought up with the father alone does not seem to lack a feminine identity. These findings reflect a more general conclusion that children seem to base their own stereotypes on the wider world around them rather than on the conditions prevailing in their own immediate family.

The future of intimate life styles

Contact with intimates in the family group seems to provide the individual, overall, with considerable benefits. Significant relationships are highly potent and there may be dangers, but generally the benefits far outweigh the costs. A variety of psychological needs are very well fulfilled in the traditional family setting. The child growing in the caring and stable family can generally develop skills and abilities and achieve a potential for happiness better than in any other setting, and the adult can fulfil with the marital partner the needs of emotional support, freedom from loneliness, sex, stability, and the building of a mutually comfortable 'social reality'. When the basic family pattern is disturbed there can be grave consequences for each of the people involved.

Yet the patterns of life style are changing and, in terms of social history, are changing rapidly. There are now fewer children in families, more single-parent families, and more divorces and separations; there is a higher incidence of transitory relationships and less contact between generations. Several lines of evidence suggest that children may be valued less than in the recent past, that women, in particular, are looking more outside the family for their role-orientation and their satisfactions, that there is now less 'family feeling' and that family duties and responsibilities impinge upon individual decision making less than was the case some decades ago.

In one way these changes represent increased independence and freedom for the individual and could be seen as likely to facilitate personal growth, yet such a view surely focusses on the young healthy adult members of society rather than on the very young, the old and the handicapped. It relates to the wishes of those who want to be independent rather than those who have to be dependent. Since one person's sacrifice may be directly related to another's fulfilment of needs, the 'best interests' of people in relationships are often, of course, conflicting. The longer-term value of stability may also be under-estimated by those who focus on their own short-term independence.

The psychological enterprise is not biassed with pre-set values, or at least tries not to be, but it can supply information about the attitudes and values which people hold and it can provide evidence which will affect the adoption of particular values and policies. The research reviewed in this chapter does suggest a highly positive evaluation of the family as an institution for the optimal happiness and well-being of individuals in society. Possible alternatives have to be seriously considered but, as yet, there is relatively little evidence on the effects of communal living or single living. What evidence there is does not suggest that any of these are likely to be a viable means to personal fulfilment, stability and happiness for the majority of people, at least at this stage. The Israeli kibbutz, which has been well studied, works reasonably well and the communal rearing of children in such a setting does not produce any strong detrimental effects, but it now appears that the parents often find their limited access to the children unsatisfying and in many kibbutzim there appears to be a move back to more traditional family styles.

There is no uniform change in western society to a single alternative life style arrangement but there is rather an increasing diversity. We may expect this variety to increase further as ideas regarding the roles of men and woman evolve, as changes in biological and 'hard' technology take place, and as patterns of employment and leisure alter. It would be premature to forecast, at this stage, what effects such changes will bring to interpersonal relationships and personal life styles. What does seem certain, however, is that there will be some important effects. To some extent these can be affected by direct social intervention and some undesired effects may be prevented.

Family life, then, is the key variable in society and adverse changes may inflict an enormous 'social bill'. For this reason the effects on individuals must be carefully monitored. To echo a former theme on the methodological realities of family studies, such monitoring may not always be based on the well-controlled studies and 'good' reliable measures which psychologists always strive to use. But the key importance of the variables concerned may force us to set these limitations in perspective and to look at the psychology of interpersonal relationships and their effects in whatever is the best way we can find. Family studies are almost always inter-disciplinary and the area is one in which co-operation between psychologists and other professionals is likely to lead to a good deal of work that is of great mutual benefit.

Reference

Brown, G.W. and Harris, T. (1978)
Social Origins of Depression. London: Tavistock Publications.

Questions

1. Write an essay on 'The family and psychology'.
2. Assess the importance of personal relationships in the lives of individuals, referring to psychological and other studies to support the analysis you present.
3. Consider some of the factors which might lead a couple to decide to remain childless.
4. Now that there are a number of highly effective contraceptive methods why do so many unwanted pregnancies occur, and how might this be changed?
5. How is a relationship between the mother and her baby likely to differ from that between the father and his baby? Why is this so?
6. Many mothers find looking after a young baby a difficult and stressful experience. Why is this?
7. Hospital births may be medically the safest, but are there likely to be psychological dangers in treating birth more as a biological than as a social and family process?
8. What are 'the needs of children' and how may they be met?
9. Critically assess the evidence relating to the effects of a mother's work outside the home on the children.
10. Write an essay on 'The family as a source of stress'.
11. Some people have maintained that schizophrenia arises as a result of problems within the family. Critically assess the evidence relating to this issue.
12. Write an essay on 'The alcoholic in the family'.
13. The family seems to be the context for a good deal of violence, particularly towards children and wives. Why should this be so?
14. Write an essay on 'The after-effects of divorce'.
15. Consider the special problems of the single-parent family.
16. Is the family an institution worth preserving?
17. Are there 'experts' in child-rearing? Is this process too important to be left to parents?
18. Some authors have claimed that the family is oppressive and that people should be liberated from the limits that it places on them. How far do you share this view? Give reasons.

nnotated reading

Herbert, M. (1975) Problems of Childhood. London: Pan.
  A comprehensive account of the problems of the early
  years, their treatment and prevention.

Kellmer Pringle, M. (1980) The Needs of Children (2nd edn).
London: Hutchinson.
  Important review of children's needs and how they may
  be met both inside and outside the family. Readable and
  authoritative book with important implications for
  social policy.

Kempe, R. and Kempe, E. (1978) Child Abuse. London:
Fontana/Open Books.
  The nature of treatment of violence and sexual assault
  on children in the family, with an account of methods
  of treatment and prevention.

Rutter, M. (1976) Helping Troubled Children. Harmondsworth:
Penguin.
  Leading British child psychiatrist examines the nature
  of the more severe problems of childhood. Provides good
  coverage of the importance of family factors and related
  methods of treatment.

elevance to the
eacher
AVID FONTANA

It is important at the outset that the reader understands
the problems highlighted by Frude in defining the family. At
one time, when geographical and social mobility were low,
reference to the family often implied not simply the
'nuclear' family of parents and children but the 'extended'
family which included close relations like grandparents and
aunts and uncles as well. The members of the extended family
tended to live near each other, and the child often saw as
much of other relatives as he did of his own parents, with
the result that he was subject to a broad range of influence. This influence is sometimes seen by modern sociologists as being all to the good in that it engendered more
of a sense of community into a neighbourhood and provided
checks upon antisocial behaviour in the young. Importantly,
it also gave children more understanding and respect for the
elderly, and perhaps more concern for the well-being of
others outside the limits of the nuclear family.
   Nowadays, however, the members of the extended family
often live long distances from each other, and effectively
the child is confined to the nuclear family for the majority
of his close early social contacts. Not only is this more
restrictive for the child, but the collapse of the extended
family leaves parents themselves more isolated, one of the
factors we have already identified as being a possible
factor in baby battering and child abuse. Frude suggests,
though, that our definition of the nuclear family as consisting of parents and children may also need revision, in
that increasingly the contemporary family consists of only
one parent and children, both because of the rise in the

divorce rate and the changing social mores that allow more women to bring up children outside marriage altogether.

Thus, when considering the family background of his children and its influence upon school progress, the teacher often needs to revise preconceived notions of what this background may be like. Coming perhaps from a happy family life himself he may be unaware of the stress placed upon a child by continual discord (and perhaps physical violence) between parents, or by alcoholism in a father or a mother, or by a single-parent home in which the child has to take early responsibility for younger siblings. He may also be unaware of the kind of demands that can be made upon children by domineering or by emotionally unbalanced parents, or of the different kind of stress caused by a parent with chronic depression who is unable to cope with the tasks of domestic life. Once he comes to study and appreciate these problems, the teacher will find it hardly surprising that children faced with difficulties of this kind within the home often present behaviour problems at school. Such problems may simply be those of physical exhaustion or of lack of motivation, but they may also take the form of withdrawal in that the child, preoccupied with his worries at home, is unable to reach out to others and participate in school activities. At their most disruptive they may take the form of extreme demands for teacher attention or of resentment and hostility towards the world in general.

The need for teacher sympathy

These and other questions relating to behaviour problems are dealt with more fully in Part IV, but our present emphasis is that the teacher should become sensitive to the potent influence upon school conduct of a child's family background. The teacher can, of course, do little to change this background. He is not a social worker and any attempts at interference would probably be resented and counterproductive (though he must be prompt to report to the headteacher and through the headteacher to the social services any instances of physical neglect or abuse). But understanding and sympathy shown towards the child in school will of itself help him to live with problems at home. It hardly needs saying the a child deeply troubled by such problems must not be further disturbed by an insensitive school environment in which no account is taken of the reasons for his failure to concentrate on class work or to get homework done or to relate satisfactorily to others. Late arrival at school, unaccountable absences, unpopularity with other children, sudden displays of violent temper, and general moodiness may all be traced back to difficulties at home, and it is part of the teacher's task to look closely into these difficulties before deciding what action to take. He should also bear in mind that children may often be reluctant to admit to domestic upsets either through a sense of shame or through a sense of loyalty to parents. Further, many children with a background of this kind may also be relatively inarticulate (due to the lack of verbal stimuli to which we have already made reference) and may find it hard to put their problems into words, particularly if they feel they are not assured of a sympathetic hearing.

The influence of sex differences

Frude also draws our attention to the unequal treatment that children of the same family sometimes receive within the home. This may be due to the kind of temperamental clash between parents and particular children to which we made reference in the discussion of Schaffer's section in chapter 1, or it may be due to age, with older children having to shoulder undue responsibility, or it may be due to sex. This last is a very real issue within many families. Most parents doubtless love their sons and daughters equally, but it is beyond dispute that they frequently do not treat them alike. Sometimes there are clear and good reasons for this. The children may develop different interests although given the same opportunities, with boys perhaps being drawn more towards sport and girls more towards artistic activities (or vice versa); or one child may show more independence than another, or need less help with school work. But research shows that the variation in treatment appears often to be primarily a consequence of the child's sex itself. Girls are, for example, from an early age taught to be more dependent upon parents than are boys. Parents are prone to give their daughters less freedom than their sons, and to involve them more in domestic pursuits and in activities associated with the home. They are more likely to intervene in the play of girls if it becomes boisterous, and are more inclined to soothe rather than distract if they become upset for any reason. Recent studies suggest that mothers even discriminate in the toys they offer young babies, tending to offer boys rattles and girls soft toys, and to encourage boys to bounce about while girls are offered more docile activities and are expected to display clever or attractive behaviour.

Perhaps not surprisingly, girls tend to grow up more sensitive to parental opinion than do boys, and to centre more of their leisure interests upon the home. As they grow older, they are often given more specific guidance on what is still taken to be the traditional female role in society, and are expected to help more in the house and to orientate themselves towards 'feminine' occupations such as nurses (and teachers!) in their play. Boys too, of course, are sometimes the losers in that they may be constrained to hide their feelings even in cases of genuine emotional upset, and may be steered away from such activities as cooking which they perhaps enjoy, but it appears that girls suffer most from this sexual stereotyping. At an early age they acquire the culture-bound view that the female sex is all right in its place but is generally inferior to the male, and in consequence they tend to set lower goals for themselves and to fail to reach their full potential. There is even some evidence that on occasions girls will deliberately under-achieve rather than be seen to outshine boys engaged on a matched task.

There are, of course, biological differences between the sexes which influence variations in behaviour. Smith (1974), for example, reviews evidence to show that in primates generally the male is more prone to engage in boisterous and aggressive activities from infancy onwards than the female, but nevertheless the greater part of the sex role appears to be learnt, and learnt in particular from within the family. Not only do children identify with the parent of the same sex, they also take over from the parent of the opposite sex his or her notion of what is 'manly' or of what is 'feminine'. Thus from both sexes they learn what is expected of them as boys or girls, and tend to adhere increasingly to these stereotypes as they grow older. Even where parents try hard to avoid this sex-typing, influences from outside are strong. Television, children's and adolescents' magazines, and adults generally are obvious examples here, but so too are the child's friends. Children are often described as being essentially conformist, and this is true in the sense that they like to feel accepted by their peers, and quickly learn that such acceptance is often dependent upon being like everyone else. In particular, they strenuously avoid acquiring labels such as 'sissy' or 'tomboy', and boys especially come in for a deal of censure if they are seen to show too much kinship with the opposite sex. Even in adolescence, where a certain amount of pairing off is regarded as appropriate, boys are often still subject to teasing from their friends and are not expected to lose their sense of manly dignity over a mere girl. Poets and troubadors may indeed have been inspired by romantic love, but if an adolescent boy feels similar noble stirrings within he quickly learns when it is politic to keep quiet about them.

Obviously the teacher cannot change these sexual stereotypes single-handed. Nor would it be right for him to expect children to engage in unisex behaviour that would hold them up to ridicule outside school. But nevertheless there is much that can be done within the classroom to help children develop more desirable attitudes, and to help girls in particular escape some of the handicaps that sex-typing lays upon them. Most obviously, all school activities should be open equally to both sexes, and there should be no question of boys being channelled, say, towards wood and metalwork while girls have to make do with domestic science, or of boys being given every opportunity to take part in organized games while girls have to make do with the odd game of netball if and when someone can be found who is prepared to take them. Of equal importance, the teacher should avoid all unecessary polarizations like the ones implied by such instructions (heard in dinner queues, PE lessons, etc.) as 'girls on one side of the room, boys on the other', or 'girls lead now', or 'girls only now' (to the accompaniment of gay, fairy-like music) and 'now the boys' (to the accompaniment of growling, heavy passages). In addition, everything possible should be done to see that girls aim as high as boys, and go for the same range of vocational opportunities. The notion that for girls a career is only something to fill in time until marriage comes along is still too prevalent both within the family and within education. Even where girls take this line themselves, it should be pointed out to them that more and more married women are now taking up careers when their children start school, and that such careers should be as rewarding and fulfilling as those enjoyed by the male sex.

The importance of parental involvement

Frude's final point is one that has particular relevance to teachers, namely that parental involvement in a child's education is associated positively with the child's school progress. It is not hard to find reasons for this. Through their interest in his education parents show the child both the importance they attach to good school progress and the importance they attach to him as a person and to his future. Such parental interest also usually leads to offers of help with the schoolwork the child brings home, and means that parents attend school functions and generally become familiar with the school and with its standards and values. It means they get to know the child's teachers and are ready to turn to them for advice, while the teachers also benefit in that they get to know more about the child's background and can discuss learning problems where the parents may be able to help. Teachers often remark, of course, that the very parents they most want to see are the ones least likely to come anywhere near the school, and this is undoubtedly true; but even where parents never attend parents' evenings or any of the other opportunities given them to meet the staff, this does not necessarily mean that they take no interest in the child's progress. Indeed, where certain parents consistently fail to attend anything held at school the school needs to ask itself why it has been so unsuccessful in attracting their attention. It may be that the parents in question feel overawed by the school and by its well-spoken and well-educated staff. Or it may be that they know their child is doing badly and are either ashamed by this or are reluctant to hear even more bad reports of him. Or it may be that they are unimpressed by the school and by what it has to offer, and by the essentially middle-class cultural activities (school orchestra and choirs, school plays and so on) that it uses to attract parents into the school.

Some schools have identified this last as a major problem and mount bingo sessions and dances as a way of bringing parents into the school and establishing the kind of informal contacts that will lead to future attendance at parents' evenings. When such attendance does take place, they are also careful to avoid subjecting parents to a disheartening catalogue of their children's inadequacies or, worse still, to a lecture on the contribution the parents themselves have made to these inadequacies. Instead, they adopt a positive line, emphasizing what can be done to help the child, and stressing those areas where the child has performed with more credit. Once parents have learnt to trust the school, and to see the improvements in their child's performance which are linked to the closer interest they are now learning to take in his education, their sense of commitment and involvement is likely to increase, to the great benefit of all concerned.

Reference

Smith, P.K. (1974)
Ethological methods. In B. Foss (ed.), New Perspectives in Child Development. Harmondsworth: Penguin.

Additional reading

Maccoby, E. and Jacklin, C. (1974) The Psychology of Sex Differences. Stanford, Ca: Stanford University Press.
A thorough examination of most of the important aspects of sex roles and of sex differences in intellectual behaviour.

Block, J. H. (1976) Issues, problems and pitfalls in assessing sex differences. Merrill-Palmer Quarterly, 22, 283-308.
This article discusses some of the problems facing the researcher in this important field.

3

Play
David Fontana

As will become apparent to the reader, we could as readily
have included this chapter under cognitive development as
under social development. Play appears to have important
implications for all areas of a child's psychological life,
and it is a mistake to see it even in older children as a
trivial, time-wasting activity. On the other hand, it is a
mistake to lose sight of the fact that the purpose of play
from the child's point of view is simple enjoyment. He does
not consciously engage in play in order to find out how
things work, or to try out adult roles, or to stimulate his
imagination, or to do any of the other things that commentators over the years have claimed to identify in various
aspect of this play. He plays because it is fun, and the
learning that arises out of play is to him quite incidental.
Even when he engages in so-called structured play (that is,
play organized by the adult with the express intention of
providing desirable learning experiences) it still appears
to him as an essentially non-serious activity offered for
his diversion.

We should not assume that play is any the worse for this
hedonistic (pleasure-seeking) element. Western society has
placed its major emphasis upon work, and activities entered
into for the sake of pleasure have been held to be of little
real worth. For the psychologist, however, anything that
contributes towards the psychological health of the individual is of importance, and in this respect pleasure-
orientated activities may at times be of greater value than
those related to work. For the teacher also, the pleasure
aspect of children's play should not be dismissed too
lightly. It is inappropriate for him to see childhood as
simply a preparation for adulthood rather than as a phase of
life to be savoured for its own sake. In childhood, emotions
often have a sharper, more intense quality than they have in
later life, and to deny a child the opportunity to experience delight is to deny him experiences that may never
present themselves again in quite the same form. Delight, in
other words, should be seen as a desirable end in itself,
rather than as diverting the child from what are held to be
more long-term and more worth-while pursuits. Those who hold
that such an argument is impossibly frivolous may wish to
console themselves with the knowledge that the experience

of happiness, which is really what we are talking about, appears to carry desirable physiological as well as psychological benefits for the individual concerned, and this in itself makes it of inestimable value for anyone concerned with the future well-being of others. By learning that play is an experience valued by the adults in his life, and one which can be indulged in without constant feelings of guilt for all the other, more serious things he should be doing, the child is also helped to develop positive attitudes towards the place of leisure in his life, attitudes which should stand him in good stead when he grows up. We should not forget that one of the shortest but perhaps most satisfactory definitions of psychological health available to us is that the healthy individual is one who can work and play and love (see Allport, 1961).

The nature of play

The young of many species of animals engage in activities which appear to have the non-serious qualities of play (i.e. they do not seem to be directed primarily towards hunting or mating, or the exercise of territorial rights, or the evasion of danger). The higher up the so-called evolutionary scale the species happens to be, the more apparent and purposeful this 'play' becomes. In the case of all animals except man, however, 'play' involves primarily intense physical movement such as chasing and romping and is usually directed towards peers or other animate objects. Only rarely does it involve inanimate objects, and only rarely does it show obvious development as the animal grows older. In man, by contrast, play increasingly involves the use of physical objects, many of them standing symbolically for objects other than themselves as the infant grows older, and follows a discernible developmental pattern involving ever-increasing complexity. This utilization of physical objects is indicative both of the manipulative skills available to man through the use of fingers and thumbs, and of the presence of imagination (i.e. of the ability to call to mind situations or objects or processes that are not physically present at that point in time), while the growing complexity of play is indicative of the development of cognitive skills and of the increasing use of language both in communication with others and in thinking.

Piaget, whose work on cognitive development we look at more closely in chapter 4, suggests that the emergence of set rules and procedures in children's play as they grow older is further evidence of the development of their powers of thought. Thus the child moves in a few short years from the apparently entirely physical play of the small baby, which is perhaps analogous to the unthinking play of animals to which attention has already been drawn, to play which involves many of the sophisticated mental processes that help to mark man out as distinct from other species. Piaget also has it that not only do the child's developing powers of thought help him develop more complex methods of play, but the methods of play help him develop more complex ways of thinking. Sadly, the play of mentally handicapped children shows only a limited developmental range, and often remains repetitive and stereotyped.

Socially, play moves from the solitary play of the very small child (solitary in the sense that it is not indulged in reciprocally with other children) to the parallel play of the three year old (where children play side by side and perhaps imitate each other but still function essentially as individuals), to the truly social play of the normal four and five year old where much of the activity depends upon interaction with peers. During each of these stages adults, of course, can initiate or participate in the play activities but, until the stage of social play is reached, the child will respond to or imitate the adult rather than interact with him in what might be termed a play partnership.

Categories of play

Various attempts have been made to classify children's play in terms of its content. One of the best known of these is that by Buhler, who suggests four main categories, namely functional, fictional, receptive, and constructive. Functional play, which is the first to emerge, involves the practice of a particular function or skill, which is usually relatively crude such as kicking or clapping hands, but can involve delicate movements of the hand. Fictional play emerges next, usually during the second year of life, and involves fantasy or pretend behaviour in which the individual gives himself or the objects with which he is playing a particular role (e.g. a doll is treated like a real baby), and shortly afterwards or at the same time comes receptive play in which the child listens to a story or looks at the events in a picture. By the end of the second year constructive play has also usually made an appearance, involving playing with bricks, drawing, and playing with sand and other natural materials. To these four categories is added a fifth, play with rules, which involves the set procedures we normally term games, and which usually becomes established by nursery school age.

Although the other four forms of play tend to reach a peak at the age of seven or eight, and show a subsequent gradual decline, play involving games increases steadily in importance, and under the heading of 'sport' may remain an abiding interest throughout life. Schools foster this interest by offering organized games as part of the curriculum, but such games increasingly include a new element: that of competition. In other words, they are not undertaken simply for the pleasure involved in the activity itself, but in order to produce winners and losers, and the prestige and disappointments associated with these categories. With the advent of competition, play could be said therefore to lose some of its non-serious quality, and consciously to serve psychological functions other than the hedonistic one to which we have already drawn attention. With the increasing professionalization of sport in adult life, and with the increasing emphasis, both social and economic, upon winning, it is doubtful indeed whether organized games as practised at a high level can really any longer be classified as play at all.

As long ago as 1949, Huizinga identified the decline of play in adult life as one of the disturbing elements in western civilization, and this thesis could be further developed now that television and the media generally have turned organized games into a multi-million pound industry in which even the rules under which teams and individuals compete are altered to suit the convenience of the cameras and of viewing schedules. Psychologists and sociologists are currently showing much interest in the implications of this shift away from play for human behaviour, not only for the kind of behaviour exemplified by soccer hooliganism and by the decline in participation in favour of spectating, but for the general attitudes and values of society. Doubtless sport reflects these values as well as perhaps helping to form them, but the moving force behind much sport currently appears to be something much grimmer than the delightful qualities that define play in childhood. The commercial values exhibited by much organized sport and by many professional sportsmen may therefore tend to lend credence to the mistaken notion that things should never be undertaken for the pleasure or diversion they bring in themselves but for the extrinsic rewards (usually monetary) they can command.

Play and learning

There is no doubt that children learn through play, just as they learn, consciously and unconsciously, from all forms of experience. In examining the nature of this learning it is important to remember, however, that for the young pre-school child there is no real distinction between play and what an adult might think of as work. Helping mother or father in the garden or in the home is a form of play to him because, like playing with toys, it is engaged in for non-serious ends. The two and three year old will enjoy making cakes with mother or father in the kitchen not because this will provide something nice to eat for tea, but because the business of mixing in the flour and adding the milk and the other ingredients is enjoyable in itself. He may in fact have lost all interest in the cakes by the time they make their appearance on the dining-room table, and in any case will see little connection between the neat objects arranged on the plate and the many-coloured, malleable substances he had control over a few hours previously in the kitchen. It is only as the child grows older, and comes to associate certain kinds of activity (e.g. helping with the housework) with certain kinds of reward (e.g. parental praise), that he will begin to see present behaviour as indulged in less for the sake of immediate gratification than for the sake of long-term benefits. This is partly a function of the strength of the reward or rewards themselves, and partly a function of the child's developing cognitive skills which enable him to see more clearly the link between cause and effect.

As was implied in the opening paragraph of this chapter, many commentators over the years have tended to see play as simply representing the child's method of learning. They identify what might be called a play drive, and see this drive, along with the hunger drive and other survival-orientated drives, as being the innate mechanism that leads a child to interact with his environment (as opposed to lying passively in his cot) and thus to learn the way in which it works. This view is not incompatible with the notion that a child engages in play for hedonistic reasons (though it hinders our ability to understand how play looks to the child himself if it causes us to lose sight of these reasons). Certainly, in the early months of life at least, playing does seem to be an innate rather than a learnt activity, and as such therefore can be classified with other drive mechanisms. It is also quite clearly a strong promoter of activity, and thus puts the child in a position in which learning is likely to take place. As Piaget suggests, it may also help him develop more complex forms of thinking as he strives to reflect upon the way things behave as he interacts with them, and may in addition be a stimulator of social learning as the child discovers what is acceptable and not acceptable to the people with whom he is playing.

Clearly, the more opportunities a child is offered during the course of his play, the more likely is it that new learning will take place. A child growing up in an environment in which there are few objects for him to manipulate, in which there is little access to materials like sand and clay, in which there are no constructional toys like bricks or drawing materials, in which there is a restricted range of textures and colours, and in which there is only limited social interaction, will learn less rapidly than if he were placed in a more stimulating environment. By stimulating in this context I do not necessarily mean a cupboard full of expensive mechanical gadgets that emit coloured lights and sparks, or lifesize dolls that wet themselves at both ends, or plastic machine-guns realistic en ugh to mount a bank raid; I mean a wealth of natural (though safe) objects that the child can explore and arrange and re-arrange and use imaginatively, natural materials that he can mix and shape and pour without fear of adult outrage at the ensuing mess and, just as important, a parent who delights in the child's company and actually enjoys getting down on the floor alongside and re-entering a once familiar magic world.

eferences

Allport, G.W. (1961)
Pattern and Growth in Personality. New York: Holt, Rinehart & Winston.

Huizinga, J. (1949)
Homo Ludens: A study of the play element in culture.
London: Routledge & Kegan Paul.

Questions

1. Why could this chapter on play have been 'as readily ... included ... under cognitive development as under social development'?
2. Do you agree with the statement that western society has placed a major emphasis upon work? What are the reasons for your answer?
3. What do we mean by hedonistic?
4. Why should 'delight ... be seen as a desirable end in itself'?
5. How can the adult best help the child to 'develop positive atttitudes towards the place of leisure in his life'? How would you define and recognize these attitudes (i) in children and (ii) in adults?
6. Attempt a definition of 'play' that holds good for both children and adults.
7. List the major differences in play as indulged in by children and play as indulged in by animals. What do these differences tell us about the psychological skills of the two groups concerned?
8. What are the differences between solitary, parallel, and social play?
9. What are the categories of play identified by Buhler? Can you suggest alternative categories which you consider may be more helpful for the teacher?
10. Suggest ways in which play can be structured for children in the nursery-infant age range to facilitate learning. Are there any possible dangers behind structuring play in this way?
11. What are the major differences between play and games?
12. What do you consider are the major implications of the shift of western society away from play? Can you suggest ways in which this shift can be counteracted?
13. Suggest some of the reasons why the child comes to make an increasing distinction between play and work as he grows older.
14. From your own experience, however limited, of babies and small children, do you think those psychologists who talk of an innate 'play drive' are justified?
15. List some of the qualities that you think good play equipment should possess (i) for children of nursery school age and (ii) for children in the infant school.

Annotated reading

Bruner, J.S., Jolly, A. and Sylva, K. (1976) Play: Its role in development and evolution. Harmondsworth: Penguin.
The most significant book to appear on play in recent years. It contains a wealth of reference and research material, and spans all aspects of play in man and animals.

Yardley, A. (1978) Play. In D. Fontana (ed.), The Education of the Young Child', London: Open Books.
   A very good short introduction to play in the nursery and infant schools.

Millar, S. (1968) The Psychology of Play. Harmondsworth: Penguin.
   A deservedly popular general introduction to the whole field, and succeeds in being both readable and thorough.

Garvey, C. (1977) Play. London: Fontana/Open Books.
   Another good general text.

Marzolla J. and Lloyd, J. (1974) Learning Through Play. London: Allen & Unwin.

Roberts, V. (1971) Playing, Learning and Living. Oxford: Blackwell.
   These two books look closely at the way in which learning experiences can be provided through play.

Matterson, E.M. (1965) Play with a Purpose for the Under Sevens. Harmondsworth: Penguin.
   A very practical book for the nursery and early infant years.

Yardley, A. (1974) Structure in Early Learning. London: Evans.
   A good examination of the use of structure in play with young children.

Huizinga, J. (1949) Homo Ludens: A study of the play element in culture. London: Routledge & Kegan Paul.
   This remains a valuable and seminal book for all those interested in the place of play in society generally.

Caillois, R. (1961) Man, Play and Games. New York: Free Press.
   Useful in much the same way as Huizinga.

Herron, R. and Sulton-Smith, B. (eds) (1971) Child's Play. New York: Wiley.
   A good account of the ways in which play is studied by researchers.

Opie, I. and Opie, P. (1959) The Lore and Language of Schoolchildren. London: Oxford University Press.
   The student interested in the verbal content of children's play and games will enjoy this book.

Relevance to the teacher
DAVID FONTANA

Detailed discussion on how best to use play within the school curriculum belongs more to a book on teaching methods than to one on psychology. Clearly, though, it is nursery and primary school teachers who are most likely to be concerned with the first four categories of play mentioned in the main part of the chapter (i.e. functional, fictional, receptive and constructive) while secondary school teachers are more likely to be interested in the fifth category (games). Accordingly, let me make some general comments applicable to teachers of younger children first, and then pass on to the work of teachers of older age groups.

Within the nursery school, play is the major component of the curriculum. This does not mean, as the uninitiated are sometimes prone to suppose, that children are allowed to run riot and do very much as they please under the eye of a teacher whose main concern is to keep them from physical harm. Though nursery (and infant) school teachers are well aware of the pleasurable aspect of play, their purpose is to provide children with the kind of experiences that are likely to lead in addition to desirable forms of learning (both cognitive and social), and since in this they do not differ from teachers of older children we can say that it is the methods of teaching rather than the aims of teaching that mark nursery and infant off from other schools. In nursery and infant schools, it is the task of the teacher to offer a range of play activities and to help children explore them to the full. Sometimes this involves initiating particular activities with particular children, while at others it entails observing the activities children have chosen for themselves and prompting them to modify and develop these experiences so that they may realize their full learning potential. Importantly, the teacher encourages the child to verbalize what he is doing: that is, to describe his actions, to say why they are being undertaken, and to offer suggestions on why certain results follow from these actions. Thus the child is helped to develop his linguistic and his cognitive skills, and to gain confidence in his own ability to command appropriate vocabulary structures, while at the same time extending his knowledge of how the physical world behaves and of the appropriate skills for dealing with this world.

Structure in the play of young children

One problem that arises is the degree of structure that the teacher should impart to children's play; that is, the extent to which he should offer the child set patterns of routine and guidance in play specifically designed to introduce the child to identifiable skills and techniques. One school of thought has it that play should remain free and spontaneous with very young children, and that the task of the teacher is to provide a range of opportunities from which the child will choose according to his inclinations and his developmental level. But another argues that by introducing an element (though not an over-obtrusive element) of structure into play the teacher renders children's learning less haphazard and therefore more efficient. This structure may involve setting aside certain blocks of time for certain definite activities (number games, word identification games, movement activities, story time, music making and so on), or simply the provision of play equipment designed with the learning of specific skills in mind.

Obviously, as the child grows older and moves from the nursery school into and through the infant school, the degree of formalization in the timetable becomes more apparent, and the emphasis upon play decreases. (Some argue that this is a bad thing, and that ideally one should throughout life make little distinction between work and play, deriving the same pleasure from both; whether such a thing is possible in an industrialized society where many jobs are dull and repetitive is another matter.) But even in the nursery school, current consensus appears to be moving towards an increased degree of structure, and towards the use of commercially prepared structured play equipment (such as the Peabody Language Kit) aimed at encompassing a wide range of important early skills. This is doubtless a good thing, as long as we do not lose sight of the intrinsic value of play as a promoter of happiness in children, and of the child's need to exercise choice and initiative in a significant proportion of what he does.

In addition to the learning that comes to the child through play, the teacher in turn can learn by observing the way in which the child responds to play experiences. We have already discussed the developmental aspect of play in the preceding sections, and the link between play and cognitive development. A child who therefore consistently employs stereotyped and unimaginative play should alert the teacher to possible signs of retardation. By watching the child at play the teacher can assess his ability to sort and categorize, to match by colour, size and shape, to recognize familiar objects and symbols, to identify the links between cause and effect, to use and modify existing knowledge in the solution of new problems, and to develop essential manipulative skills such as using pencils, paintbrushes, scissors and constructional toys. Of equal importance, the teacher can also gain some insight into the child's personality and social development. A child who consistently plays alone, or who shows marked destructiveness or aggression, or seems unable to share or wait his turn, or constantly demands adult attention, or who cannot tolerate minor frustrations, may be giving indications of some psychological disturbance. More subtly, the child's use of roles when involved in domestic play may give some insight into his relationships with parents or brothers and sisters at home. At all times, the observation of children's play helps the teacher listen for the child's use of language, both as a medium for expressing his own thoughts and as a way of communicating fluently and responsibly with others.

Play in older children

Turning now to teachers of older age groups, where the
emphasis is upon games rather than upon play, we find that
again there are some general psychological points that offer
the possibilities of practical help. The first of these is
that games do not involve only what goes on in the gymnasium
or on the games field. There is increasing evidence that
games are an aid to learning in most school subjects, just
as it has been found that they are of value in business and
industry, and in particular in the learning of management
skills and techniques. The use of games in classroom-based
learning, and in particular of the kind of games known as
simulation exercises, is covered in chapter 8. All we need
say at present is that these games can prove highly enjoyable both to children and teachers, and can be used to mimic
the real-life situations in which children may one day put
their classroom-based knowledge to practical use. One problem that faces education at all levels is that so much
teaching and learning takes place in the artificial environment of the classroom: that is, in an environment divorced
from the outside world and therefore from the context to
which school learning really applies. This problem can be
partly solved if, through the use of carefully organized and
planned games, the child can be enabled to see the direct
practical relevance of what he is learning for the tasks
that may one day face him in his future career, or for
the tasks that face him in everyday social life, or for the
tasks that face society and western civilization as a whole.
As chapter 8 stresses, learning is most likely to take place
where the learner can see the immediate relevance of what
he is learning, either by putting it to practical use or by
relating it to problems that he has already identified (or
is readily able to identify) as being of importance.

Games

Moving on now from the classroom to the games field, we find
that great emphasis has been laid over the years on the
belief that sport is not only good for physical development
and physical fitness but for personality growth as well. We
are told that sport develops 'character', that it teaches
the value of teamwork and co-operation, that it teaches fair
play and all the other good things that come under the
heading of 'sportsmanship', that it teaches unselfishness
and helps the individual to take knocks in life, and so on.
If sport is indeed good for personality growth then this is
a strong argument for its inclusion in the school curriculum, since education is concerned with the personal
development of the individual as well as with the transmission of knowledge. Unfortunately, there is no consistent
evidence that sport does have this desired effect or that
such lessons as it does teach are generalizable to situations occurring off the sports field. Attention has already
been drawn to the apparent decline of play in modern society, and to the doubtful values that motivate much organized

sport, and it therefore seems fair to suggest that, in any case, even if these values are generalizable their influence may not always be for the good.

It seems possible that the reason why such an extensive mythology has grown up around the educational value of sport is that, in view of the strong emphasis upon work and the relative neglect of play in western society, some justification had to be found when sport was first introduced into the school curriculum. It was not sufficient to put it there because children for the most part enjoyed it, since enjoyment was not seen as a necessary part of education. Nor was it sufficient to lay stress simply upon its physical benefits, since physical development was held at that time to be very much secondary to mental growth and the training of the so-called mental 'faculties'. So in Britain, to take one example from western culture, we have the paradox of a sport-loving nation which yet was reluctant to admit that sport was there for sheer pleasure, and that the experience of such pleasure was sufficient justification in its own right.

With changing patterns of employment in modern society, and with the prospect of an extensive addition in leisure time for most of us, it may be that games will come increasingly to be seen as conferring social benefit. They have the potential to occupy the individual's time pleasantly and to give him physical exercise, thus promoting both bodily and psychological health. They can also be a way of bringing people together, and of providing opportunities for co-operation and mutual support. It may be that when these benefits are fully appreciated, the value of play will be recognized not only for small children but for adolescents and adults as well. One hopes, too, that individuals with no great aptitude for sport will perhaps be less likely to be turned against games during their school careers if this happens, since the criteria under which they take part would then become not how they compare with the standards of their peers but how much pleasure they actually derive from the experience themselves.

dditional reading

Taylor, J.L. and Walford, R. (1972) Simulation in the Classroom. Harmondsworth: Penguin.
    A good introduction to use of the simulation exercise.

Dunn, L.M., Horton, K.B. and Smith, J.O. (eds) (1968) The Peabody Language Development Kit. Circle Pines, Minn.: American Service Inc.
    Contains the Peabody Language Development Kit.

Wood, D., McMahon, C. and Cranstoun, Y. (1980) Working with Under Fives. London: Grant McIntyre.
    This has a particularly good section on how teachers can 'tutor' young children's play. Part of a series arising out of the Oxford Pre-school Project, it contains much of practical value for teachers of young children.

Part two

Cognitive Factors and Learning

Introduction
The term cognitive, which derives from the Latin 'cognitio', to know, refers to all those psychological abilities associated with thinking and with knowing. These abilities attract particular attention within education since they help determine the facility with which a child can learn, and therefore whether he comes to be classed as forward in his work or as backward or perhaps even as educationally subnormal (ESN). Cognitive abilities include a child's measured intelligence, his levels of thinking and even, to a certain extent, his creativity and the manner in which he conducts interpersonal relationships. Since language is the medium through which thinking usually takes place, and since much intelligent and creative activity is expressed through language, this too is usually regarded as a cognitive activity.

In Part II each of these aspects of cognitive functioning is studied, and the processes by which learning takes place are also examined, since learning and cognition are obviously closely related. The starting point is thinking, and the child's ability to develop and use concepts.

63

4

Concept Formation and Development
David Fontana

Thinking and education

The ability to think clearly and sensibly, which involves being able to follow a line of reasoning, to grasp concepts and to initiate lines of enquiry oneself, is obviously central to a child's educational progress. No matter what subject he is studying, failure to understand what is required of him, and to identify and tackle the problems it involves, are obvious barriers to any real progress. Although they are fully aware of this, some teachers are unclear of the level of thinking they can reasonably expect of a child at a given age. Much educational failure, indeed, stems from the fact that forms of thinking are demanded of children that they are incapable of supplying.

The work of Piaget

The most sustained and ambitious attempt at studying children's thinking is that of the Swiss biologist-turned-psychologist, Jean Piaget. Piaget's findings led him to propose an essentially developmental theory of how children form the concepts involved in thinking. That is, a theory which proposes that children develop more sophisticated patterns of thinking as a consequence primarily of maturation, and according both to a set pattern and a more or less stable timetable. His theory is necessarily somewhat complex and elaborate in detail, but its basic ingredients can be understood readily enough.

Before we look at these ingredients, however, we must first define what we mean by a 'concept'. A concept is the idea an individual has about a particular class of objects (including animate objects) or events, grouped together on the basis of the things they have in common. It is through concepts that we make sense of the world. Thus a small child will have a concept of 'big things', a concept of 'small things', a concept of 'wetness' and of 'dryness', a concept of 'things I like' and of 'things I don't like', and so on. When he encounters novel objects or experiences, or is faced with problems of any kind, he attempts to make sense of them by fitting them into the range of concepts that he already has. If these concepts prove inadequate, he may have to modify them in some way, or perhaps try to develop a new concept altogether (as, for example, when he encounters a live dog or a snowstorm for the first time). Usually even

new concepts can be related back in some way to concepts
he already holds (e.g. the dog moves of its own accord like
people do, the snow is wet like cold water), but if the
relationships he thinks he sees are not the right ones, and
he thus cannot interpret anything important about the new
experience correctly, then he may be unable to develop a
concept for dealing with it appropriately (e.g. the child
may tear up a £10 note or Daddy's contract for his new book
because he classifies them along with chocolate wrappers and
newspapers which he knows to be expendable).

Piaget's theory has it that the way in which we are able
to form and handle concepts changes as we go through childhood into adolescence. Thus the child's thinking is not
simply an immature version of the adult's, but differs from
it in a number of radical and important ways. These ways can
be classified in terms of several different stages which the
child apparently passes through on his way from the thought
patterns of the infant to those of the fully developed
adult. Piaget has it that the child goes through each of
these stages in turn, at approximately the ages shown below,
and that the speed at which he moves through each stage,
though influenced by environment and by the richness or
otherwise of the experiences it offers, is essentially
governed by biologically determined maturational processes.
Each of the stages is characterized by a particular cognitive 'structure' (or structures): that is, by the particular strategy (or strategies) manifested by the child in
his attempt to organize and make sense of experience. The
stages are discussed in their chronological order below.

Stage 1. Sensori-motor. Approximately birth to two years
In the early weeks of life, the child's activity appears to
be purely reflex in character. He sucks, he grasps objects,
he cries, he throws out his arms and legs when startled and
so on. Such actions are apparently entirely involuntary. The
child is presented with a stimulus (e.g. something to suck,
something to grasp) and the reflex response is evoked. There
is no thinking on his part, just as there is no thinking on
our part if we snatch our hands away from something hot or
blink if something threatens our eyes.

At first these reflex activities are directed towards
the child's own body, but somewhere between four and eight
months of age he comes increasingly to direct them towards
objects external to himself as well. This is an important
development in that it indicates that an element of purpose
is now being introduced into the child's behaviour, that is,
he is now apparently using sequences of movement directed
towards the attainment of definite goals. Piaget calls such
sequences schemata, and claims they are evidence of
cognitive structures which allow the child to link actions
together into stable and repeatable units. Between the ages
of 12 and 18 months these schemata become increasingly
elaborate as the child experiments with them to attain
desired ends.

During the sensori-motor period, Piaget claims the schemata used by the child are principally circular reactions. These in turn are broken down into primary circular reactions which occur in the early period of reflex activity, secondary circular reactions which occur when the child starts more purposive activity, and tertiary circular reactions which happen when this activity becomes more elaborated. These labels are important if we wish to understand the development of thinking because they indicate that the child's reactions throughout the sensori-motor stage remain both overt and physical. That is to say, the child does not think about doing a particular action, he simply does it. As Piagetians express it, his relationship with the action is not a mental one, but is contained entirely within the action itself. It is only later on that he is able to internalize his actions (i.e. to rehearse them mentally, to decide consciously to do A rather than B), and to think, rather than simply to do.

Stage 2. Pre-operational thought. Approximately 2–7 years
This stage is divided by Piaget into two sub-stages, the pre-conceptual sub-stage (approximately age two to age four) and the intuitive sub-stage (approximately age four to age seven).

1. PRE-CONCEPTUAL SUB-STAGE: the child's cognitive development during the years from two to four is increasingly dominated by the emergence of symbolic activity. The child becomes able to use symbols to stand for actions, and therefore is able to represent these actions to himself without actually doing them (i.e. it becomes possible for him to internalize his actions). We see this, for example, in the child's play, where dolls come to stand for babies, where a toy car stands for the real thing, and where the child can assume the role of 'mummy' or 'daddy'. With the development of language skills he also comes to possess what Piaget calls signs: that is, sounds which, although they have no intrinsic relationship with objects and events (different languages use quite different sounds) nevertheless are used to represent them. Mathematical notations are another example of signs.

Note that Piaget holds the distinction between symbols and signs to be an important one. The child is able to use symbols before signs, and therefore we must not equate the development of symbolic activity with the development of language, though the two tend to become increasingly linked as the child grows older. Nor, Piaget insists, does the emergence of symbolic activity indicate that the child is able to form concepts as adults and older children can (hence the title 'pre-conceptual' for this sub-stage). For example, he cannot form generic concepts, that is classes of objects, correctly (e.g. he may refer to all men as 'Daddy'), nor can he make transitive inferences (e.g. A is bigger then B, B is bigger than C, therefore A is bigger than C). The form of reasoning he employs is known as 'transductive' reasoning, since it goes from the particular to the particular (e.g. because A goes with B in this instance then A must always go with B; because we caught a bus to meet Daddy in town, then every bus goes to meet Daddy in town). Although such transductive reasoning is incorrect, it is clear evidence of the child's attempt to make sense of the world.

2. INTUITIVE SUB-STAGE: of all stages and sub-stages, this is the one that has been most extensively studied by Piaget and his colleagues, and as it covers the early school years it is of particular interest to the teacher. The principal cognitive structures now employed by the child are labelled by Piaget egocentrism, centration, and irreversibility respectively.

* Egocentrism is characterized by an inability to see the world from anything other than a self-centred, subjective viewpoint. Therefore the child at this time is unable to be critical, logical, or realistic in his thinking. This is not selfishness, it is simply that the child is not yet aware that there can be points of view other than his own. This can be demonstrated experimentally if, for example, the child is asked to say what someone sitting across the classroom from him is likely to be able to see (typically he will describe things from his own perspective only) or to name the brothers and sisters of a sibling in his own family (again he will typically see things only from his own standpoint and leave himself off the list).
* Centration involves focussing attention (centring) upon only one feature of a situation and ignoring others, however relevant. Investigation of centring has spawned a number of interesting experiments, many of which the teacher can try out for himself. In one of the best known the child is presented with two plasticine balls which he agrees are the same size, and one is then rolled out into a sausage shape. When asked which is the larger now (or which has the more plasticine now), he will usually point to the sausage. In other words, he has focussed upon only one aspect of the problem, namely the longer length of the sausage, and based his answer upon this. As a consequence of such centring, the child is unable to practise what Piaget calls conservation: that is, he is unable to grasp in our example the fact that the amount of plasticine is conserved (remains the same) whatever happens to its shape. A similar instance of the inability to practise conservation is produced if we take two identical beakers each filled to the same point with liquid and pour the contents of one into a tall thin glass. The child will now usually claim that we have 'more' liquid than we had before, and more liquid than we have in the remaining beaker, simply

because the level has now risen higher. If we next pour the liquid into a square fat beaker so that the level falls he will now claim that we have 'less' liquid than before.

* Irreversibility entails the inability to work backwards to one's starting point. Thus having gone, say, through a given sequence involving three steps, the child finds it hard to go back to step two and then to step one. Thus although he can add two and three in order to make five, he finds it often impossible to reverse the procedure and subtract two from five in order to arrive back at three. It is not that he is incapable of carrying out the computation if it is presented to him as a separate sum; it is simply that he cannot grasp that because two and three make five then five minus two must make three. Similarly, he is also still unable to grasp the transitive inferences that eluded him in the pre-conceptual sub-stage.

Stage 3. Concrete operations stage. Approximately 7-11 years

This important stage, which essentially covers the junior school period, sees the child achieve an organized and coherent symbolic system of thinking which enables him to anticipate and control his environment. This system still differs from that employed by the majority of adults, however, in that it is tied to concrete experiences (hence the term concrete operations). This means that although the child can formulate hypotheses in the absence of any actual concrete evidence in front of him, and can go at least a step or two beyond the evidence by abstract reasoning, he nevertheless must have experienced such evidence in one form or another concretely in the past if he is to be able to do so. Essentially he is still limited in his thinking, and tends to describe his environment rather than to explain it (one reason why he finds it much easier to give examples of things than to provide definitions of them). He also finds it hard to test a hypothesis against reality correctly, often changing a perfectly correct view of reality to make it fit rather than altering his hypothesis. Thus, for example, if he believes the football team he supports is the best in the league he will continue to maintain this no matter how often it loses (a fault to which many adults are often by no means immune)!

Nevertheless the child's thinking moves forward considerably during this stage. It becomes less ego-centric, and he develops the ability to show both de-centring and reversal. With de-centring comes conservation, and Piaget maintains that this conservation takes place in a definite order, with conservation of substance coming first at approximately age seven or eight, conservation of weight coming next somewhere between ages nine and ten, and conservation of volume being achieved by about age 12.

The main cognitive structure underlying these and the various other advances made during this stage is grouping

(or categorization). The child is able to recognize the
members of a true logical class, and thus organize objects
and events into sets in terms of their common defining
characteristics. Grouping increasingly enables him to make
sense of experience, to solve problems, and to move towards
a more realistic and accurate picture of the world. With the
ability to group also comes what Piaget calls seriation:
that is, the ability to arrange objects in rank order in
terms, for example, of size or weight. We can sum this up
by saying that grouping and seriation indicate that the
child is now able to see the correct relationship between
things, and to use this knowledge to solve problems. Since
this is remarkably like the definition of intelligence
offered later in chapter 5, it is appropriate to point out
that for Piaget intelligence is indeed the result of the
various genetically determined activities that we have been
discussing under the various stages in this section, and
that for Piaget intelligence is itself therefore closely
bound up with the maturation of innate characteristics.

Stage 4. Formal operations. Approximately 12 years and onwards

The onset of adolescence usually sees the emergence of what
Piaget calls formal operations, which is the final stage in
the developmental programme. Though the child's thinking may
still differ from the adult's in degree, it now begins to
resemble it in kind. The child becomes able to follow the
form of an argument or to set up an hypothesis without
requiring actual experience of the concrete objects or
situations upon which it depends. Of equal importance,
having come to understand individual concepts or categories
in isolation during the previous stages of his development,
he is now able to see that these may be interdependent in
certain circumstances. For example, he may realize that
speed, weight and time might all have to be considered in
arriving at the answer to a particular problem, or that one
might have to be varied while the others are held constant
and so on.

The cognitive structure that underlies formal operations
is called by Piaget lattice-group structure, to indicate that it is a form of thinking in which everything is
capable of being related to everything else, thus allowing
the individual to try out various combinations of hypo-
thetical propositions when considering a problem or possible future event. The kind of reasoning thus generated is
known as hypothetico-deductive reasoning, because the individual is able both to set up hypotheses and make deductions
from results, thus furthering his understanding of the
material with which he is dealing.

There is one further important aspect of Piaget's thinking that we must touch on if we are to have a good grasp
of his theory, namely the processes that he terms functional
invariants. It will be appreciated that all the forms of
thinking described so far are dependent upon age and

development. The child changes his cognitive structures as he grows older (hence Piaget sometimes terms them functional variants). But he also has other cognitive processes that are inborn and remain constant throughout life (hence the term functional invariants). The most important of these are known as accommodation, assimilation, and organization. Borrowed from biology, the term accommodation implies that the individual has at times to adapt his functioning to the specific qualities of the things with which he is dealing. There are many things about the world that even at an early age the child realizes he cannot change (e.g. the force of gravity, the properties of water and of fire), and therefore he has to accommodate his behaviour to them rather than attempt to alter them to suit himself. Assimilation, on the other hand (which is another term borrowed from biology), refers to the process by which objects or their attributes are incorporated into the individual's existing cognitive structures, often altering and developing these structures somewhat in the process. Assimilation and accommodation always go together, although at any one time one of them may be more important than the other. The reason why they go together is that the individual can only assimilate those elements of his environment to which he is able to accommodate himself. If accommodation is impossible, then so is assimilation. For example, the child accommodates himself to a substance like water, assimilating in the process that water is wet, that you cannot breathe in it, that it makes a mess on Mummy's nice clean floor and so on.

The third of Piaget's functional invariants, organization, concerns the way in which cognitive acts are grouped and arranged to form sequences or schema. In any intellectual act there is always a schemata of some kind present, a kind of cognitive plan which the individual uses to help him tackle a given problem. If a certain schema proves inappropriate for a certain task, then the individual will try to re-organize it: that is, try to alter or add to or subtract from or re-arrange the cognitive acts which it contains in order to try again more successfully. Obviously his ability to organize, just as his ability to accommodate and assimilate, develops as he grows older, but the three functions remain unchanged as processes from birth to maturity.

ther approaches to gnitive development

Although Piaget's work has attracted by far the greatest amount of attention within education, he is not the only psychologist who has made relevant contributions to our knowledge of the development of thinking in children. The American psychologist, Jerome Bruner, in a number of important publications, suggests children go through three main stages on their way to acquiring the mature thought processes of the adult. These are enactive (in which thinking is based upon doing), iconic (in which imagery comes increasingly to be used) and symbolic (in which complex symbolism including language is employed). These stages have obvious parellels with those of Piaget, but where Bruner differs markedly is in his insistence that although we acquire these three stages in chronological order, with symbolic coming last, we nevertheless retain and use all three throughout life. We do not 'grow out of' the earlier stages, as in Piaget's model, and although the major emphasis in adult thinking is upon the symbolic level, we can and do employ enactive and iconic thinking when the situation is appropriate.

Bruner's work is discussed in more detail in the chapter on learning (chapter 8), which includes some of the implications of his ideas for the teacher's work. There remains one other worker in this field to whom we must draw attention, however, and that is the Russian, Lev Vygotsky. Vygotsky differed from Piaget and Bruner in that his main concern was with the relationship between thought and language. His experimental apparatus consisted of a number of blocks of wood with nonsense syllables written on the hidden undersides. Each block was a variant of two heights (tall or squat) and of six shapes (circle, semi-circle, square, trapezium, triangle, and a six-sided shape). The experimenter turned up one of the blocks and showed the child the nonsense syllable written underneath, and then asked him to pick out all the other blocks that he considered would carry the same syllable. Thus the child was being asked to isolate the particular combination of shape and size that appeared to go with a particular syllable (or more technically to isolate the spatial attributes that appeared to accompany a particular verbal concept).

Broadly, Vygotsky's conclusions were similar to those of Piaget, though his terminology was different. He identified three main stages in the development of a child's thinking, namely the vague syncretic stage (in which the child depended primarily upon actions, and turned the blocks up on a random trial and error basis until he had found the right ones), the complexes stage (in which the child used strategies of varying complexity but still failed to identify the desired attributes), and the potential concept stage (in which the child was able to cope with the individual relevant attributes of the blocks but could not manipulate all of these at one and the same time). When he could do so, the ability to form concepts was judged to have reached maturity.

Like Piaget, Vygotsky's ideas are complex, and there is considerable debate on the precise relationship of his three stages to those of Piaget. Nevertheless, from the practical standpoint of the teacher, it is easy to see the link between vague syncretic behaviour and Piaget's emphasis upon the child's need for physical activity before that activity can be internalized into thought. It is also easy to see the link between what Vygotsky saw as mature thinking and the lattice-group structures said by Piaget to be used when the child reached the stage of formal operations. In both there is an emphasis upon the child's ability to manipulate mentally several different ideas at the same time, and to see the relationships between them. Vygotsky also agrees with Piaget and differs from Bruner in that he sees the child as moving through the earlier stages of thinking rather than as carrying them with him throughout life (though as with Piaget's stages there is always the possibility of regression to earlier, immature forms of thought in the face of extreme problems and stresses).

Questions

1. What do we mean by the term 'concept'? Why are concepts so important in the development of thinking?
2. What is the process by which a child makes sense of novel objects or experiences?
3. List Piaget's stages of cognitive development and give the approximate ages associated with each.
4. What is the relationship between thought and action in the sensori-motor stage of development? How do we recognize when an element of purpose is being introduced into the child's behaviour?
5. Piaget claims that during the sensori-motor period the child's relationship with an action is not a mental one but is contained within the action itself. What do you think this really means?
6. Why is symbolic activity so important in the development of pre-operational (and later) forms of thinking?
7. Distinguish between 'symbols' and 'signs'.
8. Consider ways in which a child's play may give you insight into his level of symbolic activity.
9. Give an example of the kind of experiment used by Piaget to demonstrate centration. What aspects of the child's behaviour indicate that centration is taking place?
10. Write short definitions of egocentrism, irreversibility, and transductive reasoning.
11. Why do you think the child tends to describe his environment rather than explain it during the stage of concrete operations?
12. Piaget considers both grouping and categorization are essential abilities in the development of complex thinking. Why do you think this is so?
13. What are the characteristics of lattice-group structure?
14. How important are Piaget's so-called functional invariants to our understanding of the processes of thought?
15. List and define three main stages which Bruner considers each child goes through on his way to the acquisition of mature processes.
16. What is the fundamental way in which Bruner's stages differ from those of Piaget?
17. What aspect of the child's activity indicated to Vygotsky that he had reached the ability to form mature concepts?

18. What is the link between Vygotsky's so-called vague syncretic behaviour in children and Piaget's emphasis upon the child's need for physical activity before that activity can be internalized into thought?

Annotated reading

Inhelder, B. and Piaget, J. (1958) The Growth of Logical Thinking from Childhood to Adolescence. London: Routledge & Kegan Paul.
    Provides a comprehensive outline of Piaget's ideas on cognitive development for the non-specialist.

Piaget, J. (1970) Science of Education and the Psychology of the Child. London: Longmans.
    A survey of Piaget's main concerns within education.

Flavell, J.H. (1963) The Developmental Psychology of Jean Piaget. New York: Van Nostrand Reinhold.
    Usually regarded as the most complete summary of Piaget's work.

Phillips, J. L. (1975) The Origins of Intellect: Piaget's theory (2nd edn). New York: Freeman.
    Shorter than Flavell, but a splendid book that makes even the more complex areas of Piaget's theories fully comprehensible.

Beard, R. (1969) An Outline of Piaget's Developmental Psychology for Students and Teachers. London: Routledge & Kegan Paul.
    Another good short survey of Piaget's ideas.

Boden, M.A. (1979) Piaget. London: Fontana Modern Masters
    A very readable brief survey of the whole range of Piaget's work and its relevance to philosophy and biology as well as to psychology and education.

Bryant, P. (1974) Perception and Understanding in Young Children: An experimental approach. London: Methuen.

Burton, A. and Radford, J. (eds) (1978) Thinking in Perspective: Critical essays in the study of thought processes. London: Methuen.
    These two books contain important criticisms of Piaget's work, essential reading for the student with particular interests in this area.

Bruner, J., Goodnow, J. and Austin, G. (1956) A study of Thinking. New York: Wiley.
    Bruner is easily tackled through his own writings, since he presents his ideas clearly and engagingly (and see chapter 8 for other references to his work). This book deals particularly with cognitive development.

Vygotsky, L. (1962) Thought and Language. Cambridge, Mass.: MIT Press.
> Sets out his own ideas fully, but not an easy book for newcomers to the field.

Turner, J. (1975) Cognitive Development. London: Methuen,
> A very useful, brief introduction to the general field of cognitive development.

Mussen, P.H., Conger, J.J. and Kagan, J. (1979) Child Development and Personality (5th edn). New York: Harper & Row.
> The chapters on cognitive development and allied topics, like the rest of the book, are first class.

elevance to the
eacher
AVID FONTANA

For Piaget, intelligent cognitive activity is an extension of basic universal biological characteristics. The whole of intellectual functioning, in fact, is seen by him as simply a special form of biological activity. This factor, together with the four-stage developmental model that goes with it, might tempt some observers to suggest that in Piaget's view the role of the teacher is relatively unimportant. Children's ability to manage their environments and solve problems, it might seem, is dependent primarily upon maturation, with the teacher powerless to influence the speed with which a child progresses through each of the identified stages. This suggestion would be incorrect for two major reasons.

The first of these is that in his research Piaget concentrates upon how a child deals with information, not upon what kind of information we choose to give him. It is the teacher who decides upon the latter, and the teacher who therefore determines the content of the cognitive structures that a child uses in dealing with the world. The second is that the ages given for each of the stages and sub-stages identified by Piaget are approximate only. Some commentators, in fact, prefer to refer to them as mental ages rather than chronological ages for this reason. Some children may move more quickly through some or all of the stages than the norm, others more slowly. Some children will never attain formal operations, and even as adults will still function at the level of concrete operations. Granted this unevenness of progress, the question inevitably arises as to whether a child can be accelerated through the stages given the appropriate educational opportunities; if such acceleration does prove to be possible, the role of the teacher will then obviously be crucial to it.

Criticisms of Piaget

There has, in fact, recently been some criticism of Piaget's work which suggests he may have significantly underestimated the possibilities of such acceleration, and also failed to pay due regard to the importance of language in the development of the child's thinking. Language, as we shall see in chapter 5, is a highly complex activity, and the intricacy of its relationship to thought is as yet by no means clear. It could be that the nature of the linguistic structures to which a child is introduced in the home and in the school materially influence the speed with which he devises and uses schemata.

Equally important, the child's answers to the kind of problems posed by Piaget in his experiments may sometimes be restricted as much by his inability to understand fully the language in which these problems are couched as by any biologically determined inability to form the necessary concepts. In other words, he is handicapped by lack of information at the very outset. For example, Povey and Hill (1975) have shown that if pictorial material is used instead of verbal material with children at the preconceptual sub-stage, they appeared to be capable of forming not only specific but also generic concepts. For instance, they appeared to have a specific concept of 'dog', since they were able to identify a dog even when it was embedded pictorially in situations quite novel to them, and they appeared to have a generic concept of 'food' since they could identify as food many different edible objects.

Similarly Bryant and Trabasso (1971) have shown that children in the pre-conceptual stage can grasp transitive reasoning provided that they are given appropriate previous training and steps are taken to prevent lapses of memory while they are carrying out the various comparisons. This means that in the 'A is bigger than B, B is bigger than C, therefore A is bigger than C' type of statement, the child can understand the reasoning involved if he is first taught the initial two comparisons very thoroughly, and then is tested for memory of these comparisons at the same time that he is told about (or questioned on) the relationship between A and C.

The task of the teacher

These findings in no way invalidate Piaget's work, or his contention that children at the identified chronological ages tend to think in the ways indicated. What they do suggest is that the scope enjoyed by the teacher for accelerating children's progress through the various stages may be greater than was at first thought provided that material is presented to them in the appropriate way. And it is when making decisions about what is and what is not appropriate that the teacher finds Piaget's work to be of maximum help to him. This work suggests to us that many of the mistakes children make when tackling problems may be caused by the fact that as presented, these problems are unsuited to their levels of thinking. Errors which may therefore at first sight seem to the teacher to be inexcusable may in fact simply be evidence of the child's attempt to make sense of his material in terms of his existing cognitive structures.

We can perhaps best summarize what this means to the teacher as follows.

* When working with children of any age the teacher should
  never make the assumption that a child's attempts to
  think through a problem are simply an immature version
  of his own. Often the answer the child produces may make
  sense to himself in terms of the way in which he is
  able to conceptualize the material in front of him. The
  task of the teacher should therefore be to assess the
  level at which the child is thinking. This does not, of
  course, mean going through a range of Piagetian experiments with each member of his class. The chronological
  age of each child is, as we have seen, some guide, and
  armed with this the teacher needs to remind himself of
  the level of thinking appropriate to this age, and then
  to ask whether the child appears to be functioning at
  this level and whether learning material is being
  presented to him in a form appropriate to it.
* Although children should be given opportunities to
  conceptualize at levels higher than that associated with
  their chronological age, failure to take advantage of
  these opportunities should not be seen as a sign of
  inadequacy (or lack of interest) on their part, and at
  no time should the individual child be left feeling
  confused or that he is to blame. Biological maturation
  takes place at its own pace, and it would be as unrealistic to expect a child to accelerate this pace in the
  cognitive sphere as it would be to expect him to
  accelerate it in the field of physical growth.
* A child's level of conceptual development should be
  taken into account when devising teaching methods. At
  all stages below the onset of formal operations, for
  example, the child's powers of conceptualization are
  linked closely to his physical activity, and he needs
  therefore to experience problems (or previously to have
  experienced their defining characteristics) in a concrete form. Placed in an over-formal, exclusively
  teacher-orientated environment, the child is therefore
  starved of the practical experience which serves as the
  raw material for his thinking. If we restrict his
  experience, we restrict his conceptualization.
* Having had the benefit of experience, a child relies
  heavily upon symbolization in developing his concepts,
  and in particular upon that form of symbolization called
  signs to which we have already referred. Of paramount
  importance amongst the signs available to him are those
  which go to make up language. We discuss language at
  length in the next chapter, and all we need stress for
  the present is that the child should be given the
  benefit of a linguistically stimulating environment, and
  the teacher should endeavour to see to it that he
  understands the correct meaning of the words he uses.
  The same also applies to the signs (i.e. numbers themselves as well as plus signs, minus signs and the like)
  involved in mathematics.
* Piaget's developmental model of thinking emphasizes that

a child must master the schemata at the earlier levels if he is to go on to more advanced work. This is not just a question of the child 'missing the groundwork' in a particular subject, but the much more fundamental issue of failing to master the patterns of thinking necessary for success in a wide range of educational endeavours.

* Closely allied to the last point, we derive from Piaget the notion that educational backwardness is bound up with the level at which the child is thinking. A so-called backward child may be functioning at a level below that of his chronological age, and it is the task of the remedial teacher to establish what this level is and to ensure that material is presented to the child in a form consistent with it.

* The onset of formal operations makes the teacher's job easier in some ways in that he can now deal increasingly in abstract knowledge, but this brings potential problems of its own. It is suggested that part of the argumentativeness shown by some children at adolescence is occasioned by the fact that abstract concepts such as 'freedom', 'justice', 'truth', 'altruism' and so on now begin to take on a newer and deeper meaning for them, and often lead to their judging and rejecting the standards of their elders. Thus the idealism of the adolescent should be seen as a genuine attempt to understand the full implications of the nobler side of man's nature for human relationships, and should be welcomed and respected by adults who have perhaps had their own understanding blunted by problems and difficulties and the need to compromise over the years.

Finally, a word of caution; we have already said that the chronological ages attached to the various Piagetian stages are only approximations, but we must also stress that a child's development may be uneven in that he may attain some of the thinking associated with a particular stage before attaining the remainder. Or, faced with a difficult problem in a stressful situation, he may revert temporarily to an earlier stage of reasoning. Children's errors should therefore be studied closely (as we stress again in our chapter on learning) for the insights they give into the child's thinking. An error is not simply a matter of a cross rather than a tick on a child's work; it is essential feedback to the teacher not only on whether a child has understood a particular point or not but on the reasons why failure has perhaps occurred.

References

Bryant, P.E. and Trabasso, T. (1971)
Transitive inferences and memory in young children. Nature, 232, 456-458.
Povey, R. and Hill, E. (1975)
Can pre-school children form concepts? Educational Research, 17, 180-192.

Additional reading

Brown, G. and Desforges, C. (1979) Piaget's Theory: A psychological critique. London: Routledge & Kegan Paul.
  Provides an excellent survey of Piaget's theory, together with detailed criticism of some of his findings and the inferences drawn from them.

5

Language Development in Young Children
W. P. Robinson

Introduction: a frame of reference

For over 15 years now a steady river of books about language development in children has flowed on to the market, while the journals have been flooded by research on the same topic. Much of this work has been clever and ingenious; not all of it has been sensible in its point of departure. It is encouraging that the more recent productions (see de Villiers and de Villiers, 1979) have begun at the starting point that common sense would have recommended; Halliday (1975) expresses the contrast between the earlier and some of the later work in terms of the questions asked by psycholinguists and sociolinguists. The former have tended to focus upon the child mastering the syntax of language (rules for combining words) at the expense of the other components of language: phonology (sounds), lexis (words), semantics (meaning), and pragmatics (significance for action). They have asked: how does the child combine units into structures (combinations of units), particularly words into sentences? What do a child's errors, in terms of what is acceptable in the adult language, tell us about the system his brain uses for generating sentences? Are these errors universal, common to all children learning all languages? Are there fixed sequences of syntactic development within and across all languages? What are the characteristics of the language acquisition device that all children are born with? With the possible exception of the last, all these questions are proper in that evidence could be and has been collected to answer them.

Flow charts have been drawn up setting out stages in the development of negation and question formation, and these have been 'explained' by writing out rules that the child's mind appears to be following in producing these forms. The grammatical errors of children learning different languages have been examined for similarities and differences, and explanations have been offered for the patterns observed.

However, this emphasis upon syntactic structure and a corresponding neglect of function is alien to the socio-linguistic stance. From that perspective the questions are liable to be asked in terms of the ways in which units and structures develop to serve functions. Function is primary: children talk to communicate. Introductory questions would be: why do children talk? What kinds of meanings do they encode to what ends? We can proceed to ask how they code meanings: that is, what units and structures they use. How do the functions and their associated structures change in development and why?

The main reason for preferring the functional/structural to the purely structural approach might be summarized by stating that young children issue commands rather than utter imperative forms ('Stand up!'); they make requests and ask questions rather than form interrogatives; they comment about themselves, about others and about the world rather than utter declarative sentence forms; they achieve purposes by communicating meanings rather than construct linguistic structures. In addition and crucially, a functional/structural approach obliges us to ask questions about the nature of children and their learning as well as about the language they are mastering.

That being so, if we wish to find out which units and structures are learned when and how, we have to turn to examine ways in which children can be encouraged to exercise functions requiring such units and structures. If we are to be able to specify what children can learn, what they do learn, and how, we have to look closely and attentively at theories of development, learning and instruction.

Three approaches have dominated thinking about the learning of children: associative principles, ideas of modelling, and the cognitive developmental. The first stresses that events occurring close to each other in terms of time and space are likely to become associated: the fact of their co-occurrence is likely to be learned. The work of Pavlov showed that new artificial stimuli could be substituted for the original stimuli to elicit responses already in the animal's repertoire, under certain conditions (classical conditioning). Thorndike, and latterly Skinner, have shown that new responses to stimuli can be learned if these are followed quickly by rewards or punishments (operant conditioning). What roles can classical conditioning and operant conditioning play for which aspects of language development? Have rewards and punishment and their contingent use a significant part which they can and do play?

What determines when and how imitation can be important? Children can and do learn through observation as well as action; how might observational learning fit into the picture? Piaget offers a portrait of the child as an active organizer of experience, building up schemes for action through processes of assimilation and accommodation. These schemes grow in number. They become co-ordinated and differentiated. They become organized so as to afford symbolic as well as physical solutions to problems. The symbolic systems themselves become qualitatively more powerful with growth, which is promoted through different interaction with a challenging environment. How is language development to be integrated into this approach and how do these developments relate to language mastery? The existence of each of these kinds of learning is thoroughly established. What we have yet to determine is whether they are relevant to language learning, and if so, how and under what conditions. Sadly, even recent texts are relatively reticent about these issues, but less so than those of earlier writers.

After closely observing the development of language, particularly the syntax, in three children over a number of years, Brown (1973) concluded: 'What impels the child to "improve" his speech at all remains something of a mystery'. At least two weaknesses in his reasoning might be offered to explain this pessimism. First, the actual tests made of the possible relevance of principles of reinforcement (rewards and punishments) and confirmation/correction, or of observational learning examined only very few linguistic features in very few children. We have, however, no reason to expect that identical processes will be of equal significance for all aspects of language learning in all children. Brown is not enthusiastic about common sense, but common sense easily observes that children learn the language and dialect of their caretakers rather than one of the several thousand other languages in the world. That being so, modelling must have some potential role to play in part of the learning process, even if we cannot as yet be precise in saying how and when it occurs. While imitation and reinforcement principles of learning and performance may not be able to explain some features of language mastery - for example, how adults become capable of generating an infinite number of novel sentences - it does not follow logically that these principles are irrelevant to everything else that is involved in learning to use language.

The second weakness in Brown's approach is revealed by the stripped-down characteristics of the data examined. Child speech was analysed as transcripted sequences of words. Prosodic features of intonation, pitch, and stress were not included. The caretaker's utterances and the non-verbal context in which utterances were made were generally but not entirely ignored. But the child's speech is only one component of the co-operative action involving conversation, and conversations are not about nothing. Imagine trying to describe and explain the learning of a trapeze artist's skills without mentioning the behaviour of his partner or of the trapeze! How can one expect to examine the role of the child's caretakers in the development of speech if their possible contribution to the interaction is not included in full measure? And how can one expect to study either without reference to the contextually embedded actions and interactions to which speech is directed? And if you have no theories of learning to test, then none will prove to be helpful in explaining the data.

The perspective adopted here recognizes that the growing child is an active self-organizing subject capable of building up action schemes, symbolic schemes, and sign systems through interaction with events, things and people (following Piaget), but we recognize that the child is at the same time an object whose behaviour can be shaped and developed through the contingent use of rewards and punishments (following Pavlov and Skinner). We also need to accept the idea that to produce and understand speech is to manifest a set of at least semi-automated skills (see Claim 7) whose mastery will need repeated and varied practice in situations where others in the environment offer corrective feedback. Accepting this eclectic view of a child as a growing person who is both agent and victim allows us to conceive of him as inventing functions as well as units and structures to realize these skills, and as discovering them to be already available in the speech of others. We can also conceive of him as being responsive to direct instruction and training, both for learning new features and for deploying these fluently in action.

What follows is a list of claims about the child's mastery of language and the role of his caretakers in this endless task. The claims may need amendment or partial abandonment in the light of advances in knowledge, but in 1981 they represent what is intended to be a balanced assessment of the evidence to hand.

Claims about language
development

Claim 1: the use of language develops out of already established non-verbal means of communication

From birth the child interacts with his caretakers; child and caretaker act upon and react to each other. This reciprocity involves an exchange of signals each to the other. The child responds differentially (e.g. with smiles or cries) to different maternal actions, such as different facial expressions (Bruner, 1975). For example, the caretakers endeavour to decode distress signals and cease to search for further solutions when their actions result in signals of satisfaction from the child. It is out of this interchange of communication through body movements, gestures, facial expressions, and vocalizations that verbal communication emerges; it does not arise suddenly with a first 'word'.

Claim 2: initial functions of language are social-interactional

If we distinguish broadly between language uses which attempt to comment upon the nature of things, for example, making statements which are either true or false, and those which appear to be attempts to regulate the states or behaviour of self and others or to define role relationships (see Robinson, 1978), then in Halliday's child, Nigel, the former began to appear over nine months after the first socially relevant language units had emerged. Halliday found that instrumental (getting things for self), regulatory (making others do things), interactional (encounter-regulation), and personal (reactions to events or states) units were the first to appear. Among these were nã (give me that), bø (give me my bird), ʒ (do that again), do (nice to see you), n͡ŋ (that tastes nice) (see glossary under Phonology). This child began to talk, it seems, because verbal interaction with others was pleasurable; it was not because he was hungry or in pain. The design of the baby includes an impetus to interact with people, an impetus to interact with other features of the environment, and an impetus to develop the schemes of interaction. If one wishes to say that the reasons why babies begin to talk are biological, then they are socio-biological: joint action with caretakers. That being so, the promotion of co-ordinated joint action may be one form of inducement to develop communicative skills.

As Halliday illustrates, Nigel later expanded his functional range to include the heuristic (finding out) and imaginative (let's pretend) functions, and he increased the number of communicative acts associated with each of these until by the age of one-and-a-half he had over 50 in his repertoire. This 50 is a misleading figure because from the outset the child had both general and specific variants of each function, for example, na͑ (give me that - general), bø (give me my bird - specific). The general form may be an important growth point as well as having general utility, in that it affords the caretaker an opportunity to respond non-verbally with the appropriate action, verbally to label the unspecified object, and to continue the conversation, all at the same time. The opportunity to learn a specific referent for the particular 'that' can be fitted into the sequence of activity, without this constituting a major diversion.

About the time Nigel reached his 50 meanings he also ceased to rely solely upon inventing his own units (mainly un-English in form and actually heavily reliant on tone). Two important changes occurred.

First, Nigel interpolated a third level of linguistic structure, the lexico-grammatical, between soundings and meanings. Individual sounds ceased to be expressive of individual meanings. Combinations of sounds were used to form 'words', and words and tones were sequenced to create 'meanings'. Thus the tri-stratal essence of language became established. (At some later point in time the child has also to learn to distinguish between the semantic and pragmatic levels; different forms can serve the same general functions and the same form can serve different functions, the appropriate choice requiring knowledge of the cultural norms of the society.)

Claim 3: the child makes deliberate effort to learn language

Second, Nigel's speech began to distinguish between using language and learning language. He deliberately solicited from his caretakers 'names' of objects, attributes and actions and he practised combinations and alterations both in monologue and dialogue. Whether all children do this we do not yet know. How do caretakers respond to these inquiries about words (and structures)? On the principles of

any associative theory of learning (see de Cecco, 1968),
supplying the requested items emphatically, clearly and with
some measure of repetition and extension should increase the
chances of the child learning the language feature and its
use. It should also encourage him in the process of finding
out more. Not supplying the requested information or supplying it in a form that the child cannot assimilate in the
short run forgoes an opportunity for learning about the specific matter in hand, and in the long run should result in
the child ceasing to make inquiries.

Claim 4: units and structures are accumulated piecemeal but inexorably

An extreme position might argue that units are mastered one
at a time, always being linked to some unit or structure
already in the child's repertoire. They may be learned and
lost again. The cycle may be repeated until the unit
disappears or becomes established. The units which become
finally established and relatively stable will be those in
the speech of the child's circle of interactants, particularly of those with whom he is most frequently in a
learning and interactive relationship.

By 'unit' is meant any feature of the language at any
level, such as phonemes, morphemes, words, groups, clauses,
sentences, utterances, rules of explicitness, rules of
politeness or rules of differential social status. It
should be remembered that a unit at one level can be a
structure at another, for example, a sequence of particular
pitches can form an intonation pattern, but this pattern
serves as a unit if it forms an interrogative; a principle
or rule can therefore become a unit when treated as such.

A new unit will be more likely to enter and remain in
the child's repertoire if he is intellectually capable of
grasping some aspect of its approximate meaning or significance. Capability is not the only factor; a unit is more
likely to be mastered if its meaning and significance is
relevant to something the child wishes to communicate or
comprehend. Reasons for a unit not entering would be that
the child may already be using his energies and available
capacity to develop other units or structures of verbal or
non-verbal behaviour. He may also be performing and living
rather than learning; there is more to life than learning. A
unit will only become stabilized in use if it is encouraged
to do so by others (see Claim 6).

Claim 5: the new is often first learned in terms of the old

An ancient Greek paradox points to the impossibility of
change, and this principle is sometimes invoked as a reason
why children cannot learn language! If understanding a word
must precede the learning of that word, how can it be
learned? If learning must precede understanding how can the
child come to understand something that has no meaning? And
yet children clearly do learn. One of several lines of
escape from the paradox is to argue that the child can

express new meanings 'badly' with old, already available units and structures, and that caretakers can reformulate the child's meaning with the new units and structures which the child may then be able to assimilate to the meaning intended. Evidence is consistent with the idea that the child learning to associate the various kinds of negation in English with the appropriate adult lexical and syntactic structures can rely on adults continuing to supply the new forms upon the occasions of the child using those already in his repertoire.

Since syntactic systems such as interrogation and negation are compound and complicated, it may follow that the developing child will only master them piecemeal, generating transitional forms, if Claim 4 is valid. The evidence pointing to the many transitional forms of syntactic construction (e.g. 'Why it is raining?'; see Brown, 1973) is probably consistent with the idea that these variants are best left to correct themselves unless particular examples of them appear to have stabilized over many months. If a child cannot learn quickly from a correction there is probably little point and may be harm in pursuing it.

Claim 6: caretakers control the probability of new features being learned and remaining in the child's repertoire

Montessori is responsible for the last observation made in Claim 5, and a second injunction of hers may be used to introduce Claim 6. Her 'cycle of three' for teaching was: This is an X - Show me the/an X - What is this? (pointing to X). The first labels the activity, event, object or attribute, the second checks the child's capacity for recognition, and the third encourages him to produce the label. She adds that repeated failures to elicit appropriate reactions from the child are best taken as suggestions for dropping the matter and returning to it later. This model can easily be abused if taken too literally, but it has considerable value if used as a framework to bear in mind when combining instruction with conversation.

How is a child to find out the conventional linguistic means of expressing meanings but from his caretakers? Why should they leave him to extract features as best he can from their discourse? Why not structure his learning opportunities as clearly as possible leaving him to accept or reject them? (Many mothers object to viewing themselves or being viewed as teachers. Whether or not they are to be seen as teaching is contingent only upon the definition of 'teach'. If the provision of opportunities for learning is enough to be called 'teaching' then all people interacting with children are teachers. If this provision has to be intended to help learning, then fewer people are teachers of children, but presumably there are some things all mothers intend that their children should learn. My own view is that mothers should accept that there is much they can teach their children and that they can enjoy this role to the benefit of all concerned.)

Two studies can be quoted to illustrate the power of caretakers at the relatively early period of language development when the child's utterances are on average between one-and-a-half and three MLU (mean length of utterance: at this stage of development the number of morphemes is closely related to the number of words).

Ellis and Wells (1980) contrasted the maternal inter- action characteristics of slow language developers (12 months to move from MLU 1.5 to MLU 3.5) with those of early fast developers (less than 6 months to make this change and achieved before 21 months old). At the outset mothers of the two groups differed, the former talking generally more during routine household activities, issuing more instructions and commands, being more likely to acknowledge their child's utterances, and more likely to repeat or correct these. By the time the children had reached 3.5 MLU, maternal differences were still present, but they were different in type, the early fast children's mothers using more statements and questions, particularly teaching-type questions, to which the mother already knew the answers. Cross (1978) found in a contrast between faster and slower developers that different maternal speech vari- ables discriminated at different ages. The implications of these two studies are several. Optimal facilitation of development may require the employment of different tactics at different points in development and may also require the application of different principles.

More basic general principles are also relevant. Mothers whose speech is more unintelligible, in that it is mumbled and incoherent with no clear breaks and stresses at custo- mary points, are likely to have children whose speech is developing more slowly.

In a study of the mother-child interaction among six year olds (see Robinson, in press) it was found that child- ren who asked more questions, more complex questions, and revealed more verbally mediated knowledge about an assort- ment of objects, games, and toys, had mothers who were more likely to:

*   set any remark in a previously shared context;
*   answer any question with a relevant, accurate reply that extended somewhat beyond the question posed;
*   confirm children's utterances which were true and well- formed and to point out or correct errors;
*   maintain themes over several utterances.

These findings probably need qualification and supplemen- tation. Pointing out and correcting errors is likely to be productive only if the child can learn from this, and provided he does not become afraid to make mistakes. One feature of maternal behaviour that was unrelated to child- ren's performance was the mother's questioning of the child; it seemed that at least in this context questioning may have been intended to re-focus the interest of children who were already actively attending to something else and were unwilling to be distracted. Hess and Shipman (1965), for example, treated questioning as motivating and found it to be positively associated with more advanced performance, but perhaps in their case the questioning was creating and achieving concentration rather than trying to re-direct attention. Questioning which encourages extension of interest may have different consequences from questions which are failed attempts to direct the child. (These two may be distinguishable in terms of quality of voice and intonation.)

If two words were to be used to sum up the contrast they would be 'push' versus 'pull'. Pushing did not work, pulling did: adults could set up the context of the situation in which activity took place, but beyond that the child decided what he was interested in. Adults can set the scene, offer suggestions, and tempt the child, but he directs the form and content of his script. The 'push' is already there; it is a design characteristic of human children. By their re-active behaviour adults can encourage and develop both this intrinsic motivation and the learning which results from its activity. They may also be able to treat it in ways which may slow down, check, deflect, distort, prevent or otherwise impede development.

Providing, tempting and modelling appear to be the main activities caretakers can offer to facilitate language (and general) development. How far the success of these actions depends upon the caretaker's genuine concern with the child and his behaviour remains unknown. One would have to say, as an act of faith, that caring in action, realized as an expression of a sincere liking and cheerful interest in what children find important, is certainly desirable, if not essential. Entering both intellectually and emotionally into the spirit and perspective of the child's orientation to his world must make the processes easier to achieve.

Claim 7: coming to 'know that' reorganizes the possibilities of developing 'know how'

Halliday (1975) noted that, at an early age, young Nigel discriminated between using the language and learning the language. Some children of four already 'know that' there are rules governing how things are to be said and can say something about their nature. We can also ask how children come to realize that speech can be ambiguous: that a speaker may send messages too vague for correct comprehension and appropriate action. At an early stage children do not realize a message should refer uniquely to its referents if it is to be acted upon appropriately. In a situation where speaker and listener have identical sets of cards, each set depicting stick-men holding flowers differing in size and colour, they will pick up a card in response to 'A man with a flower' without necessarily asking for more information. If their choice turns out to be wrong they will state that the speaker had said enough (told properly) and that it was their fault that the mismatch had occurred (phase 1 below). When older they will be more likely to demand more information by asking questions, and if a mismatch does still occur they can blame the inadequacy of the message and the speaker for the failure. They 'know that' messages can be inadequate. They can reflect upon and analyse the efficiency and precision of their own speech and that of others (phase 2 below).

At present we can only speculate about the general significance of this work, but the possible implications are considerable and can be represented roughly in a three-phase model that could apply to many aspects of language development. Let X be a truth, principle or fact about language.

* PHASE 1: the child is mainly a victim of X. His capacity for being an agent with control over X is limited by his ignorance of the character of X and how it functions in the language in communication. However, he achieves a measure of mastery of X in use (know how) as a result of associative learning both in its classical and instrumental conditioning guises, and he may also learn about X in use through observation. He is additionally an agent and can purposefully use X, relying on corrective feedback from others for the development of context-bound rules of use. These various processes acting separately and in combination may lead to the child using X successfully much of the time. However, limitations of intellectual capacity and an absence of opportunitites and/or capacities for reflecting upon the workings of X will be manifested when his rules for using X fail. He will not be able to diagnose the reasons for failure and will not be able to formulate a diagnosis and act effectively upon it.

* PHASE 2: either through his own reflective efforts or as a result of a competent other teaching and telling him about the workings of X, he will come to realize how (and perhaps why) X works as it does. As a result of reflective analysis, in particular new situations or through a consideration of past events, or through imaginative rehearsing of situations involving X, he will consciously develop and organize his knowledge about X. We might expect an associated period of learning-practice in which the use of X is tried out with care and awareness. The child (or adult) has become a reflecting agent in respect of X organizing his 'knowing that' - and perhaps temporarily less efficient in his 'know how'.

* PHASE 3: the use of X will become reduced to an automated skill except for situations where for various reasons it might be important not to make mistakes with X and for situations where trouble in using X occurs. In the face of trouble the problem can be raised to a conscious reflective analysis, diagnoses made and corrective action taken, other things being equal. The 'know

how' is greater than at the transition from phase 1 to
phase 2 and is in a potential dialectic relation to a
'knowing that' of understanding.

We are thinking in this fashion only about the child's
control of ambiguity in verbal referential communication,
but see a range of possible applications to a whole variety
of behaviours within the orbit of language in communication:
learning the meanings of words, rules of spelling in the
written language, rules of pronunciation in the oral, rules
of grammar, rules for varying forcefulness and politeness of
requests, rules of etiquette more generally, rules for
taking the listener into account and rules for telling jokes
well.

Perhaps one important set of reasons why school children
have difficulty in learning to use language more competently
is that we ourselves cannot formulate the rules for them.
Instead we leave them to continue to operate at a particular
and concrete level, learning many instances rather than
fewer principles and rules. And when we do find out the
rules and principles we do not necessarily set up conditions
of learning and practice that carry the child's competence
through to the phase of out-of-awareness efficient use with
reflective facilities for analysis when trouble occurs or is
anticipated. It is worth comparing the relative ease of
learning a game like chess or tennis with and without the
help of information about rules. To learn how to play will
require observation, practice and correction, but knowing
the rules renders these easier. Discovering them for yourself could be simply a frustrating waste of time and effort.

Erroneous beliefs

The most fundamental, and possibly the most common, false
assumption is that the rate and extent of younger and older
children's learning how to use language is not affected by
the behaviour of their caretakers; that some innate features
of the child's brain or temperament determine what emerges.
(We have avoided mentioning ages of children at points where
readers might have preferred them to be specified. The arguments in the section on backwardness offer some reasons why
it is misleading and dangerous to hold firm expectations as
to what individual children ought to have achieved at particular ages. The educational problems with children are to
advance their knowledge, understanding, values and motivation, not to categorize them.) While systematic investigations of parents' and teachers' beliefs about language
development have yet to be made, it is quite clear that
within some cultures, some parents believe that the child
will become what it will become regardless of what they do.
The empirical evidence is that these beliefs do not cor-
respond to reality; while many facts about relations between
caretaker behaviour and language development have yet to be
discovered, the positive results already established are too
numerous and theoretically plausible to be discounted.

Unfortunately, academic thinking about these matters is still dominated by a simplicity that is naïve. One common assumption in research seems to be that if a certain kind of caretaker behaviour can be shown to be beneficial then the more of it the better: that its efficacy will hold true for all children at all phases of language development regardless of the context of operation and the state of relationship between caretaker and child. Neither the basic assumption nor its presumed generality is likely to be true.

For example, it is likely that caretakers can talk too much with children as well as too little. And they can overteach particular features. Developmental social psychologists have been slow to appreciate that many relations between variables are likely to be curvilinear rather than monotonic. 'The more the better' may have a limit beyond which 'more' may mean worse or nothing and not better.

Just as caretakers may talk too much as well as too little, they can talk at or past children instead of with them. They can initiate and control without responding. Some adults seem anxious to hurry their replies without having listened first; they act, but do not react or interact. One of the first lessons to be learned in dealing with young children is not to impose oneself too quickly upon them, and this applies to continuing as well as initial encounters. While the child has to learn how and when to listen, he needs to be listened to as well. It has been argued that mothers listen attentively to children, trying to decipher the meanings of their cries, but one can be sceptical about the continuing and pervading applicability of such parental commitment to all children as they grow older. Brown (1973) showed that 40 per cent of his children's questions were met with replies that were unrelated to the sense of the question: one therefore wonders how many caretakers make serious efforts to listen to children, encourage them to talk about their activities, and maintain interest and cohesion in such conversations. Those caretakers who are concerned to promote development may push too hard or pull too hard. On the evidence to date, 'pushing' is not productive; 'pulling', pitched at the right level with not too high or low a frequency, is an important facilitator of development, however. Caretakers can pitch their initiations and reactions to children at too low a level or too high a one. Too low may be generally uncommon, but certainly some mentally retarded children appear to be kept at a lower standard of performance by adults unwilling to extend their conversation with them. But how are caretakers to judge what is too much, too often, or too hard?

Caretakers can solve these problems only in context. A monitoring of the child's actions and reactions in combination with an appraisal of the verbal interaction itself should suffice to indicate whether the child is attentively involved. Adults should be able to appraise whether or not their remarks are understood by the child both from his nonverbal reactions and from his succeeding remarks. Adults should be able to judge whether they themselves are understanding and reacting appropriately to the child's utterances. Does the child have great difficulty constructing replies? Are there many disfluencies and intervening silences? Are themes maintained over a succession of utterances? In short, does the conversation have an orderly structure? Does the talk relate to the contextual features of the situation in which it is occurring? If it does, and if the adult is injecting new information about the world and about language at such a rate that the child can take up and use some of the features being introduced, the worst mistakes are being avoided.

This capacity to adjust speech to a developing child is itself a skill that has to be learned. Child-rearing manuals (Leach, 1978) or pre-school teachers' advice (Tough, 1977) offer much constructive (and some wrong!) advice on such matters. Perhaps both under-estimate the value of two activities: conversation as such, and the appropriate injection of small doses of teaching about language during conversations.

Finally, the conversation has to be anchored to the outside world of actions and events and/or the inner personal world of wishes, intentions, feelings and ideas. The talk has to be more than wording. Experiences have to be arranged and/or exploited. Topics have to be selected. If they are not, the child is in danger of separating rhetoric from reality (or fantasy). He can come to believe that he has to accommodate to a world of words and another world of things and fail to realize that the two ought to be in a dialectical and corresponding relation to each other.

Special problems

Backwardness

Backwardness is not an absolute concept but a relative one. Backwardness can exist only after a norm is defined. For various reasons our society has selected biological age from birth as a reference point. For many aspects of growth and development we have devised ways of measuring characteristics of children that give a spread of scores about an average norm of some kind for children of a particular age. Then we use our tests to obtain scores for individual children. However, to expect then that each individual child should score close to the average is importantly irrational: such an expectation is logically and empirically inconsistent with the spreading procedures adopted to construct the test.

This is not to say that it is foolish to ask why a child or group of children is below (or above) average. Answers to such questions may enable us to take constructive action to facilitate the development of particular children who are unnecessarily and undesirably backward in certain respects.

Many people in our society may also adopt a moral position that special efforts should be made to promote more rapid development in some sub-sample of the population

defined as 'backward'; say, the lowest ten per cent. That is
defensible. However, it is not logically or empirically
possible to eliminate a bottom ten per cent. We can take
action to raise the absolute performance or characteristics
of children; what we cannot do is use norm-referenced tests
and eliminate the variation about the norm.

We must also accept the fact that, at any moment in any
society, there are limits both to what can be done and what
the members of society think it is important to do. There
are biological, sociological-historical and economic limits
to what can be done. There are moral limits as to what we
might consider it proper or fair to do.

We can also observe that there are wrong ways of conceptualizing these problems. Over the last 20 years and
before, questions have been asked about why children fail at
school. Some have blamed the biology and psychology of
failing children. Others have blamed bad homes. Bad teaching
and bad schools have been cited, as have curricula. The
government and the social structure of the society have not
escaped blame. In reality, the reason why n per cent of
children fail CSE, O level or A level is that the examiners
have set a fail rate of n per cent: and that is the sole
reason. We can sensibly proceed to ask why children from
certain identifiable groupings are particularly at risk of
failure.

We ought also to note that explanations for such failure
have generally made appeals to deficiency models of some
kind, deficiency in language being a frequently cited
factor. Oddly, we have only resorted to this kind of
explanation within age groups, particularly for social
categories such as social class, rurality, cultural minori-
ties and psychological categories such as the mentally
retarded or the maladjusted. We do not see infant school
children as language-deficient adults who need to be brought
up to a state of adult competence forthwith. Education is
normally seen as promoting and facilitating development and
not in terms of removing deficiencies. And yet, within a
particular age cohort, we have tended to apply the deficiency model to the backward, even for 'normal' children.
Whether a glass of water is seen as half full or half empty
is a fact about the observer, not the water. The fate of
water may not be affected by that perception. However, when
a child is seen as more empty (or filled with the wrong
stuff) than he ought to be, there are likely to be consequences for himself, his family, his teachers and ultimately
the society of which he is to become a citizen.

However, need we consider the language of a developing
child normatively, and if so, against which norms? If we are
to make special educational or other provision for those
defined as being in special need then testing individuals
against norms is essential as a diagnostic means of some
objectivity. Age-based norms may constitute the single most
efficient screening frame of reference for operation. Once
the presenting characteristics are defined by reference to

test scores, the hard work of explanation and decision making starts. Are the scores deviant enough from the age per norm to warrant further inquiry? Are the scores deviant enough from what might be expected from this individual to warrant further inquiry? If either is true, are the scores themselves what are important or are they symptoms of something else? If the scores are judged to be indicators of problems rather than problems in themselves, are these best treated by being left to remedy themselves with subsequent monitoring? Or should we intervene? Where intervention is judged as desirable, the norm-referenced tests are likely to have played a crucial role in detection and perhaps in diagnosis, but not in the explanation or specification of treatment as such.

Dialects and accents
'Standard English' (SE) can be usefully thought of as that dialect of British English whose rules of prosody, grammar, lexis, semantics and pragmatics have become institutionalized as the variety of English towards whose mastery the educational endeavour aspires. 'Received Pronunciation' (RP) refers to the accent that defines the corresponding phonology. The components of standard English which are stressed most frequently are its grammar and lexis; it is usually in respect of those characteristics that SE is contrasted with other regional and social dialects. When a variety is accorded the status of a dialect is not closely defined. Dialectologists have mapped out the distribution of regional dialects in Britain, particularly rural ones. Socially-stratified dialects have not been well investigated. And for both we have yet to learn what their similarities and differences are. Are dialects more alike than they are different in each of their components? The number of differences in grammatical rules is probably few in relation to the total in the language.

Those responsible for educating children need to distinguish between features in their speech that indicate ignorance of language and its workings and those which mark social identity, through the dialect of the child's home. If teachers denigrate the local dialect while teaching SE, they are denigrating the people who speak that dialect and may eventually force a child to choose between SE and the local dialect. Is he to equip himself for upward social mobility at the cost of social separation from his family and local community? But why create conditions where a choice has to be made?

One false belief is that people can master only ore dialect. Where the need for mastery of two different languages exists, children learn two, often without the benefit of schools to teach them. The factors that operate to prevent children mastering several dialects are mainly socio-cultural and not biological-cognitive.

If education is to open up opportunities rather than to close them down, that system has to facilitate the

development of control of the dialects and languages of
greatest potential significance to the child, of which the
two most important are his local social/regional dialect or
language and SE, so that he may be able to use each as and
when appropriate.

Similarly, arguments can be advanced for the educational
support of more than one accent. It is now well documented
that people do not always utter the same sound in the same
way; it is a matter of proportion. And the proportions vary:
this has been shown most frequently through manipulations of
the formality-casualness of the situation.

Moreover, we also converge towards and diverge away from
the speech of our fellow conversationalists (Giles and
Powesland, 1975), such movements being interpreted as indicative of goodwill and separateness respectively. Giles and
Powesland review studies which show how accents are evaluated in Britain. Evaluation can be along more than one
dimension, and in this case two emerge that may be most
simply summarized as expertness and trustworthiness. Unfortunately these are not independent, RP speakers being
seen as untrustworthy experts and broadly-accented country-
folk as trustworthy but ignorant. But children as well as
adults are judged by their accents, and it must be incumbent
upon the expert caretakers to increase their knowledge and
understanding about these matters.

In sum, we need to extend and disseminate our knowledge
about the way language functions in our community. We need
to develop and act upon policies that enable children to
master in sufficient measure those varieties of language
which will both promote their learning and enable them to
retain or gain access to membership of those social groups
in and through which their identity is realized.

Conclusions

One common complaint made by members of the public, their
elected representatives and their paid servants is that
academics address problems rather than solve them; they
spend too much time posing questions and too little answering them. At least in language development we have now moved
to a position where the types of question being asked begin
to embrace a comprehensive functional-structural framework.
We have begun to ask how children learn units and structures
to communicate meanings which have significance for action.
We are confronting language as a four-component system
(language in its pragmatic, semantic, lexico-grammatical and
phonological aspects), just as the developing child himself
confronts, copes with and learns to use all four inter-
dependently. We have appreciated that, although function may
be a useful primary focus, we have to note that a child who
can distinguish between 'knowing how to' and 'knowing that'
is in a strong position to hold and develop both structures
and functions in a dynamic interactive relation to each
other, and that this capacity in fact predates the conscious
onset of this discrimination. The questions being posed now

are more likely to lead to progress than some of those narrower and stranger questions of 20 years ago.

Furthermore, we have begun to answer quite a number of questions. The claims made here are a distillation focussing on processes and mechanisms of development rather than content. What is now known about the content and sequence of language development is considerable, especially in young children. The claims made are couched in a form at as low a level of abstraction as appears to be compatible with the evidence. To be more specific would require the prior specification of more details of the particular children, caretakers, context of situation, and learning problems under consideration; the claims are principles that may guide practice but cannot prescribe its concrete characteristics. They also mark a departure from what might be called the 'one-answer-only' mentality. Psychologists have tried to look for the process that converts all substances to gold, or in this case all pre-linguistic babies into verbally competent toddlers. We have seen the invalid logic that takes the form of arguing that, because process X may not be invariably necessary for mastering Y, it has no relevance. It is likely that all learning processes are relevant or can be made relevant to some aspects of language development in some children. Once we ask whether, when, and how a process can be used to facilitate development, our answers may become more positive and useful.

But are the claims made here any improvement on common sense? They are, in two ways. Unfortunately, a particular form of sense is not common to all people, as can be speedily demonstrated by revealing the extent of individual subcultural and cultural differences as to what it is sensible to believe. At present we know next to nothing about parents' (or even teachers') beliefs about language development, but we do know they differ. Some are wrong. This is not to insult them. We are all wrong in some of our beliefs, and none of us is omniscient. Appeals to common sense will not yield the truth. At present, too, the experts continue to disagree among themselves as to ways and means likely to facilitate language development. If we mean by 'common sense' the accumulated wisdom of experienced caretakers, then experts would surely be well advised to solicit their opinions; if they have learned through observing the consequences of their teaching methods then they are a prime population for ideas. But the convictions that have derived from their private experience have then to be checked in the publicly demonstrable contexts of systematic investigation. While the evidence obtained through scientific procedures is prone to errors of various kinds, investigators are trained to try to avoid these. Hence the evidence and the interpretations they offer should be less prone to error, especially when empirical studies conducted in a variety of settings yield results which can be shown to be consistent. The claims put forward have been subject to systematic scrutinizing activity, and that is why they, rather than others, are presented.

Accommodation

A Piagetian term referring to the development of new schemes arising out of the failure of current schemes to regulate action. Hence sensori-motor schemes for sucking will not enable an infant to drink from a cup: new schemes have to be constructed.

Adaptation

In Piagetian development, adaptation is the combination of the processes of assimilation and accommodation.

Assimilation

The application of currently available schemes to inter-action with the environment. If a baby has a sucking scheme used for breast feeding, it may readily assimilate the sucking of a bottle teat to this scheme. The sucking scheme will also be applied to fingers and toys but this transfer will not, in the long run, be adaptive. New schemes will be required to accommodate to the use of toys.

Intonation

Patterns of variation in pitch and stress that distinguish (i) between what is believed to be accepted already by conversation partners and what is new, and (ii) the charac-ter of utterances as questions, statements, commands, etc.

Lexico-grammar

The rules governing what is generally acceptable within a language system. Grammar is said to have two components: morphology and syntax. Rules in morphology define changes to words themselves as their functions in sentences change; for example, 'he' is subject, 'him' is the form for object. Syntax defines the possible sequences, substitutions and co-occurrences of words, phrases and clauses permitted in the construction of sentences.

About 150 special words in English (conjunctions, pre-positions, pronouns, etc.) are sometimes seen as having predominantly grammatical/semantic significance. The remaining half-million or so are lexical items. Both are listed in dictionaries.

Morpheme

The smallest unit of meaning in language.

Norm

In its descriptive sense, norm refers to the typical or most common behaviour of members of a group. It is also used evaluatively to assert what is to be expected of such members. The failure to separate the two can lead to the idea that everyone has to be average, which is self-contradictory.

Phonology

The study of sound systems of languages. Within a language,

which sounds make a significant difference to meaning? What are the rules which define which combinations of sounds can occur? To aid these descriptions, linguists have devised an International Phonetic Alphabet that attempts to write down sounds so that their pronunciation is defined. This does not yet include conventions that represent stress or pitch.

Pragmatics
See semantics. Pragmatics is concerned with the significance for action of utterances. To use language effectively, people have to be able to interpret the speech of others and to know how their own utterances are likely to be interpreted. This requires a knowledge of rules of the culture and not just the semantics.

Psycholinguistics
The study of the psychological processes that underlie speech performance. The main focus in child development has been upon the encoding and decoding of syntax, but a comprehensive study would include comparable analyses of sounds and written symbols and meanings. Some people would also include pragmatics.

Scheme
The procedures that regulate an action or set of actions. Hence if an infant has a sucking scheme, his brain must contain a set of instructions for action that result in a co-ordinated sequence of movements that relate his body, mouth and hands to nipples. Not all schemes relate to sensori-motor skills: they can also relate to intellectual products.

Semantics
Units at and above the level of morpheme have meanings. A cat is not a dog; 'on' does not mean the same as 'in'. It is through their combinations, in accordance with lexico-grammatical rules, that sequences of sounds come to have meaning. Some people have difficulty in grasping the distinction between semantics and pragmatics; pragmatics is concerned with action. 'The door is open', uttered by a teacher in a classroom means what it says. The semantics declares a state of affairs to be true. The pragmatic significance could be 'The last child to have come in should get up and shut the door'. Unfortunately, we can use the question 'What did he mean?' to refer to both the semantics and the pragmatics. 'Meaning' is ambiguous.

Sociolinguistics
Traditionally the study of language variation in relation to variations in the nature of the setting, participants, ends, aesthetics, key, modality, norms, and genre, within a speech community. The focus is upon pragmatics and how functions relate to the forms used. Sociolinguistics and psycholinguistics overlap.

Syntax
The rules for combining words into phrases, clauses and
sentences.

References

Brown, R. (1973)
  A First Language: The early stages. London: Allen &
  Unwin.
Bruner, J.S. (1975)
  The ontogenesis of speech acts. Journal of Child
  Language, 2, 1-19.
Cross, T.G. (1978)
  Mother's speech and its association with role of
  linguistic development in the young child. In N.
  Waterson and C. Snow (eds), The Development of
  Communication. Chichester: Wiley.
De Cecco, J.P. (1960)
  The Psychology of Learning and Instruction. Englewood
  Cliffs, NJ: Prentice-Hall.
De Villiers, R.A. and De Villiers, J. (1979)
  Early Language. Glasgow: Fontana/Open Books.
Ellis, R. and Wells, C.G. (1980)
  Enabling factors in adult-child discourse. First
  Language, 1, 46-62.
Giles, H. and Powesland, P.F. (1975)
  Speech Style and Social Evaluation. London: Academic
  Press.
Halliday, M.A.K. (1975)
  Learning How to Mean. London: Arnold.
Hess, R.D. and Shipman, V. (1965)
  Early experience and the socialization of cognitive
  modes in children. Child Development, 36, 860-886.
Leach, P. (1978)
  Baby and Child. London: Michael Joseph.
Robinson, W.P. (1978)
  Language Management in Education. Sydney: Allen &
  Unwin.
Robinson, W.P. (ed.) (in press)
  Communication in Child Development. London: Academic
  Press.
Tough, J. (1977)
  Talking and Learning. London: Ward Lock.

Questions

1. What can adults do to facilitate language development in
   young children?
2. Write a government leaflet giving advice to young
   mothers about language development in their children.
3. If mothers wish to facilitate language development in
   their children, which is it more important for them to
   know: details about the nature of language, or rules of
   interaction?
4. Is it the ignorance of parents and teachers rather than

the incapacity of children that delays their
development?
5. Describe and comment upon the child's development of
syntax.
6. What learning processes underlie which aspects of
language development?
7. What roles can imitation play in language development?
8. Why do children stretch familiar units to cope with new
meanings?
9. Why encourage language development in children?
10. What should be done in infant schools about the dialects
of children?

nnotated reading

Ausubel, D.P. (1978) Theory and Problems of Child Development (2nd edn). New York: Grune & Stratton.
A general textbook about child development from an
educational perspective.

Coulthard, C.M. (1977) An Introduction to Discourse
Analysis. London: Longmans.
What are the relations between linguistic form and the
discourse functions of speech? Coulthard offers some
suggestions.

De Stefano, J.S. (ed.) (1973) Language, Society and
Education. Worthington, Ohio: Charles Jones.
A collection that brings life to varieties of American
English and discusses learning simply and clearly. No
comparable book on British English, alas.

De Stefano, J.S. (1978) Language, the Learner and the
School. New York: Wiley.
Introductory books about language are still liable
to concentrate upon syntax and ignore language in use.
This is a welcome exception. Examples of language
varieties are mainly American.

De Villiers, J.G. and de Villiers, P.A. (1978) Language
Acquisition. Cambridge, Mass.: Harvard University Press.
The most balanced, comprehensive clear, introduction to
language acquisition. Cognitive rather than social
emphasis.

De Villiers, J.G. and de Villiers, P.A. (1979) Early
Language. London: Fontana/Open Books.
A simplified and highly readable version of the authors'
more substantial text. Compulsory reading.

Moerk, E.L. (1977) Pragmatic and Semantic Aspects of Early
Language Development. Baltimore: University Park Press.
The emphasis on pragmatics is compatible with
contemporary concerns.

Waterson, N. and Snow, C. (eds) (1978) The Development of Communication. Chichester: Wiley.
>A collection of papers illustrating the kinds of questions being posed and answers being offered in respect of the communicative development in young children.

Relevance to the teacher
DAVID FONTANA

Robinson starts off with a timely warning. Much research into language has concentrated upon how a child builds up words and sentences, how he develops syntax, whether there appears to be a universal pattern in the way in which children make errors and build up syntax, and whether children appear to be born with what is termed a Language Acquisition Device (LAD) or not. Though proper in themselves, these approaches neglect language as a function. Why do children talk? What do they use language to convey? How does their use of language change with age? Clearly, it is the function of language that is of the greatest practical value to teachers, concerned as they are with language as an aid to thought and as a method of communication, and it is with the function of language that Robinson is primarily concerned.

Much of the research into language function, as with research into other areas of linguistic competence, has focussed upon early childhood and the pre-school years. This should not be seen as providing mere background knowledge for the teacher, however, because results provide us with invaluable pointers to how language is used in later childhood, since such usage is a development of, rather than a departure from, what happens in these early years. This is illustrated if we examine closely the first six of the seven claims that Robinson advances about the child's mastery of language and the role of his caretakers in this mastery. These claims suggest essentially that the child is an active participant in the development of his linguistic skills: that is, that language is not simply something that 'happens' to him as a result of the activities of others. He actively sets out to acquire language, initially as an extension of his social interaction with those around him, and later as a deliberate attempt to find out more about, and increase his control over, his immediate environment. The response of his caretakers is, however, crucial to the level of success which greets his efforts. Failure to supply the child with the linguistic information he requests (e.g. the names of objects, the meaning of words), or to supply it in a form which he can assimilate, may result in the child's ceasing to make these requests, with obvious negative consequences for his speed of development. It must be said that some adults actively discourage children in their quest for language, for example by ignoring their questions, by laughing at them in their attempts to use new words, by censuring them too strongly for their errors, or just by making them feel guilty for 'chattering' or for using language at times which the adult finds inconvenient or irritating.

In all contexts, a child is more likely to master language units if these units are relevant to his daily life; if they help him communicate the things he wants to communicate, or understand the things he wants to understand. Thus a child with a culturally stimulating environment will have more urge to acquire language than a child with an unstimulating one since there are more things around him to be questioned and understood, and therefore a greater objective necessity to use words frequently and with a grasp of their correct meaning.

The role of the caretaker

On the question of specific intervention by the caretaker in a child's linguistic progress, Robinson suggests that a child uses many transitional forms of syntax; he uses parts of known (though, in the new context, incorrect) syntactical structures when attempting to master novel and more difficult ones. If frequently furnished with correct examples, the child will soon abandon these transitional structures in favour of more advanced and suitable ones, but continual specific attempts to correct him may do more harm than good if he is unable to grasp and profit from them reasonably quickly. The disapproval implied by these corrections before he is able fully to profit from them may prompt him to abandon his transitional grammar structures and revert back to better known, more primitive ones.

Robinson also sets out from known research findings (Claim 6) four characteristics noted in mothers who have verbally advanced children, and these might be taken as the four 'golden rules' for any adult concerned with a child's linguistic development. We can summarize these rules in a form appropriate for the teacher as follows:

* embed any new verbal structure to which a class is being introduced in structures that are already familiar to the children;
* answer children's questions about language with relevant accurate replies that go beyond what is barely necessary. For instance, the child might be furnished with examples of how the new word or the new syntactical structure might be used, or he might be invited to provide such examples himself, or his attention might be drawn to words similar in meaning to the one about which he is enquiring, or he might be shown a helpful way of remembering the new linguistic skill he has just acquired;
* provide the child with helpful and appropriate feedback on whether he is expressing himself correctly or not (though keep in mind the qualification already made and take care not to discourage him by showing undue disapproval of his errors);
* maintain linguistic themes where possible over several utterances, both when talking to individuals and to the whole class (i.e. keep the theme of a particular conversation going by prompting and responding to further

contributions from the child or children, rather than simply giving short replies that close the discussion).

The rules of language

Another of Robinson's claims with direct practical relevance to the teacher is Claim 7. Expressed in educational terms, it emphasizes that there is great value in teaching children the rules of language. From an early age (and certainly by the time they start school) most children are aware that there are rules underlying the construction of what they say, but their ignorance of these rules handicaps them in formulating new utterances to deal with novel situations. Over a period of time, by listening to others, they may gradually become sensitive to these rules so that they use them without conscious deliberation (i.e. their use becomes an automated skill), but this is a slow process. Often parents and even teachers are less help than they might be because they themselves are unable to formulate these rules and, importantly, to set up conditions in which the child can put them into practice. Thus the learning of language becomes an essentially haphazard process, based upon the amassing of instances of a particular rule rather than upon learning the rule itself and then gauging through direct experience the extent to which it enhances communicative skills.

Clearly this indicates the importance of linguistic teaching. By such teaching we do not imply the kind of formal grammar lesson in which theory may be taught divorced from practice, but the lesson in which theory and practice are closely linked, in which rules are related to the child's ability to understand, and to the practical necessities of his particular stage of development. Once the child has been introduced to these rules, then the adult can use them in his dealings with the child to prompt the latter into developing new and ever more ambitious utterances. These utterances will help him communicate his ideas and feelings more clearly and comprehensively, and give him confidence in his ability to tackle new situations and new challenges verbally.

Maintaining the right balance between theory and practice in linguistic teaching, and helping the child appreciate the immeasurable advantages of linguistic fluency, is not easy. Too often children see language work as 'boring' or 'irrelevant', rather than as a means towards the acquisition of a priceless tool which serves both practical and aesthetic ends. Precise guidance on how to go about language teaching belongs to a book on teaching methods and techniques, but the important psychological principle to bear in mind is that children should experience the tangible reward of an increasing command of language. They should be enabled to see that their developing linguistic skills help them to express more fully and precisely the things they want to say, rather than simply helping them tackle academic exercises in text books. Language should be a means towards the articulation of their problems and sentiments, the statement of their point of view, the greater comprehension of the written word and of the exciting ideas it seeks to convey. As Robinson says, if we do not present language to the child in its correct context, 'he can come to believe that he has to accommodate to a world of words and another world of things and fail to realize that the two ought to be in a dialectical and corresponding relation to each other'.

Erroneous beliefs about language

In his section on 'erroneous beliefs' Robinson gives a number of suggestions on how the adult can assess whether he is fully communicating with the child or not. These suggestions are all of great practical importance to the teacher. Robinson quotes Brown's disturbing finding that 40 per cent of the questions asked by his sample of children received irrelevant replies from adults, and there is no reason to believe that this finding is an unrepresentative one. Robinson also, when discussing 'dialects and accents', makes the important distinction between aspects of a child's speech that indicate ignorance of its workings and those which simply mark social identity: that is, which are the marks of his home and sub-cultural group. The latter habits of speech may certainly be 'incorrect' in terms of Standard English, although the child uses them not because he knows no better but because they help render him acceptable to his family and friends. Where teachers treat these habits of speech with censure they run the risk of contributing to-wards the home-school conflict to which we made reference in Part I, a conflict in which the values of school and those of the home are seen to be in sharp contrast, and the child is forced to make some form of choice between the two. The school should certainly concentrate upon teaching Stan-dard English, but should recognize, as Robinson insists, that children are readily able to learn both this and their own dialect, and use whichever is appropriate to the situa-tion in which they find themselves. The school should be happy to see both exist side by side in the linguistic repertoire of the individual child, since he needs both if he is to communicate fully and appropriately in the diverse circumstances that go to make up his social life.

The same is true of the use of accents. People are often judged (quite inappropriately) on their accents, and again a child may need to equip himself with more than one method of pronouncing words if he is to find himself fully accep-table to different groups of people. The important thing is that children should understand why there is this possible need to acquire more than one form of pronunciation, instead of being left to feel that one way of expressing their native language is inferior to another, or that one way marks them out as being 'affected' or 'ignorant' or 'ridiculous' as the case may be.

Language and intelligence

Further reference is made to language when intelligence is discussed in the next chapter. Our concern here has been to discuss language as a function, as a method of communication between the child and his world. However, the part that it plays in intelligent behaviour can in part be inferred from this discussion, with the linguistically fluent child possessing obvious advantages when it comes to conceptualizing and solving problems, and it is against this background knowledge that much of what we say in the next chapter must be viewed.

dditional reading

Boyle, D.G. (1971) Language and Thinking in Human Development. London: Hutchinson.
   A good introduction to the relationship between language and thought.

Greene, J. (1972) Psycholinguistics. Harmondsworth: Penguin.
   One of the best texts for those wishing to brave the waters of psycholinguistics.

Luria, A.R. and Yudovich, F. (1971) Speech and the Development of Mental Processes in the Child. Harmondsworth: Penguin.
   A most interesting case study of the extent to which language impairment can impoverish the development of thought.

Robinson, W.P. (1972) Language and Social Behaviour. Harmondsworth: Penguin.
   A good short examination of language within the social context.

6

Intelligence
David Fontana

Of all aspects of psychology, none has achieved more attention within education than intelligence. The reason for this
is not hard to seek. If we define intelligence as the
ability to see relationships, and to use this ability to
overcome new problems, then we can see that there are few
aspects of a child's formal work in schools that do not
appear to be influenced by it in some way. Add to this the
fact that high or low intelligence can carry important
social and vocational significance, and it is not surprising
that parents as well as teachers take a deep interest in the
subject. It is probably in part because of this deep interest that many misconceptions have grown up about the nature
of intelligence and its measurement, some of them actively
detrimental to the child's educational progress.

Let us start with the problem of measurement because, unless
we can understand this, we can have no clear idea of the
limitations placed upon our attempt to study the origins of
intelligence and the way in which its development can be
best fostered and encouraged. Because intelligence is not
something that can be directly observed, like a person's
height or weight, we are only able to infer its presence by
watching people's behaviour. If we bear this in mind we can
see that any measurement of intelligence that we may be able
to produce is less a measure of what a person has than of
what he does. If we take a crude analogy with running we
can say that one person runs fast and another runs slowly,
but the running is essentially something they do, and not
some identifiable physical quality that we can point to at
any time whether they happen actually to be out on the running track or at home in their beds. True, the running may
be the product of definite physiological characteristics,
just as intelligent behaviour may be the product of neuro-
physiological characteristics in the brain, but it cannot be
said to have any objective existence outside the activity
itself.

This makes it very difficult for us to conceptualize
what is meant by being a 'good' and a 'bad' runner in any
absolute sense: that is, in the sense in which we can, for
example, say that a tall man is tall by virtue of the fact

that at all times and in all conditions his intact body
is longer from head to toe than the bodies of the vast
majority of his fellows. We may say that being a 'good'
runner simply means running faster than the majority of
one's fellows, but do we measure speed over 50 metres, 100
metres, or over 500 metres or a mile or a marathon of 26
miles and 385 yards? Do we measure it with the runner on
the flat or going uphill or downhill; at altitude or at sea
level; on a hot day or on a cold; after a big meal or
before? It is quite clear that even with the same group of
runners, measuring speed under all these different conditions would produce quite different results, with first one
runner doing best and then another. Nor would it be sufficient simply to take the average results over all these
conditions, since we could hardly say that one individual is
'best' when he can easily be beaten by one person over 100
metres and by another over the mile. Nor could we even
necessarily pick out the best sprinter, since although one
runner might be fastest over 100 metres someone else might
beat him if we shortened the race to 50 metres or lengthened
it to 120.

We said at the start that the analogy between intelligence and running is a crude one, and it must not be supposed for one moment that we are suggesting that as
abilities they come into similar categories. But our analogy
serves to show that if we are measuring and placing judgements upon behaviour in this way then the answer to the
question 'who is best?', or 'how good is this person as
compared to that?', depends very much upon the conditions
under which we stipulate the behaviour must take place. And
there cannot fail to be an arbitrary element about these
conditions. To turn to running again for a moment, why
should the shortest official sprint race run by adults out
of doors take place over 100 metres? Why should it not be
over 99 metres or 105 or over any other distance we like to
suggest? So it is with intelligence. The designers of intelligence tests stipulate the conditions (i.e. they set the
questions, determine the time limit by which these questions
must be answered, and decide which answers are 'right' and
which answers are 'wrong') under which intelligent behaviour
is to be manifested; but we could if we wished propose quite
different sets of conditions, and perhaps produce a quite
different set of marks. Which set is the more appropriate
would depend upon which gave us a better indication of how
well the individuals performed when faced with problems
solvable by intelligent behaviour in real life, but the
range of these problems is so vast and their solution often
dependent upon so many other factors in addition to intelligence (e.g. opportunity, the encouragement of others, motivation, degree of anxiety) that it is not always possible to
allow such indication to emerge with any clarity.

All this is not an argument against the importance of
intelligence or the attempt to measure it, just as it is not
an argument against running races and using the results to

predict how well someone might perform in real-life situations where running is required. But it is intended to highlight the problems associated with such measurement, and to indicate that the decisions we make on how measurement is to be undertaken inevitably influence the way in which we conceptualize the ability itself. It is for this reason that some psychologists define intelligence as simply the ability to do intelligence tests, a splendidly circular definition which is of little real help to us but which does serve to remind us of our difficulties.

The development of intelligence testing

These points are further clarified, together with other important issues, if we now turn and look at the origins of practical intelligence tests for general use back in the early years of the present century; back, in fact, in 1905 when the French psychologist Alfred Binet and his collaborator Theodore Simon were asked by the Parisian education authorities to devise methods of identifying children who were too 'feeble-minded' for education in normal schools. Binet decided, sensibly enough, to compile a series of simple verbal and practical problems designed to test qualities of comprehension, reasoning, judgement and adaptation, all of which could be tackled by older children better than by younger, and by children classed as 'bright' by their teachers better than by children classed as 'dull'. A further sensible decision by Binet was that scores should be standardized so that each individual's mark could be compared to the norm for his age. This led eventually to the concept of MENTAL AGE (or MA), a child's mental age being the chronological age at which most children obtained scores similar to his own (thus, e.g., a child of eight obtaining a score usually achieved only by ten year olds would have a mental age of ten).

Later, in 1916, the concept of mental age was developed by the American psychologist Lewis Terman of the University of Stanford into what came to be known as an intelligence quotient (or IQ). A child's IQ was arrived at by taking the ratio of mental age to chronological age and multiplying it by 100. Thus a child with, say, a mental age of ten and a chronological age of eight would have an IQ of:

$$\frac{10}{8} \times \frac{100}{1} = 125$$

The great advantage of this method was that if a child's mental age matched his chronological age (no matter what these respective ages happened to be) he would always have an IQ of exactly 100, and such an IQ would tell the psychologist or the teacher at a glance that the child's measured intelligence was 'average' for his chronological age. This method of computing the IQ was used for many years, but it had one major disadvantage. Experience showed that mental age does not appear to improve after about age 15 (i.e. in terms at least of intelligence test scores we seem to peak at around 15), and therefore an adult's chronological age had always to be entered as 15, since to do anything else would mean that, for instance, even the most able 30 year old would have an apparent IQ of only 50, well down in the feeble-minded category! In consequence we now use what is called a deviation IQ, which expresses an individual's score simply in terms of its deviation from the norm for his age, with the norm still being scaled to equal the convenient score of 100.

ater developments in ntelligence testing

Although systematic intelligence testing may be said to have begun in a rather chancy, imprecise way, the same cannot be said for subsequent work in the field. The original Binet-Simon intelligence test has undergone a number of careful revisions at the University of Stanford and various other, now more widely used, tests have emerged since. Space does not allow us to go into great detail on how these tests are constructed but the teacher needs to know one of the basic principles behind them if he is to appreciate the true nature of this construction. This principle derives from the assumption that intelligence is normally distributed in the general population, just as are most physical attributes such as height and weight and size of feet. Normal distribution implies that if we, say, measured the height of every adult in Britain and plotted the results on a graph we would obtain a neat bell-shaped curve, with the hump in the middle representing the majority of people and the distribution on either side of the mean tailing off in a regular, symmetrical pattern. Such symmetry would stem from the fact that the distribution of people with feet larger than average would be exactly matched by the distribution of people with feet smaller than average.

The assumption that intelligence is normally distributed means that intelligence tests have been so designed that if a large and representative sample of people is tested then scores will lie along this bell-shaped curve (usually called the normal curve). If they fail to do so (i.e. if many more people get high scores than get low scores or vice versa) then the difficulty levels of the tests are adjusted up or down until the required distribution is produced. There is only one snag, of course, and that is that intelligence may not be normally distributed amongst the population after all. There may indeed be more people with intelligence levels above the average than below (perfectly possible if the average is depressed by a relatively few very low-scoring individuals), or perhaps more with levels below the average than above, and it may be, therefore, that the principles upon which our tests are constructed serve to impose a pattern of IQ distribution upon the population that has no basis in fact. This could be important, for example, in 11+ selection exams or indeed in any exams where the assumption is that only people with scores above a certain standard will be able to profit from the opportunities offered, or master the skills necessary to make a success of a particular job.

Again, this is not an argument against the assumption that intelligence is normally distributed. Given the evidence from other human characteristics (such as the examples of height and weight referred to above), it is not easy to see in fact what other assumption could be made, but it is a strong caution against interpreting IQ test scores too rigidly, and assuming that small differences between one given group of children and another necessarily mean very much in practical terms. Test scores should ideally be viewed against a background of other measures, which may be tests of attainment in appropriate school subjects if we are making educational decisions, or perhaps tests of personality and motivation if we are concerned with some form of vocational guidance.

The importance of standard deviation

A further consequence of standardizing intelligence tests along the normal curve is that we have to take careful note of the standard deviation quoted by the test constructors. The standard deviation is a measure such that if we move one standard deviation above the mean and one standard deviation below we will have encompassed approximately 68 per cent of the sample, and if we move two standard deviations above and below we will have encompassed about 95 per cent. The standard deviation is thus a measure of dispersal, telling us how spread out the marks of a representative sample are likely to be. An example will make this clear, and also show why we need to know the standard deviation used by the authors of an intelligence test before we can interpret what a child's results on that test actually mean. Suppose one intelligence test (Test A) used a standard deviation of 10 and another (Test B) a standard deviation of 20. Using the normal curve we know that in the case of Test A sixty-eight per cent of children would be expected to have scores between 90 and 110, because these two scores represent respectively one standard deviation below the norm and one standard deviation above (the norm of course being 100). In the case of Test B, however, which has a standard deviation of 20, we know that 68 per cent will now have scores between 80 and 120, since on this test it is these scores which represent one standard deviation above and below the mean. If we now look at the scores of an individual child on both tests, and find that he has 110 on Test A and 120 on Test B we can see that these two scores, although apparently quite different, are in fact only telling us the same thing. They are telling us that the child is at the upper end of the 68 per cent of people who have scores (i.e. IQs) dispersed around the mean.

We can see the kind of confusion that can arise if we take the case of a child transferring schools. Let us assume that both schools keep records of children's IQs along with

their attainment test results, and the first school attended
by the child uses Test A while the school to which he
transfers uses Test B. The headteacher of the first school
forwards the child's records to the headteacher of the
second school, and when the latter peruses them he sees that
the child has a quoted IQ of 110. Now an IQ of 110 on Test
B would indicate that the child is some way from the upper
end of the 68 per cent of children with scores dispersed
around the mean, and the headteacher may well assume that
this is therefore the information that such an IQ score is
seeking to convey. However, if he has details of Test A, and
looks up the standard deviation, it will be found that this
is not the case, and that on Test B the child's equivalent
score would be 120.

Group and individual tests

Another feature of intelligence tests is that some are individual tests while others are of the group variety. The
former are adminstered to the child individually by the
tester, and sometimes involve structured apparatus such as
bricks or cards, while the latter are essentially paper and
pencil tests which can be given to more than one child at a
time. Individual tests are more time-consuming for the tester, of course, and since the child has to respond to him
orally the tester himself can become an important variable
in the exercise, since the child may find him intimidating
or perhaps liable to give inadvertent clues through facial
expressions, nods, etc. They do, however, have the advantage
of not relying on the child's own ability to read the questions or to write down answers, and are particularly useful
with younger children or with children who appear retarded
in the basic subjects. One of the best known individual
tests is the Wechsler Intelligence Scale for Children
(WISC), which also exists in an adult form. The original
Binet Scale which we discussed above is still in use in the
revised Terman-Merrill versions of 1937 and 1960, while the
British Intelligence Scale, devised over a number of years
at the University of Manchester and standardized on British
children, is also now available.

More widely used and more readily available outside
child guidance clinics are the various group intelligence
tests. So popular are these that their use has proliferated
outside education and into the world of job selection, vocational guidance, and management training (along with individual tests, they have also long been used in the armed
forces). On one authoritative estimate (Vernon, 1979), over
200 million tests of intelligence or achievement are administered annually in the USA alone, though whether such colos-
sal investment of time and money is altogether justified is
another matter. Of the group tests currently available those
devised by Alice Heim at the University of Cambridge are
among the most useful, with versions available for use with
children of school age and with students in higher education
(e.g. the AH4 and the AH5).

Models of intelligence

Together with the advance in intelligence testing has gone an advance in attempts to build models of the intellect that help us understand how it may work. In the same year that Binet began his labours in Paris, Carl Spearman advanced what became known as the two-factor theory of intelligence. We can see how this theory operates if we go back briefly to our analogy with running earlier in the chapter. It is possible to suggest that there is one general ability that underlies every performance of the running act and several more specific ability factors that come into play in particular kinds of running tasks (sprinting, middle distance, long distance, etc.). Similarly with intelligence, Spearman suggested the existence of a general intelligence factor (which he called 'g') and a range of specific ability factors (which he called 's' factors). Thus in any intelligent act, 'g' is involved, plus the 's' factor or factors appropriate to that particular act. Specific abilities are quite separate and distinct and it is 'g', argued Spearman, that accounts for all correlations between cognitive abilities.

The measurement of 'g'

A problem arises, of course, when it comes to trying to measure 'g'. For example, are verbal tests of intelligence a better measure of 'g' than spatial tests of intelligence or vice versa? We are told by Spearman that the level of correlation (i.e. the level of agreement) between the scores achieved by a child on the two sets of tests would be accounted for by the presence of 'g', but if we wanted to test for 'g', which would be the better test to use? We have no way of knowing. Moreover it would seem to be impossible to develop a test just to measure 'g' since as we have seen each intelligent act involves 'g' plus one or more 's' factors. Thus a verbal test of intelligence would involve 'g' plus the 's' factor of verbal ability; a spatial test of intelligence would involve 'g' plus the 's' factor of spatial ability, a mechanical test of intelligence would involve 'g' plus the 's' factor of mechanical ability; and so on. There seems to be no way of getting at 'g' on its own.

For this reason, alternative models of intelligence have been advanced that abandon the idea of 'g' altogether and propose instead a series of distinct clusters of intellectual abilities that may or may not be correlated with each other but which in measurement terms are better thought of as separate (e.g. verbal abilities, numerical abilities, spatial and mechanical abilities, or memory abilities). Generally, opinion these days, particularly in the USA, tends towards these alternative models, though for practical purposes tests yielding an overall composite IQ score, such as the ones we have been discussing (rather than separate tests for each of these clusters of ability), are still the more widely used. However, some of them do yield sub-scores which can be examined separately, such as v:ed scores (verbal and educational intelligence) and k:m scores (mechanical and spatial intelligence). But we must assume that if the alternative models become generally accepted then we may see the demise of the IQ test and the IQ score, and see instead a range of marks produced for each child, with each mark representing competence in a different area of intellectual skill. The practical advantage of this would be that a child who might perhaps score poorly on certain of these areas (and therefore who might have ended up with a relatively low IQ score) could get a good result on one or more of the remainder, thus giving us clear evidence of giftedness in certain departments.

The use of factor analysis

The arguments in favour of these alternate models are based upon more than mere practical considerations, however. Recent research using factor analysis rather suggests that such models may approximate closer to reality than Spearman's 'g' and 's' model and the other so-called 'hierarchical' models based to a greater or lesser degree upon it. Briefly, factor analysis is a technique that examines a range of scores to establish whether groups of them correlate more strongly amongst themselves than they do with the rest. Thus, for example, in a range of scores that we can label A to Z, we might find that scores A, D and G form a group with this quality, while scores J, L and P form another and scores R, T and W a third. We would then say that each of these three groups has an underlying factor which accounts for the intercorrelation of the scores that it contains. Using tests of intelligence, we would expect that if there is such a factor as 'g', then instead of separate groups we would find that all the scores cluster together into a single group (i.e. that they all intercorrelate strongly due to the fact that all of them contain a high unifying measure of 'g'). In the event, such does not appear t o be the case. When we correlate the results of various different measures of intelligence we find that not one but several separate factors emerge; hence the term multi-factorial that is given to the models of intelligence that reject the notion of 'g' and put in its place a range of separate abilities.

The value of 'g' to the class teacher

Yet, in spite of this, the idea of 'g' lives on. Its supporters point to the finding that the separate factors to which we have just referred nevertheless show some correlation with each other, suggesting that there may be yet another factor (a second-order factor) in turn underlying all of them. At the educational level it is also pointed out that, like it or not, the IQ score is a pretty accurate prognosticator of academic success, suggesting that the notion of 'g' remains a useful one for certain purposes. It is also argued that some of the multi-factorial models, such as that of Guilford which postulates no fewer than 120 mental factors which singly or in combination are said to be

involved in any given intelligent act, are highly complicated and often lack any very immediate appeal to busy class
teachers. In any case, although teachers may make considerable use of the concept of 'g', they nevertheless are well
aware that on its own it cannot account for all intellectual
differences between children. Though a child who is good at,
say, verbal reasoning is also likely to be good at tasks
involving numerical ability, rote memory, inductive reasoning and so on, there will be fluctuations in his performance
from one to another, suggesting that there is some degree of
difference between the intellectual abilities involved. Thus
although a teacher may well describe a child as 'highly
intelligent' or 'of average intelligence', he will make the
reservation that this does not mean the child will perform
uniformly at all tasks involving intelligent behaviour.

In practice, the use the teacher makes of the concept of
'g' will depend in no small measure upon the age of children
with which he is concerned. Vernon (1979) considers the
evidence and suggests that there is an increasing differentiation between abilities as the child grows older. The very
young child's performance in different areas of intelligent
behaviour tends to be relatively uniform, but in adolescents
and adults there is often a marked discrepancy from one
area to another. This may in part be the result of the increasing pressures towards specialization with which we meet
after our primary school days, but there could also be other
developmental factors involved. It could be that as our
powers of thinking become more complex (see our discussion
of Piaget's work in chapter 4), so our ability to tackle
certain kinds of intellectual problems develops more rapidly
than our ability to tackle others, and our natural tendency
to concentrate upon areas in which we are successful, at the
expense of areas in which we are not, lends further impetus
to the process.

The origins of intelligence

Early researchers were in little doubt that intelligence was
an inherited ability. It might vary in its rate of development from individual to individual (as one child may grow
physically more slowly than another or may perhaps put on
less weight), but it was held to be essentially stable in
its nature, susceptible to accurate assessment even in
childhood, and a reliable indicator of future academic and
vocational attainment. Such a viewpoint had important implications for education and for society in general since it
supported strongly the notion that if the individual was not
born clever then he could not be made so, and it tended to
fit in with the hierarchical view that each person was born
to a particular station in life.

It would be wrong to suppose that these early researchers deliberately set out to strengthen this socially
divisive view of man. On the contrary, one of their main
arguments for the development of intelligence tests, and in
particular for their use in such educational contexts as the

11+ examination, was that these tests would identify innately able children who had been born in economically straitened circumstances and allow society to give them a chance, through scholarships and so on, to make full use of their potential. But there is little doubt that their emphasis upon the prime importance of heredity did fit in neatly with the most influential social and political views of the time, and did help to perpetuate an educational system in which children with low or average IQs were given much poorer facilities and much less attention than children with IQs significantly above the mean.

In the 1930s, however, things began to change within psychology as a consequence of the so-called behaviourist movement, which argued that if psychologists were ever to turn their subject into an exact science then they must study the observable facts of human behaviour (i.e. what people actually do) rather than introspection and consciousness (i.e. what people tell you about their private mental world). With such a change in emphasis came a greater interest in learning (see chapter 8), since the effects of learning can become immediately apparent in a person's behaviour. Once it was appreciated what a profound effect learning could have upon human behaviour, the door was opened to a new model of man which argued that we become the people we are (intelligent behaviour and all) largely as a result of the particular learning experiences to which we are subjected from birth onwards. As a result, the view that intelligence was essentially an innate quality began to give ground to the notion that it was largely an acquired one. The stress upon nature was replaced by a stress upon nurture.

Obviously this change of emphasis is of great interest to the teacher, concerned as he is with the child's ability to learn. The more a child can develop his ability through learning, the greater the scope of the teacher. However, though the critical part played by learning in psychological development is not now open to dispute, it is still not clear whether the ability (or abilities) we call intelligence owes more to learning than it does to innate endowment; and in recent years the debate has been vigorously reopened, with some commentators now suggesting that the pendulum may have swung too far and that we may be in danger of neglecting the contribution made by inherited characteristics to the individual differences in behaviour between children. In a sense, of course, the existence of such a debate, with strong views on either side, may make us lose sight of the fact that it is not the separate contributions of either nature or nurture that are important so much as the interaction between the two. Whatever a child's innate potential may be, if he is denied the environmental stimuli necessary for its development then it will be of little use to him. Similarly, whatever the environmental stimuli, if a child lacks the necessary degree of potential he may never be able to reach the same standards as a child more generously endowed. If we may return briefly (and for the last time) to our example of running we can readily see that without the right training experiences no athlete would be able to break the world 1500 metres record. On the other hand, no matter what training we are offered, most of us would not be able to break the record because we do not have the (largely inherited) basic physique for the job.

Nevertheless, the debate on the relative importance of the contributions of nature and nurture to individual differences in intelligence between children has achieved so much attention, and carries such profound implications for the political decisions that determine national educational policies, that the teacher must be familiar with some of the major issues raised by both sides. Let us start by looking at some research that appears to favour the greater importance of nature, the so-called twin studies.

Twin studies
Genetically, all twins come in one or other of two categories, known popularly as identical and fraternal. Identical twins (known technically as monozygotic or MZ for short) are formed from the same ovum and sperm and therefore enjoy virtually identical genetic endowments, while fraternal twins (known technically as dyzgotic or DZ) come from separate ova and sperms and are therefore genetically no more alike than any other brothers and sisters. Researchers have therefore postulated that if MZ twins are significantly more alike in terms of measured intelligence than DZ twins, then this is a strong argument in favour of the importance of inheritance, since twins in general receive very much the same kind of environment within their family and within their school. (It is often argued this is untrue, and that MZ twins are treated more alike by family and teachers than DZ twins, but this would probably only be sufficient to account for relatively minor differences in measured intelligence.) Another approach adopted by researchers is to study groups of MZ and DZ twins who have been separated at birth and reared apart in different homes. In this case both MZ and DZ twins will have received different environments, and if MZ twins are still significantly more like each other in terms of intelligence test scores, then this again will strengthen the argument in favour of inheritance.

A number of twin studies of both kinds have been carried out over the years, and some of the data have been collected and tabulated by Jarvik and Erlenmeyer-Kimling (1967). In table 1, which is adapted from their findings, the column headed 'genetic expectation' refers to the correlation in intelligence tests scores between the respective twin pairs we would expect if inheritance were the only factor. Thus, on the basis of genetic theory, MZ twins would be expected to show a correlation of 1.0, while DZ twins and siblings would be expected to correlate at 0.5 and unrelated children to show no correlation at all. Any deviance from these expected correlations, on the purely genetic argument, would be due to the unreliability of the tests used. On the other hand, if environment plays a major role then we would predict a major deviance from these correlations, with MZ twins in fact failing to correlate any more closely than DZ.

Table 1

Correlation in measured intelligence between various kinship relations
(Based on Jarvik and Erlenmeyer-Kimling, 1967)

Kinship relation	Number of studies	Median obtained correlation	Genetic expectations
MZ twins reared together	14	0.87	1.00
MZ twins reared apart	4	0.75	1.00
DZ twins of like sex reared together	11	0.56	0.50
DZ twins of opposite sex reared together	9	0.49	0.50
Siblings reared together	36	0.55	0.50
Siblings reared apart	3	0.47	0.50
Unrelated children reared together	5	0.24	0.00
Unrelated children reared apart	4	-0.01	0.00

The table indicates that, even when raised apart, MZ twins show a much higher correlation in their measured intelligence than do any of the other groups. Furthermore, it shows that DZ twins reared together are no more alike than siblings (though being of the same age they probably receive more similar environments), and that both DZ twins and siblings are more alike than unrelated children reared together. Results of this order appear pretty conclusive and have prompted some experts to suggest that, of the measured difference in intelligence between individual children, some 80 per cent is likely to be due to differences in inheritance and only some 20 per cent to be due to differences in environment.

However, the issue is not really as clear-cut as this after all. Data such as those summarized in the table have been severely criticized on a number of important counts. Most notably Kamin (1974) points out the following:

* although raised separately, many of the identical twins included in twin studies were in fact placed in very similar homes: sometimes even raised by members of the same family. Thus it is incorrect to assume that they received very different environments;
* some of the data are themselves suspect, in particular those produced by the late Sir Cyril Burt. The evidence suggests that Burt may have, for various reasons, recorded inaccurate data for various groups of twins raised together and apart, data which have suggested the case in favour of inheritance is very much stronger than it is;
* even the data for siblings reared apart is inconclusive. In one study, for example (Freeman, Holzinger and Mitchell, 1928), we find that siblings raised apart but in similar homes show a correlation in measured intelligence of 0.30, while those raised in dissimilar homes show one of 0.19.

The problem is that it is very difficult to come by samples of twins and even of siblings raised apart and in quite different environments. And if we study twins raised together, and find that MZ twins are consistently more alike than DZ twins similarly raised, this is always open to the criticism that the environments of the former may be more similar than the latter. We have already suggested that this greater similarity may only account for relatively minor differences in measured intelligence, but nevertheless it remains what is called a 'contaminating variable' in the research, and must leave all findings open to dispute.

Other studies

Is there some other way of solving the nature-nurture controversy, therefore, that is not subject to this kind of objection? Studies using animals are one possibility, though we must always be extremely cautious in the lessons for human behaviour that we derive from them. Quite apart from other major differences animals lack language and, as we have already seen, language is of critical importance in the development of thinking and of intelligent behaviour in humans. Nevertheless, such studies are not without interest, and appear to indicate that selective breeding over a few generations can significantly improve certain animal skills (such as learning to find a way through a complex maze) which are possibly analogous to intelligence in humans, and this tends to support the importance of inheritance. Studies involving certain forms of mental subnormality in humans are another possibility, since it is known that some kinds of handicap (such as Down's Syndrome and Turner's Syndrome) are directly linked to genetic factors. The inference is that if genetic abnormalities appear to play a part in low measurable intelligence, then it is likely they also play a part in measurable intelligence across the whole spectrum of abilities.

One of the most interesting arguments in favour of the role played by inherited characteristics is that advanced by Vernon (1979), however. Vernon suggests that champions of the extreme environmentalist viewpoint have yet to explain the marked differences in intelligence often noted between children within the same family. These children in most cases received similar or very similar environments, yet their measured intelligence can differ by 10, 20 or even 30 IQ points on the same tests. Genetically we would expect this, as each child will have drawn a different combination of genes from his parents, but environmentally it is not what we would predict. Similarly, we sometimes find a very bright child born to relatively dull parents. This can be explained genetically as due to recessive genes (i.e. genes carried by parents which do not affect their behaviour but which can become dominant again in the child, just as two brown-eyed parents can have a blue-eyed child), but environmentally it is something of a puzzle, as the child will not have received a particularly stimulating upbringing. By the same token, we sometimes find highly intelligent parents who produce a relatively unintelligent child in spite of providing a great deal in the way of environmental stimuli.

Summarizing the evidence in all its different manifestations, Vernon concludes that it demonstrates a strong genetic component in the development of individual differences in intelligence. Although environment has a very important role to play, measurable IQ seems to 'depend more on genetic endowment than on favourable or unfavourable environmental opportunities and learning, at least within white culture'. But lest it be thought that this is an argument in favour of élitism in education, with genetically favoured children being given the best opportunities and the rest left to gravitate towards the social levels to which nature has called them, it must be stressed again that nature and nurture complement each other. In an educational sense, one is meaningless without the other. As Vernon goes on to say on the same page, 'both are essential, and neither can be neglected if we are to plan children's upbringing and education wisely'. To this we can add that the élitist argument can just as easily be turned the other way round. We can as readily argue that children with lower intellectual potential warrant better educational opportunities than children with higher, since it is important that they do not waste any of this more limited potential.

The approaches of Hebb and Cattell
Rather than spend more time discussing the precise percentage contributions of nature and nurture to human intelligence, we should turn now to a suggestion advanced by Hebb: namely, that instead of talking about intelligence in a general sense we should talk of Intelligence A, which is inborn potential and which we have no way of measuring, and

Intelligence B, which is that part of Intelligence A actually developed by environmental influences. Thus one child, with a larger Intelligence A than another, might yet end up with a smaller Intelligence B due to environmental deprivation. This model has been augmented by Vernon, who suggests that since intelligence tests are imperfect instruments we should also talk of Intelligence C, which is that part of Intelligence B that we actually manage to measure.

A model along somewhat similar lines is proposed by Cattell (1963), who talks of fluid (gf) and crystallized (gc) intelligence, the former representing the influence of biological factors on intellectual development and the latter the outcome of environmental experiences. Where Cattell differs from the Hebb-Vernon model is that he claims both gf and gc can be measured, in that they emerge from factorial analysis of the results of a range of ability tests. Further, he considers that such measurement indicates a deterioration of gf with age, which is an important point since, as we have already said, measured intelligence does not appear to increase much in most people after the age of 15, and in fact shows something of a decline from early adult life onwards. Cattell's findings would seem to show that the biological mechanisms involved in intelligence reach full maturity by this age, and then are subject to the ageing process, whereas crystallized intelligence (gc) can go on developing with experience throughout life. Within the context of the nature-nurture debate this would suggest that, given appropriate experiences, people are capable of increasing their capacity for certain kinds of intelligent behaviour long after leaving school, and this perhaps helps to explain the great success of many mature students who performed with only limited success during their earlier formal education.

Before leaving this section we must stress that, although we have been talking about the nature-nurture controversy and its possible implications for educational policy, intelligence is only one of the many psychological variables that influence a child's progress at school. Motivation, creativity, vocational aspirations, child-teacher relationships, personality, self-esteem, peer-group pressures and many others all have their part to play, and these are, of course, dealt with at the appropriate points throughout this book.

Intelligence and race

It will be noted in our quote from Vernon a few paragraphs ago that we used the words 'at least within the white culture', and this unfortunately raises the whole vexed question of whether or not genetically determined differences in intelligence exist between the different races of the world. With so many factors creating distrust and dislike between races we could well have been spared this one, but a lively controversy has sprung up in recent years, with some bitterness on both sides, and as with the nature-nurture controversy it is important that the teacher should know the issues involved.

Our starting point must once again be with the difficulties in defining and measuring intelligence. If intelligence is the ability to solve problems, which in summary is what we have suggested, then the Australian aborigine or the Kalahari bushman, for example, would regard the average westerner as highly unintelligent in view of his lack of ability to survive unaided for long in their harsh environments. And so indeed might the Eskimo. These examples might seem extreme, but they illustrate the point that, historically, different races have been faced with different kinds of problems, and it is therefore inappropriate (and unfair) for one race to claim that its intelligence tests are the correct way of measuring intellectual ability (i.e. problem-solving ability) in any part of the world. An aborigine child might well smile at a psychologist who expects him to answer one of the standard items on a western intelligence test (e.g. 'complete the sequence of numbers 8, 20, 50, 125, ?') yet who could not find the nearest source of water in order to save himself from an agonizing death. Similarly, a Buddhist monk might doubt the intelligence of the whole of western society, with its emphasis upon material possessions and upon weapons of fearful mass destruction, and its inability to solve the problems of living at peace with oneself and one's fellow men.

What we are saying, therefore, is that our concepts of intelligence and our methods for measuring it are 'culture bound', and may not have validity ouside western White society. In the light of this, it should come as no surprise to find that in one piece of research a sample of White American children emerged with an average of 14 IQ points higher than a sample of American Indians on verbal reasoning tests, but that the position was more than reversed when non-verbal intelligence tests such as the Goodenough or the Harris were used (Gaddes, McKenzie and Barnsley, 1968). The latter tests, it would seem, with their emphasis upon visual detail, are more suited to the culture of the American Indian than are the verbal tests with their extreme emphasis upon linguistic skills.

The most extensive investigations into racial differences in intelligence have been carried out, however, not with American Whites and American Indians but with American Whites and American Blacks. Literally hundreds of studies using these two populations have been undertaken over the last half century, and Vernon (1979) considers the consensus which emerges from them is that Black IQs are, on average, 15 points below those of Whites (85 as opposed to 100). In a study that aroused great controversy, Jensen (1973) attacked the argument that differences of this magnitude can be caused by environment alone, and pointed out that even when steps have been taken to improve the environments of Black communities these differences have not fully disappeared.

Does this mean, therefore, that the supposed intellectual inferiority of American Blacks as compared to American Whites must be taken as a proven fact, and that the genes which cause differences in skin pigmentation and the other superficial differences which mark one race off from another are also connected in some way with the development of intelligence? No, it emphatically does not. The picture is much more complex than this, and the closer one studies it the more anomalies one finds. For example, Vernon (1969) shows that IQ gains of 15 points and more are by no means uncommon amongst West Indian children who have attended London schools for six or seven years. In addition, the observed gap between White and Black children in America is nowhere near as marked in the pre-school years as it is later on. Although it is not easy to test intelligence very reliably in children as young as two years, the available evidence we have using the Gesell test in fact shows no difference at all between the two groups. Summarizing worldwide evidence, Werner (1972) even suggests that on psycho-motor tests (i.e. tests involving the solution of physical problems) both African and American Black races show the highest mean scores of any group tested while western Whites show the lowest. It is only at school age, when intelligence tests come to involve more verbal problems, that the gap begins to open up in the other direction.

The implications of these and the various other issues involved are far too numerous to pursue in detail here, but it is fair to conclude that there are no conclusive grounds for supposing genetic differences in intelligence exist between races. Such measurable differences as do exist would seem to be far too strongly contaminated by environmental variables to allow us to explain their origins with any confidence. Western White culture is highly verbal in its current orientation, and success in many walks of life seems to go to those who are able to use language at a fluent and complex level. Groups who themselves place a lower emphasis upon the importance of language (and after all language is not the only form of communication), or who have less opportunity to acquire and use it to a high standard, will therefore inevitably appear to be less able on tests demanding verbal reasoning and other verbal skills. Until such time as we develop genuinely culture-fair tests, or until such time as we decide money spent on exploring racial differences in intelligence is better spent in other areas of human need, there is little that one can usefully add.

Other between-group differences in intelligence

Socio-economic factors

From the educational standpoint, probably the most important differences in measured intelligence between groups are those associated with socio-economic status. Socio-economic status (SES for short) is usually determined by reference to paternal occupation. In the UK the Registrar General classifies such occupations into five groups, starting with Group

I which includes such luminaries as doctors, politicians and university teachers and proceeding down through managerial, skilled, and semi-skilled to the unskilled workers who make up Group V. Research has consistently shown that the higher one moves upwards through these groups the higher the mean IQ becomes, both for parents and children (the mean for children of parents in Group I for example is reported to be about 115, while for those in Group V it is around 92).

The reasons for these differences are again by no means clear. Children from low SES homes are, of course, less likely to have the material possessions that stimulate intellectual activity, such as books and constructional toys. They are also less likely to be read to, to have a room where quiet study is possible, to hear complex verbal structures in the speech of their parents and siblings, and to be motivated to do well at school by parents who have high ambitions for them. But it has also been suggested that there may be genetic factors at work, with people of lower intelligence tending to gravitate to SES Group V and to pass on lower intellectual potential to their children, while people of higher intelligence tend to move up towards SES Group I and to pass on a higher potential. Lest it be thought that this will result in a steady widening of the gap between the two groups, geneticists suggest we should take account of an interesting phenomenon known as 'filial regression to the mean'. Put simply, this represents the tendency of children, over a wide range of genetically determined factors, to score nearer to the mean for the whole population than do their parents in instances where the latter obtain unusually high or unusually low ratings. With height, for example, the average stature of sons of very tall fathers is 50 per cent nearer the mean than is that of their fathers, while the sons of very short fathers again show an average height nearer the mean by the same percentage than do their fathers. This is nature's way, if you like, of ensuring that the race remains relatively uniform, and does not consist of giants and dwarfs. If filial regression to the mean operates in the field of intelligence (and the evidence that it does has been hotly disputed) this would mean that parents in Group I would on average have higher IQs than their children, while in Group V the reverse would be the case.

Urban and rural differences in intelligence

Turning away from socio-economic status, we find that differences in measured intelligence also exist between urban and rural children. One study (McNemar, 1942) found that at school entry the difference is some 5.7 IQ points in favour of urban children, and rises to 10.4 by top junior age and to 12.2 in school leavers. Again, this could be a compound of genetic and environmental factors. The trend since the eighteenth century has been for people to seek their fortunes in the cities and the large towns, and it could be that historically it has been the intellectually more able who have tended to up and leave the quiet rural life. Thus the genetic pool could have been gradually depleted of its high intelligence genes in country districts, while the pool in towns and cities was constantly being augmented. On the other hand, it could simply be that there is more environmental stimulation in the cities (at least of the kind that leads to success in intelligence tests!), better school facilities, and higher motivation. Or it could simply be that in the urban-rural dichotomy we see in miniature the kind of things we suggested may exist between races: that is, country people place less emphasis on the verbal and other skills measured in intelligence tests, and prefer to develop a more measured and perhaps profounder way of life which is more in keeping with the kind of problems that present themselves for solution in their environment.

Sexual differences in intelligence

A third between-group difference in measured intelligence that has attracted research interest is that between the sexes. The extensive literature that this research has spawned is extensively reviewed by Maccoby and Jacklin (1974), but if we summarize their findings and those of more recent workers we can say that no conclusive general difference in IQ scores appears to exist between boys and girls, though in certain specific intellectual skills such differences do seem to be apparent. Of most direct interest to the teacher are those differences in reading and mathematics. In the former, twice as many boys as girls are diagnosed as backward in the USA, while the picture is probably not substantially different in the UK. Girls also tend to be more verbal and articulate than boys at first, though these differences disappear by around age 16 or so. However, cross-cultural studies show that this picture is not duplicated in all societies, and it may therefore be primarily a culturally induced one. In western societies girls spend more time within the home than do boys, and are more concerned for parental approval. They are thus more likely to be exposed to a verbally stimulating environment and to good parental reading habits. With less in the way of physical activities open to them, they may also turn to reading as a way of employing their time.

In support of this culture-orientated argument there is some evidence that when boys are presented with reading books that have a high interest content (i.e. are orientated towards a boy's pursuits), differences in reading ability between boys and girls tend to disappear (Stanchfield, 1973). There is also some evidence, though it has not gone undisputed, that when boys are taught by men in the early schoolyears, and therefore come to identify school with masculinity rather than with femininity, they perform up to the same standards as girls in reading and other verbal skills.

In mathematics, we find the position reversed, with boys showing significant superiority over girls, this time right up to school leaving age. But here again, this may primarily be a culturally-induced phenomenon. Mathematical and spatial skills traditionally (and unfairly) are associated with the male world and with male vocational choice. Even in the early school years, the more interesting and exciting mathematical problems tend to be presented in terms of masculine occupations and preoccupations rather than in terms of feminine (the latter being restricted to problems to do mainly with shopping and household budgets). As with boys and reading, there is evidence to show that where these and other opportunity and emotional variables are held constant there is no evidence that one sex is markedly superior to the other, and findings of this kind should make educationists reflect very carefully on the degree to which girls (and boys) can be handicapped by the very agencies that are supposed to be helping them develop their potential and widen their occupational choice.

In particular, we should stop believing that girls are naturally more literate than boys and boys naturally more numerate than girls, as it seems that teacher attitudes and expectations can materially influence child performance. If we expect one child for some reason to be better at something than another child then we will, consciously or unconsciously, tend to convey this expectation to the children themselves, who will allow it to influence their own views as to their ability. We will also tend to expect higher standards from the first child than from the second, and perhaps work that little bit harder ourselves as teachers to get the him to achieve them. Very few teachers are ever consciously sexist in their approach at any level, but misconceptions about the relative abilities (and interests, inclinations and emotions) of boys and girls lead without doubt to a great deal of unconscious bias within the school, as indeed they do within society in general.

References

Cattell, R.B. (1963)
Theory of fluid and crystallized intelligence: a critical experiment. Journal of Educational Psychology, 54, 1-22.

Freeman, F.N., Holzinger, K.J. and Mitchell, B.C. (1928)
The influence of environment on the intelligence, school achievement and conduct of foster children. In Twenty-Seventh Yearbook of the National Society for the Study of Education, Part 1. Bloomington, Ill.: Public School Publishing.

Gaddes, W.H., McKenzie, A. and Barnsley, R. (1968)
Psychometric intelligence and spatial imagery in two northwest Indian and two white groups of children. Journal of Social Psychology, 75, 35-42.

Jarvik, L.F. and Erlenmeyer-Kimling, L. (1967)
Survey of familiar correlations in measured intellectual functions. In J. Zubin and G.A. Jervis (eds), Psychopathology of Mental Development. New York: Grune & Stratton.

Jenson, A.R. (1973)

    Educability and Group Differences. New York: Harper & Row.

Kamin, L.J. (1974)

    The Science and Politics of IQ. Harmondsworth: Penguin.

Maccoby, E. and Jacklin, C. (1974)

    The Psychology of Sex Differences. Stanford: Stanford University Press.

McNemar, Q. (1942)

    The Revision of the Stanford-Binet Scale. Boston: Houghton Mifflin.

Stanchfield, J. (1973)

    Sex Differences in Learning to Read. Bloomington, Ind.: Phi Delta Kappa Educational Foundation.

Vernon, P.E. (1969)

    Intelligence and Cultural Enviroment. London: Methuen.

Vernon, P.E. (1979)

    Intelligence: Heredity and environment. San Francisco: W. H. Freeman.

Werner, E.E. (1972)

    Infants around the world: cross-cultural studies of psychomotor development from birth to two years. Journal of Cross-cultural Psychology, 3, 111-134.

Questions

1. Can you account for the great interest that educators and parents have taken in intelligence over the years?
2. What particular problems does the measurement of intelligence present?
3. In the chapter we used 'running' as an analogy in our discussion of the measurement of intelligence. Can you think of any other analogies we could usefully have employed instead?
4. Why do some psychologists simply define intelligence as 'the ability to do intelligence tests'? Why is this definition of little real help to us?
5. What are the origins of formal intelligence tests? Why is it of value for us to know about these origins when discussing the concept of intelligence within education?
6. What is meant by mental age? How was this originally used in the computation of IQ?
7. What was the disadvantage of this method of computation and what is the method that has superseded it?
8. How has the notion that intelligence is normally distributed affected the design and construction of intelligence tests?
9. Why is it important to know the standard deviation of an intelligence test before we try interpreting the result produced by it?
10. What is meant by 'g' and what part does this concept play in models of intelligence?
11. Why is the term 'multi-factorial' given to certain models of intelligence?

12. How does age apparently affect the usefulness of the concept of 'g'?
13. Why is the nature-nurture controversy over the origins of intelligence of interest to teachers?
14. Give examples of some of the methods psychologists have used to try and resolve the nature-nurture controversy.
15. Give some of the objections raised to the data on nature-nurture yielded by twin studies.
16. How do the models proposed by Hebb and Vernon on the one hand and by Cattell on the other deal with the relative influences of nature and nurture?
17. What do we mean when we say that our methods for measuring intelligence are 'culture bound'?
18. Give some reasons why children from LSES backgrounds may show lower measured intelligence then children from USES.
19. What is meant by 'filial regression to the mean'?
20. Discuss the apparent differences in intelligence and ability between girls and boys noted by some researchers. Can you account for these differences?

Annotated reading

Vernon, P.E. (1979) Intelligence: Heredity and environment. San Francisco: Freeman.
> The student keen to find a good general text on all aspects of intelligence need look no further. In spite of its title, this book covers virtually all areas of the subject of interest to the teacher and does not concentrate solely on the heredity versus environment debate. It is scholarly, fair-minded, and eminently readable.

Butcher, H.J. (1968) Human Intelligence. London: Methuen.
> An earlier survey but still of value.

Kamin, L.G. (1974) The Science and Politics of IQ. Harmondsworth: Penguin.
> The book that sparked off the current debate over the relative contributions of nature and nurture to measured intelligence.

Block, N. and Dworkin, G. (1977) The IQ Controversy. London Quartet Books.
> Contains much of the relevant evidence thrown up by both sides.

Wiseman, S. (ed.) (1973). Intelligence and Ability (2nd edn). Harmondsworth: Penguin.
> A good collection of papers on intelligence.

Eysenck, H.J. and Kamin, L. (1981) Intelligence: The battle for the mind. Harmondsworth: Penguin.
> An excellent debate between two of the major proponents of nature and nurture theories of intelligence respectively.

Richardson, K., Spears, D. and Richards, M. (1972) Race, Culture, and Intelligence. Harmondsworth: Penguin.
    Deals with cross-cultural issues in intelligence and intelligence testing.

Watson, P. (ed.) (1973) Psychology and Race. Harmondsworth: Penguin.
    Also of interest, and concerned rather more closely with racial issues, though it deals with other psychological matters in addition to intelligence.

Relevance to the teacher
DAVID FONTANA

Gains in IQ

We have seen that measured intelligence appears to be a consequence of both genetic and environmental factors, and since the teacher's concern is with the second of these the question that immediately arises is by how much, and in what ways, can measured IQ be improved by education? The answer to the first part of the question cannot be given with any precision, of course, but the consensus amongst both geneticists and psychologists seems to be that for children with similar genetic backgrounds a difference of up to 25 IQ points could be apparent at maturity given highly stimulating and very unstimulating backgrounds respectively. This could mean, for example, that a child averaging an IQ of 95 points at age four could reach the 100-105 range by school-leaving age if he received the right stimuli, or he could slip back to the 80-85 range without it. This might well represent the difference between a well-paid skilled or lower managerial job, or an unskilled occupation offering neither fulfilment nor prospects.

Whether the school on its own can ensure that each child reaches the upper end of his ability range is another matter. As with all social and academic factors, the school is limited in what it can do without the help of the home and, if need be, of other social services. Various ambitious intervention programmes based upon the school and designed to help under-privileged children have been tried (such as the Head Start programme in the USA) but have failed to eliminate all environmentally induced differences in IQ ratings. What they have sometimes succeeded in doing, however, is to maintain the IQ levels that these children show upon first being admitted to compulsory schooling (Lazar et al, 1977). Since such levels tend to show the greatest deterioration in disadvantaged children in the years after leaving infant school (perhaps because in these years they are left increasingly to rely upon their own efforts) it seems essential that these programmes should therefore not be confined to the early school years, but should follow children right through to the time they leave.

It might be thought that the maintenance of IQ scores is only a kind of marking time, but this is not so. The items in an intelligence test presented to an 11-year-old child are much harder than those presented to a five year old. To maintain his IQ score he must, therefore, be able to solve increasingly difficult problems and keep up with the intellectual development of his peers: no mean achievement for the child from a disadvantaged home. The child will also come to possess more knowledge as a result of good educational programmes than he otherwise would. Education, after all, is not simply a matter of the skills required to do well in an IQ test, but of the accumulated factual and experiential knowledge necessary to understand an increasingly complex society. Even in his more dispirited moments (which luckily will come but seldom) the teacher should never under-estimate the importance of his role in the child's life. Such under-estimation is likely to lead not only to career dissatisfaction but to a lowering of expectation, and we have already touched on the influence that teacher expectation can have upon children themselves.

Coaching for IQ tests

At one time, when the 11+ examination was widespread in Britain, teachers frequently used to ask whether a child's IQ score could be improved if he were given specific practice in answering intelligence test items. The answer is that some improvement in score (up to about ten per cent, in fact, with brighter children showing proportionally the greatest gains) can be achieved by systematic coaching of this kind, though whether such improvement also enhances the child's ability to deal with the real-life problems that intelligence test items are supposed to mimic is unclear. It is possible, in any case, that some at least of this improvement comes about simply as a result of greater confidence. We see in the chapter on learning that anxiety can have a deleterious effect upon educational performance, and when a child is preparing for an examination such as the 11+, anything that helps to allay this anxiety to some degree is therefore likely to have consequences for the standard achieved. The problem faced by administrators of the 11+, however, was that children from schools which did not go in for coaching (and for the most part coaching was officially discouraged) tended to be at something of a disadvantage compared with those who came from schools which did. Now that the 11+ has become a relative rarity, coaching is only likely to be a problem if it is given to a child who subsequently is to be tested by the educational psychologist for possible placement in a special school. It could be that parents (or even a well-meaning teacher) might be tempted to offer such coaching in the belief that they are in some way helping the child. The opposite would be the case, of course, since the psychologist could be misled by an enhanced score and might be wrongly influenced in his recommendations as to placement.

Value of IQ tests to the teacher

This chapter has dealt in detail with the development and nature of IQ tests, but the teacher sometimes asks whether, for all the time and money that have been spent on them, they are really of very much value within the educational context. The answer is that for all their faults they remain one of the most (if not THE most) accurate predictors of educational achievement, in that test scores correlate highly with both children's present and future levels of academic success. They thus serve as very useful diagnostic instruments. For example, a child scoring high on an intelligence test but doing much less well at school than that score would predict is likely to be suffering from problems other than those caused by lack of cognitive ability. He might have problems at home or be unhappy with his teacher or his classmates, or have missed vital groundwork through absence. An unusually high IQ score might indicate that he is in fact bored with school because it under-extends him. Or he might have undiagnosed physical problems such as poor hearing or poor eyesight, or he might be an immigrant child who has problems with language (this would be indicated by much higher scores on non-verbal than on verbal test items), or he might be setting his sights too low in order to remain with his friends or because of lack of confidence for some reason.

Thus the intelligence test could alert us to the real cause of a child's problems, allowing us to plan the right kind of remedial programme. Two qualifications need to be made about the diagnostic role of IQ tests, however. The first is that there is nothing to be gained (and much possibly to be lost) by trying to diagnose IQ levels in children who are already performing satisfactorily. There is sometimes a feeling on the part of headteachers and their staff that it would be of value to test children's intelligence routinely and keep records of the results. But we have already said that teacher expectations of individual children's performances can be influenced by a knowledge of IQ scores, and there is always a danger that a teacher will lower the standards demanded of a child who comes out with a score below the mean for his classmates, even though to date he has been meeting these standards without difficulty. As was stressed earlier on, intelligence is not the only variable affecting school performance, and to know that one child scores five IQ points less than his neighbour is meaningless if the child is coping well with his work.

The second qualification is that the value of IQ tests for diagnostic purposes is only seen to best advantage where individual rather than group tests are used and where the administration and analysis is done by the educational psychologist or by a teacher trained in test usage. Many group tests, with their reliance upon reading and vocabulary skills, may fail to give a sufficiently accurate picture of the child's cognitive abilities. And, needless to say, even these individual test results must be treated themselves with great caution, and viewed ideally against a background of results from a variety of other diagnostic tests.

Improving intelligence

The second part of the question we posed in the opening
paragraph of this section concerned the way in which
measured IQ can best be improved within the educational
context. The answer lies in part in doing the things that
the good teacher will already be doing; that is, providing
the child with interesting and stimulating learning material, presenting him with problems that demand careful
thinking strategies, encouraging his use of verbal skills
and specifically of verbal reasoning, and motivating him
generally to make best use of his cognitive abilities. But
there may be more to it than this. In the main part of this
chapter reference was made to multi-factorial models of
intelligence and, in particular, to the model of Guilford.
Guilford's model is, as was suggested, a complex one, but
the basic elements are of considerable value to the teacher
who is trying to formalize his thinking on how best to
encourage intellectual development in children.

Guilford's research (e.g. 1968) suggests that in any intelligent act there are three elements, namely contents,
operations, and products. The individual is first presented
with the contents of a problem, which become the subject of
his mental operations, and which in turn produce certain
products. Guilford recognizes four sub-categories under the
contents category, five under the operations category, and
six under that of products. These sub-categories are given
below.

Contents	Operations	Products
figural	cognition	units
semantic	memory	classes
symbolic	divergent thinking	relations
behavioural	convergent thinking	systems
	evaluation	translations
		implications

This means that the contents of the problem facing the
individual can be of a figural or symbolic or semantic or
behavioural kind (or a combination of these), that the
operations he performs upon these contents involve cognition or memory, etc. (or again a combination of these),
and that he produces units, classes, relations, etc., in his
attempt to understand and solve the problem. Since the four
content categories, the five operational categories and the
six product categories can all interact with each other we
get 4 x 5 x 6 = 120 possible mental factors.

For the teacher, the importance of this model lies in
the fact that where a child fails to solve a particular item
(and it could, of course, be an item from an intelligence
test itself) the failure can be ascribed to one or other of
the sub-categories or to the interaction between them. The

child might, for example, be unable to cope with the symbols or the semantics involved in the contents (this would certainly happen if he could not understand the language in which the problem was couched), or with the memory task or the evaluation involved in the operations, or with the units or the systems in the products. Obviously, there is a limit to the amount of time a teacher can spend in diagnosing each individual failure of each individual child in his class, but a model of this kind has the virtue of directing the attention of the teacher towards the likely variables occasioning difficulty with an intellectual problem, and therefore of helping him make decisions as to the kind of assistance he might best offer.

Clearly, not all the sub-categories in Guilford's model make equal demands upon the child. Jensen (1969) believes that operations involving memory, for example, contain little in the way of reasoning and can be referred to as Level I skills. Such skills are apparent in the recognition of symbols (arithmetical notation, vocabulary) and in the learning of physical movements, and are particularly evident in the early years of school life. Level II skills, on the other hand, involve operations that require the child actually to do something with the information acquired (such as evaluating it or adding to it through the use of divergent thinking), and are likely to lead to products rather than to the simple regurgitation of information in the same form in which it was assimilated. These skills become increasingly important as the child moves up the school, and are sometimes referred to as 'higher order skills' or as 'learning how to learn'.

The work of Edward de Bono

One psychologist who lays particular emphasis upon skills that require the child to change or re-structure the information he receives if he is to solve complex intellectual problems is Edward de Bono. De Bono maintains that, faced with one of these problems, the child typically attempts to work through it using a sequential pattern (i.e. going from what seems to be one logical step to the next). Often he finds, however, that each time he does this he reaches a point where the sequence breaks down and he is unable to proceed further. What he requires, de Bono argues, is some method of disrupting the sequence so that a new one is allowed to form. De Bono calls this method lateral thinking as opposed to the vertical thinking involved in sequential patterns.

De Bono's ideas are fully set out in his own books, to which the reader's attention is drawn at the end of the present chapter; and space does not allow us to look at them in great detail. Essentially, however, de Bono's argument is that both vertical and lateral thinking have their place and are involved in intelligent behaviour, but that too often we use the first where the second would be more appropriate. He also believes that in schools we teach vertical thinking but make little attempt to teach lateral. The child should be helped to see that at the point where a sequence of vertical thinking breaks down he needs to move sideways, as it were (i.e. laterally), and pick up another vertical track going in a different direction. He may have to do this more than once in order to arrive at the desired solution, but each time he does so a better cognitive pattern emerges, involving not only movement towards the solution but also a better understanding of the critical issues involved in the problem, an understanding that will generalize to new problems in the future.

Lateral thinking therefore allows the juxtaposition of ideas which have no apparent logical or sequential connection. Such juxtaposition does not necessarily make sense in itself at first sight, but it triggers off something else that will do so. The reader will no doubt be able to think of examples of the value of this kind of thinking from his own experience, not only in academic life but in day-to-day living. A good example might be the gadget recently arrived through the post which we try to assemble following the manufacturer's meagre instructions. Each time, we reach a point where the thing stubbornly refuses to come together, and the experimental application of a little force produces only ominous noises. At this stage, in desperation, we try something that on the face of it looks ridiculous, like turning the object upside down or inside out, and to our relief it falls into place without further ado. In retrospect, the process of assembly looks so easy that we cannot understand why we did not think of it in the first place. The answer is that in following the inadequate instructions we were making certain false assumptions (e.g. that what looked like the top really was the top) that sent us off on the wrong vertical track each time. It was only when, in desperation, we introduced a lateral element like turning the item upside down that we were able to proceed along the correct vertical sequence.

Undoubtedly one of the best ways to come to grips with lateral thinking, and to see the implications it has for intelligent behaviour within one's own teaching subject, is to tackle some of the problems devised by de Bono to demonstrate its importance. These problems, of the brain-teasing variety, usually set the conventional thinker (or rather the person who is allowing himself to think conventionally) off on the wrong vertical track, and it is only by exploring lateral possibilities that he is eventually able to reach his goal. By working through a number of these problems de Bono maintains that the reader is able to give scope to his lateral thinking abilities, and thus to put himself in a much better position to tackle any problems requiring intelligent behaviour. In a very real sense we can say, therefore, that de Bono's work supports the notion that by exposing children to carefully constructed problems (which could, of course, be problems framed within the context of any school subject) we can maximize their intellectual potential surely and divertingly.

References

Guilford, J.P. (1968)
The structure of intelligence. In D.K. Whitla (ed.),
Handbook of Measurement and Assessment in the
Behavioral Sciences. Reading, Mass.: Addison-Wesley.

Jensen, A. (1969)
How much can we boost IQ and scholastic achievement?
Harvard Educational Review, 39, 1-123.

Lazar, L. et al (1977)
The Persistence of Pre-school Effects: A long-term
follow-up of fourteen infant and pre-school experiments:
final report. Denver, Colorado: Education Commission of
the States.

Additional reading

De Bono, E. (1978) Teaching Thinking. Harmondsworth:
Penguin.
> All his books are fun to read. This is one of the best
> for the teacher, and gives a variety of strategies that
> the teacher can adopt with his class.

De Bono, E. (1971) The Mechanism of Mind. Harmondsworth:
Penguin.
> Deeper and more theoretical, though setting out fully
> his ideas on mind.

De Bono, E. (1970) Children Solve Problems. Harmondsworth:
Penguin.
> An interesting, amusingly illustrated record of how
> children tackle some of the problems presented to them
> using de Bono's methods.

De Bono, E. (1969) The Five Day Course in Thinking.
Harmondsworth: Penguin.
> Readers interested in sharpening their own wits might
> like to work through this.

De Bono, E. (1980) Future Positive. Harmondsworth: Penguin.
> Discusses the ways in which positive and lateral
> thinking can be put to good use in planning for the
> future and solving our environmental and social
> problems.

De Bono, E. (1979) Word Power. Harmondsworth: Penguin.
> An illustrated and highly diverting dictionary of the
> key words used in the world of business and management
> today. Of obvious relevance to education.

7

Creativity
David Fontana

Creativity is a familiar yet oddly elusive concept. We all
think we can recognize creativity in others (and even in
ourselves at times), since this is regarded as one of the
abilities of the good teacher, but we woud probably be hard
pressed to advance a definition acceptable to all our colleagues. And we might find some disagreement over whether
one can be creative in the sciences as well as in the arts,
in the home as well as in the potter's studio, in bringing
up children as well as in writing books. Further disagreement would probably arise if we began to discuss ways of
teaching creativiy to children, or even whether such teaching is possible, whether in fact creativity can be learnt at
all or whether it is a precious gift with which we are born
(or not as the case may be).

Creativity as thinking
One approach to the problem is to see creativity as a
special kind of thinking, a kind of thinking that involves
originality and fluency, that breaks away from existing
patterns and introduces something new. Obviously, on this
count de Bono's lateral thinking (which was discussed in the
last chapter) would involve creativity, whereas his so-
called vertical thinking would not. Indeed, creativity would
also be involved in the divergent thinking included in
Guilford's model of the intellect which was also discussed
in the last chapter. In fact, it is this divergent thinking,
together with other aspects of Guilford's work, that has
tended to attract maximum attention in the debate over the
nature of creativity that psychologists have been conducting
during the last three decades.

Guilford claims that divergent thinking is the ability
to generate a range of possible solutions to a given problem, in particular to a problem to which there is no single
right answer (like 'think of all the meanings you can for
the word bolt'). It will be readily seen that such an ability is likely to play a part in the creative act, where the
artist will often need to explore a range of possible ways
of painting his picture, or finishing off his novel, or
writing his poem before he finally decides on the one that
pleases him the best. Obviously we also expect a creative
act to bear the stamp of originality (at least in the sense

that the individual himself has not thought of the idea before), but here again divergent thinking will play a part, in that the wider the range of possibilities we are able to generate the more likely it will be that one of them will carry originality.

Creativity and intelligence

It will be noted that in his model Guilford also refers to what he calls convergent thinking. In convergent thinking the individual is said to converge upon the single acceptable answer to a problem rather than to diverge and throw up as many solutions as he can. It is sometimes said that conventional intelligence tests concentrate only upon convergent thinking in that there is only one single acceptable correct answer to each item, and that divergent thinking can only really be demonstrated in tests of the so-called open-ended type. This is probably true, and it is always an interesting exercise to ask children to look at certain intelligence test items (particularly those of the 'underline the odd man out' type) and see whether they can find reasons for more than one acceptable solution to each. In doing so we are asking them to think divergently rather than convergently, and the results might come as something of a surprise to intelligence test designers.

Nevertheless, we are not suggesting that divergent thinking is in any way superior to convergent, or that we have made mistakes in the past by emphasizing convergent thinking in schools. Often the latter is the more appropriate to a particular problem, and we should therefore at the outset regard divergent thinking as complementary to convergent rather than as some kind of competitor. The point that Guildford and others have tried to make is that, in our emphasis upon convergent thinking, we have tended to neglect divergent altogether, and in consequence we have done little to teach (or develop) creativity in schools.

The problem is, however, that we have no conclusive findings as to the degree of correlation between the ability to perform well on divergent thinking tests (more will be said about these tests shortly) and the ability to achieve success in obviously creative subjects such as fine art, writing, and musical composition. Nor is it as yet clear whether convergent and divergent thinking are separate operations as suggested by Guilford, or whether they are part and parcel of the same group of mental abilities. In an early work, Getzels and Jackson (1962) studied groups of children having on the one hand high divergent thinking scores and relatively low IQ scores (the 'high creative' group), and on the other high IQ scores and relatively low divergent thinking scores (the 'high IQ' group). Both groups were found to have similar school achievement records, but the former emerged as less conformist than the latter, less popular with teachers, more prone to over-achieve (i.e. to exceed expectations), and more likely to have a lively sense of humour. Importantly from our point of view, there appeared to be no significant correlation in the sample between divergent thinking and IQ scores.

One drawback to this study, however, was that the children were all in the high ability range (the mean IQ for the whole sample was 132). Using a broader ability band, other psychologists have failed to replicate these findings, and have concluded that convergent and divergent thinking abilities do appear to be linked, though it is not yet clear how strongly. Supporters of Getzels and Jackson have countered by saying that this link is a consequence of test procedure rather than of psychological fact. Divergent thinking tests, they argue, should be administered untimed, and in a deliberately light-hearted and playful atmosphere, since the serious exam-orientated climate in which IQ tests are undertaken is inhibiting to creative thinking. If we insist on producing such a climate, we penalize the diverger and end up with inaccurate results. In support of this argument they point to a study by Wallach and Kogan (1965) which showed that younger children, in particular, seem to produce their best divergent thinking results when there is an absence of stress in the air.

In the light of present knowledge, the fairest conclusion seems to be that the link between convergent and divergent thinking abilities appears to be strongest for children with moderate or low IQs, where a straightforward linear relationship may apply. Above an IQ threshold somewhere in the 110-120 range, however, the relationship becomes a much more complex and even random one. That is, we become much less able to predict whether a given highly intelligent individual is likely to score at a comparable level on divergent tests. Up to this threshold level, therefore, increased intelligence seems usually to go with increased divergent abilities, but above this level gains in the former do not necessarily appear to go with gains in the latter. Assuming that divergent thinking abilities do go with recognized creative ability in the arts, this means that, for example, a painter with an IQ of 150 would not, simply by virtue of that fact, emerge as a greater artist than a painter with an IQ of some 30 points less.

We must not lose sight of the fact, though, that certain activities may demand IQ and high divergent ability. This could well be true of certain areas of science. In this chapter's opening paragraph it was suggested that there might be disagreement on whether creativity is apparent in science as well as in arts, but the examination of the creative act in due course below (together with common sense) would indicate strongly that it is so apparent, particularly in areas of scientific research and invention. One of the differences between high level performance in science, as opposed to high level performance in the arts, is that more convergent ability may be needed to understand the grammar of science, to identify and clarify research problems within it, and to see the relationship between these problems and other relevant issues.

Having read this far, the reader may consider that we have ducked rather neatly out of the attempt to provide a precise definition of creativity. Certainly there is a tendency to avoid the issue, since any definition is likely to be some way short of perfect. Some definitions advanced in the past, with their emphasis upon the ability to see relationships, look in fact very similar to those associated with intelligence, while others are so vague that they cover almost every informal thought and action. A definition that has some merit, however, is that creativity is the ability to generate fluent and novel ways of tackling problems and of organizing material. Such a definition shows quite clearly that one can have creativity in the home as well as in the art room, in dressing a shop window as well as in writing a symphony, in educating children as well as in advancing scientific theory and practice. What it cannot do without becoming unwieldy, however, is to stress that by 'novel' we mean novel for the individual concerned. Thus a child who spends happy hours inventing something only to be told someone else thought of it years ago is nevertheless being creative. He has gone through the creative process just as did the original inventor, and probably derived as much value (though regrettably not in financial terms) as did this worthy individual.

Divergent thinking tests

We have already indicated that divergent thinking can only be assessed by tests of the open-ended variety: that is, by tests that have no set right and wrong answers. They can, of course, be of the verbal kind, but can also be spatial or even musical. In each case the emphasis is the same. The child is asked to think of as many appropriate ways as he can for solving some particular problem. For example, we can have what is called the 'Uses of Objects' test, in which the subject is invited to write down as many uses as he can for everyday objects such as a housebrick, a paper clip, a barrel, a blanket, a book and so on. Another example is the 'Meanings of Words' test in which he is invited to record all the meanings he can for appropriate words like 'iron', or 'carpet', or 'bolt', and yet another is the 'Consequences' test in which he is asked to think of as many results as he can for a particular change in the usual order of things (e.g. the caretaker losing the school keys, or everyone living to be 100 years old).

Turning to non-verbal tests, we have such things as the Guilford 'Circles' test, in which the subject is confronted by a sheet of small uniformly-sized blank circles and is asked to use his pencil to turn as many of them as he can into recognizable objects. Tests using a random pattern of lines instead of a circle are also popular, while a simple musical test would be to ask the subject to think of as many endings as he can for a given musical phrase. Commercial tests (such as the Torrance 'Tests of Creative Thinking') are available, but it will be readily appreciated that the teacher can devise his own without much difficulty. Scoring is simple in that marks are usually given for fluency (the number of appropriate responses the subject makes), originality (the novelty of these responses) and flexibility (their variety). The usual method for arriving at the originality score is to compare each child's responses with those of the rest of the class, and award, say, 5 marks for every response that is offered by one child only, 4 marks if it is offered by two children and so on down to zero. Flexibility is scored by grouping responses into categories (e.g. 'domestic', 'sporting', 'animal'), and counting how many of these categories a subject has offered.

Since divergent thinking tests lay emphasis upon individuality of response, far less work has been done on standardization than is the case for intelligence tests, and in consequence most commentators regard them still as rather crude devices. They are also criticized as being somewhat dull, which may inhibit the full creative response from subjects. To date, results on these tests do not always correlate very well with proven success in creative work or with peer group ratings of creativity, and it is probably as a consequence of this that research in the field has tended to taper off after the hectic activity of a few years ago. It would seem at the moment to be badly in need of fresh impetus and of a new sense of direction.

he creative act

Turning now from the definition and the measurement of creativity to the creative act itself, we find that studies of creative men and women suggest that a creative act typically involves four stages.

* PREPARATION, which is primarily concerned with the recognition that a particular problem is worthy of study, or a particular theme is suitable for a book or a picture or a piece of music.
* INCUBATION, during which the problem or the theme is mulled over, often at an unconscious level.
* INSPIRATION, when the possible solution to the problem or a flood of ideas for the book, etc., come abruptly into the conscious mind.
* VERIFICATION, when the solution is put to the test or the ideas are tried out on paper or on canvas.

Each of these stages carries its own importance. The ability of the highly creative person to recognize the importance of a problem or of a theme which has lain disregarded under the noses of other men and women often for very many years is legendary: Pavlov spotting the anomaly that dogs salivated on hearing the footsteps of the attendant bringing their food rather than solely on seeing or smelling the food itself; Freud recognizing the existence of infantile sexuality; Cervantes spotting the absurdities in the medieval system of chivalry; Dvorak realizing the symphonic potential of simple folk songs; in fact, practically any artist's or research scientist's work that leaves us wondering, 'Now why on earth didn't I think of that?'

During this preparation stage the creative person explores various possibilities associated with his problem or theme, and then often comes to a full stop. The solution, or the precise methods of procedure, fail to come to mind, and there then follows the period of incubation during which the creative person often puts the whole subject out of his mind, sometimes only for days, at other times perhaps for years. We can only guess at what happens during this incubation period, but if the model of the unconscious suggested by Freud and other depth psychologists is correct, then the processes of thought continue at the unconscious level, though without employing the kind of logic which characterizes conscious thought. This apparent illogicality perhaps assists the lateral thinking we discussed in connection with de Bono's work in the last chapter. Freed from logical, sequential thought, the mind is able to rove freely over its accumulated store of knowledge, trying new permutations and new juxtapositions until one eventually makes recognizable sense and in a surge of creative excitement comes up into the conscious mind in the form of illumination.

This flash of illumination (or inspiration, though perhaps this term should apply to the whole of the creative act) has been well illustrated by, for example, the poet Houseman, who maintained that most of his verses came to him 'ready made', or the mathematician Poincaré who solved the problems associated with Fuchsian functions in a series of inspirational flashes which occurred at odd moments when he was engaged in quite different activities, or the scientist Kekulé whose revolutionary discovery of the chemical structure of benzene came to him in a dream. Illumination is then followed by verification, which is the perspiration stage of the creative act. The scientific theory must now be put to the test in the laboratory, often over careful months or years, or the novel or the symphony has to be worked out in detail and revised and re-revised.

This four-stage model of the creative act sometimes comes as something of a surprise to the layman, who supposes that the scientist, in particular, works carefully through his data and only arrives at his theory by a process of deduction when he comes to the end. In reality science, just as much as the arts, seems to rely for its major advances upon the creative leap of the brilliant mind. Obviously such a leap is only normally possible (we say 'normally' because there are exceptions) where the scientist concerned is already steeped in his subject, and has the accumulated knowledge necessary not only for the permutations and the juxtapositions that we have suggested take place at the unconscious level, but also for recognizing the potential value of his illumination and for undertaking the verification procedure. But the importance of the incubation period and of the moment of illumination do not seem open to doubt. If the reader wants to test this personally he has only to remember the occasions when, stuck over a particular form of words or a particular idea in an essay, he puts it to one side and banishes it from his conscious mind, and then finds on returning to the fray a little later that the problem now resolves itself without difficulty.

Does this mean, therefore, that it is impossible to have a creative act without incubation followed by illumination? Since, as we have seen, creativity appears to cover such a wide area of human endeavour, and to be practised to a greater or lesser extent by each individual member of the human race, it would be unwise to generalize to this extent. The process of incubation may, in any case, often be very brief, particularly when we are working with very familiar material or where the problem to be solved is a relatively simple one. The journalist regularly meeting the editor's deadline with his copy can hardly afford himself the luxury of long periods of incubation, and neither can the teacher attempting to deal creatively with a wide range of classroom problems. Again, some creative people work very much more quickly than others, and the time from the conception of a creative idea to its final delivery in book (or whatever) form may be relatively short. But as a model for formalizing one's thinking about the creative process and developing strategies for helping children work creatively, the four-stage model of preparation, incubation, illumination and verification seems to approach most closely to what creative people themselves feel to be happening when they engage in creative activity. It also leaves us wondering whether formal examinations where the candidate has both to read the questions and produce the answers all within the space of three short hours or so really allows much scope for creative thinking. Along with the nervous stress of the examination situation itself, the absence of sufficient time for incubation may well be one of the reasons why all the best answers seem to come to us after leaving the examination room.

References

Getzels, J. and Jackson, P. (1962)
Creativity and Intelligence: Explorations with gifted children. New York: Wiley.
Wallach, M. and Kogan, N. (1965)
Modes of Thinking in Young Children. New York: Holt, Rinehart & Winston.

Questions

1. How would you define creativity?
2. What are the differences between so-called 'convergent' and 'divergent' thinking?
3. How would you convert a question which calls upon convergent thinking into one which calls upon divergent? Give examples.

4. Do convergent and divergent abilities appear to be correlated?
5. Is creativity as important in advanced work in science as it is in advanced work in the arts?
6. What is an 'open-ended' test?
7. What are the usual variables used in marking divergent thinking tests?
8. Give the four stages that appear to be associated with the creative act.
9. What appears to happen during the 'incubation' stage of the creative act?
10. Give further examples of the ability of the creative person to recognize the importance of a problem that has lain disregarded under the noses of other men and women for years.
11. Is the notion that creative scientists work systematically through their experiments and only arrive at a new theory when they come to the end generally an accurate one?
12. Is it appropriate to talk of creativity in the bringing up of children and in the work of the teacher, for example, or is creativity confined to the work of the artist?

Annotated reading

The 1960s and early 1970s saw a flood of books on creativity, most of them saying the same kind of things. The flow has dried up somewhat in recent years, while a new initiative is awaited.

Vernon, P.E. (ed.) (1970) Creativity. Harmondsworth: Penguin.
This book gives a good survey of the field.

Kneller, G.F. (1965) The Art and Science of Creativity. New York: Holt, Rinehart & Winston.

Cropley, A.J. (1967) Creativity. London: Longmans.
These two provide a well-written short introduction.

Torrance, E.P. and Myers, R.E. (1970) Creative Learning and Teaching. New York: Dodd Mead.
Highly recommended for the teacher to try out methods for enhancing creativity.

Foster, J. (1971) Creativity and the Teacher. London: Macmillan.
Also useful.

Hudson, L. (1966) Contrary Imaginations. London: Methuen.
Although, in light of subsequent research, it tends to overstress the arts-science dichotomy, this book presents interesting evidence on creativity in schoolchildren (and see also 'Frames of Mind' by the same author, published by Methuen in 1968).

Wallach, M.A. and Kogan, N. (1965) Modes of Thinking in Young Children. New York: Holt, Rinehart & Winston.
Harder going, but also gives interesting evidence on creativity research with schoolchildren.

Torrance, E.P. (1962) Guiding Creative Talent. New Jersey: Prentice-Hall.
A very influential book in its day, and still well worth reading.

Ghiselin, B. (1952) The Creative Process. New York: New American Library.
An excellent book on the creative process itself, containing first-hand accounts by creative individuals in the sciences and the arts.

**Relevance to the
teacher
DAVID FONTANA**

Just as all teachers are teachers of language, whatever their actual subject, so all teachers are teachers of creativity. This applies to science teachers as much as to those in the arts field. Earlier findings by Hudson (1966) that at sixth-form level high divergers tend to be on the arts side and high convergers on the science side are now thought primarily to be due to encouragement and opportunity rather than to anything inherent in either the academic disciplines concerned or in the pupils themselves. It seems arts students, in certain schools at least, are simply allowed to operate divergently more often than science students because the disciplines they are studying are held to be more subjective (more 'inspirational' perhaps) than those followed by the latter. Where science students are given examples of what is meant by divergent thinking, their scores on divergent thinking tests show immediate improvement. Assuming that such tests are a good measure of creativity, this would indicate that science students have no lack of creative ability, but simply need the impetus to bring it out.

The encouragement of divergent thinking
The first point for the teacher to bear in mind, therefore, is that whatever his subject he must be alive to opportunities for the encouragement of divergent thinking in his students. It is argued by both Bruner (to whom we made reference in chapter 4 and to whose work we return in more detail in the next chapter) and de Bono that within education we tend to reward only the 'right' answers and penalize the 'wrong'. This makes children reluctant to attempt novel or original solutions to problems, since the chances of error are inevitably greater when they do. In other words, they play for safety. Yet the imaginative leap, the production of an answer different from the conformist one, the readiness to take what we might call cognitive risks, are inseparable from creative endeavour. The teacher should be prepared to operate in an atmosphere where this endeavour

is encouraged and rewarded, rather than in one where only cautious, convergent solutions are countenanced.

This does not mean, of course, that we have no regard for accuracy or precision. Remember that in the creative act the final stage is one of verification. The solution must be put to the test to see if it will work. If it fails it must be discarded, though the child can still be praised for an imaginative attempt. And even this failure may spark off fresh ideas which in turn can be tested and which may lead to the desired solution. In de Bono's terminology, the creative act is often a lateral endeavour that moves our thinking out of its narrow path and on to a new tack, while Bruner has it that creative thinking is holistic (i.e. productive of responses greater than the sum of their parts), while rational, convergent thinking is algorithmic (i.e. productive of responses that are unambiguously themselves). Both kinds of thinking have their vital roles to play, but they should be used to complement and support each other, and not be regarded as in some sense mutually exclusive.

Before we protest too strongly that we already understand the value of both forms of thinking in the classroom, and would never penalize the child for holistic endeavour, we should remember that one of Getzels and Jackson's findings was that high divergers were less popular with teachers than high convergers. Schools have their rules and regulations, their patterns of procedure and conduct, and often the conformist child is more comfortable to live with than the nonconformist, highly imaginative one. In addition, divergent ideas may often be original and valuable, but they can also be bizarre and silly, leading the teacher to suspect the child may just be playing up. Unfortunately (or fortunately), creativity is an unpredictable thing, and we cannot expect it always to emerge in a form appropriate to the circumstances of the moment. By studying children's responses, and in particular by watching where ideas that initially appear silly actually lead, the teacher can soon recognize when a child is trying to use his imagination and when he is simply trying to be difficult. By neglecting such study, the teacher runs the risk of stifling the good ideas along with the not-so-good, and giving the class the impression that originality quite simply is not welcome when he is around.

Classroom organization and creativity

If the first point in encouraging creativity is therefore to be open to its operation in the classroom, the second point must be concerned with the nature of classroom organization itself. Does creativity flourish better in an informal classroom, where children are responsible for much of their own work and for initiating a great deal of what goes on, or is it at its best in a more formal, structured context? Before we automatically plump for the former it is as well to remember that many artists have talked of the need for

discipline in their subject, of the need for set work routines and for hard work and sustained application. The great
teachers of the arts, whether they be dancers, musicians, or
painters, have all insisted on their pupils learning the
grammar of their subject, and of putting their creative
gifts to constructive use rather than dissipating them without discipline or dedication. It is one thing to encourage
creative expression, quite another to take that expression
and mould it into a form that does it full justice.

With this in mind, it is perhaps not surprising to find
that the evidence does not unequivocally support the informal classroom as the best way of nurturing creativity. Haddon and Lytton (1977) did indeed find that children from
informal primary schools out-performed those from formal on
divergent thinking, and that the differences persisted even
after transfer to secondary schools, but in a more extensive
study Bennett (1976) found that when he used actual creative
endeavours (such as creative writing) instead of divergent
thinking tests as his variable, results did not differ significantly between formal and informal primary schools. It
could be that these apparently conflicting findings are
fully explained by the different experimental variables
used, divergent thinking tests as opposed to creative
writing and so on, but it could be that the teachers themselves were far more important than the simple matter of
classroom organization. Wallach (1970) showed that creative
adults appear in general to have been exposed in childhood
to a rich variety of experiences, and to an environment in
which they were encouraged to ask questions, to test out
their ideas by active experimentation, and to pursue their
interests through hobbies and through the development of
special talents and skills. Since this can be done as
readily in the good formal as in the good informal classroom
this seems to suggest that we should look first at the
teacher's general approach to his task.

The role of the teacher in creativity

We have already seen that the teacher should encourage the
generation of ideas in his work with children, but the above
suggestion indicates that we should also ask what kind of
personal interests and enthusiasms does he bring into the
classroom? Teachers who themselves have wide interests, and
who enjoy sharing them with children both in and out of
timetabled school hours, who themselves have lively enquiring minds and enjoy playing with ideas, and above all who
like posing and listening to questions, would seem much more
likely to prompt creative development in their children than
teachers who are stereotyped and rigid. Torrance (1962)
suggests specifically that the teachers should help children
to indulge in speculation along the 'What would happen if
...?' (or 'What would have happened if ...?') line, and to
teach them that everyone has creative potential and not just
a few outstanding individuals.

Parnes (1967) proposes a method called 'brainstorming'
which has achieved wide popularity in industry and which has

obvious educational implications. Participants in a brain-storming session work as a group and are encouraged to generate ideas in response to a particular problem. Nothing is regarded as too wild or inappropriate, and no criticisms of any kind are offered. The session can be tape-recorded, and at the end the tape played back and allowed to stimulate further inspiration or work of the verification kind. Often seemingly intractable problems are solved in this way, with each participant sparking off creative ideas from the rest of the group. The non-judgemental atmosphere allows each person to let his thoughts on the problem come without check or censure, and at school level it is this process, as much as the solution of the problem itself, that has educational value.

The importance of this open-ended approach is emphasized further by Davis (1976) who presented three student groups with a problem (how to change or improve a doorknob) and then tried different methods with each to stimulate their creative thinking. The first group was presented with a list of specific examples of how the problem might be solved, the second was given a number of possible general strategies (e.g. try thinking about changing the materials from which the knob is made), while the third was given a matrix with which to work. This matrix allowed one set of variables to be placed along the first axis (e.g. the various materials from which a doorknob can be made) and another set along the second (e.g. the various possible shapes a doorknob can take), thus making it possible to combine the variables into new arrangements.

Not surprisingly, in view of the points we have been making so far, individuals within the third group produced the most ideas and individuals within the first the least. The latter individuals in fact spent all their time working through the long list of specific possible solutions which they had been given instead of trying to think up something new. The implication of this for the classroom is that if we constantly present students with our ideas, even if these are simply offered as examples, the situation becomes less open-ended in that they will concentrate upon these to the exclusion of any new ideas of their own. Present them with stimuli by all means, but in a form which allows for re-arrangement and juxtaposition. Even if we are concerned simply with a classroom discussion or debate, the teacher must beware of 'closing' the situation by constantly attempting to sum up or to offer his own solutions. Carrying as they do the authority of the teacher, these will inevitably be regarded by many children as the 'right' answers, and will put an end to further creative individual thinking. Even at the end of the debate the teacher should avoid the temptation of providing his own judgement on the virtues of the ideas that have been put forward. Far better to leave things deliberately rather open, and send children away thinking further, than to give the class the impression that the last word has now been uttered and nothing further remains to be said.

Finally, it is essential that children should be helped
to see the distinction between different kinds of thinking,
and to come to decisions as to which is appropriate in a
given context. A number of studies show that, faced with the
same problem, children produce different kinds of solutions
if they are asked on the one hand to be creative and original about it, and on the other to be practical. Practicality
is usually interpreted as meaning, 'stick to the known
methods', while invitations to be original prompt the child
to use his imagination in the search for something new. In
creativity, as in so many other classroom activities, the
things we get out of children depend not only on their own
abilities but on our cleverness in phrasing the questions we
put to them.

References

Bennett, N. (1976)
Teaching Styles and Pupil Progress. London: Open Books.
Davis, G. (1976)
Research and development in training creative thinking.
In J. Levin and V. Allen (eds), Cognitive Learning in
Children: Theories and strategies. New York: Academic
Press.
Haddon, F.H. and Lytton, H. (1971)
Primary education and divergent thinking abilities -
four years on. British Journal of Educational
Psychology, 41, 136-147.
Hudson, L. (1966)
Contrary Imaginations. Harmondsworth: Penguin.
Parnes, S. (1967)
Creative Behavior Guidebook. New York: Scribner's.
Torrance, E. (1962)
Guiding Creative Talent. Englewood Cliffs, NJ: Prentice-
Hall.
Wallach, M. (1970).
Creativity. In P. Mussen (ed.), Carmichael's Manual
of Child Psychology (3rd edn), Volume 1. New York:
Wiley.

8

Learning
David Fontana

In spite of its critical importance within education, the problem of explaining how learning takes place, and analysing the factors that influence it, remains a confused area. Teachers, and educators generally, often blame the psychologist for this, and claim that he either presents them with several conflicting explanations of learning, each one based upon a different psychological theory, or a single coherent explanation with which he has to admit other psychologists would probably not agree. Yet perhaps this blame, though understandable, is a little unfair. The problem is that learning is such a highly complex activity. We each of us receive a constant and varied stream of experiences throughout our waking moments, each one of which potentially can give rise to learning, yet most of which apparently vanish without trace from our mental lives. What is it that makes some things memorable and others not? Why is it that a particular event can prompt learning in one person yet have no measurable effect upon someone else? Why does an individual learn readily from one teacher but not from another? How is it that we are able to make sense of our experience, and put that knowledge to good effect when it comes to tackling new situations and problems? Questions such as these and many others make the psychologist's task of understanding and explaining learning, and above all of advising on how learning can be made more efficient and more permanent for all types and conditions of learner, an almost herculean one. Perhaps the wonder is not that the psychologist has so far failed to come up with all the answers during the 50 years or so in which he has made a systematic study of learning, but that he has come up with as many as he has done.

The definition of learning
Since it is always helpful to start with a definition, let us say that most psychologists would agree that learning is a relatively persistent change in an individual's possible behaviour due to experience. This definition draws attention to three things: first, that learning must change the individual in some way; second, that this change comes about as a result of experience; and third, that it is a change in his possible behaviour. The first of these points of

emphasis is obvious enough. Unless we are changed in some way, learning cannot be said to have taken place. This change can, of course, be at a relatively simple level (as, for example, when we learn a skill like tying a shoelace) or at a more complex one (as, for example, when we encounter a great work of art for the first time), but the principle remains the same. The individual is in some definable way a different person with his learning from the person he was without it. The second point of emphasis stresses that the change must come about as a result of experience. This therefore excludes the kinds of change that accrue from maturation and physical development. The third point stresses that although a change has taken place, it is a change in potential rather than in actual performance. We may learn something, but give no hint of this learning in our actual performance until months or years later (as, for example, when a child sees some facts about a foreign country on television and surprises everyone by trotting them out when his class starts to study that country at a later date).

Armed with this definition, we can now look at the psychologist's attempt to develop a convincing theory of how learning comes about. At this point we must acknowledge the existence of the sharpest divergence between psychologists, a divergence which in effect sometimes puts them into two opposed camps, neither of them prepared to accept the potential usefulness of the other's point of view. Without wishing to become drawn too deeply into the issues that divide these two camps, we can say that one adopts an essentially connectionist (or behaviourist) approach and the other a cognitive (or cognitive-field) one. The behaviourist approach maintains that if psychology is to be an exact science it must restrict itself to the study of observable behaviour: that is, to the responses made by the individual and to the conditions under which they occur. Such an approach sees learning in terms of connections between stimulus and response or between response and reinforcement, and places great stress upon the role played by the environment. Structure the environment correctly, and learning will follow, irrespective of the particular volition of the learner. The cognitive approach, on the other hand, holds that if we are to understand learning we cannot confine ourselves to observable behaviour, but must also concern ourselves with the learner's ability mentally to re-organize his psychological field (i.e. his inner world of concepts, memories, etc.) in response to experience. This latter approach, therefore, lays stress not only upon the environment, but upon the way in which the individual interprets and tries to make sense of his environment. It sees the individual not as the somewhat mechanical product of his environment, but as an active agent in the learning process, deliberately trying to process and categorize the stream of information fed into him by the outside world.

As we attempt to show, these two sets of theories are not mutually contradictory. The teacher, concerned as he is with the practicalities of learning, can draw usefully upon them both, and see each of them as having greater or lesser relevance dependent upon the level at which he intends learning to occur. To clarify this we must first look in turn at one example from each of these sets of theories, examples which have direct practical relevance for education and which will provide us with a theoretical underpinning for much of what we have to say in this chapter.

heories of learning

Although usually referred to as theories, the two views of learning that we are about to discuss are really descriptions. That is, they confine themselves to describing what actually happens when learning takes place, instead of entering into theoretical speculation on why and how it happens. This will come as something of a relief to the teacher, since it is a common complaint that theories of learning, for all their undoubted complexity, are not really that much help when it comes to the practicalities of helping students learn. Descriptions of learning, on the other hand, are of much more immediate benefit because they describe the kinds of activity carried out by both pupil and teacher that appear to lead to enhanced levels of learning on the part of the former. They thus assist teachers to plan classroom strategies, to monitor pupils' learning, and to isolate the possible reasons for the success and failure of this learning.

The first of these descriptions of learning is drawn from the behaviouristic school of thought and is known as operant conditioning.

Operant conditioning

The principle of operant conditioning is most clearly expounded by the American psychologist B. F. Skinner, who has spent over 40 years in the experimental investigation of learning. Skinner (1969) holds that the learning act involves three identifiable stages: first, the stimulus or situation (S) with which the learner is confronted; second, the behaviour (B) which it elicits from him; and third, the reinforcement (R) which follows this behaviour. Such reinforcement can best be thought of by the teacher as the results that follow on from B. Obviously these results can either be favourable to the learner (in which case they are known as positive reinforcement or R+), or they can be unfavourable (in which case they are known as R-). R+ increases the likelihood of the learner producing the same piece of behaviour again in the future, while R- decreases this likelihood. To take a straightforward example; a student is asked by the teacher to give the present participle of the verb 'avoir' (S), he answers 'ayant' (B), and the teacher says 'correct' (R+). When confronted by the same question in the future, the likelihood of his answering 'ayant' is accordingly increased. Had he responded with 'avant', however, the teacher would have said 'incorrect'

(R-),and he would have been less likely to offer this answer again.

Obviously R+ and R- need not always come from the teacher. The learner can find out in all sorts of ways whether his answer to a particular task or problem is right or wrong. But the principle that R+ increases and R- decreases the likelihood of behaviour recurring remains the same. The reader may regard this as self-evident, but Skinner and his associates consider that the relative inefficiency of much school-based learning stems from a basic failure to grasp both the S-B-R (or operant conditioning) model itself and its many implications. We look at some of these implications in due course, but first we must examine an example of the cognitive-field approach to learning.

Instrumental conceptualism
This somewhat intimidating title is used by Bruner to define his own attempt at a coherent and consistent description of learning (Bruner, 1966). Bruner's approach is very much in the cognitive tradition since it sees learning not merely as a passive unit of behaviour elicited by a stimulus and strengthened or weakened by reinforcement, but as an active process in which the learner infers principles and rules and tests them out. Learning, in other words, is not simply something that happens to the individual, as in the operant conditioning model, but something which he himself makes happen by the manner in which he handles incoming information and puts it to use. For the teacher, the main difference between Bruner's model and that of Skinner is that, while not denying the potential importance of the stimulus and the reinforcement in the S-B-R paradigm, Bruner considers that Skinner pays insufficient attention to the element that comes in between, namely the learner's own behaviour (B). This behaviour is not simply something 'elicited' by a stimulus and strengthened or otherwise by the nature of the reinforcement that follows, it is in fact a highly complex activity which involves three major processes, namely:

* the acquisition of information;
* the manipulation or transformation of this information into a form suitable for dealing with the task in hand;
* testing and checking the adequacy of this transformation (Bruner, 1973; Bruner and Anglin, 1973).

The learner achieves transformation by codifying and classifying incoming information: that is, by fitting it into (and sometimes thereby modifying) the categories he already has for understanding the world. This codifying and categorizing is therefore an internal mediating process that comes between the stimulus (S) and the learner's overt behaviour (B) in response to it. As this process becomes more developed through age and experience the learner increasingly transforms the stimulus and gains freedom from stimulus control. What this means - and we must understand it if we are to grasp fully the differences between Skinner and Bruner - is that whereas Skinner sees the stimulus as a relatively discrete unit, an objective event distinct from the learner himself and evoking a fundamentally mechanistic response from him, Bruner sees it as something identified and recognized by the learner in his own individual and subjective way. Thus the stimulus, in a sense, becomes a personal thing, which the individual interprets (or mis-interprets) and transforms in his own fashion dependent upon the previous experiences, thoughts, aspirations and so on he has about it. Far from his response being purely mechanical, therefore, the learner can ignore a stimulus altogether if he regards it as inappropriate, or he can use it to help construct internal hypotheses and models ('anticipatory categories' as Bruner calls them) which allow him to predict future events and which in turn influence the way in which he perceives and transforms fresh stimuli. Similarly, he can also become increasingly independent of immediate reinforce-ment (R), and work towards long-term goals since such goals are essentially the anticipatory categories which he predicts will give him the greatest satisfaction.

Before leaving this theoretical discussion and moving on to more practical matters, we must say something about the manner in which the learner transforms incoming informa-tion. Bruner believes this transformation is linked to three methods of representation (i.e. systems for representing past experiences in the memory and utilizing them to deal with the present). The mature person is capable of using all three systems, and acquires them one by one in childhood at ages determined both by environmental opportunities and by maturation. These systems, in the order in which they are usually acquired, are labelled by Bruner, Goodnow and Austin (1965) the enactive, the iconic and the symbolic respectively.

The enactive is a highly manipulative mode, using neither imagery nor words. It operates through action, and is apparent in, for example, motor skills, which we learn by doing and would find difficult to represent internally in terms of language or pictures.

The iconic mode is more developed in that it does use imagery, though still does not employ language. This ima-gery, which depends upon visual or other sensory organi-zation, represents a concept without fully defining it. A child of five, for example, has mental and aural images of a wide range of things which allow him to recognize and use them, though he would be unable to define or describe them in terms of words. Similarly an adult may, for example, have a clear picture of the geographical route from A to B, yet find himself hard put to it to give verbal directions to a stranger.

Finally, the symbolic mode goes beyond action and imagery and employs representation through language. Such representation leads to thought and learning of a much more abstract and flexible kind, allowing the individual to engage in reflective thinking, to consider propositions as well as concrete examples, and to arrange concepts in a hierarchical structure. Symbolic representation can, of course, employ symbolic systems other than language, such as the symbolism used in mathematical and scientific logic.

Bruner (1966) considers that Skinner's operant conditioning model may be an adequate account of the way learning takes place when the learner is operating in the enactive mode, but that it tells us little about the iconic and symbolic modes. Whether this is correct or not, the teacher may well find that Bruner's description of learning is of more practical help than Skinner's when it comes to dealing with the problems of facilitating pupils' abstract learning, though as we see both have their place in helping the teacher plan learning experiences at different levels.

Finally, Bruner and Anglin (1973) consider that when we undertake such planning, or indeed when we think about any learning activity, we must consider three important variables, namely the nature of the learner, the nature of the knowledge to be learned, and the nature of the learning process. Although we are not concentrating simply upon Bruner in the remainder of this chapter, this threefold division forms a convenient and productive way of ordering our thinking on the practical aspects of learning, and accordingly we examine each of these variables in turn.

The nature of the learner

There are a number of factors within the learner himself that influence his ability to learn. Perhaps best known of these are cognitive factors such as intelligence and creativity, but there are many others of equal relevance to the teacher with which he is often much less familiar. These include affective (i.e. emotional) factors, motivation, maturational factors, the learner's age, sex and social background, study habits and, above all, memory.

Affective factors

Strictly speaking, the term 'affective' refers only to the emotions, but psychologists tend to use it more broadly to cover all the things related to personality. Of particular importance amongst these from our point of view is the learner's level of anxiety. From general classroom experience the teacher soon discovers that a mild degree of anxiety can be a useful aid to learning, but that too much can have an inhibiting effect and interfere with it. Precisely what degree of anxiety motivates and what degree inhibits varies from child to child and from task to task (the more difficult the task, the more likely a given degree of anxiety is to interfere with it). One of the most potent sources of anxiety in children is the fear of failure. We see this particularly in exams where a great deal is often at stake, or in unhappy classrooms where teacher anger or ridicule from classmates is the usual consequence of failure. But some sources of anxiety are less obvious than this. Trown and Leith (1975) and Bennett (1976) produce evidence that suggests habitually anxious children may find the informal classroom, where they are often unsure of what is expected of them, more anxiety-provoking than a more formal, less ambiguous environment. Even in higher education, where habitual anxiety seems to be more of an advantage than it does at school (for the possible reason that it motivates students to make better use of their time outside lectures!), recent research (Franson, 1977) indicates individuals do better at specific learning tasks in the presence of low rather than high anxiety.

Closely linked to anxiety is the question of self-esteem (i.e. the regard in which we hold ourselves). In a number of studies, Coopersmith (e.g. 1968) has demonstrated that children with high self-esteem consistently perform better than children of similar ability with low self-esteem. They also set themselves higher goals, show less need for adult approval, are less deterred by failure, and have a more realistic view of their own abilities. High self-esteem seems to be due in large measures to parental attention, encouragement, physical affection, consistency, and democratic behaviour (i.e. to the things that make a child feel a valued, significant and responsible member of the family), but the teacher can help to give the child confidence in his own abilities by giving him opportunities for success, by encouraging rather than censuring him when he is confronted by failure, and by demonstrating personal belief in his competence.

High and low self-esteem can be referred to as a dimension of personality. Another such dimension that has implications for learning is that of extraversion-introversion. Typically the extravert is an individual who enjoys change and variety and is orientated towards the external world of people and experiences, while the introvert is more concerned with stability and with the inner world of thoughts and feelings. All of us find our place at some point on this dimension between extreme extraversion and introversion, and research with children (Entwistle, 1972) suggests that success in primary school (where the emphasis is often upon group work and social activity) may be linked to some extent to extraversion, but that the balance swings towards introversion (more rapidly for girls than for boys) in the secondary school and even more markedly in higher education (where the emphasis is more upon solitary, static activity). Further evidence that extraverts prefer unstructured and introverts structured learning environments comes from Rowell and Renner (1975), while Lewis and Ko (1973) demonstrate that introversion may be of most value in terms of school learning and achievement when it is combined with high levels of intelligence.

Note that the relative progress of introverts and extraverts at school level appears determined, partly at least, not so much by some quality in themselves as by the way in which we organize the learning environment for them. The inference for the teacher is that just as he adopts different approaches for children of differing cognitive ability, so should he for children of differing personality, making sure that the introvert enjoys ample opportunities for quiet, structured work and the extravert for more active, socially orientated activities. In particular, he should avoid ordering his classroom (and his value system) so that only children with personalities similar to his own find it a suitable environment for learning.

Motivation

Satisfactory school learning is unlikely to take place in the absence of sufficient motivation to learn. We have already mentioned one possible source of motivation, namely anxiety, but there are many others. For convenience we can divide these into intrinsic forms of motivation, which come from the individual himself, and extrinsic, which are imposed upon him by the environment. Taking intrinsic first, research studies suggest (e.g. Harlow and Harlow, 1962; Charlesworth, 1966) that there may be a natural curiosity drive in animals and man, a drive that does not appear to be directed towards an apparent material end but is engaged in for itself and which prompts exploration and discovery from an early age. As the child matures, so the response of others to this drive will help determine its development. If his attempts at exploration are met with adult disapproval and consequent frustration to himself, then through operant conditioning such attempts are likely to become less frequent, and to be replaced by apathy or possibly by random purposeless activity. If, on the other hand, they are frequently rewarded and reinforced by discovery, excitement, and adult approval they are likely to continue, and to become more directed and productive.

Closely linked to a child's curiosity as a motivator is the degree of interest that he derives from a learning experience. If we had to say why some things capture a person's interest and others do not we would probably argue that the former have direct relevance to his daily life. Either they make him feel better by amusing him or taking his mind off unpleasant thoughts, or they enable him to cope more effectively with the tasks and people he meets. As he grows older they may also help him to understand himself, and develop some coherent and consistent philosophy of life. But the problem with much school learning is that it appears to lack this relevance. It takes place in an environment distinct from the outside world, and much of what it teaches is a preparation for tasks way ahead in the future rather than in the present (or for tasks which the child meets only in school and nowhere else). By knowing both his subject and his children the lively, imaginative teacher can do much to make school work appeal directly to children's interests. Essentially, this means starting from what children already know, their curiosities, their ambitions, their problems, and showing how these relate to what is studied in school, and how such study can provide answers that will help them lead more satisfying lives.

Nevertheless, however stimulating the teacher, there will always be occasions when the children's intrinsic motivation is insufficient and recourse has to be made to motivation of an extrinsic kind. Such motivation usually consists of marks, grades, school reports, tests, examinations and, of course, teacher approval. Success at such things helps build up a child's prestige in his own eyes and in the eyes of teachers, peers, and parents, and thus assists the development of what is called achievement motivation (sometimes called need for achievement, or nAch for short). The child finds success to be rewarding, and builds up expectations which he has to work ever more purposefully to fulfil. But extrinsic motivation raises a number of important considerations at school level (quite apart from the danger that it may increase anxiety to an inhibiting level), the most important of which we summarize below.

* Instead of success, some children experience only failure. This tends to produce either low self-esteem or a rejection of school as 'boring' and 'stupid' (i.e. a defensive attempt to convince everyone that 'I could do the work if it was worth doing'). In combatting the harmful effects of constant failure, the golden rule of the class teacher is to provide opportunities for success at however low a level. Through this experience of success the child gradually builds up a new self-image, and can be encouraged to set his sights progressively higher.
* Sometimes motivation suffers because children have to wait too long for the results of their work. The operant conditioning model demonstrates that the longer the gap between performance and results the less efficient the learning, and the greater the likelihood that the child will lose interest in the task and in how well he has done it.
* Competition between children is a useful motivator, though if it becomes too intense it can lead to bad feeling and the harmful effects of failure. A situation where the child competes against himself, steadily improving his performance, is often more helpful, as is a spirit of co-operation where children adopt group norms and work together to achieve them.
* Wherever the pressures of extrinsic motivation are too strong, children may resort to strategies like cheating, absenteeism, or feigned illness to avoid the consequences of failure.

Age, sex and social factors
Age variables in learning bring us to the concept of readiness. Such a concept has it that children are unable to undertake certain kinds of learning (whether it be simple

skills like colour discrimination or more complex ones like classification and seriation) until their cognitive processes have matured to the appropriate levels. Piaget's well-known developmental stages of sensori-motor operations, concrete operations, and formal operations (with their various sub-divisions) provide a context within which to study this concept, as do the enactive, iconic, and symbolic systems of Bruner referred to above. Both Piaget and Bruner stress that learning is related closely to thinking. As the child becomes more capable of complex thinking, so the nature of the learning he is able to undertake changes in a range of important and subtle ways. For the teacher the most important difference between the developmental psychologies of Piaget and Bruner is that although Bruner believes we acquire the stages proposed by his system in a set order and we continue to use each of them throughout life, Piaget argues that generally we progress beyond each stage as we acquire the next one above it. The subject is too complex to debate fully here, but the teacher should study both the systems of Piaget and Bruner and ensure that learning experiences are presented to a child in a form suited to his particular level of thinking. Thus, for example, a child in the early stages of concrete operations (Piaget) and capable only of iconic thinking (Bruner), should not be taught by methods that employ elaborate linguistic definitions, and highly abstract concepts. Bruner, in particular, stresses that a child is ready to tackle virtually any subject provided it can be presented to him in a form appropriate to his level of thinking.

Just as the ability to learn is influenced by age variables, so is it influenced by sex. Girls are generally more verbal than boys at school age, and have fewer reading, speech, and general backwardness problems (Davie et al, 1972), while boys are more advanced in number skills. These verbal and speech differences tend to disappear by age 16, and boys between five and ten years old also appear twice as likely to show an increase in measured intelligence as girls (Kagan, Baker and Nelson, 1958). Throughout school life, however, girls tend to be better all-rounders, while boys are better at the subjects they enjoy and spurn those they do not. These sex-related differences could be in part genetic and in part related to the home (where girls are taught to be more dependent, and more concerned for parental approval), but research in the USA summarized by Mussen, Conger and Kagan (1979), suggests they could also be due to the fact that most early school teaching is done by women, and boys therefore associate school with feminine values. Where such teaching is done by men, the higher rate of backwardness and school rejection shown by boys apparently declines. Sadly, at all ages, girls tend to show lower self-esteem than boys, and may even artificially depress their levels of performance in conformity with an outmoded and unfortunate social conception of the inferiority of the female role.

A number of studies (e.g. Davie et al, 1972) show that children from deprived social backgrounds lag behind children from more favoured environments in every aspect of school learning. Extended discussion of the reasons for this belong elsewhere, but obviously poorer economic circumstances, fewer facilities, less parental interest and encouragement, and a higher level of emotional upheaval will all play their part. It may be also that since schools, for better or worse, uphold the so-called middle-class values of thrift, respect for authority, professional ambition, politeness, and deferral of satisfaction (i.e. the willingness to put off short-term gain in the interest of long-term), then children who share these values are more likely to fit in successfully than those who do not.

Memory

Clearly, learning depends intimately on memory. At the practical level psychologists recognize the existence of two kinds of memory, short-term and long-term respectively (a further sub-division into immediate or sensory memory is of little practical importance to the teacher). All information received by the senses and to which we pay attention seems to enter short-term memory, but it can only be held there briefly and is either then forgotten (as when we look up a telephone number and forget it the moment we have dialled it) or transferred to long-term memory where it can be held more permanently (though it is still, of course, subject to forgetting). Obviously this transfer from short- to long-term memory is vital for the teacher. Available evidence suggests it involves some form of consolidation, typically a short pause during which the information is held consciously in the mind. Even after an interesting lesson children often remember little, probably because each piece of information is so quickly followed by the next that there is no time for consolidation. However, a number of strategies exist both for helping consolidation and for increasing the efficiency of long-term memory generally.

* Pausing, repeating, and questioning: each of these prompts children to dwell sufficiently upon material for transfer from short- to long-term to take place.
* Relevance and interest: children best remember those things that appeal directly to their own experience and feelings.
* Attention span: the process of concentrating on a task for any length of time is difficult for some children. Their attention wanders, and material is neither listened to nor remembered. A rough rule is that the teacher can expect to hold attention with a normal class at any one point, even with interesting material, for no more than a minute to a minute-and-a-half for each year of the children's age (e.g. 10-15 minutes for a class of ten year olds).
* Practical use: material that is put to practical use

tends to be remembered better than material which is
not.

* Meaning: material which is understood by the child is
more memorable than material which is not.

* Overlearning: skills or knowledge that the child goes on
practising and revising even after he has apparently got
them off to perfection (i.e. material that is overlearned) persist better in the memory than material that
he does not. This is especially true of material required to be remembered in a stressful situation (e.g.
in the examination room, on the concert platform).

* Association: unfamiliar material is remembered more
effectively if it is associated with something
familiar. Realization of the truth of this lies behind
the old (and good) primary school adage that learning
should always go from the known to the unknown; that
is, that new material should be keyed in by reference to
the association between it and something already known.
Research (e.g. Bugelski, 1968) indicates that visual
association is particularly helpful: hence the importance of visual aids. Such aids need not necessarily be
closely linked in terms of meaning to the material to be
learned (witness the highly successful advertisements on
television!), but they must be presented concurrently
with this material so that a strong association is built
up.

* Recognition and recall: there appears to be a functional
difference between recognition (where we spot as familiar some stimulus physically presented to us) and recall (where we have to retrieve some word or fact from
memory itself). Recognition appears to come more readily
than recall (e.g. it is easier to recognize a face than
to recall a name, to recognize a word in a foreign
language than to recall it from memory), and in consequence, where practical, the teacher should aid children's recall by providing appropriate recognition cues.

So much for the factors that aid long-term memory. Now
for those that appear to interfere with it. One of these,
anxiety, has already been touched upon. Material that can
readily be recalled in a relaxed state may prove elusive
when in a stressed state. Two others of importance are known
as retroactive and proactive interference respectively.
Retroactive interference occurs when recently learned
material appears to inhibit the recall of that learned
earlier. The phenomenon appears to take place at all levels
of learning and is apparent in the student, for example, who
crams for an examination and finds the facts he learned the
night before keep coming back when he tries to recall those
he studied earlier in the week. Proactive interference, on
the other hand, occurs when earlier learning seems to block
the recall of later, as when, for example, a child starts
learning a second foreign language and finds himself unable
to remember the word he wants because the equivalent in the

first foreign language keeps coming to mind. We shall discuss ways of minimizing the risk of retroactive inhibition when we deal with study habits below, but little can be done, within the confines of the classroom, to lessen proactive interference in the early stages of a new learning task. Such interference is more likely where the two subjects being studied share certain similarities, but it is generally less of a problem than retroactive interference and tends to disappear as the new material becomes more familiar and overlearning takes place.

Finally, we come to the subject of memory training. Some teachers still assume they are 'training' children's memories when they require them to learn long pieces of poetry, as if the act of memorizing in itself effects improvement. There is no consistent evidence that it does. True, actors and others who spend their professional lives memorizing material seem to become extra good at it, but this comes from acquiring skills on how to memorize rather than from memorizing per se. Some of these skills have already been mentioned, and others are discussed in the next section, but some reference should be made here to mnemonic devices, which are devices created specifically to aid recall. They range from simple tricks like tying a knot in a handkerchief and short jingles like 'thirty days hath September ...' to the elaborate devices used by stage 'memory men'. One such device is the so-called peg-word system, where the digits 1-10 (or more) are each associated with a rhyming word (e.g. 1 is a bun, 2 is a shoe, 3 is a tree, etc.). These associations are learned, and then facts to be memorized are associated with them in turn, preferably using visual imagery. Thus, for example, if we wished to learn (for some reason) the agricultural produce exported by New Zealand we could visualize first butter spread on a bun, second a lamb wearing shoes, and so on. Such devices are remarkably effective in the learning of lists of facts, but their use beyond this is limited.

Study habits

As the child grows older and comes to take more responsibility for his own learning, so good study habits become increasingly important. Some of these habits, like working in an environment free from distraction, are obvious while others, like overlearning, have already been covered. We can summarize the remainder as follows.

* Realistic work targets: realistic work targets, which the student plans in detail, are far more effective than impossibly ambitious or vague commitments. Ideally these targets should be expressed publicly, so that he will stick to them to protect his prestige.
* Rewards: the student can build small rewards, as reinforcers, into his work schedule, like a cup of coffee and a five-minute break after every hour of solid work. He should be strong enough to withhold the reward from himself if he fails to earn it.

* Punctuality: work should be started promptly at the appointed hour. This forestalls the elaborate (and plausible) strategies we each develop to put off actually sitting down at our desks and getting on with it.
* Whole and part learning: a new learning task should be read through first in its entirety, to get the general drift of it, before being broken down into small units and learned methodically.
* Organizing material: often textbooks (and lecturers) do not present material in a way which accords best with the learner's own experience and understanding. Time spent making notes and reorganizing the material into a more palatable form is never wasted. Similarly, time spent in ensuring that notebooks are attractive and neat is also time well spent. Scruffy notes, with pages out of order, are a powerful disincentive to learning. Revision notes should also contain all important references and information likely to be needed later. Many things that seem unforgettable at the time soon fade from memory, as does the meaning of the cryptic, home-made shorthand that many students employ in lectures!
* Revision: a programme of phased revision throughout the duration of a course is of far more value than an attempt to cram everything in during the final few weeks before an exam. Retroactive inhibition is the almost inevitable consequence of such cramming. Phased revision, however, leads to a growing mastery of the whole course as the student works his way through it, with each new piece of knowledge being placed in its proper context. When it comes to final examination preparation the student is therefore looking back over material that has already been overlearned. Revision is best done before material has actually been forgotten. This is known as maintenance revision.

The nature of the knowledge to be learned

From time to time one still hears the view expressed that the experienced teacher can teach any subject, no matter how unfamiliar, simply by keeping one page ahead of the class in the textbook. The fallacy of this view is most clearly emphasized by Bruner (1966), who insists that the ultimate aim of teaching a subject is to help children understand its structure: that is, the basic principles that help define it, give it identity, and allow other things to be related to it meaningfully. Without a thorough specialist knowledge of the subject himself, the teacher can neither understand its structure nor help others achieve such an understanding. By knowing the structure of his subject the teacher is able to abstract from it material that is suited to the level of comprehension of his class, and that represents coherent, logical, and meaningful elements of the whole. This material can then be expressed in terms of clear

learning objectives which state the 'purpose and point of
the whole enterprise'.

Emphasis upon the essential nature of such objectives,
if learning is to be rendered efficient, also comes from
operant conditioning theorists who argue that such objectives must be couched in behavioural language so that we can
judge by the changes in student behaviour whether or not the
desired learning has taken place. In other words, objectives
must state clearly what a student should be able to do at
the end of a successful lesson. The most detailed attempt to
provide guidance on the preparation of learning objectives
comes from the work of committees under the direction of
Bloom (1956) and Krathwohl (1964) working respectively in
the cognitive domain (the area of learning concerned with
intellectual outcomes) and the affective domain (the area
concerned with feelings and emotions). Bloom and Krathwohl
and their colleagues have produced a set of general and
specific categories that encompass all the learning outcomes
that might be expected in the class or lecture room. These
categories are arranged in hierarchical order, from the
simplest to the most complex. Each of the higher categories
includes the outcomes at the levels inferior to it (e.g.
outcomes at level 2 will include those at level 1 also), and
we now summarize them in ascending order, taking the cognitive domain first.

Categories in the cognitive domain (after Bloom et al, 1956)

* Knowledge: simple knowledge of facts, of terms, of
  theories, etc.
* Comprehension: an understanding of the meaning of this
  knowledge.
* Application: the ability to apply this knowledge and
  comprehension in new and concrete situations.
* Analysis: the ability to break material down into its
  constituent parts and to see the relationships between
  them.
* Synthesis: the ability to re-assemble these parts into a
  new and meaningful relationship, thus forming a new
  whole.
* Evaluation: the ability to judge the value of material
  using explicit and coherent criteria, either of one's
  own devising or derived from the work of others.

Armed with this taxonomy the teacher is able to examine
whether or not he is keeping a balance between his expectations. For example, is he placing too great an emphasis
upon expectations connected with level 1 of the taxonomy
(e.g. by concentrating the attention of his class upon the
memorization of facts and figures) at the expense of the
more complex outcomes? More important still, is he able to
separate educational outcomes (i.e. the behaviours expected

of children at the end of the learning task) from educational processes (i.e. the behaviours expected of children -
and of the teacher - during the task itself)? Educational
processes are, of course, a major concern, and we deal with
them in the next section, but the tendency to confuse these
processes with outcomes is a prime cause of the vague and
well-nigh valueless objectives with which many teachers and
student teachers preface their lesson notes. For example, a
teacher may state that his objective is to demonstrate to
his class a particular skill (whether it be in science,
craft, PE or whatever). But this is not really a learning
objective at all. It is simply a statement of what he plans
to do, and therefore belongs more properly under the heading
of process (or methodology). It fails to say why he is going
to demonstrate this skill, and how children's behaviour is
going to be changed as a consequence. Instead of a mis-
stated objective of this kind, therefore, the teacher should
have said that his objective was one or more of the following (dependent upon the level of Bloom's taxonomy at which
he planned to work). At the end of the lesson the class
should be able:

* to recognize and identify the various elements involved
  in the particular skill (these elements would then be
  specified: this is an objective at the knowledge
  level);
* to define these elements and to know the part they play
  in the particular skill (an objective at the comprehension level);
* to practise the skill itself (an objective at the
  application level);
* to describe what is happening - and why - during this
  practice (an objective at the analysis level);
* to utilize elements of this skill in solving a particular novel problem (an objective at the synthesis
  level);
* to assess the degree of success achieved in this
  solution and to propose improvements (an objective at
  the evaluation level).

Note that if we were using objectives at more than one level
we would not necessarily always deal with them in their
hierarchical order. To do so would lead to formal and
stereotyped lessons. We might prefer, at times, instead of
first presenting the class with knowledge and then going on
to the practical activities, to start by confronting the
class with the problem and then feed in the knowledge (and
the comprehension) as the objective necessity for it arose
during the course of problem solving. Note also that the
verbs in our above extended example of objective writing are
of an essentially unequivocal behavioural kind. Bloom and
other workers in the field lay great stress upon the need
for this. It is all very well for the teacher to write that
he wants his class 'to appreciate' a particular thing, or

'to become proficient' at something else, but what do these terms actually mean when translated into directly observable changes in children's behaviour? Instead of such imprecision, Bloom proposes examples of the kind of concrete verbs that should be used, with appropriate variations dependent upon the level at which we are working. Thus if we were working at level 1 (knowledge) we would express objectives in terms of class members being able to state, or list, or identify, or reproduce; at level 2 (comprehension), we would talk of their being able to explain, or distinguish, or infer, or give examples; at level 3 (application), we would expect them to be able to demonstrate, or operate, or show, or solve, or use; at level 4 (analysis), to describe, or break down, or discriminate, or select; at level 5 (synthesis), to combine or compile, or design, or create, while at level 6 (evaluation), we would expect behaviour that would show them able to appraise, to contrast, to criticize and to justify.

The categories in the affective domain are rather different from those in the cognitive, and can be taken to refer not just to classroom learning but to all those values and attitudes that a student derives from the institution of which he is a member. Thus the affective domain must not be seen as something quite separate from the cognitive. The affective categories advanced by Krathwohl and his colleagues are summarized below, and this time we include in each of the categories the kind of concrete verbs in which objectives might be expressed.

Categories in the affective domain (after Krathwohl et al, 1964)

* Receiving (willingness to attend): the student listens, or asks, or sits erect, or looks at.
* Responding (willingness to participate actively): the student answers or complies, or helps, or obeys, or reads, or writes.
* Valuing (the ability to assign value to things; this differs from evaluation in the cognitive domain in that it involves attitudes and moral and social judgements rather than the application of the specific principles of a given subject or discipline): the student joins, or justifies, or prefers, or commits himself, or shares.
* Organization (the ability to bring separate values together and compare and relate them): the student modifies, or relates, or organizes, or accepts responsibility.
* Characterization by a value or value complex (the ability to take the organizational level a step further and build up a coherent value system or philosophy of life which informs all of one's behaviour): the student serves, or acts, or influences, or shows self-awareness.

The committees that met under Bloom and Krathwohl originally intended to produce a taxonomy of educational objectives in the third major domain, the psycho-motor, in addition to those produced in the cognitive and affective domains. This work was never finished, but various attempts have been made to remedy this omission, the best known probably being that by Simpson (1972). The psycho-motor domain is concerned with motor skills, such as those used in sport, in operating machinery and equipment and in manipulative exercises such as handwriting. Simpson's taxonomy, in ascending order, consists of perception (the acquisition by the senses of cues to guide motor activity), set (the readiness to take a particular kind of action), guided response (the ability to copy an instructor or to be guided by knowledge of results), mechanism (the ability to carry out simple movement patterns with confidence and proficiency), complex overt responses (the ability to carry out more complex patterns with smooth and accurate control), adaptation (the ability to modify established movement patterns to meet special situations and problems), and finally origination (the ability to create new movement patterns).

It would be wrong to suggest that all psychologists and curriculum theorists interested in school-based learning agree that with the help of the above (or any other) taxonomies it is necessarily possible to write specific objectives for all learning situations. Stenhouse (1970) argues, for example, that the teacher cannot plan in advance the precise impact that great literature is likely to have upon young minds and behaviour, and this argument is perfectly valid. Indeed, it would not be a good thing if the teacher could. Great literature is an intensely personal experience and it is not the teacher's job to circumscribe this experience by imposing too many of his own reactions upon his class. Nevertheless, even with great literature the teacher should have a good idea of the kinds of responses from children that can be regarded as appropriate and those that cannot. He will expect, to give an instance, that even those who reject the literature will be able to show some knowledge and comprehension of it, that they will be able to analyse the plot, the characterization and perhaps the techniques that it contains, and that they will be able to offer some considered evaluations and take part in informed debate.

Assessment

The preparation of specific learning objectives plays an important part in helping the teacher to structure the learning experience and evaluate its success. Such evaluation, however, involves more than the teacher sitting back and observing whether or not the children evidence the kind of behaviour for which he hoped. Often he will want to offer them specially devised opportunities for such behaviour, and this brings us to a consideration of assessment in its various forms.

The first point to stress is that the teacher's choice of assessment techniques will be strongly influenced by the level (in terms of the taxonomies discussed above) at which he intends learning to take place. All too frequently, particularly in arts and social science subjects, assessment simply takes the form of a written essay, which may be ideal for gauging progress at the more complex cognitive and affective levels (such as synthesis and evaluation, or valuing and organization), but which is a very limited measure of such things as knowledge and comprehension. It may also be that students have little idea of the kind of essay likely to appeal to a particular teacher, or the precise meaning of a given title, or of the criteria which will be employed in marking it. Thus their essays may be a poor reflection of the actual learning that has taken place, and of the use to which they can put this learning in environments other than the classroom. The value of essays in assessment can be increased considerably if teachers pay attention to these points, making their expectations clear to their students and explaining the details of their marking schedules.

The main alternative to the essay, in the cognitive domain at least, is the so-called objective test, each of whose items carries only a single right answer. The principles behind the construction of such a test can be simply stated.

* From the objectives of the various lessons that the teacher wishes to assess, a list is made of the student behaviours that represented the desired outcomes of these lessons. These behaviours yield the general area to be tested.
* From the contents of these lessons a list is made of the knowledge and comprehension (or whatever) that were expected to figure in these behaviours. For example, the lesson objective may have stated that the student should be able to quote the terms or the parts of speech or the procedures associated with a particular skill, while the lesson content will have stated what these various things actually were. This knowledge and comprehension yield the precise subject matter to be tested.
* From these two points, a schedule is drawn up of the relative importance of each of the various items of subject matter to be tested. This provides guidance on the number of test questions that will be constructed for each item.
* Finally, the test questions are prepared. In an objective test these are usually of the multiple choice variety, with the student being asked which of a range of possible answers is the correct one: for example, 'The Theory of Association was first advanced by: Herbart/William James/Francis Galton/none of these.' However, some operant conditioning theorists claim that in getting a multiple choice question wrong, a student may unwittingly form an association in his mind between

the question and the incorrect response. To avoid this, it is sometimes suggested that the question should be left to stand on its own, without the addition of a range of possible answers. The reader will note at once that in this form such a question would be testing recall, whereas when presented in its multiple choice guise it is testing recognition.

It is often objected that tests of this kind take much longer to construct than does a test of the essay type. There is no gainsaying this, but on the other hand they are much quicker to mark, and the teacher is left with the satisfaction of knowing that he has adequately tested the knowledge, comprehension and application that he set out to test. Further, the student is motivated to acquire this knowledge since he knows it is to be comprehensively tested, rather than fractionally sampled as in an essay. He is also left with the reassurance that good marks really do mean that he knows the field and is equipped with the basic grammar of his subject.

The nature of the learning process

Consideration of the practical aspects of the learning process brings us to the question of teaching methods and techniques. Many of these are specific to the particular subject or subjects being taught, and therefore lie outside the scope of a text in psychology. However, there are a number of general points to which we can draw attention. Gagné (1974), who draws upon both Skinner's operant conditioning model and (though to a lesser extent) the kind of conceptual model associated with Bruner, suggests that the learning act typically consists of a chain of eight events, some internal to the learner and others external. These are, in their usual order of occurrence:

* motivation (or expectancy);
* apprehending (the subject perceives the material and distinguishes it from the other stimuli competing for his attention);
* acquisition (the subject codes the knowledge);
* retention (the subject stores the knowledge in short- or long-term memory);
* recall (the subject retrieves the material from memory);
* generalization (the material is transferred to new situations, thus allowing the subject to develop strategies for dealing with them);
* performance (these strategies are put into practice);
* feedback (the subject obtains knowledge of results).

Where there is a failure in the learning process, Gagné argues, it will take place at one of these eight levels, and it is the task of the teacher to ascertain which. We have already discussed motivation at some length, but Gagné

considers that the teacher can help avoid failure at the
other levels by bearing in mind that a learning sequence
should consist of five steps:

* STEP 1: the learner is informed of the performance to
  be expected of him at the end of the learning
  experience. This is best done by presenting him with a
  list of the teacher's objectives. Neglect of this basic
  step, suggests Gagné, is a frequent cause of learning
  failure. The learner is unsure of teacher expectations
  and thus unable to monitor his own progress adequately;
* STEP 2: the learner is questioned in a way that requires
  a re-statement of earlier concepts upon which the
  current learning depends;
* STEP 3: the teacher provides cues that help the learner
  put together the current learning as a chain of concepts
  in the correct order;
* STEP 4: the learner is questioned in a way that allows
  him to demonstrate concrete applications of his
  learning;
* STEP 5: the learner is questioned in a way that allows
  him to make statements of the rule or rules that he has
  learned.

Note that the 'questions' referred to in Steps 2, 4 and
5 can take the form of project work and discovery learning
as well as simple verbal presentations on the part of the
teacher. Such project and discovery work is also likely to
incorporate Step 3, and here we can turn from Gagné to
Bruner (1966) for further helpful comment. Bruner believes
that far too often when providing the learner with the cues
mentioned in Step 3 we deal only in the 'middle language' of
our subject: that is in the facts, formulae, techniques,
ideas and so on developed by other people. The learner is
not allowed to discover these facts for himself. True, if we
do allow him to discover these facts for himself they are
not 'new' discoveries in any absolute sense, but this,
suggests Bruner, is not the point. The point is that they
are new for him, and by going through the discovery process
he is much better able to grasp the concepts and the
structure that underlie them.

By allowing the learner to use the discovery method,
Bruner argues, we are also closing the gap between elementary and advanced knowledge. After all, the university professor and the higher degree student employ the discovery
method, and if we deny it to learners functioning at a less
exalted level we are preventing them from really experiencing the subject they are attempting to study. An academic
subject is defined not just by the knowledge that it has
amassed over the years, but also by the methods used to
amass it. If we teach merely the middle language of the
subject we are teaching the one without the other, and
hindering genuine understanding on the part of the learner.

Bruner is aware that too often discovery learning is
used as an excuse for vague and haphazard goings on, with

neither teacher nor class very certain of what is supposed to be happening. This is one of the reasons for his emphasis upon objectives. The teacher should hold the ends of learning constant, while providing a scaffolding within which the means can be varied to suit the level of thinking and of conceptualization of the class. For example, when teaching the working of an electrical circuit the teacher will be quite clear on the principles that have to be learned, yet instead of simply listing these principles to the class he will present them with the necessary wires, bulbs, and batteries and set them a problem which can only be solved when they are connected up correctly. Having done these connections, the class will then be expected to state the rules that can be derived from the experience (Step 5 of Gagné's learning sequence above). It is sometimes objected that this approach is less suited to arts and social science subjects than to mathematical, technical and scientific subjects, but here Bruner stresses the value of simulation exercises. Such exercises present the learner with imaginary problems designed to mimic those faced, for example, by historical figures, economists and social workers, and ask him to produce solutions. These solutions are then compared with genuine case histories, and comparisons and contrasts are drawn which promote debate, understanding and the efficient workings of memory.

Naturally it is not possible to carry out all classroom learning by means of the activities advocated by Bruner. However, whatever the nature of the lesson, the teacher can ensure that the questions he directs at his class (whether verbal or in the form of written exercises) contain a fair proportion designed to prompt the kind of reflective thinking that leads to discovery. Too often questions invite only middle language answers, such as 'What is the population of Great Britain?'; 'What is the formula for water?'; 'In what metre is this poem written?' Such questions are useful at their own level, but they demand nothing from the student other than a single answer delivered in the form in which he first heard or read it. On the other hand, reflective questions (or 'springboard' questions, as they are often called) usually contain an element of controversy or contradiction. They introduce material which may not fit in with the student's knowledge or beliefs, and which therefore disturbs him and stimulates him to produce an answer which is more personal and original. Good springboard questions often contain the word 'why'. For example, 'The north and south poles are equidistant from the equator yet it is colder at the south. Why?' 'Christianity teaches you to love your enemies, yet many of the most terrible massacres have been carried out in its name. Why is this?' 'The higher an aeroplane flies, the nearer it gets to the sun, yet the colder the air becomes. Why?' Springboard questions can also take the form of statements, such as 'You have to be unscrupulous to succeed in business', 'Milton was a greater poet than Shakespeare', or 'There is no such thing as a scientific law'.

Creating springboard questions is, of course, best done by a teacher who is an expert in the subject being taught, and who knows its structure and its challenges. Their essential feature is that, by making the student reflect upon some critical aspect of the subject he is studying, they help him to understand the subtle ways in which the subject works, the relationship between cause and effect, and the methods of procedure and enquiry. Thus is he helped actively to advance his understanding of the subject and of the structure that underlies it. As a consequence, not only does he acquire knowledge, he acquires a grasp of the way in which that knowledge is generated, and of how it may be generalized to solve new problems. By contrast, PROGRAMMED LEARNING concentrates upon providing the learner with a simple unit of knowledge and then testing his retention of it. It owes much to the operant conditioning techniques of Skinner, with their emphasis upon learning by small steps and immediate knowledge of results. An example of an item from a programme on electrical wiring illustrates the principles behind this form of instruction.

Stage 1 (information): in wiring a 13 amp plug the brown wire is connected to the live terminal.

Stage 2 (question): what colour wire is connected to the live terminal of a 13 amp plug?

Stage 3 (response):
   A. the blue
   B. the brown
   C. the green and yellow

Stage 4 (answer): the brown

The student looks at each of these stages in turn, and if he gets the answer wrong turns back and re-reads Stage 1. Programmed learning is a vast subject in its own right, and we have no space to deal with it fully here. However, since the principles behind it are so simple the teacher can easily select programmes suitable for his class or, indeed, construct his own programmes which children can work through individually. Programmed learning theorists criticize discovery learning because it allows children to make frequent mistakes, thus setting up incorrect associations which may persist in the child's mind. Advocates of discovery learning, on the other hand, claim that mistakes are an essential part of learning, because they prompt the learner to ask questions of his own in an attempt to discover why and how he went wrong. Too often the teacher instils in the child a fear of making mistakes and of showing his failure to understand, and this leads to conservative and stereotyped patterns of learning which inhibit reflective thinking and a genuine grasp of the principles upon which knowledge is based. Doubtless the reader will want to make up his own mind on these matters, but a crucial consideration could be the level at which learning is intended to take place, with programmed learning proving particularly effective where the objective is to impart straightforward knowledge, and the reflective springboard approach where the aim is to stimulate thinking and further enquiry.

ferences

Bennett, N. (1976)
Teaching Styles and Pupil Progress. London: Open Books.
Bloom, B.S. (1956)
Taxonomy of Educational Objectives. Handbook 1: The cognitive domain. London: Longmans Green.
Bruner, J.S. (1966)
Towards a Theory of Instruction. Cambridge, Mass.: Harvard University Press.
Bruner, J.S. (1973)
The Relevance of Education. New York: Norton.
Bruner, J.S. and Anglin, J.M. (1973)
Beyond the Information Given: Studies in the psychology of knowing. New York: Norton.
Bruner, J.S., Goodnow, J.J. and Austin, G.A. (1965)
A Study of Thinking. New York: Wiley.
Bugelski, B.R. (1968)
Images as mediators in one-trial paired-associate learning. I: Self-timing in successive lists. Journal of Experimental Psychology, 77, 328-334.
Charlesworth, W.R. (1966)
Persistence of orienting and attending behavior in infants as a function of stimulus locomotion uncertainty. Child Development, 37, 473-491.
Coopersmith, S. (1968)
Studies in self-esteem. Scientific American, February.
Davie, R., Butler, N. and Goldsmith, H. (1972)
From Birth to Seven. London: Longmans.
Entwistle, N.J. (1972)
Personality and academic attainment. British Journal of Educational Psychology, 42, 137-151.
Franson, A. (1977)
On qualitative differences in learning: IV - Effects of intrinsic motivation and extrinsic test anxiety on process and outcome. British Journal of Educational Psychology, 47, 244-257.
Gagné, R.M. (1974)
Essentials of Learning for Instruction. Hinsdale, Ill.: Dryden Press.
Harlow, H.F. and Harlow, M.H. (1962)
Social development in monkeys. Scientific American, November.
Kagan, J., Sontag, L., Baker, C. and Nelson, V. (1958)
Personality and IQ change. Journal of Abnormal and Social Psychology, 56, 261-266.
Krathwohl, D.R. et al (1964)
Taxonomy of Educational Objectives. Handbook II: The affective domain. New York: David McKay.

Lewis, D.G. and Ko, P. (1973)

Personality and performance in elementary mathematics with special reference to item type. British Journal of Educational Psychology, 43, 24-34.

Mussen, P.H., Conger, J.J. and Kagan, J. (1979)

Child Development and Personality (5th edn). New York: Harper & Row.

Rowell, J.A. and Renner, V.J. (1975)

Personality, mode of assessment and student performance. British Journal of Educational Psychology, 45, 232-236.

Simpson, E.J. (1972)

The Classification of Educational Objectives in the psychomotor domain. The Psychomotor Domain, Volume 3. Washington: Gryphon House.

Skinner, B.F. (1969)

Contingencies of Reinforcement: A theoretical analysis. New York: Appleton-Century-Crofts.

Stenhouse, L. (1970)

Some limitations of the use of objectives in curriculum research and planning. Paedogogica Europaea, 6, 73-83.

Trown, E.A. and Leith, G. (1975)

Decision rules for teaching strategies in the primary school: personality-treatment interactions. British Journal of Educational Psychology, 45, 130-140.

Questions

1. An individual may learn readily from one teacher yet not from another. Assuming both teachers are equally knowledgeable in their subjects, and generally produce comparable results with their classes, suggest possible reasons for this.

2. Think about the definition of learning offered in the text. Can you suggest ways in which it could be made more satisfactory?

3. Identify your own attitude towards the behaviourist and the cognitive approach to learning respectively. Which seems to accord more closely with your own experience?

4. What is the difference between a theory and a description of learning? Which appears to be of more potential practical value to the teacher and why?

5. What are the three identifiable stages in Skinner's description of learning?

6. What is meant, in Bruner's language, by freedom from stimulus control? Skinner considers such freedom is illusory. Why?

7. Is there any way in which we can prove that freedom of choice is possible?

8. Bruner suggests it is not enough to regard behaviour as simply something elicited by a particular stimulus. Why?

9. Give examples of Bruner's three modes of representation as you might witness them in normal classroom work.

10. Sometimes anxiety is an aid to learning and sometimes the reverse. Why is this? Do you think the teacher is ever right to encourage even mild anxiety in a child?

11. Make a list of the strategies that the teacher can adopt to help the growth of self-esteem in children.

12. The debate on formal versus informal class teaching has tended to ignore the variable of the child's own personality. In what ways do you think this variable should influence the debate in the future?

13. Both parents and teachers often fail to encourage children's curiosity and love of exploration. Why? What effect might this have upon a child's learning?

14. Make a list of some of the topics that you have found particularly interesting in your own education. Can you say why they captured your interest?

15. Make a list of the extrinsic motivators in common use in schools. Can you decide what effect they are each likely to have upon different types of children?

16. Why is it that the experience of consistent failure is so damaging to a child's readiness to learn?

17. From your own experience do you think operant conditioning theorists are right to lay such an emphasis upon immediate knowledge of results?

18. If you found a child cheating in your class what action would you take? What would his cheating tell you about himself?

19. Bruner maintains that a child is ready to tackle virtually any learning task provided it is presented to him in a form appropriate to his level of thinking. Is that realistic? Can you think of exceptions?

20. List some of the factors both in the home and in the school that may influence the respective rates at which boys and girls learn.

21. Define short- and long-term memory respectively. What are the strategies the teacher can use to aid children in effecting transfer from one to the other?

22. What is meant by overlearning and why is it a valuable strategy?

23. Write short descriptions of three television advertisements that you have seen recently and that appear to apply association as an effective aid to memory. Consider ways in which similar techniques can be used in the classroom.

24. Define the difference between recognition and recall. How can the teacher convert a recognition task into a recall task (and vice versa)?

25. When and in what circumstances must the teacher be alert to possible interference with the process of remembering?

26. Write down as many examples as you can of well-known mnemonics. Construct a mnemonic for helping children remember important details in your own subject.

27. List the six suggested ways in which study habits can be improved. Can you think of any further ways of your own?

28. An experienced teacher should be able to teach virtually

any subject as long as he is able to keep ahead of his students in the textbook. Comment on this statement.

29. Write a set of learning objectives for teaching students to do one or more of the following: (i) make an omelette; (ii) become more aware of nature by reading a particular poem; (iii) solve simultaneous equations; (iv) mend a bicycle puncture; (v) construct a simple histogram.

30. Write out the six categories in Bloom's taxonomy of educational objectives and list against each one some of the verbs in which objectives can be expressed. Repeat the same exercise with Krathwohl's and with Simpson's taxonomies.

31. Why do correctly written educational objectives lay stress upon learning outcomes rather than upon learning processes?

32. Take each of the major subjects in the school curriculum in turn and discuss in which of the three domains it predominantly lies.

33. Discuss some of the problems a teacher of handicapped children (e.g. deaf, blind or ESN) would have in using a taxonomy in one or more of the three domains.

34. Discuss the respective functions of the essay and of objective tests. Can you think of the particular problems that confront the teacher in preparing these two kinds of assessment exercises?

35. Construct a simple multiple choice test designed to establish whether a student has correctly learned the principles and/or facts behind one or more of the following: (i) propagating plants by means of softwood cuttings; (ii) starting a motor car and drawing away safely from the kerb; (iii) tuning a particular musical instrument; (iv) swimming the crawl; (v) the parts of speech; (vi) the symbols on a map (or a weather map); (vii) the events leading up to an important historical occurrence; (viii) the conjugations of a French verb.

36. What are the eight events in a learning chain according to Gagné?

37. Select a particular aspect of your teaching subject and indicate how it can be taught either (i) in a direct practical way using Bruner's discovery method or (ii) through the medium of a simulation exercise.

38. How can we ensure Bruner's discovery method does not lead to classroom activities in which the children appear to be busily occupied but where there is little clear purpose and little identifiable learning?

39. Construct a list of knowledge questions and a list of reflective (or springboard) questions on some aspects of your own teaching subject. Indicate the purpose behind each question.

40. What are the arguments for and against allowing children freedom to make mistakes during the learning processes? Which set of arguments do you most favour and why?

Annotated reading

Bigge, L. (1976) Learning Theories for Teachers (3rd edn).
New York: Harper & Row.
> One of the best and most comprehensive surveys of
> learning theories and their application to teaching.

Hintzman, L. (1978) The Psychology of Learning and Memory.
San Francisco: Freeman.
> A good choice for those who want to take their study
> of learning theories rather further, and examine their
> relationship to memory.

Rachlin, H. (1976) Introduction to Modern Behaviourism (2nd
edn). San Francisco: Freeman.
> An excellent and very readable statement of the
> behaviourist position within psychology.

Neisser, U. (1976) Cognition and Reality. San Francisco:
Freeman.
> Contains some of the major tenets of the cognitive
> position.

Skinner, B.F. (1969) Contingencies of Reinforcement. A
theoretical analysis. New York: Appleton-Century-Crofts.
> Sets out Skinner's own theoretical position fully.

Skinner, B.F. (1972) Beyond Freedom and Dignity. London:
Jonathan Cape.
> Covers the application of his ideas to learning within
> society generally.

Wheeler, H. (ed.) (1973) Beyond the Punitive Society.
London: Wildwood House.
> Provides a full debate on Skinner's ideas.

Bruner, J.S. (1961) The Process of Education. Cambridge,
Mass.: Harvard University Press.

Bruner, J.S. (1966) Towards a Theory of Instruction.
Cambridge, Mass.: Harvard University Press.

Bruner, J.S. (1973) The Relevance of Education. New York:
Norton.
> Bruner's ideas are expounded in a number of highly
> readable texts, of which these three are good examples.

Marjoribanks, K. (1979) Families and Their Learning
Environments. London: Routledge & Kegan Paul.
> Provides a thorough and scholarly survey of the research
> into the relationship between intelligence, personality,
> family variables and learning.

Fontana, D. (1977) Personality and Education. London: Open
Books.
> Gives a more general discussion, with an examination of
> the implications for the teacher.

Hunter, I.M.L. (1964) Memory (rev. edn). Harmondsworth: Pelican.
> Difficult to beat as an examination of all aspects of memory.

Klatsky, R.L. (1980) Human Memory (2nd edn). San Francisco: Freeman.
> A more up-to-date picture of this subject.

Rowntree, D. (1976) Learn How to Study. Harmondsworth: Pelican.

Mace, C.A. (1968) The Psychology of Study (rev. edn). London: MacDonald.
> Both these are highly recommended among the good books currently available on study habits.

Gronlund, N.E.R. (1978) Stating Objectives for Classroom Instruction (2nd edn). London: Collier Macmillan.
> There are also many books available now on the writing of educational objectives and on the taxonomies produced by Bloom, Krathwohl and Simpson respectively. This is one of the best - and shortest - of them. It also has something useful to say on the construction of objective tests.

Vernon, P.E. (1964) An Introduction to Objective-type Examinations. London: Schools Council Examinations Bulletin No. 4.
> Remains one of the most valuable short introductions to objective tests.

Gagné, R.M. (1975) Essentials of Learning for Instruction. Hinsdale, Ill.: Dryden Press.

Gagné, R.M. (1977) The Conditions of Learning (3rd edn). London: Holt, Rinehart & Winston.
> Gagné's work is best tackled through his own writings, particularly these two books.

Jones, R.M. (1972) Fantasy and Feeling in Education. Harmondsworth: Penguin.
> Contains a good discussion of Bruner's ideas within the practical classroom context.

Taylor, J.L. and Walford, R. (1972) Simulation in the Classroom. Harmondsworth: Penguin.
> Gives a comprehensive explanation of simulation exercises with examples.

Rowntree, D. (1974) Educational Technology in Curriculum Development. London: Harper & Row.
> Provides a good introduction to programmed learning and the whole field of educational technology.

**Relevance to the
teacher
DAVID FONTANA**

Since the chapter is concerned with learning and teaching,
attempts have been made throughout to point out the relevance of psychologists' work on learning for the teacher.
The concern of this section is therefore not to go back over
ground that has already been covered but to extend the
practical relevance of the chapter by looking at specific
learning difficulties in the classroom and at strategies for
dealing with them.

The slow learner
Children are individuals, and each of them works at his
own pace. Thus each child at some point or other is likely
to be 'slow' when compared with classmates, and thus the
label slow learner therefore does not of itself tell us very
much. It may mean simply that a child is falling behind the
other members of what is a very able group, or that he is
slow at grasping new work (but tends to catch up later). For
practical purposes, however, 'slow learner' is usually taken
to mean any child who is consistently unable to cope with
the work of his age group to the satisfaction of his teachers. Far from being pejorative, the earlier a child who is
having difficulties of this sort is diagnosed as a slow
learner and offered appropriate help the better. As was
stressed very firmly in the main part of the chapter, consistent failure in itself has a handicapping effect upon a
child because it lowers his esteem in his own eyes and in
those of his classmates and teachers, and usually leads to
reduced self-confidence, reduced aspirations, and often
reduced effort as the chi ld resigns himself to the belief
that he just 'can't do' the required work.

Having identified a child as a slow learner, the next
task of the school is to have this identification confirmed
by the use of attainment tests, and to establish why the
child is having difficulty. Often an intelligence test is
useful at this point, administered together with other
diagnostic instruments by the educational psychologist.
Viewed against the child's attainment age scores, the
results of this administration help place the child in one
or other of the two main categories of slow learner, namely
mental dullness and retardation. The mentally dull child is
someone who appears by nature to have limited intellectual
endowment, and who is unlikely ever to develop into a bright
child whatever educational provision is offered. The retarded child, on the other hand, is one whose intellectual endowment appears to be within or above the normal range, but
whose speed of work is held up by some factor or factors in
his background. Such a child, with appropriate help, is well
capable of making up lost ground and rejoining his classmates. These two categories need now to be looked at
separately and in more detail.

The mentally dull child
Many teachers are put off by this intimidating label, and
for the best motives strenuously resist having it placed

upon one of their children (we are talking here about teachers of young children, since it is usually early in a child's career that such a diagnosis is made). It is unfortunate that attempts to find an alternative label (such as 'exceptional children') tend to be too vague to be of much general use. However, as we have indicated, the sooner a child who comes in this category is recognized as such, the better his chances of avoiding the psychological damage that constant failure can bring.

Some mentally dull children are eventually categorized as educationally sub-normal (ESN), and transferred to a special school where the ratio of pupils to teachers is lower and where the staff are specially trained for their remedial role. In terms of measured IQ (see chapter 6), ESN children usually fall within the 50-80 range. Below 50, the child is usually categorized as severely sub-normal (ESN(S), more commonly referred to now as SSN), and it is unlikely that the teacher will encounter any children in this category in the normal school. Usually the handicaps shown by SSN children (which often include physical handicaps) are so severe that they are diagnosed before the child reaches school age, and he is entered at a special school designed to cope with these particular problems. An intermediate category ESN(M), with the 'M' standing for 'moderately severe handicap', is now also recognized and usually covers children in the IQ range of 50-70. Only some 3.7 children per thousand fall into the SSN category, whereas some ten per cent fall within the broad mentally dull category.

Mentally dull children, then, have special needs and require special help. Recently, however, it has been argued with increasing conviction that for children simply classed as ESN (i.e. not as ESN(M) or SSN), this help might be better provided in remedial classes within the normal school than in the special schools to which we made reference above. One of the problems of special schools, no matter how good, is that the child becomes labelled, in his own eyes as well as in those of adults and other children, as being 'different' from his fellows in an undesirable way. This kind of stigma places additional burdens upon the child and his parents, and it is ironic that it should arise from the way in which we organize the child's formal education, since the purpose of such education after all is enhance the child and not to handicap him further.

Remedial classes within the normal school, the argument has it, go some way towards lessening the stigma of being mentally dull, particularly if the child works with the rest of the school wherever possible, and only joins the remedial group for certain subjects. True, he may still be labelled to some extent by his fellows, but it is up to the school and its general system of values and behaviours to see that this labelling is kept to a minimum. Perhaps the most important variable here is to let everyone see that the children in the remedial groups are prized by the school. This means they should at all times enjoy just as good (perhaps better) classroom and general facilities as everyone else, that they should be given positions of trust and responsibility, that their expertise and qualities as individuals should be praised at every opportunity, and that they should be taught by teachers who are respected and admired by all school members and who take a full part in running the school and helping with general school activities. Above all, the remedial groups should at no time be treated as units 'set apart' from the rest; for example, by putting them in a separate part of the school buildings, by giving them different break or lunch periods, by time-tabling them separately for games or sports activities, by denying them access to school facilities such as laboratories and work-shops, or by refusing them subject options which are given freely to the rest of the school. Obviously, in many of these situations remedial children may need special help and supervision, but they must be seen by all (themselves inclu-ded) as members of the school first, and as members of remedial or of any other groups very much second.

Teaching the mentally dull
A detailed discussion of the teaching skills necessary for use with mentally dull children lies outside the scope of this book, but in every context it is vital for the teacher to keep in mind that these children, as we emphasized earlier in this chapter, must be allowed to experience success at however low a level. The experience of success itself is the important thing, rather than the absolute standard achieved. Through such experience the child gains in confidence, escapes from the 'can't do it' syndrome, and is encouraged gradually to raise his sights until he is performing up to his maximum potential. The teacher must also remember that in Piagetian terms (see chapter 4) mentally dull children are usually operating at conceptual levels below their chronological ages. They may never, for example, reach the stage of formal operations, and this means it is valueless to expect them to grapple with abs-tract concepts, or to grasp the principles behind sets and categories simply because these are crystal clear to the teacher himself. Often it is difficult for the teacher, if he has no special training for remedial work, to avoid be-coming irritated if a child seems particularly obtuse in the face of an apparently simple idea. But such irritation only makes matters worse, with all concerned ending up frustrated and with a sense of defeat. The teacher should instead re-mind himself that the child would do the work if he could. It can be little fun to sit in a classroom and fail, espe-cially if one's peers find no difficulty in forging ahead. Where the child experiences particular problems, therefore, the teacher needs first to look at the way in which material is being presented to him, and to ask whether this is appropriate to his level of thought.

With his lower developmental stage of conceptualization and his problems with abstract ideas, the mentally dull child profits particularly from practical activities. He likes to be doing things, not only art and craft and domestic skills but also music, where a low IQ does not appear to be a necessary barrier to high levels of performance. He may also enjoy working outdoors with animals and with plants, and taking part in sport and physical activities. In fact, the curriculum can be made so interesting and exciting that the child will come to take a particular pleasure in school, and see himself as performing there relevant and socially useful skills. The absence of examination pressures, and the more favourable teacher-pupil ratios within remedial groups, can also mean that the child comes to have a much closer and less formal relationship with his teachers than does the child engaged in more academic work, and the realization that he is liked and respected by these teachers can further enhance the growth of his self-esteem and self-confidence.

This close relationship also means that the child's opportunities for linguistic communication with verbally fluent and articulate adults are greatly increased. We have already stressed in earlier chapters the critical importance of language to cognitive development, and we need only remind the reader here that far too often the mentally dull child, by virtue of the fact that he probably comes from a verbally unstimulating home, mixes mostly with other verbally retarded children, and experiences reading and comprehension difficulties, usually has few chances outside the classroom for improving his linguistic skills. Thus the teacher carries a particular responsibility for providing such a child with good examples of appropriate verbal communication, and for encouraging the child to respond in kind. Good linguistic development will not only help the child's cognitive growth, it will help him avoid the frustration of being unable to communicate his feelings and ideas in a form comprehensible to those around him. It is this frustration that lies behind a good many of the behaviour problems that mentally dull children often develop.

The retarded child

We have already suggested that the retarded child is one whose failings do not appear to be due to low intelligence. Generally such children have IQs from about 80 upwards, and may even fall into the very superior category. The teacher's first task, therefore, once it has been established that a slow learning child does not belong to the mentally dull category, is to isolate the factor or factors responsible for his retardation. Often the school psychological service, together with social workers and school welfare officers, may be of some help here, but the teacher usually remains the person who knows the child best, and his role in this diagnostic procedure is therefore a crucial one. The major factors likely to lead to retardation are as follows.

1. PHYSICAL PROBLEMS: the child may suffer from some ailment which has led to long absences from school, or which

renders it difficult for him to perform certain of the motor skills associated with learning. Ailments in the second category (e.g. poor sight, poor hearing, bronchial problems, or mild brain damage affecting motor co-ordination) may have gone unrecognized for some years, even by the child himself. Alternatively, in the case of stammering or stuttering for example, they may be all too painfully obvious, and may hold the unfortunate child up to ridicule from other children or (unforgivably) from the teacher himself.

2.   PERSONAL PROBLEMS: these could include such relatively simple factors as frequent changes of school or of class, or more complex ones such as limited attention span and high distractability. Frequent changes of schooling lead to problems of adjusting to new teachers, new syllabuses and new teaching methods, and to new peer groups and surroundings. Such changes, in addition to the cognitive strains they impose, leave the child feeling emotionally insecure and vulnerable. He has to re-establish his status in his new environment, prove his competence to strange teachers, learn new rules and standards (both formal and informal), and make new friends. Small wonder that he is often left struggling, and it is the teacher's job to ensure that he is integrated into the life of the school as soon as possible. This means seeing to it that he gets all his new textbooks and exercise books at once, that trouble is taken to find out what he already knows about current work and to give him guidance on where some catching up is necessary, that immediate interest is shown in him as a person, and that he is warmly welcomed in front of the class and a sympathetic child asked (formally or informally as appropriate) to show him around and see to it that he is not left on his own at break and lunch times.

Limited attention span and high distractability are not dealt with so easily. Children faced with these difficuties find it extra hard to settle to work, to concentrate for any length of time, and therefore to undertake learning tasks successfully. In some cases, where the distractability is of a particularly marked kind and accompanied by almost constant physical activity, the child is labelled hyperactive, and it is recognized that he presents particular problems. At one time it was thought that such hyperactivity was a symptom of brain damage, but it is by no means clear that this is necessarily the case. Children obviously vary innately in their activity levels, and problems are sometimes caused by the fact that a particularly active child is made to keep unnaturally quiet at home or school leading to frustration and explosions of random and undirected activity. The remedy with such children is simple. Too much should not be expected of them in the way of passive behaviour. Given free range for their activities and their energies, and provided with as much interesting and stimulating material as possible, their attention span gradually increases as they grow older, and they show themselves well able to cope with school and its demands.

With some children, however, the picture is not as straightforward, and there seems to be a genuine psychological problem that may need specialist help. Typically such children (and they are the only ones who genuinely merit the term hyperactive) are retarded from an early age in important skill areas such as language and reading, and show an inability to concentrate (or even to stay in one place) for any but the very briefest interval, placing great strains upon parents and upon nursery and infant teachers. Usually these strains become so severe that in the end the child is referred for specialist diagnosis, and may be recommended for transfer to a special school. In such a school the child is given more scope for his restless behaviour without the fear that he may be disrupting the rest of the class, and often special schooling is therefore the best solution for all concerned.

Typically, however, if the child is not made to feel excess frustration or guilt as a result of his behaviour, hyperactivity tends to lessen as he grows older, and may disappear as a major problem by about the age of eight or so. Retardation in speech and reading may also disappear, often even before this age is reached, allowing the child eventually to be transferred back to normal schooling. It is as if hyperactivity is due to some neurological immaturity that eventually corrects itself, and if the child has not been allowed to develop psychological problems or to fall too far behind his peers in those areas where he needs to develop competence, then his long-term educational prospects may be good.

3. ENVIRONMENTAL PROBLEMS: these include a poor or depressed background in which the child has no encouragement to read or to use language, in which there are no facilities for homework or private study, and in which the values of the school are rejected and perhaps even held up to ridicule. There may also be cases of actual physical deprivation (such as shortage of food or extreme shortage of sleep), of physical abuse, or of outright physical rejection, perhaps brought about by a broken home or by alcoholism in one or both parents. These issues have all been fully discussed in chapters 1 and 2, and the task of the teacher in relation to them outlined.

4. EMOTIONAL PROBLEMS: the cause and treatment of emotional problems will be dealt with more fully in chapter 14 and again when we come to look at discipline and class control in chapter 15. Mild emotional problems can, however, be caused by any or all of the three categories of problems that we have been discussing above. They can also arise from the fact that a child may feel disliked or rejected by his classmates or teachers, or even because he happens to take a rooted dislike to one teacher in particular and finds it hard to remain in his class (such apparently irrational over-reaction is not uncommon, particularly at adolescence). This dislike can stem from a real or imagined injustice, or

from some mannerism of speech or dress on the teacher's part. Alternatively the child may develop an exaggerated fondness for a teacher, and become too eager to please, or too hurt by the slightest suggestion of criticism. More rarely, a child may feel acute physical fear of a teacher, and go in dread of his lessons and indeed of any mention of his teaching subject, and find that even the general school atmosphere becomes a source of disturbance and anxiety to him.

Whatever their cause, emotional problems can become a major hindrance to learning, and if allowed to go untreated can lead to a syndrome in which the child and his teachers become increasingly alienated from each other. The child's parents, disappointed by his lack of progress in school, may unwittingly make matters worse by bringing pressure upon him to work harder, thus leaving the child with the feeling that no one understands his difficulties nor takes an interest in helping him to solve them. Thus what perhaps started out as only a minor problem, which could readily have been solved given the appropriate action on the part of those concerned, becomes a major crisis which perhaps permanently affects the child's chances of making a success of his school career.

Helping the retarded child

Having diagnosed the reasons for a child's retardation, the teacher is part way towards providing the solutions. Usually allowance can readily be made for physical problems, with the child being referred to the relevant medical authorities, moved nearer to the board, given extra time to complete his work or extra help to catch up with what he has missed and so on. Frequent changes of school and/or of class teachers can also be made good with appropriate remedial assistance and encouragement. Where the problem is environmental the teacher cannot, as we saw in chapters 1 and 2, put things right on his own. What he can do, however, is to convince the child that the school is there to help him. Even if the child appears to reject this help, it is nevertheless important to his self-esteem to know that the school considers him worth bothering about, and is anxious not to make his life any more difficult. A child who feels at odds with both home and school is likely to develop rapidly into the maladjusted category (see chapter 15), and present extreme behaviour disorders in addition to his retardation.

Where the teacher suspects that his own behaviour may in part be the cause of slow learning in one or more members of his class (and there is no need to feel shame on this score; we cannot expect to be perfect all the time any more than we can expect this of the child) it is a useful exercise to tape-record all or part of a lesson or, better still, videotape it if this is possible. By studying the tape the teacher may be surprised to hear how complex (or unstimulating or confused) some of his questions to the class are, or how little he gives praise or encouragement to certain members of it, or how many irritating little mannerisms he has developed or is developing. We will look more closely at these matters in chapter 13, but the point we are stressing here is that the more the teacher knows about what is actually going on between him and the individual members of his class (as opposed to what merely seems to be going on), the better will he be able to assess his own role in slow learning, and take steps to remedy it where these are seen to be necessary.

Finally, at no point should slow learning be seen exclusively as the child's own problem. It is the school's problem, and all associated with the child are equally involved. If the child fails to respond to help, then questions must be asked as to whether this is after all the most appropriate kind of help, whether causal factors have been correctly identified, whether the child himself perceives the help in the same light as do his teachers (he may, for example, see any extra work he has been given as a punishment rather than as a learning aid, perhaps because the motives behind it were not correctly explained or because it was handed out in an unsympathetic way), and perhaps even whether other children are playing the constructive role that they should. Slow learning is, as we have said, the school's problem, and that means classmates as well as teachers. Have these classmates been helped to understand the slow learner's problems? Have they been shown how they can offer assistance? Have they been taught, through the value systems operating throughout the school and through the example set by the staff, that it is the job of everyone to offer sympathy and help to those less well off than oneself? The school is there to enable slow learners to become quick learners, and this means a constant reappraisal by staff of the methods they use and the values they uphold.

Additional reading

Furneaux, B. (1973) The Special Child. Harmondsworth: Penguin.
    A deservedly popular short introduction to the whole question of the special child and his problems.

Laing, A.F. and Chazan, M. (1978) Educational handicap. In D. Fontana (ed.), The Education of the Young Child. London: Open Books.
    Deals more specifically with the young child, but is also well worthy of study.

Gulliford, R. (1971) Special Education Needs. London: Routledge & Kegan Paul.
    Another excellent general text.

Francis-Williams, J. (1970) Children with Specific Learning Difficulties. Oxford: Pergamon Press.

Kirman, B.H. (1968) Mental Retardation. Oxford: Pergamon Press.
    Two more very good general texts.

Brennan, W.K. (1974) Shaping the Education of Slow Learners. London: Routledge & Kegan Paul.

Chazan, M. (ed.) (1973) Compensatory Education. London: Butterworth.
    Both of these are more specifically geared to the task of the specialist teacher of slow learners.

Shakespeare, R. (1975) The Psychology of Handicap. London: Methuen.
    Gives a more general examination of the whole question of handicap.

Mittler, P. (ed.) (1970) Psychological Assessment of Mental and Physical Handicap. London: Methuen.
    Strongly recommended for those interested in finding out how levels of handicap are assessed.

Part three

Affective Factors

The term 'affective', strictly speaking, applies to the
emotional factors associated with human behaviour, but is
generally taken to refer more broadly to all those elements
which go to make up personality. Personality can be
defined as the relatively stable and persisting characteristics of a person's non-cognitive psychological life. As
such, it covers his attitudes and value systems, his
emotions and feelings, his ambitions and aspirations, and
his complexes and self-regard. It takes in both conscious
and unconscious elements, and incorporates many of the
things that help define people as individuals.

At this point the reader may argue that the distinction
between cognitive and affective factors is surely an artificial one, since thinking (cognition) must enter into many
of the things we have just listed. There is some force in
this argument, since obviously we cannot disregard the
individual's patterns of thinking - or allied factors such
as his intelligence and powers of creativity - when we are
considering his personality. But we all know highly intelligent people who are nevertheless petulant and childish for
much of the time, or given to uncalled-for displays of
temper, or prey to all kinds of anxieties that rationally
they know are quite unjustified. Conversely, we all know
people of apparently modest measurable intelligence who
are serene and well-balanced, helpful to friends and to
strangers alike, philosophical and realistic in the face of
problems. Similarly, if we turn to value systems, we all
know intelligent folk who are devious and vindictive, who
use their cognitive abilities to deceive and beguile others,
and who delight in scoring off those they consider inferior
to themselves. By the same token we know people of much
lesser intelligence who are honest and courageous, and who
speak ill of no one.

I could develop these examples further by pointing to
highly creative individuals whose gifts are expressed in a
form indicative of internal turmoil and anguish, and to
others whose works of art bring tranquillity and delight to
the onlooker, but the point being made should already be
clear. Affective factors interact with, and are modified by,
cognitive factors, but the two nevertheless have a functional independence. We cannot take the measure of a man

or a woman by simply looking at their results on cognitive tests, however good these tests are for their own purposes.

Within formal education the main emphasis has been upon cognitive factors though, as was indicated in the last chapter, the child's emotional state (together with other personality variables) may have a profound effect upon his school performance. Within the last few years psychologists have been urging that this fact be recognized, and that teaching strategies be adapted to the child's personality as well as to his cognitive abilities. In the chapter that follows Kline goes into detail concerning the ways in which psychologists go about the measurement of personality, since an understanding of the techniques of measurement is essential if the teacher is to be in a position to assess the practical value of personality research in the classroom. Kline then looks at descriptions of personality and at theories of personality: that is, at the models advanced by psychologists to explain how personality develops and influences the individual's behaviour.

9

Personality
P. Kline

Personality tests

Personality tests can be divided into tests of temperament and mood. Temperament tests measure how we do what we do, and temperamental traits are usually thought of as enduring and stable, such as dominance or anxiety. Dynamic traits are concerned with motives: for instance, why we do what we do, and include drives such as sexuality or pugnacity. Moods refer to those fluctuating states that we all experience in our lives: anger, fatigue or fear. Let us now look at each of these three categories in turn, and discuss how the psychologist attempts to measure them.

Temperament tests

The most used type of temperament test is the personality questionnaire. This consists of lists of items concerned with the subject's behaviour. Typical items are: 'Do you enjoy watching boxing?', 'Do you hesitate before spending a large sum of money?' Items come in various formats. Those above would usually require subjects to respond 'Yes' or 'No'; or 'Yes', 'Uncertain' or 'No'. Sometimes items are of the forced choice variety. For example, 'Do you prefer: (i) watching boxing; (ii) going to a musical; or (iii) sitting quietly at home reading?'

CONSTRUCTION OF PERSONALITY QUESTIONNAIRES: the reader may wonder how personality questionnaires are constructed and how the various kinds of item are chosen. Accordingly, the selection of items by what is called 'item analysis' is briefly described because this gives an insight into the effectiveness of personality questionnaires.

* Item writing: in the first place, items will be written which are face valid, that is, they appear to be relevant to the variable which we are trying to measure. For example, if we were attempting to measure anxiety we should include items that seemed to touch on the symptoms and feelings of anxiety both as we experience it and as we have found it delineated in the literature, such as finding it difficult to get to sleep, worrying over things one has done, feeling miserable for no good reason, having palpitations, poor appetite, and so on.

* Item analysis: in the construction of tests, the item analysis by which items are selected for a test is the critical issue. The rationale of item analysis is simple: if we are trying to measure a variable (say anxiety) then each selected item should be shown to measure anxiety. Furthermore, if the test is to be discriminating, then each item should be answered in one way (yes or no) by not more than about 80 per cent of the sample. Obviously, our sample for item trials should be drawn from the population for whom the test is intended. Item analysis therefore requires a statistical procedure which will establish that each item measures a common variable, and that each item is discriminating. Three possible procedures are used: (i) factor analysis: the items are correlated and the correlations are then subjected to factor analysis. Items loading on a general factor (unless we are constructing several scales at once) are selected. This method automatically eliminates items of low discrimination, since they will not load up properly. The items are then tried out again on a new sample to eliminate those loading by chance in the first item trial. (ii) Correlations of item and total score: a more simple method and one with less technical problems than factor analysis is to correlate each item with the total score for each scale separately. Items are chosen which correlate beyond 0.3. The endorsement rate for each item is also checked and any items of poor discriminatory power are removed. Finally, all results are checked on a new sample. Results from this method are similar to method one. (iii) Criterion-keying: here the items are administered to criterion groups and those items that can discriminate between the groups are selected. The problem here is to establish sufficiently clear criterion groups to make the technique robust. Thus an anxiety scale might be given to a group of anxious patients and a control non-anxious group. In addition, if the groups differ on more than one variable - if, for example, anxiety is confounded with intelligence - the resulting scale could be heterogeneous. Thus this method is not, in our view, as powerful as methods one and two.
* Validation of the scale: finally, the scale produced by the item analysis must be validated.

These methods are used in the construction of all psychometric tests which contain items (therefore excluding projective tests: see below), not only personality questionnaires. Method one was used to construct Cattell's 16PF personality questionnaire, method two for our own Ai3Q, a far less well-known test than the former, and method three was used to construct the MMPI (the Minnesota Multiphasic Personality Inventory).

The disadvantages of questionnaires are considerable, in spite of the fact that many valid and highly useful personality questionnaires have been constructed. These disadvantages are: (i) they are easy to fake; that is, subjects may not tell the truth for one reason or another, and this makes them difficult to use in selection, although for vocational guidance or psychiatric help where subjects have no reason to fake this is not too serious; (ii) they require a degree of self-knowledge, and some subjects (while attempting to be honest) may respond quite unrealistically; (iii) they are subject to response sets, such as the social desirability set, that is, the tendency to endorse the socially desirable response and to present oneself in what one considers to be the most favourable light. For example, to the item, 'Do you have a good sense of humour?', the response 'Yes' would be given by about 95 per cent of subjects. The other serious response set is that of acquiescence, the tendency to put 'Yes' or 'Agree' as an answer regardless of content. Balanced scales, with some responses keyed 'No', obviate this to some extent.

OBJECTIVE TESTS: these, defined by Cattell (cf. Cattell and Kline, 1977) as tests of which the purpose is hidden from the subject and which can be objectively scored, have been developed to overcome the disadvantages of questionnaires. The aim is to reduce the possibility of faking response sets or acquiescence though the reader might wish to challenge their face validity. Ironically, because their purpose is hidden from subjects, considerable research is necessary to establish their validity, and as yet most are still in an experimental form. These tests will probably take over from questionnaires when the necessary research has been done. The following examples indicate their nature.

* Balloon-blowing: subjects are required to inflate a balloon as much as they can. Measures taken are the size of the balloon, time taken blowing it up, whether they burst it, and if they delay in beginning the task. This test may be related to timidity and inhibition.
* The slow line-drawing test: subjects are required to draw a line as slowly as possible. The measure is the length of line over a fixed time.

In fact more than 800 such tests have been listed and more can easily be developed depending upon the ingenuity of the researcher. The technique is to administer a large battery of such tests, and to determine experimentally by so-called 'validity studies' what each of them measures.

PROJECTIVE TESTS: these tests essentially consist of ambiguous stimuli to which the subjects have to respond. They include some of the oldest personality tests and one, the Rorschach Test (the so-called 'inkblot' test), has achieved a fame beyond psychology. The rationale of projective tests is intuitively brilliant: if a stimulus is so vague that it warrants no particular description, then any description of it must depend on what is projected on to it by the subject. Projective testers believe that projective tests measure the inner needs and fantasies of their subjects. Their ambiguity disarms the subject, thus enabling the tester to sidestep the latter's defences, or his desire to please or to fake.

A serious problem with projective tests lies in their unreliability, however. Very complex responses have to be interpreted by scorers, and often considerable training, experience and expertise is necessary. Inter-marker reliability is low. Generally, too, it is difficult to demonstrate test validity. However, the present writer has experimented with entirely objective forms of scoring these tests and some evidence has now accrued that this is a useful procedure.

PROJECTIVE TEST STIMULI: although any ambiguous stimulus could be used as a test, generally the choice of stimulus is determined by the particular theory of personality the test constructor follows. For example, a psychoanalytically orientated psychologist would select stimuli relevant to that theory, such as vague figures who could be mother and son (the Oedipus complex) or figures with knives or scissors (the castration complex). The TAT (Thematic Apperception Test) developed by Murray uses pictures which, it is hoped, tap the inner needs held by Murray to be paramount in human behaviour.

Mood and motivation tests
Mood and motivation tests are essentially similar to temperament tests, but relatively little work has been done on them and their validity is not so widely attested as that of temperament tests.

Mood tests generally use items that concentrate, as might be expected, on present feelings rather than on usual ones. With such tests, high test-retest reliability is therefore not to be expected. However, fluctuations in scores should not be random but should be related to external conditions. Thus experiments can be conducted in which scores, if the tests are valid, can be manipulated. For example, subjects can take the mood test and then some can be angered, others sexually aroused, and the tests can be retaken. If the experimental manipulations are good and the tests valid, the relevant scores should change in response to these changes in mood.

The results of motivation tests should be similarly fluctuating, according to whether drives are sated or frustrated. In a well-known study by the present author the scores of a single subject over a 28-day period were related to a diary recording all that happened to her and everything she felt or thought, and it was found that the relations of scores to diary events were close. For example, the fear drive rose each weekend, when the subject went touring in a dangerous car. The career drive was flat except on the day when the subject was interviewed for a course in teacher training, and so on.

Motivation tests can be of the questionnaire variety, although objective and projective tests are more frequently used. For moods, questionnaire tests are more usually employed, though they suffer, of course, from the same response sets as bedevil questionnaire measures of temperamental traits.

Interest tests

The tests of motivation described above are very general: that is, they measure variables thought to account for a wide variety of human behaviour. Vocational and industrial psychologists, however, have long felt the need for more specific measures of motivation which assess the variables deemed to be of immediate relevance to them, such as interests. For example, we all know of motoring enthusiasts whose interest in cars also appears to account for much of their behaviour and conversation.

Thus a number of interest tests have been developed which attempt to assess the individual's major interests: outdoor, mechanical, or an interest in people for example. In some tests, the scoring of items is in terms of occupational groups. The performance of specific occupational groups on the tests is known and if, for example, foresters score high on a particular item then this item contributes to the 'interest in forestry' score. In other tests, the scoring involves little more than subjects having to rank jobs. In other words, interest tests of this type are like formalized interviews.

Generally, as has been pointed out in Buros (1972), the correlations of interest test scores with success in a job relevant to the interests are modest and little better than the correlation obtained between job success and the subject's response to the question of whether he thinks he would enjoy the job or not.

Attitude tests

Social psychologists have attempted to measure attitudes for many years now. Generally, the attitudes tested are important aspects of a person's life, such as attitudes to war, or to coloured people (in white populations) or to religion. Obviously, if efficient measures of such attitudes are possible then progress can be made in understanding how such attitudes arise and are maintained; important knowledge, it is thought, in a complex multi-racial society. There are three kinds of attitude test, differing in their mode of construction.

*   THE THURSTONE SCALES: in these tests proposed items are given to judges to rank 1-11 (favourable-unfavourable) in respect of an attitude. Items on which there is good agreement among the judges are then retained. The subject taking the test receives the score

assigned to the strongest item with which he agrees, and we can disregard his other responses. The reason we can do so is made clear if we consider a few examples. (1) 'War is totally evil' would probably be ranked high as unfavourable to war. (2) 'Wars sometimes have to be fought if there is no alternative': this is clearly against war but not strongly. (3) 'Wars are not always wrong': this is yet further down the scale, while the item (4) 'Wars are good: they select the finest nations' is favourable. Thus a subject who agreed with (1) would not agree with (2), (3) or (4). Similarly, a subject agreeing with (3) would not agree with (4).

These tests are difficult to construct because much depends on obtaining a good cross-section of judges. A more simple alternative is the Likert Scale.

* LIKERT SCALES: in the Likert scales statements relevant to the attitude being measured are presented to the subject who has to state on a five-point scale the extent of his agreement. Thus 'a Hitler' would score 100 on a 20-item attitude to war scale; 'a Ghandi' would score zero, one presumes. To make the scale less obvious, items are so written that to agree with items represents both poles of the attitude.

* THE GUTTMAN SCALE: this is a scale so constructed that if the items are ranked for positive attitudes, then any subject who endorses item 10 will also endorse items 1-9 below it. While this tends to happen by virtue of its similarity to the Thurstone scale, such perfect ordering rarely occurs in practice. Guttman scales are not much used because they are extremely difficult to construct, and as Nunnally (1978) has pointed out, this perfect ordering of items can usually only be achieved by leaving huge gaps between the items (in terms of attitude) which means few items and rather coarse measurement.

The factorial description of personality

Personality questionnaires have been subjected, over the years, to factor analyses in the hope of discovering what are the basic temperamental dimensions. The main researchers in this area have been Cattell (working in Illinois), Eysenck (in London) and Guilford (in California). Although superficially each has produced what looks like a separate set of factors, recent research in this field has enabled some sort of consensus to be arrived at (see Cattell and Kline, 1977; Kline, 1979, for a full discussion of this work). In effect, we now seem to have established the main dimensions of personality. These dimensions are therefore those that demand study, and they are accordingly outlined below.

Extraversion
The high-scoring extravert is sociable, cheerful, talkative, and does not like to be alone. He enjoys excitement, takes

risks and is generally impulsive, and an outgoing optimist, active and lively. The introvert is the opposite of this: cold, retiring and aloof. This dimension has been related by Eysenck to the arousability of the central nervous system, and scores on tests of this factor have a large genetic component.

Neuroticism (or anxiety)

The highly anxious subject is one who worries a lot, is moody and often depressed. He is highly emotional and takes a long time to calm down. He tends to sleep poorly and to suffer from psychosomatic disorders. This variable is claimed to be related to the lability of the autonomic nervous system.

These variables are both measured by the Cattell 16PF test and Eysenck's EPQ (the most recent version of the Eysenck personality tests). If we know an individual's status on these two factors, then already we know a good deal about his temperament.

Psychoticism (P)

This variable has not been as extensively studied as extraversion and anxiety and only recently (1975) has it appeared in a published questionnaire, the EPQ. Nevertheless, the nature of psychoticism is clear. The high scorer on this dimension is solitary, uncaring of people, troublesome, lacking in human feeling and empathy, thick skinned and insensitive. He is cruel, inhumane, hostile and aggressive, reckless to danger, aggressive even to his own family. Naturally enough, most normal individuals score low on P, but many criminals score high. This factor has been related by Eysenck to 'maleness' because it seems to embody extreme examples of 'tough-minded' male characteristics.

Of course, this factorial analysis of personality is essentially a theory of personality postulating that these three factors, physiologically and largely genetically determined, account for most of the differences in behaviour between individuals. It is interesting, therefore, to contrast this theory, which is closely based upon measurement, with some earlier theories of personality based on clinical observation and inference.

Psychoanalytic theories and theories of personality

Perhaps the most famous theory of personality is the classical psychoanalytic theory of Freud. Freud was a psychiatrist working in Vienna from the turn of the century to just before the outbreak of the Second World War. Eysenck has attacked psychoanalysis because it lacks quantification, is hard to verify and is not, in his view, highly successful as a therapy. Against this one must bear in mind the fact that it has attracted intelligent men all over the world because of its ability to throw light on a diverse array of human behaviours, such as motivation, painting, scientific

endeavour, literary production, dreams and neuroses. Our
brief description can do little justice to Freud's 24
volumes of collected papers.

Data base

The data on which psychoanalytic theory is based are the
free associations of patients and in particular their free
association to dreams (Freud called the dream the 'royal
road to the unconscious'). Free association is the process
by which the subject is requested to say whatever comes into
his head, regardless of its nature, taking as his starting
point either a word presented to him by the psychoanalyst or
an event (or character or object) from one of his dreams.
The idea is that in the course of his rambling free association he will reveal clues to the material down in his
unconscious mind.

The unconscious

A critical feature of Freudian theory is the emphasis placed
upon unconscious mental activity, which is held to be highly
important in determining behaviour. Unconscious mental activity (termed by Freud primary mental processes) is chaotic,
illogical and bizarre, demanding immediate satisfaction of
the drives and needs within the unconscious. Only by understanding the unconscious can we therefore understand personality. Freud distinguished the unconscious from what he
called the 'preconscious', which is that part of our mental
life which contains all our thoughts and memories that are
not currently conscious but that are not subject to
repression and can be recalled at will.

The mind

In psychoanalytic theory the mind is divided into three
parts. The id, unconscious, is the repository of basic
drives, sex and aggression, and what has been repressed into
it. The id is the source of mental energy, demanding immediate expression. This, however, in modern society cannot
be permitted. To kill and copulate at whim leads only to
prison. The id is controlled, therefore, by two other mental
provinces, namely the ego, developed by identification with
the same sex parent and the repository of our conscious life
and moral values (these being those of our parents as seen
at about the age of five when the super-ego develops).
Mental health depends upon the correct balance of these
three systems: too much control and the individual leads a
narrow inexpressive life. If the super-ego is too strong we
feel guilt-ridden and anxious, yet if there is too little
control we become psychopathic criminals. The aim of
psychoanalytic therapy is to make man as rational as possible. As Freud puts it, where id was, there shall ego be.

The ego maintains control by the use of mechanisms of
defence, which satisfy the conflicting demands of id and
super-ego and which are unconscious. The system of defences
we use profoundly affects our behaviour.

Successful defences (sublimation) allow expression of the instinctual, forbidden id drive: unsuccessful defences simply prevent its expression. This is important because in Freudian theory an instinctually barred expression still demands outlet. Hence unsuccessful defences have to be used over and over again, as the id drive persists in seeking expression, and this is the basis of the tension and weariness of neurotic illness.

Defence mechanisms

1. SUCCESSFUL DEFENCES utilize what Freud called sublimation, which involves the deflection of instinctual drives so that they are expressed in a manner acceptable to the ego. For example, in Freudian theory anal drives, the desire to smear and handle faeces, are sublimated in the exercises of painting and pottery-making. Children's love of playing in mud and puddles is another example of such sublimation.

If drives are blocked, the energy remains in the system and demands different outlets. Sublimation is important because it allows the expression of otherwise forbidden drives. Indeed, Freud (1933) regarded sublimation as the cornerstone of civilized life: the arts, the sciences, all are sublimations of sexuality. Free expression of the id, sexuality and aggression is the road to barbarism.

2. UNSUCCESSFUL DEFENCES

* Repression: one of the most important mechanisms of defence. There are two phases in repression: primal repression, where the ego denies the instinct entry into consciousness, and repression proper, where the instinct and all connected with it are kept out of consciousness. The energy still remains in the system and is expressed as anxiety. Thus repression is critical in the development of neurosis. It is, of course, unconscious.
* Denial: this is similar to repression, except that here the ego wards off the external world by altering perception. Denial of age is a common example: the middle-aged paunch crammed into tight jeans, combined with an Afro hair-cut and cowboy boots.
* Projection: here unacceptable impulses are attributed to others. A woman's neurotic fear of sexual attack may result from her projection of her own sexual drive and may even lead to agoraphobia.
* Reaction-formation: the feelings in the conscious are the opposite of those in the unconscious. Thus love becomes hate, while shame, disgust and moralizing are reaction-formations against sexuality. The delusions of persecution found in paranoia are in Freudian theory attributed to reaction-formation against homosexuality. Thus, 'I love him' becomes 'I hate him', which becomes, by projection, 'he hates me'.

* Regression: to avoid conflict, people resort to earlier
  modes of behaviour. Thus the person regresses to earlier
  modes of responding which were appropriate then, but not
  in the present. The ego cannot solve the conflicts created by the need to develop new responses appropriate
  to present circumstances.
* Isolation: here feelings and emotions are separated from
  the experiences which normally produce them: for example, the man who can only have sexual relations with
  women he despises, and who isolates love from sex.
* Undoing: here an action 'undoes' an imaginary or real
  action. For example, the obsessional who washes everything he touches because he feels, being himself dirty,
  that he has made them dirty.

From this, the importance of defence mechanisms in understanding personality must be obvious. The quality of the
dynamic balance depends upon the strategy of our defences.
However, another aspect of psychoanalytic theory relevant
to personality is Freudian psychosexual developmental theory
and this is described below. As we shall see, it is in this
that the importance of the first five years is emphasized.

Psychosexual development

'Sexual life does not begin at puberty, but starts with
plain manifestations soon after birth' (Freud, 1940). Indeed
Freud described the infant, to the outrage of his
contemporaries, as a 'polymorphous pervert'. This is
because, as Freud (1940) continued, 'sexual life includes
the function of obtaining pleasure from zones of the body –
a function which is subsequently brought into the service of
reproduction'. The infant derives pleasure initially from
the stimulation of any part of the body, and this pleasure
is sexual: hence the term 'polymorphous pervert', for Freud
defined any sexual activity which does not have reproduction
as its aim as a perversion.

* The oral stage: very soon in the infant's life the
  sexual drive begins to manifest itself through the
  mouth, which becomes the principal erotogenic zone.
  There is an oral-erotic phase, sucking, and an oral-
  sadistic phase, biting. The erotogenic pleasure is known
  as oral eroticism.
* The anal stage: at about two years of age, the anus
  becomes the most important erotogenic zone. Anal erotism
  also has two phases: there is pleasure in expelling
  faeces (anal-expulsive) and later in retention (anal-
  retentive).
* The phallic stage: around the age of four the penis and
  clitoris become the chief erotogenic zones; this is
  phallic erotism. Then, after the Oedipus and castration
  complexes (see below), the child enters the latency
  period, during which he usually experiences less sexual
  conflict, until the final stage of sexual organization
  is established at puberty.

*   The mature genital stage: here previous stages are reorganized and subordinated to the adult sexual aim of reproduction.

The Oedipus complex

Freud regarded the Oedipus complex not only as his greatest discovery but as one of man's greatest discoveries. It explains how, in spite of our instincts, we become law-abiding citizens, strive for perfection, and develop a conscience. Every male child is fated to pass through the Oedipus complex. At the phallic stage the boy becomes his mother's lover; he desires to possess her physically, to assume his father's place: his father becomes a rival.

However, the Oedipus complex is 'doomed to a terrible end'. It is repressed through fear of castration - a punishment for infantile masturbation - which the boy imagines will be inflicted on him by his powerful rival, his father. The result of this is that the boy identifies with his father (through fear of castration), and thus the super-ego is born. Since the child cannot have his mother sexually (as the id wishes), he adopts the compromise of vicarious pleasure through identifying with his father. This identification involves not only sexual pleasure but subsequently the father's ideas and beliefs. Thus the cultural values of our generation are passed on to the next. Clearly, these complexes are critical for the development of the male personality.

Penis envy

For the girl, however, there is a different process. At the phallic phase she suffers from penis envy: inferiority feelings about the clitoris vis-à-vis the penis. She then turns against her mother who, she feels, has castrated her; in her mother's place she puts her father as an object of love. Thus the Electra complex begins. Oedipal attitudes are more likely to remain in women, as there is no castration complex to end them. It is through fear of losing love that the girl identifies with the same sex parent and develops the super-ego which, according to Freud, is likely to be less strongly developed in women. It follows that women are less idealistic and less troubled by conscience.

Psychosexual theory and personality

Two facts contribute to the importance of psychosexual theory in understanding personality.

*   Pregenital erotism cannot all be directly expressed. Thus defence mechanisms have to be used, producing other apparently unrelated behaviours. For example, direct expression of anal erotism (sodomy) is actually illegal in Britain, though direct expression of oral erotism is allowed, as in connoisseurs of food and specialists in oral sex. Permanent character traits, according to Freud, are either unchanged expressions of these original instincts or defences against them. Defences

against oral erotism are the oral traits of dependency, talkativeness and optimism. Defences against anality embrace the famous anal character of parsimony, perseverance, obstinacy and orderliness. Parsimony is a sublimation of the desire to retain the faeces, orderliness a reaction-formation against the desire to smear them.

* Fixation at the pregenital level: we may become fixated at a particular level, as a result of being over-indulged or not sufficiently indulged during the relevant stage of infancy. Thus fixation at the oral level can be caused by sudden weaning or indulgent demand feeding. Similarly, different kinds of toilet training can cause fixation at the anal level. Fixation implies that undue importance is attached to a particular developmental phase. Fixation is also partly determined by constitutional factors, such as the sensitivity to stimulation of the particular erotogenic zone. This, of course, interacts with the environmental variables discussed above.

* The Oedipus complex: this is regarded as the kernel of neurosis. For Freud, true maturation involves breaking away from the parents. In the neurotic this is never done. The unconscious conflict that results affects our lives in ways of which we are unaware. Attitudes to women (do we like women like our mother?), attitudes to employers and superiors and attitudes to authority itself (rivalry of father) are all examples of this. The castration complex, too, is also powerful. This may be reflected in attitudes to vivisection, to surgery, to blood itself. Homosexuals in psychoanalytic theory are held to have the castration complex. Their homosexuality stems from their inability to face penisless beings or beings that bleed from their private parts (i.e. women).

This brief account of psychoanalytic personality theory makes clear its complexity in that it can account for a huge variety of behaviours. However, it does so with a surprisingly small number of concepts.

Objections to Freudian theory
We have already mentioned the objections on scientific grounds to psychoanalysis, objections most widely broadcast by Eysenck. These include:

* the lack of clear raw data;
* the poor sampling: the patients under Freud's care were clearly not samples of all mankind;
* the lack of statistical analysis;
* the ambiguity and vagueness of the concepts;
* the difficulty of falsifying the theory;
* the failure of the therapy to show itself efficacious.

Even if all these objections are admitted, does this

inevitably mean that Freudian theory should be abandoned as worthless?

The scientific study of psychoanalytic theory

A previous work (Kline, 1972) has dealt extensively with this problem. The essence of the case that psychoanalytic theory has some scientific validity and is deserving of further investigation is set out below.

* Psychoanalytic theory can be broken down into sets of testable hypotheses. In this sense, Freudian theory is a collection of theories as has been claimed.
* When this is done and the theories are put to a scientific test, using proper samples, validated tests and adequate statistics, certain of the psychoanalytic propositions can be shown to hold. For example (see Kline, 1972), there is reasonable evidence for repression and the Oedipus complex, and we can say in summary that much of Freudian theory has received some objective support and it would be flying in the face of the evidence to reject it out of hand.

Other psychoanalytic theories

Of course, over the years there has developed a large number of variants of Freudian theory, the work of Jung, Adler, Fromm, Horney, Sullivan and Melanie Klein being amongst the most well known. In general, these theories have differed from those of Freud in their lesser emphasis on sexuality. For Adler the great drive was the aim of achieving superiority (hence his use of the term 'inferiority complex'). For Jung the profoundest aspects of the mind were the contents of the collective unconscious, the accumulated wisdom of the ages. While Freud believed that mental health lay in controlling the instincts of the id, Jung believed that only by allowing oneself proper contact with the collective unconscious could one develop one's full potential.

Other theories of personality

Psychoanalytic theories, especially those of Jung and Freud, have had enormous effects on the Zeitgeist; their ripples have spread far beyond the confines of psychology. For this reason alone psychoanalytic theory deserves critical scrutiny.

However, there are many other personality theorists whose work, even if influenced by dynamic theories, can in no way be called psychoanalytic. To summarize these briefly and with justice is hardly possible. However, many of these theories are old, so that a brief acquaintance is perhaps all that is necessary. More recently theories of personality have been eschewed because the field is so large. The age of grand theorizing is gone. Indeed, the nearest thing to a coherent modern personality theory is in fact the factor-analytic work of Eysenck and Cattell, which we have already

discussed. To conclude this brief account of theories of
personality, let us simply select a few items from various
different theories to illustrate the range and scope.

The work of McDougall

McDougall, a psychologist not now held in high repute,
claimed that the mainsprings of human activity lay in a
number of native propensities and of sentiments within which
these propensities are organized. McDougall (1932) listed
18 propensities among which were food seeking, rejecting
noxious substances, sexual propensities, fear, exploratory
drive, protective and gregarious propensities, to name but
seven. However, McDougall regarded one sentiment as all
important, namely the self-image, the master sentiment
around which much of what we do revolves. Other sentiments
are (for example money-seeking, job-seeking and so on)
cultural avenues for expressing the basic propensities.

This kind of psychologizing is mainly of historical
interest (i) because it is speculative rather than empirical
and (ii) because the very concept of propensity is circular:
that is, we observe a behaviour, such as food seeking,
explain it by hypothesizing a food-seeking propensity and
then use the behaviour which it seeks to explain as confirmation of the hypothesis. However, we mention it because
recent factor-analytic work by Cattell in Illinois (see
Cattell and Kline, 1977) gives some support for there being
a number of basic propensities and sentiments, although by
no means as many as McDougall claimed. It could be the case
that McDougall will become more highly esteemed as more
empirical work is carried out. McDougall's theory suffered
neglect because of a distaste among psychologists, which
lasted from the Second World War until quite recently, for
any theory which was based on the notion of inborn
propensities or instincts.

The work of Murray

Murray was another important personality theorist who, in
'Explorations in Personality' (1938), attempted to develop a
new subject called 'Personology'. His work was based on the
analysis of interviews, biographies, projective and experimental tests and involved brilliant clinical intuition from
a huge amount of data from each subject. He postulated a
large number of needs to account for human behaviour, together with corresponding environmental presses. Although
the factor analysis of motivation has not supported his list
of needs (which included to abase, to affiliate, to achieve,
to be aggressive, to be different), it seems likely that
Murray was looking at surface clusters of behaviours rather
than the larger more basic factors of factor analysis. One
of his drives, nAch, the need to achieve, has been extensively studied by McClelland and colleagues and does seem an
important determinant of entrepreneurial performance at
least. Murray's work is valuable because it lays stress on
the importance of studying the whole person in all his

aspects, yet not to the extent that generalizable laws of behaviour cannot be formulated. This is a good counter-balance against large-scale statistical studies where the unique individual can be lost.

Physique and personality

Two researchers, Kretschmer (1925) and Sheldon (Sheldon and Stevens, 1942) have claimed that physique is related to temperament. Kretschmer observed from his clinical work that schizophrenics tend to be thin, and manic depressives fat, extreme examples, in his view, of tendencies in the normal population that moody individuals are likely to be rotund, and aloof, withdrawn people of slender build.

Sheldon in his work on physique and character attempted to classify body build into three dimensions, each on a seven-point scale. Most individuals are high on one of these dimensions which are measured precisely from different parts of the body. A cluster analysis (a simple form of factor analysis) of ratings of temperament carried out by Sheldon showed a close relationship between body build and charac-ter, findings which have, however, been challenged on grounds of computing error (not that uncommon in large-scale correlational studies calculated by hand). The results were in accord with common sense and literary stereotypes. The fat individual was of Falstaffian temperament, the muscular rugby-playing type was pushy and insensitive, and the thin ectomorph cold and withdrawn.

Modern studies conducted by Eysenck and colleagues at the Maudsley, and by Cattell and co-workers at Illinois, give only modest confirmation of this physique-personality link. Nevertheless, it is research that has been largely neglected, perhaps surprisingly, and large-scale investi-gations of Sheldon's typology relating it to the main personality dimensions might prove useful.

In all these theories which we have so far mentioned it must be noted that there are common problems. These relate to the proper quantification of temperament and dynamics, in that none of these researchers had personality tests of proven validity and reliability.

Finally, the approach of two other psychologists must be mentioned so that psychological testing in relation to personality can be put into a different perspective. Our view, as is obvious, is that precise measurement is the 'sine qua non' of any adequate personality theory. Concomi-tant with this is our claim that factor analysis is the instrument by which good tests can be constructed and validated. This indeed is the psychometric view, the imp-licit underpinning of the work of Eysenck and Cattell.

The work of Allport

Allport (1938), however, has explicitly argued against this. He admits that statistical analyses of tests can reveal common dimensions, but he stresses the importance of the unique components of personality that each individual alone possesses, and dependent upon the experience that he alone has undergone. For Allport it is these personal data that are critical to understanding personality.

Two important points are raised here. First, if Allport were correct, a science of personality would be impossible, for each individual is essentially unique. We can, given sufficient time, understand him but this would not help us to understand anyone else. Thus no statements about regularities of behaviour can be made. The second point follows from this. If Allport were correct, it would not be possible to predict real-life behaviours from tests of personality. In fact, however, this can be done, as the extensive handbooks to the better personality inventories, the 16PF test, the EPQ and the MMPI, illustrate. Allport, therefore, must have exaggerated his argument. In any case, the existence of personality scales is not incompatible with the notion of uniqueness. In any one sample, individuals will have very different profiles across a range of scales, but this does not mean they will not share certain characteristics or groups of characteristics in common with other members of the sample.

Situationalism
Mischel (e.g. 1977) has been influential in recent personality theory to such an extent that many writers have come to abandon the notion of traits entirely, and hence to regard the measurement of personality as impossible and worthless.

Mischel attacks traits on the old behaviourist ground of redundancy. We see a man violently attacking another and say he is high on aggression, and that this aggression is causing the behaviour. While this logical argument is sound, it can be refuted empirically if in fact wide clusters of behaviour do not cohere together such that a concept of aggression can parsimoniously account for them.

His second argument is empirical. He argues that in fact there are few cross-situational similarities in behaviour. Behaviour to Mischel is situation-specific. To understand a behaviour we must examine the stimuli which elicits it.

Intuitively this is not sensible since in everyday life we do find people to be consistent. We think of A as cheerful, B as testy and so on. This is regarded by Mischel as but a halo effect, reflecting the stereotype of the observer. Thus we form a view of an individual and remember the behaviour that confirms it, forgetting what fails to fit our picture: fighting Irishmen, sad Russians, loudly-checked English gentlemen, just for example. Thus our everyday observations are set at nought.

Further, Mischel argues that the traits which raters use reflect only the categories of behaviour which raters hold, rather than any real categorization of observed behaviour, citing as evidence studies where ratings of virtually unknown subjects revealed the same factor structure as ratings of known subjects.

Finally, situationalists cite investigations where traits and ratings fail to correlate with observed criterion behaviours, thus casting doubts on the cross-situational generality of such measures.

The answer to situationalism is again an empirical one. If there is no cross-situational generality, if the responses to personality questionnaires are specific to the tests, how can it be that there are meaningful educational, clinical and occupational discriminations and correlations? These, if Mischel were correct, should not occur, yet they do and this fact alone seems to us to refute the situationalist case.

Enough has been said about theories of personality. Generally, most flounder through a lack of sound quantification and a consequent reliance on clinical impressions. Those theories that argue that common traits can never reveal the uniqueness of the individual are destroyed by the evidence, as is situationalism. The fact is that personality traits can be reliably and validly measured and these do have substantial correlations with a wide variety of external criteria. As such they should become the data base of any theory of personality.

References

Allport, G.W. (1938)
Personality: Psychological interpretation. New York: Chilton.

Buros, O.K. (1972)
VII Mental Measurements Year Book. New Jersey: Gryphon Press.

Cattell, R.B. and Kline, P. (1977)
The Scientific Analysis of Personality and Motivation. London: Academic Press.

Freud, S. (1933)
New Introductory Lectures. London: Hogarth Press & Institute of Psychoanalysis.

Freud, S. (1940)
An Outline of Psychoanalysis. London: Hogarth Press.

Kline, P. (1972)
Fact and Fantasy in Freudian Theory. London: Methuen.

Kline, P. (1979)
Psychometrics and Psychology. London: Academic Press.

Kretschmer, E. (1925)
Physique and Character. London: Methuen.

McDougall, W. (1932)
The Energies of Man. London: Methuen.

Mischel, M. (1977)
On the future of personality measurement. American Psychology, 32, 246-254.

Murray, H.A. (1938)
Explorations in Personality. New York: Oxford University Press.

Sheldon, W.H. and Stevens, S.S. (1942)
The Varieties of Temperament. New York: Harper & Row.

Questions

1. What are the main types of psychological test of personality? Give a brief description of them.
2. Compare projective and questionnaire personality tests.
3. Discuss the main types of attitude tests.
4. Outline the main arguments concerning the heritability of intelligence.
5. What are the main factors of personality?
6. Compare the work of Eysenck and Cattell on the factor analysis of personality.
7. Outline the Freudian developmental theory as applied to the first five years of life.
8. Discuss the Oedipus complex.
9. Discuss the castration complex.
10. Write an account of the Freudian theory of dreams.
11. Write an account of the Freudian theory of slips of the tongue.
12. Discuss defence mechanisms.
13. Discuss the objections to trait psychology by situationalists.
14. Compare the work of McDougall and Murray.
15. Give a simple description of factor analysis.
16. If individuals are unique, how can they be measured by tests of universal dimensions?
17. If individuals are unique, how can there be a science of personality?

Annotated reading

Cronbach, L. (1976) Essentials of Psychological Testing. Chicago: Harper & Row.
    A clear comprehensive discussion of psychological testing and tests.

Cattell, R.B. and Kline, P. (1977) The Scientific Analysis of Personality and Motivation. London: Academic Press.
    A full account of the factor analysis of personality, in which the results are related to clinical theories.

Freud, S. (1978) New Introductory Lectures. Harmondsworth: Penguin.
    A brilliantly told account of Freudian theory by the Master himself.

Hall, G.S. and Lindzey, G. (1973) Theories of Personality. New York: Wiley.
    A good summary of a variety of theories of personality.

Vernon, P.E. (1979) Intelligence, Heredity and Environment. San Francisco: Freeman.
    Another useful book on this topic.

Relevance to the
Teacher
DAVID FONTANA

In this chapter Kline has divided personality tests into
three kinds, namely tests of temperament, of mood, and of
dynamics. These refer respectively to the individual's
enduring emotional characteristics (how he does what he
does, e.g. timidly, domineeringly), to his motivational
state (why he does what he does, e.g. because of hunger,
desire for parental approval), and to his moods (the fluctuating feelings of the moment). The teacher is concerned
with test results in all three of these areas, since these
results tell him a great deal about children's behaviour and
their likely response to the challenges and issues that face
them within school. He may not actually use personality
tests with his own class, but a study of research results
allows him to make important deductions about children in
general, and then to apply these deductions where
appropriate in his work with his own class.

Of the three areas, that of temperament demands particular attention because it includes many of the stable and
persisting characteristics which, as we saw in our definition at the start of Part III, go to make up what we
generally recognize as personality. And in studying this
area, as with cognitive factors, the first question we need
to ask is to what extent can temperament be shaped by
education? Is it, in other words, fixed at birth, or is it
largely learnt in response to environmental circumstances?
Let us examine the evidence in some detail.

The origins of temperament
Many parents remark on the fact that they see identifiable
differences between their children in behaviour as early as
the first few weeks of life. One child may be a happy,
contented baby while another, though enjoying the same kind
of parental care and in apparently equally good physical
health, may be inclined to be demanding and awkward. A third
child may be much quieter than the other two, while another
may be particularly active and involved in all that goes
on. Clearly, since these characteristics are evident so
early in life, they are far more likely to be due to
inheritance than to learning, but the question is whether
they form the basis of the individual's mature personality
in later life, or whether they are simply superficial
variations in behaviour that quickly become superseded by
more enduring qualities as he begins to react with the world
around him and commences the process of learning.

A major study that has set out to answer this question
was inaugurated some years ago by the American paediatri-
cians Thomas, Chess and Birch. They took an initial sample
of 141 children at the age of 12 weeks, and with the co-
operation of parents studied them closely in their own homes
and rated them on a number of different behavioural characteristics. These included such things as activity levels,
regularity of bodily functions (e.g. feeding, sleeping,
excreting) and general disposition (e.g. cheerful, cranky).
Results (e.g. Thomas, Chess and Birch, 1970) showed that

65 per cent of the sample could be assigned at this early age to one or other of the following three groups.

* THE EASY GROUP (40 per cent of sample), characterized by regularity of bodily functions, by a high level of adaptability, by a generally friendly and positive disposition, and by a normal reaction to stimuli.
* THE DIFFICULT GROUP (10 per cent of sample), characterized by irregularity of bodily functions, by low adaptability, by negative response to new people and situations, by a general crankiness of disposition, and by an over-reaction to stimuli (i.e. they tended to fuss if everything was not quite right).
* THE SLOW-TO-WARM-UP GROUP (15 per cent of sample), characterized by low activity and adaptability levels, by an inclination to withdraw in the face of novelty of any kind, by a slight general negativity of mood, and by mild reaction to stimuli.

The children were then followed through into later childhood and adolescence, and it was found that membership of the three groups remained remarkably constant. 'Easy' children at 12 weeks tended still to be easy children at 12 years, while 'difficult' children remained difficult and those 'slow-to-warm-up' remained slow-to-warm-up. Obviously the precise aspects of behaviour studied by the researchers changed as the children grew older, but they still focussed upon the same general areas. Perhaps not surprisingly, it was found that 70 per cent of the 'difficult' group had developed distinct behaviour problems by adolescence, as opposed to only 18 per cent of the 'easy' group.

Of particular practical relevance to the teacher, it was found that when the children first started school the easy group quickly adapted to the new routine, participated cheerfully and readily in all activities, and showed the general friendliness and sociability that had been apparent in their early weeks of life. The 'difficult' and 'slow-to-warm-up' groups, on the other hand, presented more problems, often showing considerable reluctance to settle in, to make friends, and to join in the various activities.

Examining the environments in which the children were reared, the researchers found there were no significant differences between the three groups. All the parents were good parents in the sense that they provided and cared for the children well (a factor, indeed, which had been taken into account when the sample was selected), and the groups each contained similar proportions of authoritarian and permissive parents. The inescapable conclusion, therefore, was that the observed differences in temperament were due to heredity. The children, it seemed, had been given the raw material of their personalities at birth.

However, lest it be thought that environment was relatively unimportant, it was found that parents exerted a major influence on the extent to which children adapted to their temperaments. In particular, children from the 'difficult' and 'slow-to-warm-up' groups were much more successful at coping with their potentially troublesome natures if they were blessed with parents who were extra patient, consistent and objective in their manner. The 'difficult' children especially tended to become even more negative and awkward when confronted by parents who were rigid and punitive, and who met childish tantrums with outbursts of their own. 'Difficult' children, it seemed, could be taken to water but could not readily be made to drink, and the more their parents insisted the more stubborn they tended to become. It appeared they responded best to parents who were gentle but firm, who were prepared to reason and explain, and who had clear standards but preferred to enlist the child's co-operation in their attainment rather than to rely on force and punishment.

The 'slow-to-warm-up' children also benefitted from this kind of sympathetic handling. If they were pushed too precipitately into new experiences they tended to withdraw into themselves. If, on the other hand, they were left to their own devices they still showed little inclination to take part. Their best responses were forthcoming if they had parents who provided a wide range of stimuli and interests, and who relied upon encouragement and support rather than upon ultimatums. They needed, it seemed, time to adjust and have their interest aroused if they were to become involved.

Thomas, Chess and Birch do not claim that their three categories are the only possible ways of classifying temperamental factors, but their general finding that these factors exist from an early age and remain reasonably constant over the years has been supported by a number of other studies. Maccoby and Jacklin (1974), in a similar approach, have also shown that there are seemingly temperamental differences between the sexes apparent at this age, with boys tending to be more active, initiatory and aggressive than girls, and girls more watchful, attentive and vocal. As we saw in chapters 1 and 2, such differences are likely to be quickly overlaid by learnt characteristics, since even in the first months of life parents tend to show subtle differences in their behaviour towards the two sexes, but at least the greater incidence of aggression in young males seems to be partly genetic in origin, since it is observable in other primates besides man.

By the time a child starts school, of course, his early temperament will have been considerably modified by learning. The 'difficult' child (using the terminology of Thomas, Chess and Birch) who has received sympathetic handling may well show determination rather than stubbornness, while the 'slow-to-warm-up' child may show interest rather than apathy. In addition, of course, we must remember that 35 per cent of the sample studied by Thomas, Chess and Birch could not be assigned to any of the categories with any consistency, which may indicate that their temperaments were more malleable (or that a wider range of variables should have been studied in the children). But this work on temperament indicates, particularly to the teacher of very young children, that account must be taken not only of the child's home background when considering individual differences in personality but also of the child's own disposition. A child can hardly be held to blame if he finds new experiences, or joining in things, or meeting new people, or distractions in his immediate environment more disturbing and upsetting than do many of his peers, or if he finds it harder to take an active and lively interest in some of the things that are on offer. The role of the teacher is to help children adapt and adjust to the social and academic demands of the school and, like the successful parents in the Thomas, Chess and Birch sample, this may mean showing particular patience and sympathy towards certain children. The so-called 'easy' child may find life rather less of a problem than do children from the other two categories, and may appear much more receptive to what the teacher is trying to do, but it is often the children in these latter categories who have most need of the understanding, supportive adult, and who in the long run may derive most benefit from their relationship with him.

The origins of motivation and mood

Obviously one of the teacher's main tasks is to motivate children to learn, and we examined the practicalities associated with this task at some length in chapter 8. For the present, therefore, we are concerned only with the origins of the general motivational states that characterize children's personalities. We say that one child differs from another in his general levels of motivation, or that he seems to be motivated to get on well with people, or to please his teachers and parents and so on, but we need some kind of theory of motivation to tell us how all this comes about and how susceptible it is to change.

Most theories of motivation take their start with the basic survival motives with which we appear to be born. Often referred to as drives, these include such things as the desire to seek for food when hungry, for warmth when cold, for physical safety when threatened in some way, for drink when thirsty, and for sexual activity when aroused. The suggestion is that hunger, thirst, etc., set up tensions within the individual, which he seeks to relieve by appropriate action. If he did not experience tension as uncomfortable, of course, he would simply stay where he is and die. In the young baby whose activity, and therefore whose independence, is limited by physical immaturity, crying is used to attract the attention of others who then initiate tension-reducing activity for him.

This is all very well and appears to make obvious sense, but in our highly complex, artificial environment these survival drives (with the exception of sex) are rarely strong determinants of behaviour once early infancy is past, since the needs associated with them are met with routine ease. Even aggression, which also seems to be a natural survival drive, rarely needs to be given physical expression in a civilized society, and indeed is often discouraged in most of its manifestations by social mores and taboos. Thus we are faced with the conclusion that for all their obvious importance, survival drives have little direct influence upon the motivational structures that help define the personalities of older children and adults. There are also a range of important motives that appear, potentially at least, to work against survival drives, and others that have no obvious relationship to them. Examples of motives in the first category would be concern for others and for society in general, self-denial and self-sacrifice and even, in many instances, conscientiousness, honesty and sympathy. In the second category we might instance love of music and of the arts, many hobbies, and a delight in beauty and in nature generally.

Motivation and reinforcement

From our discussion of learning theories in chapter 8 it can be seen that one possible explanation of these motivational systems is that they develop in response to strong reinforcement. Thus the individual's love for a hobby, for example, might come about because the activities connected with it received generous praise and encouragement from parents when he was a child. Parental praise (and even parental attention) is, as we have seen, a potent form of reinforcement, and the child may well have found that turning to these activities was an excellent way of attracting such praise. In consequence, the activities became an established part of his behavioural repertoire, and soon produced further reinforcers unconnected with the home (e.g. teacher praise, success in competitions, the establishment of new friendships, prestige, release from boredom). Similarly, helpful actions and concern for others could also have attracted adult approval initially, and then gone on to attract wider reinforcers that serve to sustain them into adult life (e.g. the grateful thanks of recipients, the feeling that one is a significant and necessary member of the community, or the warm feeling of self-approval).

Obviously the reinforcement model can account for many motives of this kind, but it cannot account for them all. It cannot account, for example, for hobbies and enthusiasms that arise suddenly and with no apparent pre-conditions in later life. Nor can it account for acts of self-sacrifice where the tangible rewards would seem to be much less than those to be gained by acting selfishly. We can, of course, say that nevertheless there must be schedules of reinforcement to account for these behaviours if we were only able to study the individuals concerned and their life histories closely enough to discover what they are. But this is simply a statement of belief, since there is no direct evidence to show that this is the case. Hence motivation remains one of those problem areas in psychology where there is no general agreement that any one model or set of models is adequate.

Maslow's theory of motivation

An alternative and less ambitious way of approaching the subject therefore is to attempt simply to describe motivation rather than to account for it. The best known descriptive model of this kind is suggested by Maslow (e.g. 1943), and takes the form of a hierarchy going from personal needs at the bottom to intellectual ones at the top as shown below.

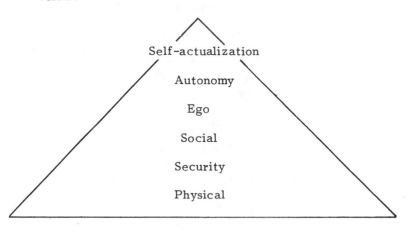

The implications are that the lower, personal levels of the hierarchy, which consist of physiological needs and needs associated with survival and security, are largely innate, while the social and intellectual levels consist of innate factors combining more and more with learnt responses. In the light of our present knowledge it is not clear how this process of combination happens, but Maslow does not rule out the possibility that innate factors may still play the more important part even at the intellectual level: that is, that the thirst for ego-strength and autonomy may be something inherent in man, and something which he will pursue even when they are not necessary for his physical or even for his social needs.

Maslow thinks that we can only attend to the three highest levels of the hierarchy, however, if the lower levels of personal and social needs have been satisfied. Thus a society living perpetually in near starvation conditions or at war with its neighbours would have little time or energy left to allow individuals to develop the creativity and wisdom associated with autonomy and self-actualization. The great upsurge in artistic endeavour noted in Europe during the Renaissance, for example, only became possible because at this point in history certain nations had advanced to the point where primary needs were reasonably easily met, and certain sections of the community had the time to divert their attention to loftier matters. Note that this does not mean that the satisfaction of primary motives will of itself lead us on to higher things, but simply that unless this satisfaction is forthcoming all of man's motivational energy goes into the simple business of keeping himself alive, with none left over for more exalted considerations.

Maslow's hierarchy therefore suggests that if the individual has his physiological needs (food, drink, shelter, etc.) satisfied, together with his need for safety from aggressors, he then becomes chiefly concerned with being accepted by his family and the social group (social needs). Once accepted, he will next concern himself with ego needs such as being well thought of in their eyes so that he may come to think well of himself. Having satisfied these ego needs, he then moves on to autonomy, that is to a sense of independence and personal freedom, and finally to self-actualization, which is a more difficult concept but one upon which Maslow lays great stress. Self-actualization means in effect that the individual develops those characteristics peculiar to mature and well-adjusted people. He becomes, for example, realistic, independent, creative, problem-centred rather than self-centred, and with a ready appreciation both of other people and of the world about him.

Locus of control

Of course, although we are each faced with this same hierarchy, some of us will climb higher up it during our lifetime than will others. We will also tend to tackle the problems associated with it in different ways. Rotter (1954) suggests that one important way in which these differences are expressed is evidenced by what he calls locus of control. This refers primarily to the way in which individuals express their successes and failures. Those with an external locus of control tend to ascribe these things to factors outside themselves (e.g. 'I did well because I had the lucky breaks', 'I failed because my teacher was no good'), while those whose locus of control is internal feel the responsibility usually lies with themselves ('I got through because of my own hard work', 'I failed because I didn't take it seriously enough'). Not surprisingly, research shows that people in the former category prefer usually to work in conditions where chance plays an important part, while people in the latter prefer circumstances where skill is the deciding factor. This does not imply that success is always more likely where the locus of control is internal. Many prestigious and lucrative occupations depend upon a high risk factor (not only sporting occupations but such things as stock-broking, starting new businesses and commercial undertakings, and being prime minister). In addition, the tendency of the internalizer to lay all his problems at his own door can lead to feelings of inadequacy and personal failure which may deter him from attempting new tasks even though they may be well within his talents. However, within the school and the educational world in general, an internal locus of control seems the more desirable. Weiner (most recently 1979), working along similar lines to Rotter, has developed what is known as attribution theory, which explores the way in which we attribute the reasons for success and failure in our personal and professional lives, and even the way in which we attribute meaning to the terms 'success' and 'failure' themselves, and has shown that the most highly motivated students are those who:

* prefer situations in which the consequences of their actions can be ascribed to themselves;
* have learnt to attribute outcome to effort;
* are sensitive and reactive to cues that indicate the importance of effort expenditure in any particular area.

In the light of present knowledge we cannot say for sure whether locus of control and the various factors associated with attribution theory are innate or acquired; probably both, but it would seem that of the two learning plays the more important part. Some children are taught by parents and teachers from an early age that it is no good putting the blame on somebody else, or complaining about bad luck when poor results are achieved. Instead, they are told, they must rely upon their own efforts, and if they meet with failure they must try extra hard to develop the skills that are lacking. Of course, blaming things on others can be a form of self-defence. If it is always somebody else's fault then we never have to face up to our own inadequacies. Children who are allowed to get away with this attitude find it a comforting one, therefore, which in itself acts as a strong reinforcer and helps to make the attitude habitual. (It is worth while pointing out that teachers who always lay the blame for classroom failure upon their children may also be exhibiting the same attitude.)

The teacher's reaction to success and failure in children
It is perhaps already clear from remarks in chapter 8 that one of the most important aspects of the teacher's role is his reaction to success and failure in children. Most teachers have few problems in recognizing and rewarding success (though they sometimes neglect the fact that success should be interpreted in terms of what the individual child can do and not merely in terms of the subject itself and the usual standards achieved in it by other children of his age), but more problems arise with failure. The point has already been emphasized very strongly indeed that making mistakes is not evidence of failure but is an integral and essential part of the learning process. By puzzling over where and how he went wrong the child learns from these mistakes, and develops strategies for dealing with them in

future. Slow learning, as has been indicated, is not failure but evidence that the child needs special kinds of help. So failure at school level, therefore, is more an attitude of mind than an objective reality. The child who develops this attitude, perhaps encouraged by teachers who give him consistently low marks and show him up in front of the class, will tend to give up and show low levels of motivation even when the work is theoretically within his grasp. If his locus of control is external he may blame his failure upon others or upon the subject itself; if it is internal he may feel it is his own fault, but the end result will be the same, with the child coming to make failure a habit. Faced with low motivation, the first question the teacher must ask therefore are what has been the child's experience of failure to date and how has this experience affected his general motivation to learn.

Mood

Turning from motivation to mood, which we can define as a state of feeling of varying duration, we find that an obvious link exists with temperament. This link, which has been confirmed by factor analysis, suggests that certain moods tend to go together in the same person. The anxious person, for example, will have a different cluster of moods from the cheerful optimistic person, the aggressive person from the serene peaceable one. It will be remembered that the 'difficult' children in the Thomas, Chess and Birch sample had a general crankiness and negativity of mood when compared with the 'easy' children, and that the 'slow-to-warm-up' children also had characteristic mood states. In part we tend to recognize people's personalities in terms of these characteristic states, and if someone is exhibiting a mood that we do not normally associate with him then we may well comment on the fact and wonder what may lie behind it.

This link between mood and temperament suggests that there may be an innate factor in the former (indeed, that body chemistry may play a part), but mood also seems to be under environmental influence. Individuals who experience happy, secure childhoods, for example, are more likely to see the world as a pleasant, optimistic place than children who come from difficult and stressful backgrounds. People who experience constant failure are more likely to show dejection and apathy than people who experience predominantly success. Children who are encouraged to discuss all their problems and feelings fully and openly with their parents, without fear of rejection, are less likely to indulge in sullen brooding than children who have always had to bottle up their feelings and keep their mouths closed. Children who are taught a humane and balanced moral code are less likely to be tortured by guilt at imagined misdemeanours than children who are brought up in an unrealistic punitive creed. At each point the child's mood is in part a response to the behaviour of people around him, and can only be understood if it is viewed within the context of this behaviour.

Moods are often thought to be at their most labile (i.e. subject to the most rapid fluctuation) at adolescence. Body chemistry again may play some part here, with the child undergoing the rapid adolescent growth spurt, and maturing in the space of some two or three short years from physical childhood to physical adulthood, with all that the latter implies in terms of bodily size and strength, sexual energy, and brain maturation. But environment is also important in that the individual often feels the restrictions that society still lays upon him are particularly irksome, and keep him in the subservient, dependent role of the child when physically he clearly belongs to the grown-up world. In addition the adolescent is, of course, trying out various new patterns of behaviour, experimenting in a sense with his personality to see how other people react to him, and to see what kind of person he really is and what kind of person he would like to become. Met with sympathy and understanding (and consistent firmness where necessary) the adolescent gradually comes to terms with his moods, and learns where self-control is preferable to self-expression. This whole phase, linked as it is to the vital question of personal identity and the development of the self, is so important that we return to it at greater length in the next chapter. Before leaving the question of moods, however, it is appropriate to point out that the teacher is himself also subject to these varying states. Some days he may feel like nothing in the world so much as tackling a lively class of children, while on other occasions there may seem to be many more desirable ways of passing the time. How the teacher feels at any given moment will depend upon a number of factors, such as his own temperament, his relationship with the children concerned and with colleagues, the way he feels about the subject to be taught, the state of his private life outside school, and so on. But sheer physical fatigue can also play an important part. Particularly towards the end of term some teachers experience what is often called a 'fatigue debt': that is, they find the tiredness of the preceding day is not fully dissipated by an evening's rest and a night's sleep, and in consequence they have to draw upon their energy reserves to keep going. At such times minor irritations which normally would pass almost unnoticed may take on major significance, and the teacher will perhaps find himself snapping at children in consequence. Far from improving matters this may only serve to irritate the children in turn, leading to further problems for the teacher and a rapidly escalating state of tension for all concerned.

The best advice that can be offered here is that the teacher should be aware of his own changing moods, and aware of the effect that these moods can have upon the class. As we have stressed already in the book, children thrive best upon consistent treatment from the important adults in their lives. Such treatment allows them increasingly to predict what is likely to happen next in their relationship with these adults, and to see their social world as an essentially lawful and understandable place. As they grow older, of course, they come to realize that a degree of fluctuation in the behaviour of those around them appears unavoidable, but there should still be sufficient consistency for them to feel secure and to learn appropriate workable strategies for managing relationships with parents and teachers and other adults in positions of authority over them. Where adults fail to show consistency of this kind children are left feeling confused and uncertain, and perhaps even resentful and hostile at what they see as the adult's inexplicable and unfair behaviour towards them.

Thus, however difficult it may seem, the teacher cannot really afford the luxury of moods that significantly alter behaviour towards individual children or towards the class as a whole. Children come to respect the teacher with whom they 'know where they stand' (one reason why even the stern, remote teacher usually commands respect), and in the long run have scant regard for anyone who fluctuates wildly from good humour to bad, from friendliness to aloofness, from sympathy to indifference, and from leniency to strictness. Provided it does not happen frequently, and therefore come to be seen by the children as a tiresome excuse, it is better for the unwell or over-fatigued teacher on a particular day to tell the class at the outset of the lesson, so that they will understand why his behaviour may be a little different from usual. Some teachers strongly condemn such a practice, and see it as a sign of weakness, but it is better that children should know and sympathize than that they should be left puzzled and hostile. Where the relationship with the class is a good one, the teacher will also be heartened at the thoughtfulness and kindness that many of the children show towards him. Needless to say, this will be particularly noticeable where the teacher himself is noted by the children as being sensitive to their problems in turn.

Interests

In addition to the above areas of personality, attention has been drawn in this chapter to interests and attitudes. It is relatively easy to test the nature and strength of both of these even in children of junior school age and below, but it is more difficult to trace their origin and to make decisions on how the teacher can best encourage the development of those deemed by society to be of most value.

If we take interests first, we have already suggested in chapter 8 that children tend to become interested in those things that help them deal with problems and difficulties in their lives because they see these as having 'relevance'. In our discussion of play (chapter 3), we also proposed that there seems to be a natural inclination towards hedonistic activities (that is activities, such as games and sports, which bring pleasure to the participant). In addition, earlier in the present chapter it was suggested that an interest in hobbies (and of course in school subjects) can come about in response to parental reinforcement, and indeed even as a consequence of association between these hobbies and parents themselves. To this we can add the possibility that innate factors also play some part, particularly in those interests demanding skills which may to a certain extent be genetic in origin. Thus the child with a good ear for music even before receiving musical training, and with good manual dexterity, might show more interest in learning a musical instrument than a child less favourably endowed, while a child with good visual imagination might be more ready to show an interest in developing his drawing skills than a child with one less good.

The development of interests would seem, therefore, to be dependent upon a number of inter-related factors, with certain of them more important in one instance and others of them in another. In helping the child to develop an aptitude or interest in things considered to be of value, however, the role of the teacher is essentially:

* to provide the relevant opportunities;
* to demonstrate the relevance of the interest concerned to the child himself;
* to refrain from passing judgements on the child's competence at the skills associated with the interest until he has been given the opportunities he requires to develop these skills;
* to show personal enthusiasm and involvement in the interest.

To these four basic points we can add a fifth, namely that the teacher should not react angrily if the child, after due opportunity, does not develop the feeling towards he interest that the teacher himself has. A negative reaction of this kind is usually counter-productive in that it turns the child further against the interest (either though hostility towards the teacher, or through anxiety, or through feelings of personal inadequacy at not experiencing the enthusiasm which the teacher claims he 'ought' to be experiencing). Sometimes, although nothing may be apparent at the time, if the child is left to himself the interest will flourish at a later date. At other times, it is as well simply to remember that each of us is an individual, with our own particular set of psychological endowments and life experiences, and it would be impossible for us all to enjoy precisely the same things.

It must be stressed that we are not talking at this point about a child's feelings towards basic school subjects. These are dealt with in the discussion of learning and motivation in chapter 8, but about the more general enriching experiences that are a part of the school's educational life. The teacher is quite right to think that the child would benefit from these experiences if he came to appreciate them to the full, but such appreciation is not something the teacher can compel. By its very nature it even lies to a great extent outside the conscious control of the child himself. He can learn to write, for example, an elegant criticism of a poem or of a painting or of a piece of music, but few teachers would regard this as the same experience as being deeply moved by the work of art concerned: that is, stirred by it emotionally because it strikes chords with important aspects of his own life history or with the dreams and hopes he has about the future. There may come a time when we will have learnt so much about the techniques of teaching that we will be able to produce this kind of reaction from children for any great work of art or for any of the interests that we feel are important for children; but I doubt it. I also think it likely that if such a day does come, many teachers will feel that the things that make their job worth doing (and the things that make the arts and most other interests worth studying) will have disappeared.

Attitudes

Turning now to attitudes, we find ourselves on rather more precise ground. Psychologists define attitudes as the relatively enduring orientations that individuals develop towards the various objects and issues they encounter during their lives, and which they express verbally as opinions. Obviously attitudes therefore contain elements of value and belief, as well as varying degrees of factual knowledge (or what the holder takes to be factual knowledge). Less obviously, they may be partly conscious and partly unconscious, with the two sometimes even in conflict with each other. Freudian theorists, in particular, lay great stress upon this conflict, and regard it as playing an important role in the development of the personality. We can see this exemplified by the ego defence mechanism of reaction-formation which was explained earlier in the chapter. In terms of this mechanism, an individual might for instance harbour hostile attitudes towards people of other races, yet refuse to admit to these consciously because they arouse in him strong feelings of guilt. The attitudes are therefore kept repressed in the unconscious, and in an attempt to make sure they stay there the individual adopts an exaggeratedly solicitous and pious attitude towards everyone from abroad he happens to meet. The presence of the unconscious attitudes are, however, revealed by surreptitious acts of nastiness (such as blocking the promotion of a coloured colleague or voting against a local councillor because of the liberal stand he takes on race), which the individual nevertheless attempts to explain away to himself as being in the 'best interests' of the person concerned or as being 'for the sake of peace' or because 'the majority would never stand for it.

The main problem here, however, is that we have no accurate way of measuring unconscious attitudes of this kind or of assessing how important the conflict between them and consciously held views is in normal life. Some psychologists hold that Freud greatly over-stressed the case, and that in the light of current knowledge we should concentrate upon conscious attitudes and keep an open mind on any other kind. However, the teacher will want to examine his own attitudes on important moral and social issues closely to see whether there are any grounds for supposing that they are influenced or affected in any way by deeper beliefs which so far he has refused to face.

Closely linked to reaction-formation is another of the Freudian mechanisms of ego defence, namely rationalization. Rationalization applies where the individual expresses a socially acceptable reason for behaviour that in fact stems from much more dubious attitudes or motives whose existence he is reluctant to admit even to himself. Thus the military man might claim he is in the services because this is the best way of deterring the aggressor, whereas in fact he is drawn to the life by a liking for violence. Similarly, the anti-pornography campaigner might claim that he watches a salacious film only because this enables him (or her) to press for legislation to prevent other people from seeing it, whereas actually he enjoys the titillation provided by the experience.

This is not to suggest, of course, that the teacher has much in common with either of these examples, but simply to urge that someone entrusted with the task of helping form the attitudes of the young should strive first for self-knowledge, and should examine his own attitudes and beliefs for signs of the things against which we have been warning. Of equal, if not greater, importance he should look closely at the origin of his conscious attitudes (particularly where these concern education or children) and at the evidence that supports them. Sometimes he may find that these attitudes have been taken over, on trust so to speak, from authority figures in his own life and have not been subjected to proper critical scrutiny. At other times he may find that they stem from his emotional reactions rather than from any reasoned argument, and demand to be re-thought in a cooler and more objective context. On other occasions he may find that attitudes lead him to pre-judge important issues (e.g. his disapproving attitude towards a certain child may lead him to presume the latter's guilt whenever trouble has been caused instead of pausing to look at the evidence), and to take action which may in the event be inappropriate and even unjustified.

Attitudes and behaviour

Before we leave this general discussion and turn to the more specific matter of attitude change in children we should add an additional word of caution, namely that behaviour does not always match up even to consciously held attitudes. This is often because such attitudes set the individual standards that appear to be beyond his reach. We see this particularly in such things as New Year resolutions, where the individual consciously vows to match his behaviour to his attitudes, but which rarely survive beyond the end of January (or beyond the first day of January in some cases). The individual knows he should work harder, or be kinder to his family, or watch less television, or take more exercise, or give up certain bad habits, but although his attitudes towards these things are right, his determination to carry these attitudes through lags some way behind. As in many important things, the spirit is willing but the flesh is unfortunately weak. Nor do changes in attitude necessarily lead to changes in behaviour. The headmaster may indeed have a fine turn of phrase, and send children away after morning assembly resolved to mend their ways and live henceforth lives of blameless purity, but the resultant changes in behaviour may not survive the first classroom skirmishes.

This means that paper and pencil tests of attitude, in which children (or adults for that matter) claim to prize desirable things like honesty, kindness towards others, thrift, and hard work, may tell us disappointingly little about how the children concerned will actually behave when faced with opportunities to live up to the attitudes in question. Certainly they may feel twinges of conscience at each failure, but these may be insufficient to make them behave differently next time. Similarly, some people may endorse the desirable things in an attitude test yet make mental reservations that under certain circumstances these attitudes may legitimately be abandoned. The businessman may endorse the virtues of fair play, for example, yet consider that these do not apply when it comes to winning business from a competitor. The child may endorse the value of honesty, yet feel this does not apply when it comes to copying homework from a friend a few minutes before it is due to be handed in.

Closely linked to such anomalies we have what Festinger (1962) calls cognitive dissonance. Cognitive dissonance is said to arise where an individual holds a particular attitude, yet finds that his behaviour (or another attitude) is at variance with it. Such variance can set up tension (dissonance) which the individual finds uncomfortable, and which he therefore tries to reduce by modifying one of the variables concerned. He may do this by distorting it, even if this means tampering with what he believes to be the truth. For example, if a person has a confident attitude towards his abilities, yet fails an examination that hitherto he has considered to be an accurate measure of such abilities, he may suddenly find all sorts of reasons why the examination after all is no good. Once having made a dissonance-reducing change of this kind he will often go to great lengths to maintain it by misinterpreting new evidence. In our example he might interpret a change in the examination syllabus the following year as 'proof' that it was unfair in the past. Or when he hears that someone who passed the examination has nevertheless failed to get a coveted job he may regard this as demonstrating that employers have little regard for the qualification it carries, and therefore must also be convinced of its worthlessness.

Dissonance-reducing changes are also apparent sometimes after an individual tells a lie. If the individual has a positive attitude towards the truth, he is now faced with dissonance between this attitude and his own behaviour. To reduce this dissonance he may decide that what he said was not really a lie at all because of the careful form of words he used (e.g. it was all right to say I did not go for a swim because in fact we only splashed about in the shallows). Individuals, it seems, will often show great ingenuity in convincing themselves that a lie was not really a lie, or in changing their recollection of events so that it appears to fit with the account of such events that they actually gave. This is particularly true, Festinger tells us, if the lie only brought very small rewards. It is as if our view of ourselves as truthful people can survive the knowledge that we have told a lie over something important more readily than the knowledge that we have told it over something trivial. To give way to great temptation, it appears, is seen by the individual as being human. To give way to minor temptation looks suspiciously like weakness (note that I am not saying that people do in general give in to great temptation more readily than to minor, or necessarily feel less badly about it if they do, but simply that the individual's view of himself as basically honest seems less subject to dissonance where the falsehood is over something important than where it is over something unimportant).

Attitude change
In effect, a great deal has already said about attitude change, both in the present chapter and in chapter 8. To interest a child in something, to motivate him to succeed at it, is usually to change his attitude towards it. To reinforce him for changes in behaviour is also often likely to lead to changes in attitude (e.g. the child finds that hard work begins to pay off in class because the teacher deliberately sees to it that every example of it is reinforced, and the child then comes round to the view that lessons are not so bad after all). We can, however, add one or two further points that the teacher needs to keep in mind when thinking about this field.

* Children's attitudes towards a particular activity benefit from seeing that activity performed (or 'modelled') for them by a prestige figure. This does not mean, of course, that watching somebody else is a substitute for the children actually taking part in the activity themselves, but to attend, say, a top level games match, or to visit a factory to see certain skills and crafts in operation, or to watch inspired acting in

the theatre, can be an invaluable experience (provided, of course, that the children are not then expected to match up to the observed standards themselves!).

* Linked to this notion of modelling, children's attitudes also benefit from the example set by the teacher, particularly in matters of social conduct. A teacher who is himself considerate and fair-minded towards his class is far more likely to see his children taking over these behaviours than a teacher who simply talks about them but does not follow his own precepts.

* Arising from the discussion of learning in chapter 8, it will be appreciated that where we have tried to change attitudes by modelling and by discussing important issues with children we should take every opportunity to watch for and immediately reinforce the changes in behaviour that arise from these new attitudes. Otherwise, like the New Year resolutions that we used as our example above, these changed behaviours may be temporary in the extreme. Often, of course, the teacher will want to engineer specific opportunities for the children to put these new behaviours into effect, and the sooner this happens after changes in attitude have been noted the better.

* Finally children, like adults, respond readily to enthusiasm in others. Provided this enthusiasm is not forced on them (we have already cautioned against the teacher expecting children necessarily to show the same interests as he does himself), they are likely to be fired by it and want to participate in the activities associated with it. The same is true of success. Where children witness success they quickly want to be associated with it through participation: as witness the upsurge in interest in a particular sport after a national competitor has won a gold medal in it for his country. One quality of the successful teacher about which there is little dispute is that such a teacher is able to inspire enthusiasm in others for his subject, and to carry them along with him until they reach the point where their enthusiasm becomes self-reinforcing and they are able to continue on their own. Another is that he gives an example of success that the children want to emulate: that he has, in other words, skills and techniques that they would dearly love to possess for themselves.

References

Festinger, L. (1962)
Cognitive dissonance. Scientific American, October.
Maccoby, E. and Jacklin, C. (1974)
The Psychology of Sex Differences. Stanford: Stanford University Press.
Maslow, A.H. (1943)
A theory of human motivation. Psychological Review, 50, 370-396.

Rotter, J. (1954)
Social Learning and Clinical Psychology. Englewood
Cliffs, NJ: Prentice-Hall.
Thomas, A., Chess, S. and Birch, H. (1970)
The origin of personality. Scientific American, August.
Weiner, B. (1979)
A theory of motivation for some classroom experience.
Journal of Educational Psychology, 71, 3-25.

dditional reading

Thomas, A. and Chess, S. (1977) Temperament and Developmen
New York: Brunner-Mazel.
The most recent publication on the work of Thomas, Chess
and Birch.

Maslow, A.H. (1970) Motivation and Personality (2nd edn).
New York: Harper & Row.

Maslow, A.H. (1968) Towards a Psychology of Being (2nd
edn). New York: Van Nostrand.
Maslow has produced a number of books, all interesting
and highly readable, on his theories of personality and
motivation. The reader might like to look initially at
either of these two.

Warren, N. and Jahoda, M. (1973) Attitudes (2nd edn).
Harmondsworth: Penguin.
Gives a good general survey of the field of attitudes.

Theories on locus of control and on attribution can be
approached through Weiner's recent paper, details of which
appear in the references.

10

Values and Moral Development
David Fontana

Definition of morals and values

Our discussion of attitudes in the last chapter brings us on to the broader issue of morals and values. Morals and values refer to those attitudes and behaviours that are generally prized by the society in which one lives. They may or may not be defined by rules, and these rules may or may not carry the force of law, but they are nevertheless seen by responsible members of society as having a binding effect in matters of conduct and of interpersonal relationships. These morals and values may be derived from religious, philosophical, or political teachings, and usually they have had an important influence upon the historical development of the society concerned, providing guidelines for the emergence of civilized patterns of behaviour and even (ostensibly) for dealings with other countries. Sometimes, within a society, sub-groups become apparent which differ from each other in the morals and values held (e.g. religious groups, socio-economic status groups), and this can lead to friction and to attempts to put down opposing value systems by force.

The origin of value systems

The generally held view amongst psychologists is that morals and values are largely learnt structures, with the young child acquiring them initially from his parents and later from teachers, peer groups, the media, and society generally. One psychologist who made a particular study of the way in which this seems to happen was Freud (see chapter 9). Freud considered that the development of moral attitudes and behaviour in the child is due to the super-ego, which is largely the internalization by the child of the moral codes and strictures taught him by his parents, but which he takes over so completely that he often loses sight of their point of origin. The super-ego becomes, therefore, not just a collection of parental 'dos and don'ts' but an autonomous part of the mental life of the individual which he may come to regard as the voice of conscience or as his own carefully formulated moral code.

Freud considered that an over-developed super-ego could lead to psychological problems such as guilt and feelings of personal inadequacy and worthlessness and even, in extreme cases, to severe neuroses. Nevertheless, he saw the formation of the super-ego as on balance a good thing, since without it the child would only behave correctly when parents or other adults were there to reinforce his good behaviour. In their absence, and when detection was unlikely, he would feel quite free to follow his own selfish interests, no matter what the consequences for others might be. As suggested in chapter 9, Freud's ideas attract much criticism nowadays in some quarters, and space does not allow us to go into them in any great detail, but it is interesting to note that he saw the super-ego as developing two distinct elements. These were the conscience, which provides the child with feelings of guilt when he does wrong and is equivalent to the punitive function of the parent, and the ego-ideal which provides feelings of satisfaction when he does right and is equivalent to the parental rewarding function. It is through the ego-ideal also that the child builds a picture of 'the person I would like to be', which may be important not only in determining day-to-day conduct but in setting long-term life goals and ambitions.

In spite of what some psychologists regard as its 'unscientific' nature (a term which implies that it cannot be demonstrated experimentally), Freud's model of the super-ego is a useful way of conceptualizing what may happen in the mental life of the child as he builds up his moral sense. An alternative view, based upon a study of the child's thinking, is proposed by Piaget (1932), however. Piaget, whose work was examined in detail in chapter 4, observed the changes in the level of moral reasoning shown by the child as he moves through the various Piagetian stages of cognitive development. His findings suggest that the child goes from ego-centric thinking, where everything is seen from the point of view of the self, to a form of thinking which allows him to put himself in the place of others. Only when he is able to engage in the latter form of thinking is he capable of true moral judgement. We need not examine this model in detail, however, because a more comprehensive one, again related to the child's levels of thinking, is proposed by Kohlberg (1969). Kohlberg has it that the child passes through six major stages in moral development, and these are summarized below.

Kohlberg's six stages of moral development

PRECONVENTIONAL MORALITY (Piaget's pre-operational stage of thinking). Age approximately 2-7 years.

1. 'Obedience'. The child has no real moral sense, but his behaviour can be shaped by simple reinforcement.
2. 'Naive egoism'. A 'right' action is one that works for the child himself. The child may appear able to meet the needs of others, but this is only because the result is directly favourable to himself.

CONVENTIONAL MORALITY (Piaget's concrete operational stage of thinking). Age approximately 2-11 years.

3. 'Good boy/girl orientation'. Children try to please
    their elders, initially only in specific situations, but
    later more generally as they come to acquire a concept
    of the 'good' child.
4. 'Authority maintaining orientation'. Moral ideas gener-
    alize even further, and the child tries to live up to
    them not simply for personal gain, but because he now
    develops a sense of duty towards authority and the
    maintenance of the existing social order.

POSTCONVENTIONAL MORALITY (Piaget's formal operational stage of thinking). Age approximately 12 years
onwards.

5. 'Contractual legalism'. The sense of duty is still
    strong, but a sense of fairness and legality become even
    more important than the simple maintenance of the status
    quo. Rules are increasingly seen as arbitrary things
    subject to possible and often desirable change.
6. 'General principles of conscience'. Moral ideas become
    integrated into a consistent and coherent philosophy.
    Moral decisions are able to take into account all the
    relevant variables, and the individual can now look
    beyond surface fairness and legality.

As with Piaget's stages themselves, the rate of progress
through these six levels can vary from child to child, and
some individuals may never reach the higher levels just as
they may never achieve formal operations. In fact, it seems
that reaching the appropriate level of thinking is an essential prerequisite for arriving at the corresponding level of
moral development, though simply because the child has
achieved the former does not necessarily mean that he will
also have achieved the latter. Learning and opportunity play
a major part, and simply because a child is capable of a
certain level of moral thinking does not mean that he will
automatically have arrived at it.

Measuring moral development
One way of measuring the stage of moral development of a
particular child is to confront him with a teasing moral
problem and see how he solves it and why. Ideally, this
should be in the form of a story, with children as the
central characters. The plot should present these children
with a dilemma of some kind, and the child taking the test
should then be asked what he thinks they should do next. An
example of one of these problems is given below.

Jane's mother promises her she can go to the dance on
Saturday if she washes the dishes all week. Jane does

the dishes, but on Saturday her mother tells her she has changed her mind and will not let her go after all. Jane steals secretly out of the house and goes to the dance, and confides in her sister Mary. Should Mary tell their mother?

Clearly there is no easy right answer to this problem. Most children tend to agree that Mary should tell on her sister, but their reasons for taking this line vary and help us to decide their level of moral development. Children at Stage 1 typically say that Mary should tell because if she does not do so and her mother finds out that she kept the information back she will be punished. By Stage 3, however, the emphasis has usually shifted and is now placed upon the relationship between Mary and her mother rather than upon the fear of punishment, and children typically say that it is wrong for children to keep secrets from their parents. By Stage 5, the reasoning is much more subtle and children tend to say that if Mary does not tell her mother then she is conspiring in her sister's lie, and lies are always morally wrong even though Mary's mother was also wrong to break her promise to Jane. By Stage 6, children show less agreement in their responses, and now tend to invoke their own moral codes. Some will argue that two wrongs do not make a right, while others will consider that Mary should not break a confidence of whatever kind, and yet others that Mary's mother has acted unreasonably towards Jane, and Mary's silence should be regarded as the lesser of two evils.

It is not, of course, possible to distinguish clearly between each of Kohlberg's stages even with tests of this kind, and the stages are therefore better regarded as guidelines in our approach to children's moral thinking than as rigid categories. We should not, for example, expect Stage 5 reasoning from a child who clearly is in Stage 2, but we should not be surprised if a child who solves one problem at a certain level reverts to a lower level when confronted with a dilemma of a different kind. A further difficulty, to which attention has already been drawn in the discussion of attitudes in chapter 9, is that a child who expresses a moral attitude in response to a Kohlberg-style problem will not necessarily behave in accordance with this attitude when faced with a similar problem in real life. For example, the real-life Mary might decide not to tell on her sister simply for fear of what Jane would do to her if she did, or simply out of loyalty to Jane, or simply because at that particular moment in time she also had been treated unfairly by her mother and carried a brief grudge against her. It is also true, paradoxically, that children sometimes feel less guilt if they do what they claim is the 'wrong' thing (e.g. refuse to tell on Jane) than if they do what they claim is 'right' (tell on her after all).

It is also true (again, this can be implied from the discussion of attitudes in chapter 9) that a child may change his values dependent upon circumstances; that is, that he may show failure to generalize his moral code. He may, for instance, find it acceptable to lie to the teacher but not to his best friend, to steal from a shop but not from his parents, to cheat in a class test but not in a public examination. His moral code may also be overriden by what appear to him to be more important considerations. Thus he may behave badly because this makes him more acceptable to a peer group, or cheat in an examination because this will get him into a higher set which in turn will please his parents, or steal from a shop because this is the only way he can get presents to give his family and friends. In our modern society, children are faced with increasingly difficult problems when it comes to moral decisions, due to constant bombardment by the media with materialistic and acquisitive concepts and to the decline in the moral imperatives that go with religious beliefs (to say nothing of the general decline in the authority of parents and of the school). Perhaps in view of all this it is a wonder not that the moral standards of the young have slipped, as we are sometimes told, but that they have held up so well.

References

Kohlberg, L. (1969)
Stage and sequence: the cognitive-developmental approach to socialisation. In D. Goslin (ed.), Handbook of Socialisation Theory and Research. Chicago: Rand McNally.
Piaget, J. (1932)
The Moral Judgement of the Child. New York: Harcourt, Brace, & World.

Questions

1. From where does western society derive its morals and values?
2. Discuss the origins and the nature of the super-ego in Freudian theory.
3. From your own personal experience and from your knowledge of children, how appropriate do you consider Kohlberg's model of moral development to be?
4. To take an example from Kohlberg's model, why do you think that the stages of 'good boy/girl orientation' and 'authority maintaining orientation' are related to Piaget's stage of concrete operations?
5. What are the characteristics of 'contractual legalism' as defined by Kohlberg?
6. Describe one method we can use to test which stage of moral development a particular child has reached.
7. Why does achievement of formal operations appear to have an important influence upon moral thinking? (Look back to our comments on formal operations in chapter 4 for further help here.)
8. Are young children likely to be consistent in their moral behaviour? Give reasons for your answer.
9. Give some of the reasons why a child may perform an act

FT - P

that he knows to be normally wrong. Do these reasons always show him up in a bad light?
10. Is a child born with moral sense?
11. Why does a child sometimes feel less guilt if he does what he claims is wrong than if he does what he claims is right?
12. Why are children these days faced with increasingly difficult decisions when it comes to moral problems?

Annotated reading

Kohlberg, L. (1964) Development of moral character and ideology. Review of Child Development Research, Volume 1, New York: Russell Sage Foundation.

Kohlberg, L. (1969) Stage and sequence: the cognitive-development approach to socialisation. In D. Goslin (ed.), Handbook of Socialisation Theory and Research. Chicago: Rand McNally.
  Kohlberg's ideas on moral development can be approached through his own work, especially these two.

Piaget, J. (1932) The Moral Judgement of the Child. London: Routledge & Kegan Paul.
  Presents Piaget's work on moral development.

Wright, D.S. (1971) The Psychology of Moral Behaviour. Harmondsworth: Penguin.
  This is a very good general text on moral development.

Ausubel, D. and Sullivan, E. (1970) Theory and Problems of Child Development (2nd edn). New York: Grune & Stratton.
  Contains some useful references.

Lockwood, A. (1978) The effects of values clarification and moral development curricula on school-age subjects: a critical review of recent research. Review of Educational Research, 48, 325-364.
  A good survey of school programmes designed to enhance moral development.

Purpel, D. and Ryan, K. (eds) (1976) Moral Education ... It Comes With The Territory. Berkeley: McCutchan.
  Also of value in this context.

Rest, J. (1974) Developmental psychology as a guide to value education: a review of 'Kohlbergian' programs. Review of Educational Research, 44, 241-259.
  A review which concentrates particularly upon Kohlberg and developmental psychology.

Relevance to the teacher
DAVID FONTANA

The task of the teacher in assisting children's moral development is never less than a delicate one. We have already discussed (chapter 9) the way in which he can help children develop desirable attitudes (in moral matters as well as in all other areas), and there is no need to go back over this ground except to stress two things: first, the enormous importance of the teacher's own example. It is of little value to emphasize to children the necessity for tolerance and sympathy if the teacher, in his own dealings with his class, shows himself to be intolerant and unsympathetic. Similarly, it is of little value to teach honesty if the teacher shows himself to be not above a bit of sharp practice when it suits him, or to teach fair play if the teacher then treats children with manifest inequality. Not only will children fail to learn the desired qualities under these conditions, they may even end up regarding them with the same disrespect with which they regard teachers who relate to them in this way.

The second thing we must re-emphasize is that the teacher must take every opportunity to reinforce the right moral behaviour when he sees it taking place. It is no good teaching children the importance of consideration for others, for example, and then sweeping past the child who rushes to open the door for us without a word of thanks, or teaching the value of honesty and then imposing a harsh penalty, without even a word of approval, upon a child who owns up to a certain misdeed. It is all very well to argue that virtue should be its own reward, but this is asking a great deal of children. As they grow into adulthood so their moral behaviour should become self-sustaining as they come to appreciate its importance to a civilized community and to their own personal (and spiritual) development, but during their less mature years, and in particular while they are still in Kohlberg's first three stages, feedback from the environment is vital in assuring them that they really are learning and applying moral codes successfully.

Some specific moral problems
In addition to these two general points, there are a number of specific aspects of his moral role that sometimes trouble the teacher. In particular he often asks what kind of action should be taken against children who contravene moral codes in important ways, such as by stealing or cheating in examinations. The answer is that, as in all aspects of child behaviour, we must look first for the underlying causal factors. If we take stealing first, we have already implied that a child may steal to compensate for material inadequacies in his own life. A child from an impoverished economic background, faced with the constant blandishments of press and television advertising and by the temptation of goods prominently on display in shops will, not surprisingly, think from time to time of helping himself. If he has been given little in the way of moral guidance by parents, he may well put such thoughts into action. Such a child must obviously be viewed in a different light from a child with a more affluent background who may be stealing simply for excitement (though he too could have real problems, such as

worry over his parents' marriage, or feelings of neglect which drive him to steal in order to draw attention to himself).

The teacher should, therefore, try to understand something of the motives of the child caught stealing, and should use this understanding to help him to decide what help needs to be given. But whatever these motives may be, the child must be shown that his action was wrong, and inevitably carries certain consequences. We discuss what these may be, and the relationship of the school to the police, etc., when we deal with counselling in chapter 15, but the basic principle to be kept in mind at all times is that the child should be shown that, whatever he may have done, he still as a person has the sympathy and support of the school. We can hardly expect to teach him the value of moral behaviour, of compassion and concern, if we abandon him to his fate at the time he needs us most. It is sometimes argued that, where stealing and other misdeeds put a child on the wrong side of the law, he becomes the responsibility of the social or probation services rather than of the school. These services are, of course, of great importance, but involve the child, who may already be insecure, in forming relationships with strangers. His teachers, however, are already familiar to him, and may be better placed to help him come to terms with his mistakes and learn desirable lessons for the future from them. The practical involvement of the school at times like this will also demonstrate to all concerned that schools are not simply there to impart academic knowledge but to serve the children with whose care they are entrusted.

Turning to cheating, the treatment of which also causes teachers some problems, again the first question to ask is why should a child engage in such a practice. Obviously, he is likely to do so for one overriding reason, namely fear of the consequences if he does badly in the work concerned. This fear could simply be fear of the teacher's anger (or of the punishment that he might mete out), in which case the teacher needs to query his own behaviour. We have already stressed on a number of occasions that making mistakes is an aid to learning, both because the rectification of such mistakes helps the child directly, and because these mistakes give the teacher clues as to where the child most needs help. If, therefore, a child prefers to cheat rather than to acknowledge his mistakes, it looks as if the teacher has in the past been misunderstanding the importance of mistakes, and has been adopting the wrong attitudes towards their occurrence. Or he may have (perhaps unwittingly) been humiliating children who receive low marks by reading these marks to the class or getting the children to read them out themselves (the reader will probably remember from his own schooldays the delighted horror with which the rest of the class greeted the unfortunate child forced to confess to zero marks out of ten).

On the other hand, the child may simply be afraid of his own anxieties. Better to have cheated than to go home with the knowledge that you got nought out of ten, since the former is perhaps more readily forgotten than the latter. Poor marks deliver a blow to the child's self-esteem if he happens to be a person who cares about his work, and if he happens to have parents who make a habit of asking him how well he got on. Or he may be afraid that poor marks will put him in a low set next year away from his friends, or in a set with an unpopular teacher instead of in one with a teacher he happens particularly to like. None of this should be taken to mean that we can condone cheating, of course; simply that we should not take a lofty moral stance in the matter and regard it always as exclusively the child's fault. We may rest assured that if he does not care in the least about his work (or about his teachers) then he will not be bothered to go to the trouble of falsifying his marks. Far better then, when the teacher finds evidence of cheating, to take the child on one side in private and try to find out the cause, than automatically to harangue him in front of the class and hand out a stiff penalty which may do nothing to help him get his work right next time by his own unaided efforts.

A third example of a common contravention of the school's moral code is the telling of tales. This is almost exclusively a problem of the primary school, since by the stage of secondary education the child is too concerned about peer group approval to attempt such an exercise. Often the teacher's response to the problem is to refuse to listen to the saucer-eyed innocents who are attempting to pour out details of some heinous crime, at that very moment being perpetrated elsewhere in the playground or school building, unless the crime involves damage to another child or to school (or to his own!) property. Sometimes the tale bearers are warned briskly not to come running on such an errand again. Not surprisingly they go away feeling a little confused, as if they themselves are in the wrong. Having tried to absorb the school's moral code, and seeing one of their number apparently breaking this code, they went to the teacher to put things right but met only with stern dismissal. Now it is perfectly reasonable that the teacher should dislike tale-telling (particularly if he suspects it is done simply for the smug delight of getting another child into trouble), but this should be explained to children as part and parcel of their normal moral education, not thrust at them out of the blue when they feel they are doing the right thing. The teacher should at the same time explain to the children why he dislikes this activity (not always easy), and may also end up having to explain why, in a law-abiding community, adults are supposed to report the misdemeanours of their fellows to the police (the majority of crimes apparently are solved as a result of information given to the police by private citizens), while children are scolded for attempting to do the same thing with their teachers.

The teaching of moral behaviour

In conclusion, we should say something about the actual teaching of moral behaviour as a formal lesson. At one time such teaching tended to come almost exclusively under the heading of religious education, but it is now recognized that many other subjects (e.g. the teaching of literature, of current affairs, of general studies, of history and of geography) can also raise moral issues, and that these should in any case not simply be left to a single period a week and to one teacher on the timetable. Where the teacher deliberately wishes to raise questions of morals and values, he can do so by inviting the class to debate the kind of question used in the measurement of moral development and exemplified above in our discussion of the work of Kohlberg. Through such debate the child is helped to see the various issues relevant to particular moral dilemmas, and to express his own views (and misgivings). The teacher might also like to consider composing springboard questions (see chapter 8) related to moral problems, and to allow children to think creatively about the answers. The emphasis at each point should be upon helping children to get at the underlying variables and to ponder the full implications of their own ideas rather than upon producing cut and dried solutions.

Since moral development, as we see from the stages isolated by Kohlberg, depends to a great extent upon seeing the other person's point of view, much of the class work should be devoted to his end. Here we can recognize two processes, namely sympathy and empathy. To sympathize with someone is to feel sorry for their plight, while to empathize with them means actually to experience the kind of emotions that they may be feeling. Empathy requires a more finely developed sensitivity than does sympathy, and obviously cannot be 'taught' in any complete sense. It comes more readily to some children than to others, but role-playing in drama lessons, together with simple imaginative descriptions of the kind of emotions we think others may be going through, both help. Unless prompted by such activities, some children even at the stage of formal operations seem never to have considered what it must be like to be the butt of class teasing, or to be old and unwanted, or to grow up against a background of family violence. To speculate on the emotions of others, and then to apply these to oneself, is an essential first step for many children in developing the sensitivity towards others that is an integral part of moral development.

No matter how good the moral education within a given school, however, some of the impact is lost unless the staff show common standards in their day-to-day dealings with children. This is easier in a small than in a large school, of course, but children need to feel they are part of an institution that has some readily definable set of values.

After all, if these values are important enough to be demanded of them, then the children are bound to reason that they should be important enough for the staff to demand them of each other. To be treated one way by one teacher and quite another by someone else leaves the child feeling that the school only pays lip service to values when it suits itself, and really does not care enough about them to ensure that they apply to adults as well as to children. Reaching a workable general consensus amongst staff on even the most important standards of behaviour is not easy, particularly where members of staff come from different backgrounds and different religious and political creeds, but this is as much a task of any school staff as agreeing on general policy matters relating to syllabuses and to teaching techniques.

Additional reading

Wilson, J. (1972) Practical Methods of Moral Education. London: Heinemann.

May, P.R. (1971) Moral Education in Schools. London: Methuen.

Sugarman, B. (1973) The School and Moral Development. London: Croom Helm.
    The above three books each provide a good introduction to the practicalities of moral education in schools. All three are highly recommended.

11

Personality and Learning
David Fontana

The idea that the affective variables that we have been
discussing in the last two chapters, and which together make
up what we call personality, have some influence upon the
child's learning is not new to the teacher. Classroom
experience shows him that it is not cognitive variables
alone which determine the child's progress. These variables
interact with the child's attitudes and interests, his
motivation, and a wide range of emotional responses such as
excitement, sympathy and empathy and, perhaps above all,
anxiety. We looked at the specific relationship between
learning and anxiety in chapter 8, and pointed out how anxiety can affect not only the assimilation of knowledge in the
first place but its recall at a later date, particularly if
this recall is demanded under test and examination conditions or in a generally unsympathetic environment. But we
need now to stress that some children have habitually higher
levels of anxiety than others, so much so that these can be
regarded as constituting an enduring personality dimension.
Thus we say that one child is timid and nervous, that
another is full of confidence, that a third is a real
worrier, that a fourth takes things as they come and so on.
We mean by these labels that, whatever the situation in
which the respective children find themselves, we would
expect them to show the behaviour patterns in question in
response to any kind of stress. Anxiety is not, of course,
the only consistent personality dimension of this kind, nor
is it the only one that has a significant influence upon
learning, and we will now look at some of these other
dimensions in more detail.

Personality dimensions

Since we have already mentioned anxiety, it will be appropriate to make this the first dimension to be scrutinized.
As pointed out by Kline in chapter 9, there are numerous
different ways of attempting to measure how anxious a person
is. Kline instances such things as tests of writing pressure
and of balloon blowing, together with the more widely used
projective tests. But the most reliable tests available to
us at present are the personality questionnaires, tests
which ask people to respond to a number of questions about
themselves. It must not be assumed that just any old

questions will do. One well-known questionnaire test of personality in Britain, the Maudsley Personality Inventory, was constructed by its author H. J. Eysenck from an original battery of 261 questions assembled after a careful examination of the literature and of the kind of behaviours that appear to distinguish one person's personality from that of another. This battery of questions was then administered to a large sample of people, and the results were factor analysed: that is, they were subjected to a statistical technique that looks for relationships between a range of responses. In this instance, the factor analysis was designed to reveal whether people responding 'yes' to one question (e.g. a question on whether the individual enjoyed parties) also tended to respond 'yes' to others (e.g. questions on whether the individual enjoyed action, took the initiative in making new friends, liked numerous social contacts and so on).

Factor analysis of the 261 questions allowed Eysenck to discard large numbers of them. Some of the questions were seen to be duplicates, others showed a poor level of discrimination (a question to which everyone answers 'yes' is of no use if we are trying to discriminate between people), while others showed no relationship with any of the other items at all. The questions that remained, 48 in number, clustered into two factors, one of which was clearly emotionality, since all the questions concerned had to do with such things as fluctuation of mood, inability to concentrate, feelings of tension at meeting new people, feelings of nervous exhaustion and so on. The inescapable conclusion was that people obtaining high scores on these questions could be classified as consistently more emotional (neurotic) in stressful situations than people who produced low scores. This finding indicated not merely that it is possible to measure such a factor reliably by a questionnaire, but that a major part of the personality differences between people seems to be accounted for by traits and characteristics associated with it. Subsequently, Eysenck developed an improved version based upon more extensive research, and known as the Eysenck Personality Inventory. This has been extensively used in further and higher education, and with samples of children in the 16+ age range, while a version for use with younger children, the Junior Eysenck Personality Inventory, has also been developed and put to wide use by S. B. Eysenck.

We said above that neuroticism was one of the two factors revealed by Eysenck in his research and measured by the Maudsley Personality Inventory (MPI for short) and by both the Eysenck Personality Inventory (EPI) and the Junior Eysenck Personality Inventory (JEPI). The other factor was what Eysenck called 'social extraversion' (see chapter 9), with the high-scoring person (the extravert) on this dimension emerging as someone who takes the initiative in making friends, who is generally fond of physical activity, likes change and variety in his life, is sociable and outgoing, is easily aroused emotionally but usually not very deeply, and who tends to be materialistic, tough-minded, and free from social inhibition. The low-scoring person (the introvert) tends by contrast to be more inward-looking, less socially orientated, less eager for change and variety, and generally the opposite of the extravert in many of his responses to the environment and the various kinds of social and sensory stimuli it offers.

The extraversion–introversion dimensions and learning
From the educational point of view, the main interest is whether or not any discernible relationship exists between either of these dimensions and classroom achievement. A number of studies have explored this relationship using the JEPI, and in reviewing the evidence up to 1972 Elliott detects an interesting pattern. This pattern suggests that as children move up the mean attainment age from top infants (mean attainment age 7.9 years) to unversity students (mean attainment age estimated at 18 years) we find an initial positive significant correlation between extraversion and scholastic attainment of 0.19 turning by stages into a significant negative correlation of -0.55. Since Elliott is pooling the results of a number of separate investigations rather than carrying out an investigation of his own using stratified samples (i.e. samples matched for all relevant variables except age), we must treat this pattern with some caution, but it seems to suggest either that extraverts are better workers than introverts in the primary school, with the position reversed by the time higher education is reached, or that some factor or factors in the primary school environment favour extraverts and some factor or factors in higher education favour introverts.

Of these two suggestions, the second would seem the more plausible, since one can readily make out a case that the sociable, outgoing, active teaching environment of the normal primary school suits the study habits of the extravert, while the more individual, even lonely, academic environment within which the student has to work in higher education suits those of the introvert. In the secondary school, where the teaching environment may vary from subject to subject, it could be argued that it is sometimes the extravert who is favoured and sometimes the introvert, so that no clear pattern emerges (though there is some evidence that introversion in girls proves beneficial quite early on in secondary school life).

However, there is a third, more subtle, suggestion that is sometimes advanced to account for this swing from extraversion to introversion as the more beneficial end of the dimension at classroom and higher education level. This cites the known evidence that in most people extraversion increases up to about age 14, and then shows a steady decline towards introversion throughout the rest of life (in other words, people become more introverted as they grow older). It could be, therefore, that children who are intellectually precocious are also precocious in terms of personality, and show an extraversion peak in the primary school (i.e. some years ahead of the average) where such a peak is at its most useful. Thereafter they become increasingly introverted, and are scoring more strongly on this quality than their peers in the upper secondary school and in higher education, where introversion is at a premium.

The neuroticism–stability dimension and learning

In the light of current knowledge it is not possible to say whether this last suggestion is more important than the more widely advocated one that the primary school environment tends to favour extraverts and higher education introverts. Possibly both have some truth in them. But before we discuss the matter further, it is as well to turn to Eysenck's other dimension, anxiety (or the neuroticism-stability dimension as Eysenck prefers to call it), and examine its relationship to educational achievement in turn. And here we find that the position is rather more complex. One way of explaining this complexity is to refer back to the Yerkes-Dodson law that we discussed in chapter 8. This law has it that moderate levels of anxiety act as motivators and improve performance, whereas high levels lead to inhibition and a deterioration in performance. This suggests that children who score highly on Eysenck's dimension (i.e. who have high neuroticism scores) will do their best work in relatively unstressful environments, while children with lower scores will receive optimum motivation in environments where the pressures are rather more severe.

There is some evidence, however, that students with high neuroticism scores tend to do better than those with low scores in higher education, where the stresses (at least around examination times) are quite intense. Since this applies particularly to students following arts courses, we could suggest (as we did in chapter 8) that there may be a subject ('subject' in the sense of academic discipline) variable at work here. Arts subjects, particularly those which have a literary basis, may demand a particular kind of sensitivity in students which goes with a certain degree of anxiety. Put rather fancifully, it may be impossible to appreciate the emotional sufferings that writers and poets pour into their work unless one has experienced at least a degree of similar suffering oneself. It may also be that anxiety is less inhibiting in an arts examination, where one is not quite so concerned with the recall of factual information, as it is in science and technology. Thus the anxious arts student is able to give a rather better account of himself than is the anxious student in these other disciplines.

The evidence, extensive as it is, leaves us with no final very clear answers. Indeed, the most important conclusion that we can reach is that personality variables cannot be viewed in isolation when it comes to assessing their impact upon learning, but must be viewed within the context of a range of other variables that interact with them at every point. This is amply demonstrated by the work of Bennett (1976), who looked at children's personality in relation to teaching styles within the primary school. We have already said that most studies show a link between extraversion and classroom success in the primary school, but Bennett seems to show that this may be an over-simplification. He found, for example, that well-motivated extraverts actually did better in formal than in informal primary schools, which calls into question the idea that it is simply the free atmosphere of the primary classroom that favours extraversion. An able extraverted child may certainly shine in a very informal primary school environment, but it seems that where he is well motivated he will do even better (at least in terms of results in reading and the other basic subjects that Bennett used as his criterion variables) in a more formal environment where presumably he finds himself better able to concentrate upon the work in hand. Bennett also found that children with high neuroticism scores did better in formal than in informal primary schools, and in fact spent only half as much time on work activities in the latter as did children with low neuroticism scores. This may again seem odd in view of our suggestion that anxious children do better in less stressful environments, but the probable answer here is that, in the formal classroom, anxious children felt less worried because they were given a more structured atmosphere in which to work and therefore knew more of what was expected of them. In the informal classroom they actually avoided work, probably because they were less sure of what they were supposed to be doing, and this uncertainty made the work itself somewhat anxiety-provoking.

Note that we are being somewhat speculative here in the absence of any firm evidence, but the point to be emphasized is that we must keep a variety of variables in mind before we try to reach any conclusions on the part played by personality in school success. Another important variable, for example, is that of sex. Lynn (1971) demonstrates that females tend to have higher neuroticism scores than males throughout the years of formal education. This may be one of the reasons why they tend to shy away from science subjects, and to concentrate upon the arts where, as we have seen, higher neuroticism may be less of a handicap (NB: we say that this is only one of the reasons; others might be the greater human interest of the arts, the cultural myths that suggest women are less good at science than men, and the fact that hitherto women's education has been regarded as less important from a career point of view). A further important variable is probably the teacher's own personality, to which we return in chapter 16.

Other personality measures and a note of caution
Before we leave this section, we should point out that, although we have looked mainly at work done in schools and

in higher education using the JEPI and the EPI, these are by no means the only personality questionnaires available to researchers. In America in particular wide use has been made of Cattell's Sixteen Personality Factor Inventory (the 16 PF) and of the three versions of this Inventory developed for use with school children (the High School Inventory for children aged between 12 and 18, the Children's Personality Questionnaire for ages 8-12, and the Early School Questionnaire for children from six to eight). Recently Eysenck has himself brought out a new questionnaire (the Eysenck Personality Questionnaire) which contains an additional dimension, namely psychoticism-normality. People with high scores on this dimension are said to be solitary, troublesome, cruel, insensitive, foolhardy, and aggressive, and the dimension would seem in consequence to have most relevance to certain kinds of mental disturbance (see chapter 9).

We should also add that, in most of the studies within education using the Eysenck or the Cattell measures, the levels of correlation between these measures and academic success is not very high. This means that although the findings are statistically significant when we are testing children in large groups, they do not tell us a great deal about the position of individuals within the groups. At best we can say no more than that if a child is an extravert there is a slight chance that he will do better in primary school than if he were an introvert, with the position reversed in higher education. This indicates clearly the need for caution when making statements applicable at class level.

Cognitive style and learning

Personality dimensions are one important way of studying the interaction between personality and learning, but they are not the only way. Another approach (which is complementary rather than an alternative) is through what is known as cognitive style. As the name implies, cognitive style is to do with thinking, and it could be argued that this topic should be dealt with in Part II, along with concept formation, language development, intelligence and so on. This is a valid point, but it is usually dealt with under the general heading of personality because it seems to link closely, as we shall see in a moment, with affective factors as well. However, it is fair to concede once again that the distinction between cognitive and affective factors is never a clear one, and there are times when we group the two under separate headings simply because this makes for convenience and (let us hope) clarity. Eysenck makes this plain when he argues that intelligence is really only another dimension of personality, and Cattell does in fact include it as one of his personality factors in the 16 PF.

Intelligence and personality
Whether one accepts Eysenck's argument or not, the link between intelligence and various personality traits is well

attested by research. Children who evidence significant increases in measured intelligence between the ages of six and ten years have, for example, been shown to be more independent, competitive, and verbally aggressive than children who evidence a decline (Kagan et al, 1958). They are also more likely, it seems, to work hard, to show a stronger desire to master intellectual problems, and to show less readiness to withdraw in the face of challenge. In their extensive longitudinal study of high IQ children, Terman and Oden (1947) found that those most likely to make good use of their gifts were high on self-confidence, on perseverance, and on work interest, and had well integrated life goals (i.e. life goals that were realistic and single-minded). The more successful children also showed themselves to be better adjusted and more socially balanced than the less successful, and to be more likely in later life to make successful marriages and to achieve satisfaction in their personal and professional lives. Comparing high and low IQ children, McCandless (1969) considers research shows the former to be taller, better looking, less anxious, more popular, and physically stronger than the latter and, not surprisingly, to be better judges of other people.

Whether it is the high intelligence that prompts the desirable personality traits or whether it is the other way round is open to debate. Probably the two interact with each other at every point, making it impossible to establish the precise nature of causal links. What we can say, however, is that certain kinds of personality traits seem to be desirable if the child is to make the best use of his intelligence, while high intelligence allows a child to be more independent, self-confident, competitive and so on.

It also seems that creativity interacts with personality in somewhat similar ways. Creative people appear to be more autonomous, self-sufficient, self-assertive, and resourceful than the average, and also to be more introverted and aware of their impulses, and more ready to confess to the irrational in themselves (Taylor and Holland, 1964). They also appear to be more prone to engage in abstract thought, and to have a higher tolerance of ambiguity (i.e. they do not demand that things always be cut and dried and issues made clear). This close link between creativity and personality has led some people to suggest that creativity (or rather the divergent thinking that apparently goes with creativity) should be regarded as a cognitive style and again, like intelligence, be seen primarily as a dimension of personality. However, research into cognitive styles has tended to focus on areas other than divergent and convergent thinking (convergent thinking, as we saw in chapter 7, being the form of thinking associated with intelligence), and it is to these areas that we now turn.

Cognitive style theorists start from the fact that we are bombarded with stimuli from the environment every moment of our waking lives, and attend to only a small part of it which we make sense of by 'coding'; that is, by assigning it to a range of categories, each of which carries its own rating of importance. In any situation, things belonging to categories relatively high in importance gain our attention while those belonging to categories relatively low do not. For example, a child sitting in a classroom will not be attending to the physical sensation of his chair being pressed against his body, or the feeling of the ground under his feet, or the air entering his lungs, or the backs of the heads around him, but he will (one hopes) be attending to what the teacher is saying, since this will fall into categories such as 'interesting' and 'important' and be further coded into categories associated with meaning as it becomes assimilated. However, if somebody has put a drawing pin on his chair, or if the air entering his lungs becomes charged with the smell of cooking from the kitchen, or if one of the heads in front of him turns round and pulls a face, then his attention may be diverted from the teacher to these other stimuli because they have suddenly moved up into categories of greater importance.

The way in which we assign things to categories will be determined to a great extent by previous experience. The child has learnt that when the teacher is talking this experience must be placed in a category of high importance and attended to, either because it gives him relevant and useful information or because the teacher has a habit of directing questions at people who are not listening. As he assimilates what the teacher is saying, he matches it with what he already knows and categorizes it accordingly (e.g. into sets if the lesson happens to be mathematics perhaps, into time-charts if it happens to be history). But such assignment may also be influenced by innate factors including how we actually perceive things. Some people, it seems, are innately more sensitive to certain stimuli (e.g. loud noises, bright colours, subtle differences in shape) than others, with the result that such stimuli may impinge on their awareness whereas to somebody else they would go unnoticed. When faced with any kind of problem, therefore, the child will attend to what he considers to be important within it, will categorize the information concerned, and will hunt through his head until he finds data coded into a similar category which will help him form a hypothesis as a means towards its solution.

Cognitive style theorists consider that there is an identifiable consistency about the way in which each of us carries out this coding process, and that we do not change our methods drastically from problem to problem. They further consider that this applies not only to how we tackle academic problems but social problems as well, and indeed all the problems with which we are confronted in daily life. It is for this reason that they see cognitive style as an integral part of personality. This is readily apparent when we say, for example, that one person lets his heart rule his head (i.e. that he tends to code information into categories associated with emotional responses rather than those associated with rational thinking), that another tends to rush into things headlong (i.e. categorize without due thought), that another is too slow in making up his mind (i.e. deliberates too long over which categories to use), that someone else is disorganized or precise or methodical and so on. Useful as these general categories are, to the teacher as much as to anyone else, cognitive style theorists have tried to go beyond them and identify certain very definite dimensions along which we can all be placed. The research is still in its relative infancy, and no one is as yet sure how many common dimensions there may be, but there are three that have obvious relevance to education, and we will look briefly at each of these in turn.

Dimensions of cognitive style

The first of these has been identified by Bruner (Bruner et al, 1956), whose work we have already looked at in chapters 4 and 8. Bruner labels this dimension focussing-scanning and argues that extreme focussers, when faced with a problem, characteristically delay hypothesis-making until they have amassed sufficient evidence, while extreme scanners form a hypothesis quickly and usually have to go back and start all over again if this hypothesis eventually turns out to be untenable. This is well illustrated if we look at the test originally designed by Bruner to place people on this dimension. The test involves presenting the subject with a number of pairs of cards, each card consisting of varying arrangements of squares, circles, lines and colours, and then telling him that one card in each pair is 'correct' and the other 'incorrect'. As each successive pair is revealed to him he is asked to determine what particular features of the squares, circles, etc., denote 'correctness' and 'incorrectness' respectively. Clearly, if we carry this over into the classroom, we can see that focussers sometimes might delay hypothesis-making longer than necessary, and therefore appear over-deliberate in their work, while scanners might make up their minds too quickly and be at a disadvantage in problems presented to them orally where they cannot go back and look at earlier information if their hypotheses prove to be wrong.

Another well researched dimension of cognitive style is that originally called field dependence-field independence, but now more often referred to as global-articulated. The discoverer of this dimension, Herman Witkin (see Witkin et al, 1954), noted that certain people (those who are now said to have 'global' cognitive styles) appear less able than others (now said to have 'articulated' styles) to separate out the relevant from the irrelevant stimuli in a given situation. That is, they appear less able to decide which information belongs to important categories in that situation, and should therefore be attended to, and which information belongs to unimportant ones and can consequently be ignored. For example, Witkin showed in early experiments that people with global styles are unable to tell very precisely whether a chair in which they are sitting is tilted. They are, it seems, unable to separate the relevant stimuli (i.e. the bodily sensation of whether one is upright or not) from the irrelevant (the visual stimuli at which they are looking). Witkin has since shown that global individuals seem less able to remember details when given recall tests, seem less perceptive, and appear to be more easily influenced by their fellows.

There seems to be some link between the global-articulated dimension and intelligence in that global individuals appear to do less well on analytical items in IQ tests than do articulated people, though there is no difference on verbal items. Witkin suggests (1965) that this imbalance between analytical and verbal skills in the global child may work to his disadvantage, in that high verbal skills may disguise inadequate analytical ones, leaving the teacher unaware of the real reasons that may lie behind the difficuties a child experiences with certain learning tasks. He suggests in consequence that cognitive style tests may be of more use to the teacher than IQ tests, and should indeed be used in place of them since they are more comprehensive and 'recognise the rooting of intellectual functioning in personality'.

A third dimension of cognitive style of relevance to the teacher is that proposed by Jerome Kagan (1966), namely that of reflectivity-impulsivity. The 'reflective' child tends to make fewer errors than the 'impulsive', particularly on challenging and difficult tasks, since he shows a strong desire to be right first time, and seems able to tolerate the ambiguity, say, of a long silence in front of the class while he thinks out the right answer before responding. Impulsive children, on the other hand, adopt a 'shotgun' approach, firing off answers in the hope that one will be right and that in any case errors will provide appropriate feedback from the teacher and help them to get nearer the solution next time.

On each of the above dimensions it might be supposed at first sight that one end is very much better than the other. This is not really true. All cognitive style theorists stress that ideally we should be able to operate at either end of a dimension dependent upon the circumstances. If we take the reflectivity-impulsivity dimension as an example, it is easy to see that an over-reflective child, unwilling to commit himself until he is sure he is right, may be showing an undue fear of ever being wrong, and may also be denying himself the valuable learning opportunities that often come from making mistakes and to which we have made frequent reference. Similarly, the analytical approach of the person with an extreme articulated style might be inappropriate in social situations where humanity demands that we respond to individuals themselves as well as to the information they are trying to convey. Again, as we have already seen, the extreme focusser may be at a disadvantage in a situation where early hypothesis making is essential, and where decisions based on only limited evidence have to be made.

Note that there may be some overlap between the e dimensions. In particular, the focusser would appear to have much in common with the person with a reflective style, but the two are not necessarily the same thing. In focussing we are talking about a situation where information is fed to the subject in a number of stages, whereas reflectivity is a response to any situation, whether the information is present at one go or whether some of it is more delayed. Note also that although we have been talking about people at the extreme ends of each of the dimensions, most people will tend to cluster towards the centre: that is, they will tend for example to make up their minds in an interval of time that does not categorize them as extremely impulsive or extremely reflective.

References

Bennett, N. (1976)
Teacher Styles and Pupil Progress. London: Open Books.
Bruner, J., Goodnow, J. and Austin, G. (1956)
A Study of Thinking. New York: Wiley.
Elliott, C.D. (1972)
Personality factors and scholastic attainment. British Journal of Educational Psychology, 42, 23-32.
Kagan, J. (1966)
Development studies in reflection and analysis. In A. Kidd and J. Rivoire (eds), Perceptual Development in Children. London: University of London Press.
Kagan, J., Sontag, L., Baker, C. and Nelson, U. (1958)
Personality and IQ change. Journal of Abnormal and Social Psychology, 56, 261-266.
Lynn, R. (1971).
An Introduction to the Study of Personality. London: Macmillan.]
McCandless, B. (1969)
Children: Behaviour and development. London: Holt, Rinehart & Winston.
Taylor, C. and Holland, J. (1964)
Predictors of creative performance. In Taylor, C. (ed.), Creativity, Progress and Potential. New York: McGraw-Hill.
Terman, L. and Oden, M. (1947)
Genetic Studies of Genius IV. Stanford, Ca: California University Press.
Witkin, H. A. (1965)
Psychological differentiation and forms of pathology. Journal of Abnormal Psychology, 70, 317-336.
Witkin, H. A., Lewis, H., Hertzman, M., Machover, K., Meissner, P. and Wapner, S. (1954)
Personality Through Perception. New York: Harper & Row.

Questions

1. What is meant by a 'dimension' of personality?

2. How would you define social extraversion and social introversion as measured by Eysenck's personality inventories?
3. What pattern does the relationship between extraversion and academic success appear to take as the child grows older?
4. Suggest possible explanations for this pattern.
5. What is meant by the Yerkes-Dodson Law? (Turn back to chapter 8 for further help if necessary.)
6. Is the relationship between neuroticism and educational achievement influenced by the particular subject the student is studying?
7. Do children with high neuroticism appear to do better in formal or informal classrooms? Give reasons for your answer.
8. Give some examples of the links that apparently exist between personality and intelligence.
9. What is meant by 'cognitive style'?
10. What are the factors that influence the way in which a child codes incoming information?
11. What are the distinguishing characteristics of 'focussers' and 'scanners' respectively?
12. Why does Witkin suggest that cognitive style tests may be of more use to the teacher than IQ tests?
13. In what circumstances might it be better to have a 'reflective' cognitive style and in what circumstances might it be better to have one that is 'impulsive'?
14. What is the apparent relationship between sex and neuroticism? Can you account for it?
15. Suggest some of the ways in which personality variables may interact with each other to influence learning and educational achievement.

Annotated reading

Fontana, D. (1977) Personality and Education. London: Open Books.
> A useful introduction to the study of personality, which looks at the relationship between personality and learning amongst other topics.

Naylor, F.D. (1972) Personality and Educational Achievement. Sydney: Wiley.
> Another introductory text, which focusses specifically upon personality and learning.

Hintzman, L. (1978) The Psychology of Learning and Memory. San Francisco: Freeman.
> A more extensive book, which ranges more widely.

Bigge, L. (1976) Learning Theories for Teachers (3rd edn). New York: Harper & Row.
> Contains much useful material.

Additional material, together with valuable references to

original sources, will be found in the Open University
course material for the Personality and Learning units
(Course E201), and particular attention is drawn to the book
of readings, published by Longmans of London, that
accompanies these units.

Warr, P.B. (1970) Thought and Personality. Harmondsworth:
Penguin.
   A comprehensive collection of material on cognitive
   style.

Witkin, H., Moore, C., Goodenough, D. and Cox, P. (1977)
Field-dependent cognitive styles and their educational
implications. Review of Educational Research, 47, 1-64.
   A very good paper by Witkin on his own work and its
   relevance to education.

Bruner, J., Goodnow, J. and Austin, G. (1956) A Study of
Thinking. New York: Wiley.
   Fully explains Bruner's ideas.

Kagan, J. and Kogan, N. (1970) Individual variation in
cognitive processes. In Mussen, P. (ed.), Carmichael's
Manual of Child Psychology (3rd edn), Volume 1. New York:
Wiley.
   Describes Kagan's ideas.

Relevance to the teacher
DAVID FONTANA

Since this chapter has been closely concerned with learning,
much of its relevance to the practical work of the teacher
should have been made apparent already. There remain,
however, a few important points still to be considered, both
in relation to personality dimensions of the kind identified
by Eysenck and to cognitive style.

Personality dimensions

Taking personality dimensions first, we need to say that as
with dimensions of cognitive style it is not necessarily
more desirable to be at one extreme end than at the other.
Extraverted people may seem to have more fun on the face
of it than introverted people because of their greater
sociability and their generally more outgoing behaviour, but
there is not much evidence that they are very much happier
or experience a great deal more self-satisfaction. And
though introverted people may seem on balance to do better
in higher education this does not necessarily mean they are
more scholarly, but simply that the way in which we organize
teaching and examination methods in universities and colleges may be more suited to their personalities than to
the personalities of extraverts. Even if we look at the
neuroticism-stability dimensions it would be inappropriate
to say that stable people are better people than those who
are on the neurotic side. A neurotic person may go through
more difficulties in life as a result of his tendency to

worry unduly, but he may, in learning to cope with these
difficulties, find an eventual maturity and serenity that
escapes the person to whom life has come more easily. He
may also be more sensitive to mental distress in others, and
perhaps (though this is conjecture) be more drawn towards
the caring professions whose job it is to alleviate this
distress. In any case, it is not part of the teacher's role
to look constantly for ways of passing value judgements on
children's personalities, but rather to understand the
manner in which these personalities affect the ways in which
children behave and learn.

This brings us on to the next point: namely, is it
possible for the teacher to change a child's personality if
this is considered to be in the child's own interests? In a
way, such a question is meaningless, because children's
personalities are constantly undergoing development and
growth, some of it doubtless in response to the work done
with the teacher, both in and out of the classroom. What I
really mean, however, is can we change the score a child
gets on a standardized test of personality such as the
JEPI? The answer is that although we have no hard research
evidence (research projects deliberately designed to 'change
children's personalities' would rightly be given short
shrift by most parents and teachers), it seems unlikely that
we could effect more than fairly minor changes. We could,
for example, urge an introverted child to be more sociable,
in the hope that he would quickly come to enjoy social
events and therefore change into an extravert, but the
chances are that he would find these events not to his
liking and would blame us for pushing him into something he
did not want to do. In any case, many introverts are just as
fond of other people as are extraverts, but prefer to mix
with small gatherings of friends rather than be constantly
meeting new people and going to new places.

More realistically, we might try to help a child to stop
worrying so much, in the hope that this would render him
less neurotic and thus lower his neuroticism score. In
theory this should certainly be possible, but in practice
many worriers already know all the reasons why they should
not be worrying, but confess that this does not stop them
from doing so. There may indeed be physiological reasons for
this, in that the neurotic person may have a more readily
aroused autonomic nervous system than does the more stable
individual. The autonomic nervous system is that part of our
neurophysiology that controls our involuntary processes
(e.g. sweating, heart rate, rises and falls in blood pressure, digestion, shivering and the like), and it can easily
be appreciated that if this system is quickly aroused then
we may find ourselves with butterflies in the stomach and
nervous shivers when confronting a situation that leaves
someone else quite unmoved. The point is that there may be
nothing in our experience to make this situation more
frightening to us than it is to him, it is just that our
bodies respond at once and send us all sorts of alarm

signals, whereas he remains physiologically unaroused and can view the whole thing with calm detachment.

It is possible that with biofeedback techniques and some forms of meditation (both of which lie outside the scope of this book and of the teacher's normal role) the neurotic person can learn to control the rate of arousal of his autonomic system, but he is unlikely to be able to do so simply by being told to stop worrying and to take things more as they come. When working with highly anxious children the job of the teacher is therefore primarily to understand and sympathize with their problems, and to give practical proof of this sympathy by not exposing them unnecessarily to stressful situations. He should also, of course, try to equip them with the skills necessary for dealing competently with most of the problems they are likely to meet, and should help to build their confidence by giving them the experience of success which, as we have stressed repeatedly elsewhere, is essential if children are to make satisfactory progress. Thus what the teacher is trying to do is not so much radically to alter the child's personality, as to help him to cope more effectively with the kind of person he is.

Passing on to the relationship between personality and academic success, it is as well to remind ourselves again that even if we could produce consistent evidence which proved the extravert does better in a formal than in an informal classroom, these are only statistical correlations. They would tell us only that this is true when we compare large groups of children in one of the categories mentioned with large groups of children in one of the others. They would not tell us that the results necessarily hold good for this particular extravert or for this particular neurotic. Depending upon the strength of the correlations they would tell us what the chances are that these children will conform to the pattern, but no more than that. Since the correlations are, as we have seen, not in fact very high, these chances are in most cases not very much better than evens. The value of the research that has been done to date in the field is rather that it alerts the teacher to the fact that there are important links between personality and learning than that it tells him unequivocally what these links actually happen to be. As we saw earlier, personality seems to be in a complex relationship with a number of other variables such as the material being taught, the teaching methods being used, the study habits open to the individual child or student, and the personality of the teacher himself. The teacher must therefore operate as his own researcher, sensitive to the individual personalities of each child in the class, and alert to the reaction between these personalities and the other variables involved.

Cognitive style

If we now turn our attention to cognitive style, we can once more ask whether it is possible for the teacher to help a child to alter his position on a particular dimension. Here the answer is rather less clear than it was when we discussed the more straightforward factors of personality. Certainly some important aspects of cognitive style would appear to be learnt, though others might be due to temperamental and emotional factors, and it seems probable that the teacher might be able to modify and develop the latter. It is illuminating to consider how much of our educational effort is directed towards the transmission of knowledge and skills, and how little of it is concerned with helping the child understand and shape his own patterns of thinking and categorization. As was pointed out in chapter 8, failures in learning are not caused only by failures in memory, in attention, in attitude and motivation and so on, but in the way in which sense is made (or not made) of the material to be assimilated. Yet, as was pointed out in chapters 6 and 7, little thought is given within education to the best methods of helping children to extend the ways in which they explore and recognize the meaning of the material in front of them, and develop the thinking strategies most appropriate to it. It is not that educationists are unaware of the importance of children's thinking, or are unaware that one of their tasks is to encourage and help shape this thinking: it is simply that to date they are by no means sure how this can best be done. It is possible that research into cognitive style will provide valuable pointers in this area, and will show besides that the child's thinking must be considered within the context of personality as well as within the context of his cognitive abilities.

References

Allport, G.W. (1961)
Pattern and Growth in Personality. London: Holt, Rinehart & Winston.
Coopersmith, S. (1968)
Studies in self-esteem. Scientific American, February.
Erikson, E.H. (1950)
Childhood and Society. New York: Norton.

Additional reading

Gaudry, E. and Spielberger, C.D. (eds) (1971) Anxiety and Educational Achievement. Brisbane: Wiley.
Contains a number of useful papers giving a good survey of the field.

Wade, B.E. (1981) Highly anxious pupils in formal and informal primary classrooms; the relationship between inferred coping strategies and: I - cognitive attainment.
British Journal of Educational Psychology, 51, 1, 39-49.
Details interesting findings of a recent study into the relationship between anxiety, motivation, extraversion and cognitive performance.

12

Knowledge of Self
D. Bannister

Introduction
DAVID FONTANA

In many ways the next chapter is one of the most important
in the book. Much of the psychological development of the
individual is bound up with the emerging sense of self, the
sense that the individual has a separate identity of which
he himself is uniquely conscious. Yet in spite of its
importance, the phenomenon of the self is one of the most
difficult for psychologists to explain, so much so that many
of them prefer to ignore it in their work altogether. The
topic is conspicuous by its absence from many basic texts in
psychology, where the emphasis is upon observable behaviour,
and it is sometimes argued that there is in fact no reliable
way of researching into it since we can only gain knowledge
of another person's self-awareness by listening to what he
is able to tell us on the subject himself. This method,
known as the introspective method, has long been suspect
amongst large numbers of psychologists because of the
difficulties involved in checking the accuracy of the
information thus gained. People may give us a deliberately
false picture, or they may be unable to put what they wish
to convey into words, or they may mean subtly different
things by the words they use from what we take them to
mean.

For the teacher, however, some understanding of how
self-awareness develops and of the factors that influence it
are crucial. Educational success depends in no small measure
upon the view a child has of himself. He is not born with
this view, but acquires it through experience, in particular
perhaps through watching how other people react towards him
and listening to the opinions they pass about him. Part of
the role of the teacher is to help the child to think about
himself positively, to recognize and develop his strengths,
to formulate life goals that he thinks will enhance his
self-concepts, and give him an awareness of personal value
and worth. More is at stake here than simply success in the
class. We are thinking of the child's life outside and
beyond school, and of his personal development throughout
his adult years.

In the section by Bannister which follows, the author
deals first with the difficult problems of how we define the
'self', and goes on from there to look at the nature of self-

252

knowledge, at the idea of personal change and development, and at the obstacles that come in their way. It repays particularly careful reading, and the reader is advised to pause frequently as he works through it in order to reflect on the meaning of what is being read in terms of his own life experience and self-knowledge. By so doing he will find not only that his understanding is enhanced but that the implications of what is being said for the education of the young become more apparent.

What is self?
D. BANNISTER

Definition is a social undertaking. As a community we negotiate the meaning of words. This makes 'self' a peculiarly difficult term to define, since much of the meaning we attach to it derives from essentially private experiences of a kind which are difficult to communicate about and agree upon. Nevertheless, we can try to abstract from our private experience of self qualities which can constitute a working definition. Such an attempt was made by Bannister and Fransella (1980) in the following terms.

Each of us entertains a notion of our own separateness from others and relies on the essential privacy of our own consciousness
Consider differences between the way in which you communicate with yourself and the way in which you communicate with others. To communicate with others involves externalizing (and thereby blurring) your experience into forms of speech, arm waving, gift giving, sulking, writing and so on. Yet communicating with yourself is so easy that it seems not to merit the word communication: it is more like instant recognition. Additionally, communicating with specific others involves the risk of being overheard, spied upon or having your messages intercepted and this contrasts with our internal communications which are secret and safeguarded. Most importantly, we experience our internal communications as the origin and starting point of things. We believe that it is out of them that we construct communications with others. We know this when we tell a lie because we are aware of the difference between our experienced internal communication and the special distortions given it before transmission.

We entertain a notion of the integrity and completeness of our own experience in that we believe all parts of it to be relatable because we are, in some vital sense, the experience itself
We extend the notion of me into notion of my world. We think of events as more or less relevant to us. We distinguish between what concerns and what does not concern us. In this way we can use the phrase 'my situation' to indicate the boundaries of our important experience and the ways in which the various parts of it relate to make up a personal world.

We entertain the notion of our own continuity over time; we possess our biography and we live in relation to it

We live along a time line. We believe that we are essentially the 'same' person now that we were five minutes ago or five years ago. We accept that our circumstances may have changed in this or that respect, but we have a feeling of continuity, we possess a 'life'. We extend this to imagine a continuing future life. We can see our history in a variety of ways, but how we see it, the way in which we interpret it, is a central part of our character.

We entertain a notion of ourselves as causes, we have purposes, we intend, we accept a partial responsibility for the consequences of our actions

Just as we believe that we possess our life, so we think of ourselves as making 'choices' and as being identified by our choices. Even those psychologists who (in their professional writing) describe humankind as wholly determined, and persons as entirely the products of their environments, talk personally in terms of their own intentions and purposive acts and are prepared to accept responsibility, when challenged, for the choices they have made.

We work towards a notion of other persons by analogy with ourselves; we assume a comparability of subjective experience

If we accept for the moment the personal construct theory argument (Kelly, 1955, 1969) and think not simply of 'self' but of the bipolar construct of self versus others, then this draws our attention to the way in which we can only define self by distinguishing it from and comparing it to others. Yet this distinction between self and others also implies that others can be seen in the same terms, as 'persons' or as 'selves'. Our working assumption is that the rest of humankind have experiences which are somehow comparable with, although not the same as, our own and thereby we reasonably assume that they experience themselves as 'selves'.

We reflect, we are conscious, we are aware of self

Everything that has been said so far is by way of reflecting, standing back and viewing self. We both experience and reflect upon our experience, summarize it, comment on it and analyse it. This capacity to reflect is both the source of our commentary on self and a central part of the experience of being a 'self'. Psychologists sometimes, rather quaintly, talk of 'consciousness' as a problem. They see consciousness as a mystery which might best be dealt with by ignoring it and regarding people as mechanisms without awareness. This seems curious when we reflect that, were it not for this problematical consciousness, there would be no psychology to have problems to argue about. Psychology itself is a direct expression of consciousness. Mead (1925) elaborated this point in terms of the difference between 'I' and 'me', referring to the 'I' who acts and the 'me' who reflects upon the action and can go on to reflect upon the 'me' reflecting on the action.

The question 'do you know yourself?' seems to call forth a categorical 'yes' by way of answer. We know, in complete and sometimes painful detail, what has happened to us, what we have to contend with and what our thoughts and feelings are. We can reasonably claim to sit inside ourselves and know what is going on.

Yet we all have kinds of experience which cast doubt on the idea that we completely know ourselves. A basic test (in science and personal life) of whether you understand someone is your ability to predict accurately what they will do in a given situation. Yet most of us come across situations where we fail to predict our own behaviour; we find ourselves surprised by it and see ourselves behaving in a way we would not have expected to behave if we were the sort of person we thought we were.

We also sense that not all aspects of ourselves are equally accessible to us. There is nothing very mysterious in the notion of a hidden storehouse. We can confirm it very simply by reference to what we can readily draw from it. If I ask you to think about what kind of clothes you wore when you were around 14 years old you can probably bring some kind of image to mind. That raises the obvious question: where was that knowledge of yourself a minute ago, before I asked you the question? We are accustomed to having a vast knowledge of ourselves which is not consciously in front of us all the time. It is stored. It is not a great step to add to that picture the possibility that some parts of the 'store' of your past may not be so easily brought to the surface. We can then go one stage further and argue that although parts of your past are not easily brought to the surface they may nevertheless influence the present ways in which you feel and behave.

The best known picture of this kind of process is the Freudian portrait of the unconscious. Freud portrayed the self as divided. He saw it as made up of an id, the source of our primitive sexual and aggressive drives; a super-ego, our learned morality, our inhibitions; and an ego, our conscious self, struggling to maintain some kind of balance between the driving force of the id and the controlling force of the super-ego. Freud argued that the id is entirely unconscious and a great deal of the super-ego is also unconscious, and that only very special strategies such as those used in psychoanalytic therapy can give access to the contents of these unconscious areas of self. We do not have to accept Freud's particular thesis in order to accept the idea of different levels of awareness, but it may well be that the enormous popularity of Freudian theory is due to the fact that it depicts what most of us feel is a 'probable' state of affairs; namely, that we have much more going on in us that we can readily be aware of or name.

Indeed, if we examine our everyday experience then we may well conclude that we are continually becoming aware of aspects of ourselves previously hidden from us.

A great deal of psychotherapy, education and personal and interpersonal soul-searching is dedicated to bringing to the surface hitherto unrecognized consistencies in our lives.

How do we know ourselves?

There is evidence that getting to know ourselves is a developmental process: it is something we learn in the same way that we learn to walk, talk and relate to others. In one study (Bannister and Agnew, 1977), groups of children were tape-recorded answering a variety of questions about their school, home, favourite games and so forth. These tape-recordings were transcribed and re-recorded in different voices so as to exclude circumstantial clues (names, occupations of parents and so forth) as to the identity of the children. Four months after the original recording the same children were asked to identify their own statements, to point out which statements were definitely not theirs and to give reasons for their choice. The children's ability to recognize their own statements increased steadily with age, and the strategies they used to pick out their own answers changed and became more complex. Thus, at the age of five, children relied heavily on their (often inaccurate) memory or used simple clues such as whether they themselves undertook the kinds of activity mentioned in the statement; 'That boy says he plays football and I play football so I must have said that'. By the age of nine, they were using more psychologically complex methods to identify which statements they had made and which statements they had not made. For example, one boy picked out the statement 'I want to be a soldier when I grow up' as definitely not his because 'I don't think I could ever kill a human being so I wouldn't say I wanted to be a soldier'. This is clearly a psychological inference of a fairly elaborate kind.

Underlying our notions about ourselves and other people are personal psychological theories which roughly parallel those put forward in formal psychology.

A common kind of theory is what would be called in formal psychology a 'trait theory'. Trait theories hinge on the argument that there are, in each of us, enduring characteristics which differentiate us from others, who have more or less of these characteristics. The notion that we or someone else is 'bad-tempered' is closely akin to the notion in formal psychology that some people are constitutionally 'introverted' or 'authoritarian' and so forth. The problem with trait descriptions is that they are not explanatory. They are a kind of tautology which says that a person behaves in a bad-tempered way because he is a bad-tempered kind of person. Such approaches tend to distract our attention from what is going on between us and other people by firmly lodging 'causes' in either us or the other person. If

I say that I am angry with you because I am 'a bad-tempered person' that relieves me of the need to understand what is going on specifically between you and me that is making me angry.

Environmental and learning theories in psychology have their equivalents in our everyday arguments about our own nature. The fundamental assertion of stimulus-response psychology, that a person can be seen as reacting to his environment in terms of previously learned patterns of response, is mirrored in our own talk when we offer as grounds for our actions that it is all 'due to the way I was brought up' or 'there was nothing else I could do in the circumstances'. Those theories and approaches in formal psychology which treat the person as a mechanism echo the kinds of explanation which we offer for our own behaviour when we are most eager to excuse it, to deny our responsibility for it and to argue that we cannot be expected to change.

Any theory or attempt to explain how we come to be what we are and how we change involves us in the question of what kind of evidence we use. Kelly (1955) argued that we derive our picture of ourselves through the picture which we have of other people's picture of us. He was arguing here that the central evidence we use in understanding ourselves is other people's reactions to us, both what they say of us and the implications of their behaviour towards us. He was not saying that we simply take other people's views of us as gospel. Obviously this would be impossible because people have very varying and often very disparate reactions to us. He argued that we filter others' views of us through our view of them. If someone you consider excessively rash and impulsive says that you are a conventional mouse, you might be inclined to dismiss their estimate on the grounds that they see everyone who is not perpetually swinging from the chandelier as being a conventional mouse. However, if someone you consider very docile and timid says that you are a conventional mouse, then this has quite different implications. You do not come to understand yourself simply by contemplating your own navel or even by analysing your own history. You build up a continuous and changing picture of yourself out of your interaction with other people.

o we change ourselves?

That we change in small ways seems obvious enough. Looking at ourselves or others we readily notice changes in preferred style of dress, taste in films or food, changes in interests and hobbies, the gaining of new skills and the rusting of old and so forth.

Whether we change in large ways as well as small involves us in the question of how we define 'large' and 'small' change. Kelly (1955) hypothesized that each of us has a 'theory' about ourselves, about other people, and about the nature of the world, a theory which he referred to as our personal construct system. Constructs are our ways of discriminating our world. For many of them we have overt labels such as nice-nasty, ugly-beautiful, cheap-expensive, north-south, trustworthy-untrustworthy and so forth. He also distinguished between superordinate and subordinate constructs. Superordinate constructs are those which govern large areas of our life and which refer to matters of central concern to us, while subordinate constructs govern the minor detail of our lives.

If we take constructs about 'change in dress' at a subordinate level then we refer simply to our tendency to switch from sober to bright colours, from wide lapels to narrow lapels and so forth. If we look at such changes superordinately then we can make more far-reaching distinctions. For example, we might see ourselves as having made many subordinate changes in dress while not changing superordinately because we have always 'followed fashion'. Thus at this level of abstraction there is no change because the multitude of our minor changes are always governed and controlled by our refusal to make a major change, that is, to dress independently of fashion.

Psychologists differ greatly in their view of how much change takes place in people and how it takes place. Trait psychologists tend to set up the notion of fixed personality characteristics which remain with people all their lives, which are measurable and which will predict their behaviour to a fair degree in any given situation. The evidence for this view has been much attacked (e.g. Mischel, 1968). Direct examination of personal experience suggests that Kelly (1955) may have been right in referring to 'man as a form of motion and not a static object that is occasionally kicked into movement'.

Psychological measurement, to date, suggests that people change their character, if only slowly, and have complex natures so that behaviour is not easily predictable from one situation to another. Psychologists have also tended to argue that where change takes place it is often unconscious and unchosen by the person. The issue of whether we choose change or whether change is something that happens to us is clearly complex. One way of viewing it might be to argue that we can and do choose to change ourselves, but that often we are less aware of the direction which chosen change may eventually take.

A person in a semi-skilled job may decide to go to night-school classes or undertake other forms of training in order to qualify themselves for what they regard as more challenging kinds of work. They might be successful in gaining qualifications and entering a new field. Up to this point they can reasonably claim to have chosen their direction of personal change and to have carried through that change in terms of their original proposal. However, the long-term effect may be that they acquire new kinds of responsibility, contacts with different kinds of people, new values and a life style which, in total, will involve personal changes not clearly envisaged at the time they went to their first evening class.

On the issue of how we go about changing ourselves, Radley (1974) speculated that change, particularly self-chosen change, may have three stages to it. Initially, if we are going to change, we must be able to envisage some goal; we must have a kind of picture of what we will be like when we have changed. He argued that if we have only a vague picture or no picture at all then we cannot change; we need to be able to 'see' the changed us in the distance. He went on to argue that when we have the picture then we can enact the role of a person like that. That is to say, we do not at heart believe that we are such a person but we can behave as if we were such a person, rather like an actor playing a role on stage or someone trying out a new style. (This may relate to the old adage that adolescence is the time when we 'try out' personalities to see which is a good fit.) He argued that if we enact in a committed and vigorous way for long enough then, at some mysterious point, we become what we are enacting and it is much more true to say that we are that person than that we are our former selves. This is very much a psychological explanation, in that it is about what is psychologically true, rather than what is formally and officially true. Thus the student who qualifies and becomes a teacher may officially, in terms of pay packet and title, be 'a teacher'. Yet, in Radley's terms, the person may still psychologically be 'a student' who is enacting the role of teacher, who is putting on a teaching style and carrying out the duties of a teacher but who still, in his heart of hearts, sees himself as a student. Later, there may come a point at which he becomes, in the psychological sense, a teacher.

However, we are also aware that there is much that is problematic and threatening about change. The set expectations of others about us may have an imprisoning effect and restrict our capacity to change. People have a picture of us and may attempt to enforce that picture. They may resist change in us because it seems to them unnatural, and it would make us less predictable. Phrases such as 'you are acting out of character', or 'that is not the true you', or 'those are not really your ideas' all reflect the difficulty people find and the resistance they manifest to change in us. Often the pressure of others' expectations is so great that we can only achieve change by keeping it secret until the change has gone so far that we can confront the dismay of others.

This is not to argue that we are simply moulded and brainwashed by our society and our family so that we are merely puppets dancing to tunes played by others. We are clearly influenced by others and everything, the language we speak, the clothes we wear, our values, ideas and feelings, is derived from and elaborated in terms of our relationships with other people and our society. But the more conscious we become of how this happens, the more likely we are to become critical of and the less likely automatically to accept what we are taught (formally and informally), and the more we may independently explore what we wish to make of ourselves as persons.

Equally, when we attempt to change we may find the process personally threatening. We may lose sight of the fact that change is inevitably a form of evolution: that is to say, we change from something to something and thereby there is continuity as well as change. If we lose faith in our own continuity we may be overwhelmed by a fear of some kind of catastrophic break, a fear of becoming something unpredictable to ourselves, of falling into chaos. Whether or not we are entirely happy with ourselves, at least we are something we are familiar with, and quite often we stay as we are because we would sooner suffer the devil we know than the unknown devil of a changed us. Fransella (1972) explored the way in which stutterers who seem to be on the verge of being cured of their stutter often suddenly relapse. She argued that stutterers know full well how to live as 'stutterers'; they understand how people react and relate to them as 'stutterers'. Nearing cure they are overwhelmed with the fear of the unknown, the strangeness of being 'a fluent speaker'.

Monitoring of self

One of the marked features of our culture is that it does not demand (or even suggest) that we formally monitor our lives or that we record our personal history in the way in which a society records its history. True, a few keep diaries, and practices such as re-reading old letters from other people give us glimpses into our past attitudes and feelings. For the most part, our understanding of our past is based on our often erratic memory of it. Moreover, our memory is likely to be erratic, not just because we forget past incidents and ideas but because we may actively 're-write' our history so as to emphasize our consistency and make our past compatible with our present.

Psychologists have tended to ignore the importance of personal history. The vast majority of psychological tests designed to assess the person cut in at a given point in time; they are essentially cross-sectional and pay little heed to the evolution of the person. It would be a very unusual psychology course that used biography or autobiography as material for its students to ponder. There are exceptions to this here-and-now preoccupation. In child psychology great emphasis is laid on the notion of 'development' and a great deal of the research and argument in child psychology is about how children acquire skills over a period, how they are gradually influenced by social customs and how life within the family, over a period of years, affects a child's valuing of himself. Additionally, clinical psychologists involved in psychotherapy and counselling very often find themselves engaged in a joint search with their clients through the immediate and distant past in order to understand present problems and concerns. This does not necessarily argue that a person is simply the end product of their past. We need to understand and acknowledge our past, not in order to repeat it but in order either to use it or to be free of it. As Kelly (1969) put it, 'you are not the victim of your autobiography but you may become the victim of the way you interpret your autobiography'.

Obstacles to self-knowledge and self-change

To try and understand oneself is not simply an interesting pastime, it is a necessity of life. In order to plan our future and to make choices we have to be able to anticipate our behaviour in future situations. This makes self-knowledge a practical guide, not a self-indulgence. Sometimes the situations with which we are confronted are of a defined and clear kind so that we can anticipate and predict our behaviour with reasonable certainty. If someone asks you if you can undertake task X (keep a set of accounts, drive a car, translate a letter from German and so forth) then it is not difficult to assess your skills and experience and work out whether you can undertake the task or not. Often the choice or the undertaking is of a more complex and less defined nature. Can you stand up in conflict with a powerful authority figure? Can you make a success of your marriage to this or that person? Can you live by yourself when you have been used to living with a family? The stranger the country we are entering the more threatening the prospect becomes; the more we realize that some degree of self-change may be involved, the more we must rely upon our understanding of our own character and potential.

In such circumstances we are acutely aware of the dangers of change and may take refuge in a rigid and inflexible notion of what we are. Kelly (1955, 1969) referred to this tendency as 'hostility'. He defined hostility as 'the continued effort to extort validational evidence in favour of a type of social prediction which has already been recognized as a failure'. We cannot lightly abandon our theory of what we are, since the abandonment of such a theory may plunge us into chaos. Thus we see someone destroy a close relationship in order to 'prove' that they are independent or we see teachers 'proving' that their pupils are stupid in order to verify that they themselves are clever.

Closely connected to this definition of hostility is Kelly's definition of guilt as 'the awareness of dislodgement of self from one's core role structure'. Core constructs are those which govern a person's maintenance processes; they are those constructs in terms of which identity is established and the self is pictured and understood. Your core role structure is what you understand yourself to be.

It is in a situation in which you fail to anticipate your own behaviour that you experience guilt. Defined in this way guilt comes not from a violation of some social code but from a violation of your own personal picture of what you are.

There are traditional ways of exploring the issue of 'what am I like?' We can meditate upon ourselves, ask others how they see us, or review our history. Psychologists have devised numerous tests for assessing 'personality', though insofar as these are of any use they seem to be designed to give the psychologist ideas about the other person rather than to give the people ideas about themselves. Two relatively recent attempts to provide people with ways of exploring their own 'personality' are offered by McFall (in Bannister and Fransella, 1980) and Mair (1970).

McFall offers a simple elaboration on the idea of talking to oneself. His work indicated that if people associate freely into a tape-recorder and listen to their own free flow then, given that they erase it afterwards so that there is no possible audience other than themselves at that time, they may learn something of the themes, conflicts and issues that concern them; themes that are 'edited out' of most conversation and which are only fleetingly glimpsed in our thinking. Mair experimented with formalized, written conversation. Chosen partners wrote psychological descriptions of each other (and predictions of the other's description) and then compared and discussed the meaning and the evidence underlying their written impressions.

Although we have formal ways of exploring how we see and how we are seen by others (the encounter group), and informal ways (the party), it can be argued that there is something of a taboo in our society on direct expression of our views of each other. It may be that we fear to criticize lest we be criticized, or it may be that we are embarrassed by the whole idea of the kind of confrontation involved in telling each other about impressions which are being created. Certainly if you contemplate how much you know about the way you are seen by others, you may be struck by the limitations of your knowledge, even on quite simple issues. How clear are you as to how your voice tone is experienced by other people? How often do you try and convey to someone your feelings and thoughts about them in such an oblique and roundabout way that there is a fair chance that they will not grasp the import of what you are saying?

Psychologists are only very slowly seeing it as any part of their task to offer WAYS to people in which they may explore themselves and explore the effect they have on others.

Role and person

Social psychologists have made much use of the concept of 'role'. Just as an actor plays a particular role in a drama it can be argued that each of us has a number of roles in our family, in work groups, in our society. We have consistent ways of speaking, dressing and behaving which reflect our response to the expectations of the group around us. Thus within a family or small social group we may have inherited and developed the role of 'clown' or 'hardheaded practical person' or 'sympathizer'. Jobs often carry

implicit role specifications with them so that we perceive
different psychological requirements in the role of teacher
from the role of student or the role of manager from the
role of worker. We are surprised by the randy parson, the
sensitive soldier, the shy showbusiness person. Society also
prescribes very broad and pervasive roles for us as men or
women, young or old, working-class or middle-class and so
forth. It is not that every word of our scripts is pre-
written for us, but the broad boundaries and characteristics
of behaviour appropriate to each role are fairly well
understood. These social roles can and do conflict with
personal inclinations and one way of defining maturity would
be to look on it as the process whereby we give increasing
expression to what we personally are, even where this
conflicts with standard social expectations.

Kelly chose to define role in a more strictly personal
sense in his sociality corollary which reads: 'to the extent
that one person construes the construction processes of
another he may play a role in a social process involving the
other person'. He is here emphasizing the degree to which,
when we relate to another person, we relate in terms of our
picture of the other person's picture of us. Role then
becomes not a life style worked out by our culture and
waiting for us to step into, but the on-going process
whereby we try to imagine and understand how other people
see the world and continuously to relate our own conception
to theirs.

The paradox of self-knowing

We reasonably assume that our knowledge of something does
not alter the 'thing' itself. If I come to know that Guatemala produces zinc or that the angle of incidence of a light
ray equals its angle of reflection, then this new knowledge
of mine does not, of itself, affect Guatemala or light.
However, it alters me in that I have become 'knowing' and
not 'ignorant' of these things. More pointedly, if I come to
know something of myself then I am changed, to a greater
or lesser degree, by that knowledge. Any realization by a
person of the motives and attitudes underlying their
behaviour has the potential to alter that behaviour.

Put another way, a person is the sum of their understanding of their world and themselves. Changes in what we
know of ourselves and the way in which we come to know it
are changes in the kind of person we are.

This paradox of self-knowledge presents a perpetual
problem to psychologists. An experimental psychologist may
condition a person to blink their eye when a buzzer is
pressed, simply by pairing the buzzer sound with a puff of
air to the person's eyelid until the blink becomes a response to the sound of the buzzer on its own. But if the
person becomes aware of the nature of the conditioning
process and resents being its 'victim' then he may not
condition at all, or at least take much longer to condition.
The person's knowledge of what is going on within him and

between him and the psychologist has altered the person and i validated the psychologist's predictions. Experimental psychologists seek to evade the consequences of this state of affairs by striving to keep the subject in ignorance of the nature of the experimental process or by using what they assume to be naturally ignorant subjects: for example, rats. But relying on a precariously maintained ignorance in the experimental subject creates only a mythical certainty in science. Psychotherapists, on the other hand, generally work on the basis that the more the person (subject, patient, client) comes to know of themselves, the nearer they will come to solving, at least in part, their personal problems.

This self-changing property of self knowledge may be a pitfall for a simple-minded science of psychology. It may also be the very basis of living, for us as persons.

References

Bannister, D. and Agnew, J. (1977)
The Child's Construing of Self. In A.W. Landfield (ed.), Nebraska Symposium on Motivation 1976. Nebraska: University of Nebraska Press.
Bannister, D. and Fransella, F. (1980)
Inquiring Man (2nd edn). Harmondsworth: Penguin.
Fransella, F. (1972)
Personal Change and Reconstruction. London: Academic Press.
Kelly, G.A. (1955)
The Psychology of Personal Constructs, Volumes I and II. New York: Norton.
Kelly, G.A. (1969)
Clinical Psychology and Personality: The selected papers of George Kelly (ed. B.A. Maher). New York: Wiley.
Mair, J.M.M. (1970)
Experimenting with individuals. British Journal of Medical Psychology, 43, 245-256.
Mead, G.H. (1925)
The genesis of the self and social control. International Journal of Ethics, 35, 251-273.
Mischel, W. (1968)
Personality and Assessment. New York: Wiley.
Radley, A.R. (1974)
The effect of role enactment on construct alternatives. British Journal of Medical Psychology, 47, 313-320.

Questions

1. Discuss the problem of defining 'self'.
2. Examine the way in which a person's idea of 'self' is affected by the nature of their work.
3. Discuss the nature of sex differences in ideas about 'self'.
4. How can we 'keep track' of ourselves?
5. What does Kelly mean by 'hostility'? Give examples.
6. Outline one theory of 'self' you have read about.

7. Describe some way in which you have increased your knowledge of yourself.
8. Comment on Radley's idea of change through role enactment.
9. Outline Freud's picture of self as made up of id, ego and super-ego.
10. How would you go about teaching a course in 'self-knowledge'?
11. How do parents influence their children's ideas about 'self'?
12. To what extent is our picture of our self influenced by our physical state and appearance?
13. Some institutions require their staff to meet regularly and formally to discuss how their personal differences affect their work. Is this a good idea?
14. We come to understand ourselves through our relationship with others. Discuss.
15. Examine the way in which social customs inhibit our revealing of 'self'.
16. Self is just a product of our environment. Discuss.
17. People are born with a fixed character which they cannot alter. Discuss.
18. Adolescence is the time when we experiment with self. Discuss.
19. Write an essay on 'roles'.
20. Can psychologists measure personality?
21. What, in your view, are the main hindrances of self-knowledge?
22. Write an essay on 'guilt'.
23. 'He is not himself today.' What triggers off this kind of comment, and does it say more about the speaker than the person of whom it is said?
24. How can we go about changing ourselves?
25. What idea about 'self', proposed by anyone (psychologist, poet, friend or whatever) has impressed you most? Why?
26. Your family teaches you what to think of yourself. Discuss.
27. Your job enables you to express yourself. Your job prevents you being yourself. Discuss.

Annotated reading

Axline, Virginia M. (1971) Dibs: In search of self. Harmondsworth: Penguin.
> A finely written description of a withdrawn and disturbed child who in the process of psychotherapy comes vividly to life. It casts light on our early struggles to achieve the idea of being a 'self'.

Bannister, D. and Fransella, F. (1980) Inquiring Man: The psychology of personal constructs. Harmondsworth: Penguin.
> The second edition of a book which sets out the way George Kelly sees each of us as developing a complex personal view of our world. The book describes two

decades of psychological research based on the theory and relates it to problems such as psychological breakdown, prejudice, child development and personal relationships.

Bott, M. and Bowskill, D. (1980) The Do-It-Yourself Mind Book. London: Wildwood House.
A lightly written but shrewd book on the ways in which we can tackle serious personal and emotional problems without recourse to formal psychiatry.

Fransella, F. (1975) Need to Change? London: Methuen.
A brief description of the formal and informal ways in which 'self' is explored and change attempted.

Rogers, C.R. (1961) On Becoming a Person. Boston: Houghton Mifflin.
Sets out the idea of 'self-actualization' and describes the ways in which we might avoid either limiting ourselves or being socially limited, and come to be what Rogers calls a fully functioning person.

Relevance to the teacher
DAVID FONTANA

The preceding section indicates how we build up knowledge of ourselves, and how dependent this knowledge is upon what other people tell us about ourselves, both directly and, through the way in which they treat us, indirectly. Bannister sums this up by saying that 'our picture of ourselves is not derived by sitting in isolation but is generated by our engagement with others'. This is illustrated for us by a number of pieces of research into various aspects of the growth of self-concepts, some of which have great practical relevance to the teacher. The best example of these is probably Stanley Coopersmith's investigation into the development of self-esteem (e.g. 1968), and it is worth looking into this in some detail.

The development of self-esteem
Self-esteem is, of course, concerned with the value we place upon ourselves, and of all areas of self-concepts it is one of the most important. It is sometimes claimed that one of the major factors (if not THE major factor) in the development of psychological ill-health is the inability of some individuals to value themselves at their true worth. We mean by this that the people concerned seem unable to regard themselves as significant acceptable members of the community, but labour instead under feelings of inadequacy and even hopelessness, and consistently under-estimate both their abilities and the regard in which they are held by other people. As we shall see from Coopersmith's work, these feelings of inadequacy are apparent by the time children reach junior school (and probably long before), and do not seem necessarily to be related realistically to the child's academic potential or to any other factors closely associated with it.

Coopersmith began his investigation with a sample of ten-year-old boys, and followed them through into early adult life. Using a battery of psychological tests and self-ratings, Coopersmith found his sample could be divided consistently into three groups which he labelled 'high', 'medium' and 'low' self-esteem respectively. High self-esteem boys showed themselves to have a positive, realistic view of themselves and their own abilities. They were confident, not unduly worried by criticism, and enjoyed participating in things. They were active and expressive in all they did, and were generally successful academically and socially. Medium self-esteem boys showed many of these qualities, but were more conformist, less sure of their worth, and more anxious for social acceptance. Low self-esteem boys, however, were described by Coopersmith as a sad little group, isolated, fearful, reluctant to join in, self-conscious and over-sensitive to criticism. They consistently underrated themselves, tended to under-achieve in class, and were preoccupied for much of their time with their own problems.

It might be thought that the high self-esteem boys were more intelligent than the rest, and had proved their ability to themselves, or that perhaps they were physically more attractive or came from wealthier homes or had some other quality that made them more popular and better liked. Careful research showed this not to be the case. Boys in all three groups came from middle-class homes (in fact, they were deliberately chosen from the same socio-economic background), and there were no significant measurable differences between them on any of the other variables just mentioned. Where they did differ sharply, though, was in the relationship which they had with their parents. The high self-esteem boys came from homes in which they were regarded as significant and interesting people, and in which respect was shown for their opinions and points of view. Their parents had higher and more consistent standards than did those in the other groups, and their methods of discipline were less erratic. Though not necessarily permissive, this discipline eschewed corporal punishment and relied instead upon rewards for good behaviour and upon withdrawal of approval for bad. Parents knew a great deal about their children (such as their interests and the names of their friends), showed physical affection towards them, and clearly signalled to them in all sorts of ways that they mattered very much as people. Interestingly, the boys regarded their parents as being fair towards them ('fairness', remember, is a quality highly prized by ten-year-old children!).

By contrast, the low self-esteem boys often regarded their parents as unfair. Within the home, discipline veered from over-strictness to over-permissiveness, and the boys were obviously not sure where they stood. There was less clear guidance than in the homes of the high self-esteem boys, standards were less apparent, and parents knew significantly less about their children. Here the signals seemed to suggest to the boys that they were not as significant and important within the home, and did not count for as much as people.

Causal factors in self-esteem

Since, as has been said, there was no apparent difference between the boys on cognitive, physical or socio-economic variables, we can conclude that their high and low levels of self-esteem were linked significantly to parental behaviour. The boys, in large measure, took over and internalized the picture that their parents appeared to have of them. The consequences of this for their performance in school were considerable. The high self-esteem boys set themselves more elevated (and realistic) goals. Because they were not unduly frightened by the possibility of failure they were much readier to meet challenge, to participate, and to express their feelings. When they met occasional failure or criticism they were undaunted by it because they had a firm conviction of their own worth. The low self-esteem boys, on the other hand, saw failure as yet another blow to their small store of self-confidence, and tended to play safe and set themselves artificially low goals. (Note that sometimes, however, low self-esteem individuals set themselves unrealistically high goals, perhaps because no one can then blame them when they fail or because of some obscure desire for self-punishment.) They were unduly wounded by criticism, and generally anxious for approval because they set great store by what others thought of them.

These findings have relevance for the teacher for two reasons: first, because they tell him a great deal about the development of the child's self-concepts within the home, and second, because they give some practical guidance on how the teacher can best influence this development for good in the classroom. If, in the previous pages, we were to substitute the word 'teacher' for the word 'parents' we would still be providing ourselves with a valid model of what goes on. Certainly the parent has more influence normally over the child than the teacher, but the child tends to take over and internalize the teacher's picture of him just as he takes over and internalizes his parents' picture. Many teachers signal to their children, consciously and unconsciously, that they value them as people, that they consider them capable of developing the necessary skills to cope with their work, and that they consider them important enough to spend time listening to their views (and advice) on most of the things that go on in the classroom. They set their children consistent and realistic standards, encourage them to be undaunted by failure, and urge them to have the confidence to act independently and responsibly when the occasion arises. Other teachers, disappointed perhaps that progress with particular individuals and groups of children is not as fast as they would like, send signals of the opposite kind, and leave children with negative feelings about themselves and their abilities. Such teachers forget that they should be concerned first and foremost not with

making comparisons between children and finding some wanting, but with indicating clearly to each member of the class
that he matters as much as does everyone else, and that he
has qualities and abilities which can be developed and which
can help him enjoy the positive things in life and cope
better with its problems and difficulties.

Other influences on self-esteem

Coopersmith has now followed this sample through into the
adult world and shown that his high self-esteem boys have
consistently outperformed those of low self-esteem and have
proved more successful vocationally as well as within their
education. One limitation of his study, however, is that he
did not examine the influence of socio-economic status or of
sex upon self-esteem (his sample, remember, consisted only
of middle-class boys). Nevertheless, there is evidence, as
was mentioned when discussing the influence of socio-
economic status in Part I, that children from working-class
homes generally suffer from lower self-esteem than children
from homes higher up the socio-economic scale, and it was
suggested that this is hardly surprising as the former
children tend to have constant reminders of their own supposed 'inferiority' in the form of dilapidated environments,
few facilities, older school buildings and so on. Much can
be done, of course, by parents and teachers to combat this
unwarranted sense of being less good than the children from
more affluent environments, but their task is not an easy
one. As we also indicated in Part I, delinquent groups tend
to suffer from low self-esteem, and often their 'toughness'
and antisocial behaviour would appear to be an attempt to
protect this self-esteem by demonstrating their power to
destroy things that society deems to be important, and thus
prove to all and sundry that they do really matter after
all. It is interesting to note that the low self-esteem
middle-class boys in Coopersmith's sample, with their
greater respect for authority, appeared to accept docilely
the negative view that others had of them, whereas working-
class boys show a greater tendency to fight back and blame
their failures at least in part upon authority itself.

Turning now to the position of girls, we find that they
generally (again as we suggested in Part I) have lower
levels of self-esteem than boys. As with most of the sex
differences that we have discussed in the book so far, this
would appear to be largely the result of cultural factors,
and the general status of women in society (though the
stronger musculature and the greater physical height of the
male sex generally at maturity may also play some part). We
find evidence for lower self-esteem in girls, for example,
in the fact that when paired with boys in a problem-solving
task they sometimes artificially depress their performance
levels so as not to outshine their partners (a phenomenon
that does not work in reverse). Some girls, it seems, feel
uncomfortable in the superior role, as it they are performing in a manner inconsistent with their true position in

life. Girls also tend to rate themselves less highly than do boys on written tests of self-esteem, to set themselves lower goals in life, and to be more inclined to underestimate their abilities than do boys even in primary school where in reading and language skills they often tend to outshine the latter. Depressingly often, even in our supposedly more enlightened times, they seem prepared to accept second best for themselves, even though they are prepared to be just as hard-working and conscientious.

Encouraging self-esteem

Both with children from working-class backgrounds and with girls the teacher can do a great deal to help the development of self-esteem if he pursues the methods outlined above, and indicates firmly the regard and respect with which he views them. It is also important, with all children, to encourage them to articulate their picture of themselves. A low self-esteem child can do little to subject his negative self-concepts to critical scrutiny until these concepts are defined and recognized for what they are, which in turn is not possible until the child has found some way of expressing them. Once the child has learnt to communicate the nature of his self-doubts to others, he can be helped to face up to them and to recognize their lack of substance. We are not suggesting by this that the teacher should spend all his time in a counselling role, or be continually taking children on one side to get them to talk about themselves, but simply that he should be at all times alert for opportunities to get at the way in which children themselves perceive their own successes and failures. Often children become quite skilled at hiding their feelings, even from themselves, and the teacher may be misled into thinking that low marks, or criticisms directed towards them in class, have no real effect upon their self-esteem or their confidence in their own abilities. He may even feel rather angry about this, and redouble these criticisms in the hope that they will finally 'sink in'. The result is often to wound the child further, or to make him defend his self-esteem by ignoring the teacher and pretending that neither the teacher's opinions nor the subject being taught are of any value.

This does not mean that the teacher should not criticize children, or mark work wrong, or challenge them to greater effort; far from it. The teacher must always be concerned to help each child reach his potential. What it does mean, however, is that the teacher should do things in such a way that the child's self-esteem is protected. Children will differ in the extent of their needs, and the robust, high self-esteem child will, as we have seen, be less sensitive than the low, but in all cases it means giving the child work that is appropriate to his competence, drawing attention to successes rather than harping upon failures, giving work back personally to children wherever possible (particularly if the marks are rather low) with a quiet word of encouragement rather than simply handing it back in class. It also means helping a child to understand and profit from his errors, choosing any words of criticism with care and making sure that they are applied to the work rather than to the child himself, and emphasizing at all times by actions as well as by words that, whatever happens, each child retains the teacher's concern and respect.

In lessons such as creative writing, the child can sometimes be encouraged to put his feelings about himself into words. One way of doing this is to invite him to write a description of himself in the third person. Such a description can start with the words 'Do you know Mary Smith (or whatever the child's name happens to be) ...?' or 'We like Mary Smith because ...', or 'Mary Smith was very happy last week because ...' or in any other similar way that the teacher feels to be appropriate. Fine art and drama lessons can also help the child to communicate his view of self, and give the teacher clues as to the kind of help he may need to rebuild any aspects of this view which appear negative. The only cautions required here, of course, are that the teacher should not invite children to reveal too much of their mental life before classmates who may scoff at them afterwards, and that the teacher should not read too much into any one thing that a child happens to say. Children have their ups and downs and a child who is feeling badly at odds with himself one day may be much happier about things the next. Similarly, children may sometimes read themselves into a part and say what they think the teacher expects of them. The wise teacher places the happenings of any one lesson or any one day within the wider context of what he knows of the child.

In any discussion of self-esteem the objection is sometimes raised that we must not give a child an inflated picture of himself which will only be rudely destroyed one day. This is a fair point, but we are not suggesting that the teacher be dishonest towards his children. Self-esteem should not be equated with conceit. It stems not from an exaggerated view of oneself but from the realization that one matters to the people one loves or who are in authority over one or with whom one works. It stems from the knowledge that one is doing the best one can with one's abilities, and that the rest of the world is not critically watching one's every move ready to pounce as soon as there is any hint of error. And, finally, it stems from the knowledge that one should extend to oneself the understanding and sympathy that one extends to others. Some low self-esteem people are full of excuses because they cannot bear the thought that something or other was their fault and is therefore further proof of their inadequacy, but many of them are quick to excuse others but never themselves. Such people (and this is easier in childhood than in later life) need to be helped towards self-acceptance and towards a realistic appraisal of themselves and of their own abilities and potential abilities. As the German philosopher Immanuel Kant pointed out, self-knowledge is the beginning of all wisdom.

Self-maturity

Bannister indicates clearly to us that in all discussion of
the self we are concerned not just with the person as he now
is, but with the person as he will one day become. The individual's notion of himself is undergoing constant change,
particularly in childhood. Sometimes this change can be
abrupt as, for example, when the individual achieves sudden
success at a task that he has been trying to master for some
considerable time, or when he experiences equally sudden
failure in an area in which he thought himself competent.
More usually, however, it takes place gradually, as the
individual reacts with his environment and ponders over the
lessons it has taught him. Obviously the teacher is particularly concerned with the nature of this change, and is
anxious to see that it takes a positive and desirable form
in the children for whom he is responsible.

One way in which we can discuss this change is to see
it as a movement towards self-maturity: that is, towards
self-concepts that are realistic and self-accepting, and
that contain an assessment of the self broadly in line with
the assessment that other people have of one (we shall have
more to say about the definition of maturity shortly). There
are various theories within psychology as to how the individual moves towards this self-maturity, but for the teacher
one of the most helpful is that advanced by Erik Erikson
(e.g. 1950). Erikson suggests that the individual is faced
by a number of learning tasks as he goes from infancy to old
age, each of which should be completed satisfactorily before
he tackles the next. If he fails in any of these tasks, then
his later development is handicapped, and he will be faced
one day with having to go back and rectify this failure if
he is ever to become fully mature. These learning tasks,
together with the approximate period of life associated with
each, are given below. It will be noted that against each
task Erikson suggests the consequences to the individual of
failure. Thus if the small infant does not learn trust he is
left with mistrust: if the older infant does not learn
autonomy he is left with shame and doubt, and so on.

Erikson's eight stages in the development of personal maturity

*   Early infancy - trust versus mistrust
*   Late infancy - autonomy versus shame and doubt
*   Early childhood - initiative versus guilt
*   Middle childhood - competence versus inferiority
*   Adolescence - identity versus role confusion
*   Early adulthood - intimacy versus isolation
*   Middle adulthood - generativity versus stagnation
*   Late adulthood - self-acceptance versus despair

We can see, therefore, that in terms of Erikson's
theory, the early infant needs to learn that other people

can be trusted, and that he can rely upon them to satisfy his physical and emotional needs. This trust gives him a secure base from which he can reach out and explore the world with confidence. In later infancy his growing physical and psychological abilities bring with them the beginnings of independence from others, and he needs now increasing freedom to express his own wishes and to make choices for himself. If he is confronted by adults who see this bid for autonomy as stubbornness, and turn everything into a battle of wills, then he feels doubtful and confused, and even ashamed of his own desire for greater independence. This is particularly apparent in the third year of life, when the child often goes through what appears to be a very negative phase in which he responds with awkwardness and disagreement to the wishes of others. Far from indicating that he is becoming difficult, this negative phase is a healthy sign of the beginnings of autonomy, and should be met by understanding, sympathy, and patient firmness where such becomes necessary. The child then learns that his autonomy is welcome to those around him, but that at the same time there are reasonable limits which he must observe if he is not to restrict other people unduly in turn.

Erikson is not precise about the ages associated with these (or any of his other) stages, and accepts that there are wide individual differences. However, late infancy probably includes the nursery school years in most cases, and by the early childhood stage the child is usually entering the infant school. In terms of Erikson's theory, early childhood is characterized by the need to develop initiative, which is an extension of autonomy into more specific, focussed activity, with the child able to take responsibility for inaugurating this activity where appropriate. As with autonomy, if initiative is thwarted, and he is made to feel in some way unacceptable for wanting to make it a part of his behavioural repertoire, the child is left with self-doubt and guilt, and the feeling that there is something seriously wrong with him for having such desires.

Having learnt the task of initiative, the child is faced in middle childhood (approximately junior school age) with learning that of competence; that is, with learning to do things well and to develop the skills necessary for coping with immediate problems. If he fails in this task (and naturally it involves what goes on in the home as well as what goes on in school, and what goes on in social life as well as what goes on in academic life), then he shows the symptoms of inferiority and low self-esteem that we discussed in the last section. The next stage, adolescence, brings with it the search for identity (which is so important that a separate section is devoted to it below), and this is followed in early adult life by the search for intimacy (close ties with another person or persons as in, for example, marriage), in middle adulthood by generativity (creative and self-fulfilling roles in the rearing of children, in one's profession, in the community at large), and in late adulthood by the self-acceptance that comes from knowing one has done one's best in life and made the maximum use of whatever opportunities and abilities have come one's way.

Allport's model of self-development

Gordon Allport, whose work shows reciprocal influence with that of Erikson at a number of points, suggests that as the individual moves through the various stages of personality development towards maturity so he becomes a more integrated and consistent person. In the early stages of this development Allport sees the child as possessing a number of rather disparate personality traits (e.g. friendliness, honesty, bookishness) which he may use inconsistently in dealing with others (e.g. he may be honest with his friends but not with his teachers, bookish at home but not at school: see chapters 9 and 10). As he grows older these coalesce into a smaller number of what Allport calls selves (e.g. the child may have one identifiable, consistent self within the school - both in terms of behaviours and self-concepts - and another within the home), which later become integrated into a single personality. To avoid confusion over terms, note that in this context Allport only uses the word 'personality' when the individual has reached self-maturity, and uses the word 'selves' to denote units that cohere to make up personality, while both in Bannister's section and in the rest of this chapter we use the word 'self' to cover all the awareness and concepts that the individual has of himself.

In terms of Allport's model, one sign that the individual has not yet reached self-maturity is that he behaves inconsistently. He seems, in other words, to shape his behaviour to the circumstances in which he finds himself. Actions towards others which he would regard as unthinkable in the context, say, of his family or his church or his golf club he may perform without a second thought when it comes to his business life. People who meet him in these different circumstances therefore see quite different sides of him. Alternatively (though less usually) he might show different selves within the same environment dependent upon moods, the state of his relationship that day with his wife and children, the difficulty of his journey to work and so on. Obviously, we all vary the detail of our behaviour from one context to another (the informality of our behaviour with close friends might be out of place, for example, at a business meeting), but if we are mature we are still identifiably the same person, with the same value system, the same self-concepts, the same attitudes and so on, no matter where we find ourselves.

In addition to this unified, consistent approach to his life circumstances, Allport sees the mature person as possessing the following characteristics (Allport, 1961).

*   An extended sense of self (the ability to identify with other people's concerns as well as with one's own; to offer sympathy and empathy).

* A warm, unselfish relationship with others.
* Emotional security.
* Self-insight (a realistic knowledge and appraisal of oneself).
* A realistic orientation towards the world (the ability to exercise sound judgement and take necessary decisions).
* A unifying philosophy of life (some consistent, coherent view of the purpose and meaning of life, whether it be religious or humanistic, that helps resolve questions of value and helps determine life goals).

We must not overlook the fact that temperamental factors may play some part in the development of this maturity in the sense that, for example, the 'easy' children in the Thomas, Chess and Birch study (see chapter 9) might find warm unselfish relationships with others come more readily to them than they do to the 'difficult' children. But in the main, most of the qualities listed would appear to be heavily dependent upon learning. Even cognitive factors such as high intelligence, though they might be helpful in the development of, for instance, a realistic orientation towards the world, are no guarantee of maturity in the absence of the right kind of learning experiences.

Of course, Allport does not suggest that we must wait until we are adults before we can show some of the qualities associated with self-maturity. These qualities may be developed at different times (with a unifying philosophy of life perhaps always coming last) and to different degrees, with a ten-year-old child perhaps showing emotional security, unselfish relationships with others, and a certain degree of self-insight, and not manifesting any of the other qualities until rather later. Since we could well have an adult who showed none of these, it is perfectly feasible to maintain that some children show greater maturity than some of their elders.

Self-identity

This is the developmental stage associated particularly with adolescence and, as was indicated above, it is of sufficient importance to warrant a section to itself. Self-identity is really the sum total of the concepts the individual has about himself. Thus there is, of course, some sense of self-identity in early infancy and in all the tasks identified by Erikson as taking place before adolescence. But when we talk of self-identity we are really also inferring that these self-concepts should band together in a coherent way and give the individual some reasonably complete picture of the kind of person he is and is to become, and this kind of coherence usually begins to emerge at adolescence. Note that this is not the same thing as saying that the personality becomes fixed at adolescence. Growth, change and development remain possible (and desirable) throughout life, but adolescence marks the transition from the fluid personality of the child (i.e. from the traits and selves of which Allport talks) to the more constant one of the adult.

Adolescence also marks the emergence of more mature life goals. Up to this time the child will have normally had few clear life goals, not only in terms of his future vocation but in terms of the ideal self, the kind of person he would like to become. We have more to say about these (and in particular about vocational goals) when we discuss educational and vocational guidance in chapter 14, but it should be clear to the reader that they are closely linked to the sense of identity, to the sense that 'this is the person I am, these are my abilities and my values, and this is what I want to do with my life'.

The search for self-identity in adolescence is often accompanied by a great deal of experimentation. The adolescent, as it were, tries out a number of different kinds of behaviour, as if asking 'Which of these different kinds of people is really me?' To help this process, he will often adopt role models, older people (friends, pop stars, teachers, sportsmen and women) whose life style and whose values he will try to copy. Since identity is often expressed through the groups to which one belongs, the peer-group also becomes very important, and the adolescent may change his behaviour (clothes, speech and habits as well as values and opinions) in order to be accepted by it. Since acceptance by the opposite sex is also important, behaviours considered to make one sexually attractive may also be adopted.

All this may appear rather amusing (or tiresome, depending upon where one stands) to the adult, who has long left this stage behind and who in any case has to have some defence against being made to feel old or out of touch; but this is often to misinterpret what is really going on. In our complex, industrialized society we keep the young in a subservient role (i.e. still at school) long after they have reached physical maturity. We do this because there just seems to us to be so much to learn, but this places heavy potential strains upon the young themselves (and upon teachers too, sometimes). In addition, in spite of their physical maturity, and their strong sex drive and other emotional changes, adolescents are really given very little help on what it is like to be grown up. They may be given adult reading matter and taken out to look at the community and at people at work, but useful as this is it does not give adolescents any real sense of natural transition from childhood to adulthood. In less complex communities than ours the child learns by working alongside mother and father, and grows up with the knowledge of what it is like to be adult and of the rights and responsibilities that go with adult status. At some point in puberty this status is conferred upon him, often at a set ceremony or initiation, and from that time on he is recognized as a full member of the community. Thus it is sometimes suggested that what we in advanced industrialized societies recognize as adolescence, with all the storms and stresses that often accompany this period, is essentially a cultural phenomenon, and that it is not the adolescent growth spurt and the physiological changes that go with it that create the rebellious teenager, but society itself with its artificial methods of relating to its young people.

It will be recalled from chapter 3 that cognitively the adolescent has also usually achieved the stage of formal operations, and is therefore now able to reason in abstract terms. As a consequence, many of the concepts associated with religion, politics, and social relationships begin to take on a deeper and more complex meaning, and the adolescent often calls into question the activities and policies of the adult generation in these important areas. Since he may find such activities and policies wanting, and wish to see them replaced by more equitable practices, adolescence is often described as a period of idealism, and this idealism may also be reflected in the kind of life goals that he chooses at this point. These goals may later have to be modified in the light of experience, but for the present the adolescent may feel passionately about them, and resent the apparent inability of his elders to understand if not actively to share this passion.

The adolescent and the teacher
There is a tendency sometimes to forget that, in spite of his apparent assurance, the adolescent is often a prey to insecurity. While he searches for identity he is never sure that the person he is becoming will prove acceptable and successful in the adult world. He has learnt to cope with being a child, but now has to find out whether he can cope with being an adult. Thus, although he may seem unimpressed any longer by parents and teachers, their support and good opinion is still vital to him. Teachers who work well with adolescents seem aware of this fact, and are often able to create a relationship with them that they will one day come to regard as amongst the most formative of their lives. Such teachers seem able to understand and sympathize with the adolescent's problems, to tolerate patiently the occasional outbursts and strange mannerisms, to excite his interest and involvement in the subject being studied, and perhaps above all to provide him with clear and consistent (and reasonable) guidelines to the kind of behaviours best suited to the adult world and to the achievement of long-term life goals. This last means, of course, that the teacher does not compromise his own standards in the interests of making himself acceptable to his class. Where these standards concern values or opinions he makes them available to the class while insisting that in the final instance these are matters of personal choice. Where they concern school rules or regulations he stands firm on them, explains the reasoning behind them (and the correct machinery for attempting to change them if this is desired), and points out that few

jobs and professions are without their rule books and codes of conduct. Where they concern the subject being taught he insists on each individual aiming for the highest levels of which he is capable. Where they concern social behaviour, he demonstrates through his own conduct the importance of an awareness of the feelings and rights of others as well as for those of oneself.

Role confusion

It will be seen from our list of Erikson's eight stages in the development of personal maturity that the consequence of failure to develop identity is role confusion. Role confusion implies that the individual has no clear idea of the kind of person he is or of the role that he should assume in life. He may show the several different selves mentioned by Allport, or the low self-esteem and insecurity of Coopersmith's boys, or even the uncertainty and the constant self-doubt and self-questioning that is a feature of some kinds of neurotic behaviour. Note, though, that Erikson does not suggest he will inevitably become a failure in life. Many apparently successful people in business, politics, and all walks of life show the symptoms of role confusion. Erikson would argue that this is amply born out by the high incidence of psychological problems that seem to beset the outwardly successful in our community as well as the apparently unsuccessful. It is estimated that one person in ten will at some point in their lives require medical help for these problems (in reality the figure is probably much higher, with many psychological problems disguised by more obvious physical symptoms), and although a failure to develop self-identity successfully is only one of the causal factors it is nevertheless a major one. Erikson is arguing therefore that the development of a consistent identity and the various other qualities that go with self-maturity cannot be inferred simply from the material position that one has achieved in life. They show themselves instead in the much subtler areas of one's relationships with one's fellows and with oneself.

References

Allport, G.W. (1961)
Pattern and Growth in Personality. London: Holt, Rinehart & Winston.
Coopersmith, S. (1968)
Studies in self-esteem. Scientific American, February issue.
Erikson, E.H. (1950)
Childhood and Society. New York: Norton.

Additional reading

Coopersmith, S. (1967) The Antecedents of Self-esteem. San Francisco: Freeman.
Discusses his work fully.

Radford, J. and Kirby, R. (1975) The Person in Pyschology. London: Methuen.
   A highly readable little book, dealing with broader aspects of the self.

Barron, F. (1979) The Shaping of Personality: Conflict, choice, and growth. New York: Harper & Row.
   Another excellent text that roams more widely in the field of personality but has a great deal of value to say about the self.

Maslow, A. (1962) Towards a Psychology of Being. London: Van Nostrand.
   This has also proved a very influential book over the years.

Allport, G.W. (1961) Pattern and Growth in Personality. London: Holt, Rinehart & Winston.
   A splendidly humane and sensitive book, dealing fully with the ideas surrounding the concept of self-maturity.

Erikson, E.H. (1950) Childhood and Society. New York: Norton.

Erikson, E.H. (1968) Identity: Youth and crisis. New York: Norton.
   Those readers interested in Erikson's work will enjoy these. The second is especially good on adolescence.

Jersild, A.T., Brook, J.S. and Brook, D.W. (1978) The Psychology of Adolescence (3rd edn). London: Collier Macmillan.
   A highly comprehensive book on all aspects of adolescence and of the challenges it poses to the self and the sense of identity.

Kleinke, C.L. (1978) Self-Perception: The psychology of personal awareness. San Francisco: Freeman.
   This gives a good survey of the ways in which the individual comes to know and understand himself.

Part four

Social Interaction and Teacher – Child Relations

Much teaching and learning is done through social interaction, with the teacher interacting with the class both as
individuals and as a group, and the children interacting
with each other. Social behaviour, particularly within the
classroom but at all points where contact is made between
people and where learning outcomes are thus rendered possible, is therefore of great interest to the teacher. The
better he understands this behaviour, the better is he able
to provide optimum learning environments for the children.

Social behaviour, however, does not mean merely the
formal interchanges between the teacher and the class and
the interchanges between children during group activities. A
teacher and his class form together a distinct social unit,
and within that unit there exists a complex and fluid
undercurrent of social relationships and social attitudes
which shape individual and group responses in a range of
subtle ways. Some children will emerge as leaders and trend-
setters, others as followers or as isolates. Some children
will pair off into close friendships, others will form larger sub-groups with group membership based upon unspoken
rules of behaviour or upon socio-economic status. The class
may develop a kind of pecking order, with 'in-groups' who
are generally admired and 'out-groups' who are generally
ignored or even ridiculed. There will be rivalries and small
feuds, sometimes teasing and perhaps bullying, sometimes co-
operation and mutual help, sometimes a sense of common
purpose, and at other times social fragmentation and a
movement towards anarchy.

Prompted by these forces the class will develop a distinct social 'character' of its own that will mark it off
even from parallel classes of similar ability. This character will often manifest itself in particular class attitudes
towards particular teachers: sometimes friendly, and at
other times less so. Sometimes it will work to the benefit
of class learning while at other times it will become a
positive handicap. Sometimes hard work and academic success
in class members will be the focus of general admiration,
while at other times they may become the focus of banter and
even of sneering. On occasions a small sub-group may develop
with positive work-orientation, and have sufficient internal
solidarity to function independently of the rest of the

class, sustained by its own enthusiasms and interests and ready to ignore the censure of the rest. On other occasions a different kind of sub-group may develop, united perhaps by feelings of failure and inferiority, and intent on bolstering self-esteem by ridiculing the efforts of their more successful classmates.

The long-term survival of these sub-groups is determined in part by the teacher's behaviour towards them, in part by the strength of response of the rest of the class, and in part by their own cohesion and motivation as a group. If they do manage to survive, then they may increasingly become trend-setters for the rest of the class, exerting a generally good or bad influence as the case may be. Sometimes, however, different teachers will experience the same class in quite different ways. One teacher may find them alert, interested, and co-operative, another may find them apathetic and unhelpful, while a third may find them downright difficult and unmanageable. Where this happens, it becomes clear that it is the individual teacher who has become the crucial variable, and that it is his social interaction with the class and with its sub-groups that is determining the general response.

In the section by Argyle which follows, the author surveys the whole varied field of social behaviour, providing us with what we might call a basic grammar of the subject that allows us to identify the units of classroom interaction and to assess the relative importance of each one.

13

Social Behaviour
Michael Argyle

Introduction: social
behaviour as a skill

We start by presenting the social skills model of social
behaviour, and an account of sequences of social interaction. This model is very relevant to our later discussion
of social skills and how these can be trained. The chapter
then goes on to discuss the elements of social behaviour,
both verbal and non-verbal, and emphasize the importance and
different functions of non-verbal signals. The receivers of
these signals have to decode them, and do so in terms of
emotions and impressions of personality; we discuss some of
the processes and some of the main errors of person perception. The sender can manipulate the impression he creates by
means of 'self-presentation'. The processes of social
behaviour, and the skills involved, are quite different in
different social situations, and we discuss recent attempts
to analyse social situations in terms of their main
features, such as rules and goals.

We move on to a number of specific social skills.
Research on the processes leading to friendship and love
makes it possible to train and advise people who have
difficulty with these relationships. Research on persuasion
shows how people can be trained to be more assertive. And
research on small social groups and leadership of these
groups makes it possible to give an account of the most
successful skills for handling social groups.

Social competence is defined in terms of the successful
attainment of goals, and it can be assessed by a variety of
techniques such as self-rating and observation of role-
played performance. The most successful method of social
skills is role-playing, combined with modelling, coaching,
VTR (videotape-recorder) playback, and 'homework'. Results
of follow-up studies with a variety of populations show that
this form of social skills training (SST) is very
successful.

Harré and Secord (1972) have argued persuasively that
much human social behaviour is the result of conscious
planning, often in words, with full regard for the complex
meanings of behaviour and the rules of the situations. This
is an important correction to earlier social psychological
views, which often failed to recognize the complexity of
individual planning and the different meanings which may be
given to stimuli, for example in laboratory experiments.

285

However, it must be recognized that much social behaviour is not planned in this way: the smaller elements of behaviour and longer automatic sequences are outside conscious awareness, though it is possible to attend, for example, to patterns of gaze, shifts of orientation, or the latent meanings of utterances. The social skills model, in emphasizing the hierarchical structure of social performance, can incorporate both kinds of behaviour.

The social skills model also emphasizes feedback processes. A person driving a car sees at once when it is going in the wrong direction, and takes corrective action with the steering wheel. Social interactors do likewise; if another person is talking too much they interrupt, ask closed questions or no questions, and look less interested in what he has to say. Feedback requires perception, looking at and listening to the other person. Skilled performance requires the ability to take the appropriate corrective action referred to as 'translation' in the model: not everyone knows that open-ended questions make people talk more and closed questions make them talk less. And it depends on a number of two-step sequences of social behaviour whereby certain social acts have reliable effects on another. Let us take further the car-driving analogy. In driving and in social behaviour the performer is pursuing certain goals, makes continuous response to feedback, and emits hierarchically organized motor responses. This model has been heuristically very useful in drawing attention to the importance of feedback, and hence to gaze; it also suggests a number of different ways in which social performances can fail, and suggests the training procedures that may be effective, through analogy with motor skills training (Argyle and Kendon, 1967; Argyle, 1969).

The model emphasizes the motivation, goals and plans of interactors. It is postulated that every interactor is trying to achieve some goal, whether he is aware of it or not. These goals may be, for example, to get another person to like him, to obtain or convey information, to modify the other's emotional state, and so on. Such goals may be linked to more basic motivational systems. Goals have sub-goals; for example, a doctor must diagnose the patient before he can treat him. Patterns of response are directed towards goals and sub-goals, and have a hierarchical structure, in which large units of behaviour are composed of smaller ones, and at the lowest levels these are habitual and automatic.

The role of reinforcement
This is one of the key processes in social skill sequences. When interactor A does what B wants him to do, B is pleased and sends immediate and spontaneous reinforcements: smile, gaze, approving noises, etc., and modifies A's behaviour, probably by operant conditioning; for example, modifying the content of his utterances. At the same time A is modifying B's behaviour in exactly the same way. These effects appear to be mainly outside the focus of conscious attention, and

take place very rapidly. It follows that anyone who gives strong rewards and punishments in the course of interaction will be able to modify the behaviour of others in the desired direction. In addition, the stronger the rewards that A issues, the more strongly other people will be attracted to him.

The role of gaze in social skills

The social skills model suggests that the monitoring of another's reactions is an essential part of social performance. The other's verbal signals are mainly heard, but his non-verbal signals are mainly seen, the exceptions being the non-verbal aspects of speech and touch. It was this implication of the social skills model which directed us towards the study of gaze in social interaction. In dyadic interaction each person looks about 50 per cent of the time, mutual gaze occupies 25 per cent of the time, looking while listening is about twice the level of looking while talking, glances are about three seconds, and mutual glances about one second, with wide variations due to distance, sex combination, and personality (Argyle and Cook, 1976). However, there are several important differences between social behaviour and motor skills.

* Rules: the moves which interactors may make are governed by rules; they must respond properly to what has gone before. Similarly, rules govern the other's responses and can be used to influence his behaviour; for example, questions lead to answers.

* Taking the role of the other: it is important to perceive accurately the reactions of the others. It is also necessary to perceive the perceptions of others; that is, to take account of their points of view. This appears to be a cognitive ability which develops with age (Flavell, 1968), but which may fail to develop properly. Those who are able to do this have been found to be more effective at a number of social tasks, and more altruistic. Meldman (1967) found that psychiatric patients are more egocentric: that is, they talked about themselves more than controls, and it has been our experience that socially unskilled patients have great difficulty in taking the role of the other.

The independent initiative of the other – sequences of interaction

Social situations inevitably contain at least one other person, who will be pursuing his goals and using his social skills. How can we analyse the resulting sequences of behaviour?

For a sequence to constitute an acceptable piece of social behaviour, the moves must fit together in order. Social psychologists have not yet discovered all the principles or 'grammar' underlying these sequences, but some of the principles are known, and can explain common forms of interaction failure.

1. TWO-STEP SEQUENCES: conversational sequences are partly constructed out of certain basic building blocks, like the question-answer sequence, and repeated cycles characteristic of the situation. Socially inadequate people are usually very bad conversationalists and this appears to be due to a failure to master some of these basic sequences.

There are a number of other two-step sequences such as joke-laugh, complain-sympathize, request-comply or refuse. There are a number of two-step sequences which take place not because there is a rule, but as a result of basic psychological processes. For example, there is the powerful effect of reinforcement, and there is response-matching, in which one person copies the accent, posture or other aspects of the other's behaviour.

There are also proactive two-step sequences, where one person makes both moves, as in accept-thank, reply-question. Failure to make a proactive move can stop a conversation, as in this example:

A. Where are you going?
B. Swindon
(end of conversation)

B should have used a double, or 'proactive' move, of the type, 'I come from Swindon; where do you come from?' These reactive and proactive two-step pairs can build up to make repeated cycles, as happens in the classroom:

Teacher: lectures
Teacher: asks question
Pupil: replies
Teacher: comments
(cycle repeats) (after Flanders, 1970).

2. SOCIAL SKILL SEQUENCES: we turn now to sequences longer than two. The social skill model generates a characteristic kind of four-step sequence.

Figure 1

Social skill sequence

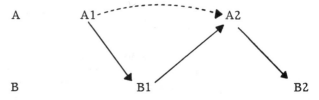

This is a case of asymmetrical contingency, with A in charge. A's first move, A1, produces an unsatisfactory result, B1, so A modifies his behaviour to A2 which produces the desired B2. Note the links A1-A2, representing the persistence of A's goal-directed behaviour. This can be seen in the social survey interview:

I1: asks question
R1: gives inadequate answer, or does not understand question
I2: clarifies and repeats question
R2: gives adequate answer

The model can be extended to cases where both interactors are pursuing goals simultaneously, as in the following example, from a selection interview:

I1: How well did you do at physics at school?
R1: Not very well, I was better at chemistry.
I2: What were your A-level results?
R2: I got a C in physics, and an A in chemistry.
I3: That's very good.

There are four two-step sequences here: I1, R1, I2, R2 and R1, I2, R2, I3. There is persistence and continuity between R1 and R2, as well as I1 and I2. Although I has the initiative, R can also pursue his goals.

3. EPISODE SEQUENCE: most social encounters consist of a number of distinct episodes, which may have to come in a particular order.
   We have found that encounters usually have five main episodes or phases:

1. greeting;
2. establish relationship;
3. central task;
4. re-establish relationship;
5. parting.

The task in turn may consist of several sub-tasks: for example, a doctor has to conduct a verbal or physical examination, make a diagnosis, and then carry out or prescribe treatment. Often, as in this case, the sub-tasks have to come in a certain order. At primarily social events, the 'task' seems to consist of eating or drinking accompanied by the exchange of information.

Verbal and non-verbal communication

Verbal communication
There are several different kinds of verbal utterance:

* egocentric speech is directed to the self, is found in infants and has the effect of directing behaviour;
* orders, instructions, are used to influence the behaviour of others; they can be gently persuasive or authoritarian;

* questions are intended to elicit verbal information; they can be open-ended or closed, personal or impersonal;
* information may be given in response to a question, or part of a lecture, or during problem-solving discussion;

(These last three are the three basic classes of utterance.)

* informal speech, consists of casual chat, jokes, gossip, and contains little information, but helps to establish and sustain social relationships;
* expression of emotions and interpersonal attitudes. This is a special kind of information; however, this information is usually conveyed, and is conveyed more effectively, non-verbally;
* 'Performative' utterances. These include 'illocutions' where saying the utterance performs something (voting, judging, naming, etc.), and 'perlocutions', where a goal is intended but may not be achieved (persuading, intimidating, etc.);
* social routines include standard sequences like thanking, apologizing, greeting, etc.;
* latent messages are where the more important meaning is made subordinate ('As I was saying to the Prime Minister ...').

There are many category schemes for reducing utterances to a limited number of classes of social acts. One of the best known is that of Bales (1950), who introduced the 12 classes shown in figure 2.

Although such schemes have been widely used, there is a fundamental difficulty with them: the same utterance may need to be classified in a number of different ways for different purposes. A discussion may include a large number of questions and suggestions, but they are different questions, and it would not be possible to trace the argument by Bales' analysis alone. Again the same utterance may be a question, which is open-ended, rude, and long; each feature may affect some aspect of the response.

Utterances follow each other in a conversation in special ways. The meaning of an utterance may depend on other utterances (e.g. 'I disagree'), or on the social setting ('forty-love'), and it may not be what it seems: 'Could you pass the salt?' is not a question; 'Come in' is not an order but a welcome. A speaker usually produces utterances that he thinks the hearer can understand, and he adjusts their technicality accordingly, and the use of local references. Encoding involves anticipating decoding. Rommetveit (1979) has shown how each utterance takes account of the shared information and objects of attention of speaker and hearer, and adds to them. The new is nested in the old.

Non-verbal signals accompanying speech
Non-verbal (NV) signals also play an important part in

Figure 2

The Bales categories (from Bales, 1950)

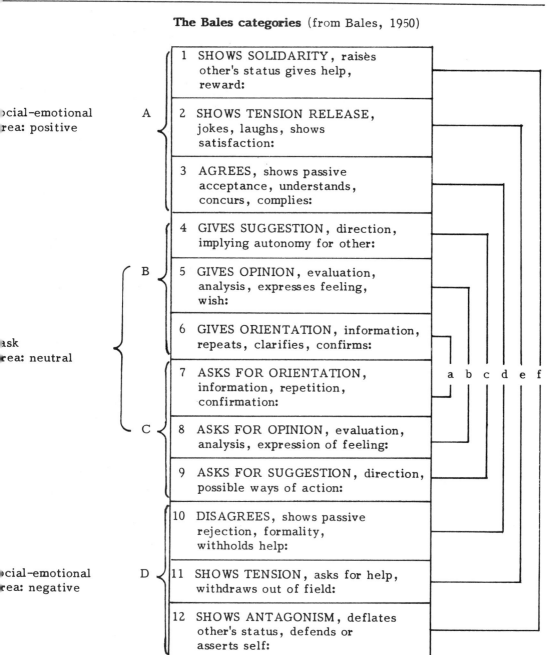

KEY

problems of communication   A positive reactions
problems of evaluation   B attempted answers
problems of control   C questions
problems of decision   D negative reactions
problems of tension reduction
problems of reintegration

speech and conversation. They have three main roles, as explained below.

1. COMPLETING AND ELABORATING ON VERBAL UTTERANCES: some utterances are meaningless or ambiguous unless the NV accompaniments are taken into account. A lecturer may point at part of a diagram: a tape-recording of this part of the lecture would be meaningless. Some sentences are ambiguous if printed: 'They are hunting dogs', but not if spoken: 'They are hunting DOGS'. Gestural illustrations are used to amplify the meaning of utterances, and succeed in doing so. The way in which an utterance is delivered 'frames' it; that is, the intonation and facial expression indicate whether it is intended to be serious, funny, sarcastic (implying the opposite), rhetorical or requiring an answer and so on; the NV accompaniment is a message about the message, which is needed by the recipient in order to know what to do with it.

2. MANAGING SYNCHRONIZING: when two or more people are talking they have to take turns to speak. This is achieved mainly by means of NV signals. For example, if a speaker wants to avoid being interrupted, he will be more successful if he does not look up at the ends of sentences, keeps a hand in mid-gesture at these points, and if, when interrupted, he immediately increases the loudness of his speech. The actual content of the speech, for example, asking a question, is also important. Not only is synchronizing usually successful, but interactors may help each other, by finishing their utterances for them. Some interruptions are mistaken anticipations of the other ending, rather than attempts to break in.

3. SENDING FEEDBACK SIGNALS: when someone is speaking he needs intermittent but regular feedback on how others are responding, so that he can modify his utterances accordingly. He needs to know whether the listeners understand, believe or disbelieve, are surprised or bored, agree or disagree, are pleased or annoyed. This information could be provided by sotto voce verbal muttering on their part, but is in fact usually obtained by careful study of the face: the eyebrows signal surprise, puzzlement, etc., while the mouth indicates pleasure and displeasure. When the other is invisible, as in telephone conversation, these visual signals are unavailable, and more verbalized 'listening behaviour' is used, such as 'I see', 'Really?', 'How interesting', etc.

Speech styles
People use different speech styles in different situations. On formal occasions they use informal speech, which is characterized by simpler structure of sentences, less accurate grammar, more verbs and pronouns, fewer nouns and adjectives and more slang.

Speech can be delivered in different accents, with different speeds, loudness and emotional tones, all of which affect the social effect of an utterance. Emotional tone is conveyed by various physical parameters; depression, for example, is conveyed by slow speech, low pitch and low volume. Accent consists of the ways in which phonemes are pronounced, such as making 'a' long or short, and conveys information about social class, education and regional origins. Research by Lambert and Giles has shown that if the same speaker makes a number of recordings in different accents, he is perceived and evaluated quite differently; stereotyped judgements about English and French Canadians, for example, will be expressed. When people who normally use different speech styles interact they converge towards a similar manner of speaking, probably in order to increase social acceptance by each other (Giles and Powesland, 1975).

Other functions of non-verbal communications (NVC)

NVC consists of facial expression, tone of voice, gaze, gestures, postures, physical proximity and appearance. We have already described how NVC is linked with speech; it also functions in several other ways, especially in the communication of emotions and attitudes to other people.

A sender is in a certain state, or possesses some information; this is encoded into a message which is then decoded by a receiver.

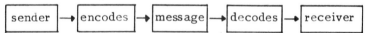

Encoding research is done by putting subjects into some state and studying the NV messages which are emitted. For example, Mehrabian (1972) in a role-playing experiment, asked subjects to address a hat-stand, imagining it to be a person. Male subjects who liked the hat-stand looked at it more, did not have hands on hips and stood closer.

Non-verbal signals are often 'unconscious': that is, they are outside the focus of attention. A few signals are unconsciously sent and received, like dilated pupils, signifying sexual attraction, but there are a number of other possibilities, as shown in table 1.

Strictly speaking, pupil dilation is not communication at all, but only a physiological response. 'Communication' is usually taken to imply some intention to affect another; one criterion is that it makes a difference whether the other person is present and in a position to receive the signal; another is that the signal is repeated, varied or amplified if it has no effect. These criteria are independent of conscious intention to communicate, which is often absent.

1. INTERPERSONAL ATTITUDES: we are concerned here with attitudes towards others who are present. The main attitudes fall along two dimensions:

FT - T

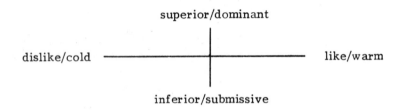

superior/dominant

dislike/cold ———————————— like/warm

inferior/submissive

In addition there is love, which is a variant of like. These
attitudes can be conveyed clearly by non-verbal signals,
such as facial expression, tone of voice and posture. Liking
is conveyed by smiling, a friendly tone of voice and so on.

Table 1

Awareness of non-verbal signals

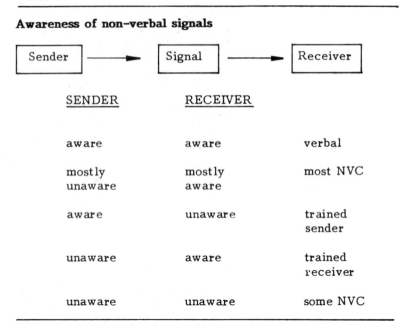

SENDER	RECEIVER	
aware	aware	verbal
mostly unaware	mostly aware	most NVC
aware	unaware	trained sender
unaware	aware	trained receiver
unaware	unaware	some NVC

The author and his colleagues compared the effect of
verbal and non-verbal signals for communicating interpersonal attitudes. It was found that the variance due to
non-verbal cues was about 12 times the variance due to
verbal cues, in affecting judgements of inferior-superior
(Argyle et al, 1970). Some of the results are shown in
figure 3. Similar results were obtained in later experiments
using friendly-hostile messages.

The attitudes of others are perceived, then, mainly from
their non-verbal behaviour. It is found that people can
judge with some accuracy when others like them, but are much
less accurate in perceiving dislike (Tagiuri, 1958). The
reasons for this are probably that expressions of dislike
are concealed to a large extent, and only the more subtle
ones remain, such as bodily orientation.

Figure 3

**Effects of inferior, neutral and superior verbal and
non-verbal signals on semantic rating**
From: Argyle, 1969.

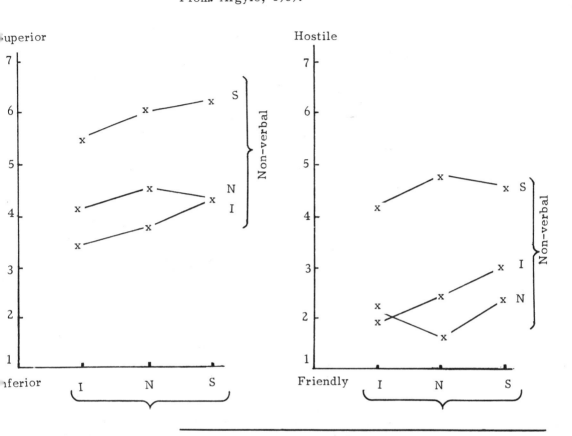

2. EMOTIONAL STATES: these can be distinguished from
interpersonal attitudes in that emotions are not directed
towards others present, but are simply states of the
individual. The common emotions are anger, depression,
anxiety, joy, surprise, fear and disgust/contempt (Ekman et
al, 1972). An anxious state, for example, can be shown by:

*   tone of voice: breathy, rapid, speech errors;
*   facial expression: tense, perspiring, expanded pupils;
*   posture: tense and rigid;
*   gestures: tense, clasping objects, or general bodily
    activity;
*   smell: of perspiration;
*   gaze: short glances, aversion of gaze.

Interactors may try to conceal their true emotional state,
or to convey that they are in some different emotional
condition, but it is difficult to control all of these cues,

and impossible to control more autonomic ones. Emotional states can be conveyed by speech - 'I am feeling happy' - but probably statements will not be believed unless supported by appropriate NVC, and the NVC can convey the message without the speech.

Person perception and self-presentation

In order to respond effectively to the behaviour of others it is necessary to perceive them correctly. The social skills model emphasizes the importance of perception and feedback: to drive a car one must watch the traffic outside and the instruments inside. Such perception involves selecting certain cues, and being able to interpret them correctly. There is evidence of poor person perception in mental patients and other socially unskilled individuals, while professional social skills performers need to be sensitive to special aspects of other people and their behaviour. For selection interviewers and clinical psychologists the appraisal of others is a central part of the job.

We form impressions of other people all the time, mainly in order to predict their future behaviour, and so that we can deal with them effectively. We categorize others in terms of our favourite cognitive constructs, of which the most widely used are:

* extraversion, sociability;
* agreeableness, likeability;
* emotional stability;
* intelligence;
* assertiveness.

There are, however, wide individual differences in the constructs used and 'complex' people use a larger number of such dimensions. We have found that the constructs used vary greatly with the situation: for example, work-related constructs are not used in purely social situations. We also found that the constructs used vary with the target group; for example, children versus psychologists (Argyle et al, in press).

A number of widespread errors, such as those listed below, are made in forming impressions of others, which should be particularly avoided by those whose job it is to assess others:

* assuming that a person's behaviour is mainly a product of his personality, whereas it may be more a function of the situation he is in: at a noisy party, in church, etc.;
* assuming that his behaviour is due to him rather than his role; for example, as a hospital nurse or a patient or a visitor;
* attaching too much importance to physical cues, like beards, clothes, and physical attractiveness;

*   being affected by stereotypes about the characteristics
    of members of certain races, social classes, etc.

During social interaction it is also necessary to perceive
the emotional states of others, for example to tell if they
are depressed or angry. There are wide individual differences in the ability to judge emotions correctly (Davitz,
1964). As we have seen, emotions are mainly conveyed by
non-verbal signals, especially by facial expression and tone
of voice. The interpretation of emotions is also based on
perception of the situation the other person is in. Lalljee
at Oxford found that smiles are not necessarily decoded as
happy, whereas unhappy faces are usually regarded as
authentic.

Similar considerations apply to the perception of
interpersonal attitudes of who likes whom, which is also
mainly based on non-verbal signals, such as proximity, gaze
and facial expression. Again use is made of context to
decode these signals: a glance at a stranger may be interpreted as a threat, an appeal for help, or a friendly
invitation. There are some interesting errors due to
pressures towards cognitive consistency: if A likes B, he
thinks that B likes him more than B on average actually
does; if A likes both B and C, he assumes that they both
like each other more than, on average, they do.

It is necessary to perceive the on-going flow of interaction in order to know what is happening and to participate
in it effectively. People seem to agree on the main episodes
and sub-episodes of an encounter, but they may produce
rather different accounts of why those present behaved as
they did. One source of variation, and indeed error, is that
people attribute the causes of others' behaviour to their
personality ('He fell over because he is clumsy'), but their
own behaviour to the situation ('I fell over because it was
slippery'), whereas both factors operate in each case (Jones
and Nisbett, 1972). Interpretations also depend on the ideas
and knowledge an individual possesses: just as an expert on
cars could understand better why a car was behaving in a
peculiar way, so also can an expert on social behaviour
understand why patterns of social behaviour occur.

The person who is perceived can manipulate the way
others perceive him by 'self-presentation'. This in turn
depends on his 'self-image'. This refers to the way a person
perceives himself. It includes roles, like occupation,
social class and religion; it includes 'personality' qualities like 'intelligent' or 'kind'; and perceptions of the
body; for example, as attractive, tall or fat. The self-
image can be assessed by the Twenty Statements Test, which
has 20 identical questions, namely, 'Who am I?...'. Another
method is the Semantic Differential: the self is rated on a
series of seven-point scales like warm ..... cold. The ego-
ideal is an important part of the self-system. It can be
assessed by asking a person to rate 'the kind of person I
would most like to be' on seven-point scales. The

discrepancies between self and ego-ideal can be readily seen. Self-esteem is the extent to which a person accepts and approves of himself. It can be deduced from the average discrepancy between self-image and ego-ideal, but it is better to use self-ratings on evaluation scales like good-bad, nice-nasty. There are also differences in the degrees of integration of the self, varying from those who have a completely integrated pattern of life from those who, like children, do not yet know who they are or where they are going.

The self is not at work all the time, but is activated by particular kinds of situation. Being in front of an audience makes people feel self-conscious and often anxious. There are many situations where people may regard others as audiences. Duval and Wicklund (1972) called this state 'objective self-awareness'; that is, being aware of oneself as an object for others. People are also made self-conscious if they are in some way different from everyone else present, such as being the only woman present. Conversely, 'de-individuation' can be brought about by dressing everyone alike. Self-awareness is brought about by penetration of territory or privacy, or unintended self-disclosure. Some people feel more self-conscious than others, and suffer more from audience anxiety. They tend to be people who are shy, have rather low self-esteem, and have failed to form an integrated identity.

When the self is activated, there is heightened physiological arousal, and greater concern with the impression made on others. This can be controlled to some extent by 'self-presentation': that is, sending information about the self. This is done partly to sustain self-esteem, and partly for professional purposes: teachers teach more effectively if their pupils think they are well-informed, for example. If people tell others how good they are in words, this is regarded as a joke and disbelieved, in western cultures at least. E. E. Jones (1964) found that verbal ingratiation is done with sublety: drawing attention to assets in unimportant areas, for example. Most presentation is done non-verbally by clothes, hair-style, accent, badges and general style of behaviour. Social class is very clearly signalled in these ways, as is membership of rebellious social groups (Argyle, 1975).

Goffman (1956) maintained that social behaviour involves a great deal of deceptive self-presentation by individuals and groups which is often in the interest of those deceived, as in the work of morticians and doctors. In everyday life deception is probably less common than concealment. Most people keep quiet about discreditable events in their past, and others do not remind them. Stigmatized individuals, like homosexuals, drug addicts and members of certain professions, also keep it dark, though they are usually recognized by other members. Goffman's theory gives an explanation of embarrassment: this occurs when false self-presentation is unmasked. Later research has shown that this is the case, but that embarrassment also occurs when other people break social rules, and when social accidents are committed: unintentional gaffes, and forgetting names, for example (Argyle, 1969).

Situations, their rules and other features

The traditional trait model supposes that individuals possess a fixed degree of introversion, neuroticism, etc., and that it is displayed consistently in different situations. This model has been abandoned by most psychologists following an increased awareness of the great effect of the situation on behaviour (e.g. people are more anxious when exposed to physical danger than when asleep in bed), and the amount of person-situation interaction (e.g. person A is more frightened by heights, B by cows), resulting in low inter-situational consistency (Mischel, 1968).

A long series of studies attempted to test trait theory and other models by finding the percentages of variance due to persons, situations and P x S interaction. This was done with reported behaviour (e.g. anxiety), and with observed behaviour (e.g. talking, smiling). Typical results were:

persons:	15-30 per cent
situations:	20-45 per cent
P x S:	30-50 per cent

(Unfortunately it is not possible to give any exact figures, since there is no way of producing equivalent degrees of variation of personality and situation; Endler and Magnusson, 1976.) These results show that a simple trait theory must be abandoned. The alternative position which has developed is known as interactionism, and recognizes the independent contribution of persons, situations and interactions between them, and accepts that the detailed prediction of behaviour requires equations of the form $B = f(P,S)$. However, the interactionist model has a number of serious limitations.

* Persons can sometimes choose the situations in which they find themselves and avoid others, so P has two different effects.
* Persons can to some extent change the situation they are in; for example, generating friendly or hostile behaviour from others.
* Although some behaviour occurs in all situations, for example, level of anxiety and amount of talk, situations also have repertoires of behaviour which are unique to them: the moves of chess are different from those in football. The interactionist equations cannot be applied here.
* There are problems about specifying the dimensions of situations to enter into the equations, as is shown below.

Whether we adopt the interactionist position or some other we need to be able to measure or assess situations. One method is to classify them in terms of the behaviour in them, but this makes it impossible to predict or explain behaviour in terms of properties of situations. Another method is to see how subjects classify situations cognitively, using methods like multi-dimensional scaling. This produces dimensions like formal-informal, friendly-hostile, equal-unequal, task-social, etc. (Wish and Kaplan, 1977). This is a good start, but does not tell us much about the behaviour required in, for example, a selection interview, a confessional, a visit to a psychoanalyst, or a judo lesson. To do this we have to study the fundamental features of the situations (Argyle et al, in press). The main features appear to be as outlined below.

Goals
In all situations there are certain goals which are commonly obtainable. It is often fairly obvious what these are, but socially inadequate people may simply not know what parties are for, for example, or may think that the purpose of a selection interview is vocational guidance.

We have studied the main goals in a number of common situations by asking samples of people to rate the importance of various goals, and then carrying out factor analyses. The main goals are usually:

* social acceptance, etc.;
* food, drink and other bodily needs;
* task goals specific to the situation.

We have also studied the relations between goals, within and between persons, in terms of conflict and instrumentality. This makes it possible to study the 'goal structure' of situations. An example is given in figure 4, showing that the only conflict between nurses and patients is between the nurses' concern for the bodily well-being of the patients and for themselves (Argyle et al, in press).

Rules
All situations have rules about what may or may not be done in them. Socially inexperienced people are often ignorant or mistaken about the rules. It would obviously be impossible to play a game without knowing the rules and the same applies to social situations.

We have studied the rules of a number of everyday situations. There appear to be several universal rules: be polite, be friendly, do not embarrass people. There are also rules which are specific to situations, or groups of situations, and these can be interpreted as functional, since they enable situational goals to be met. For example, when seeing the doctor one should be clean and tell the truth; when going to a party one should dress smartly and keep to cheerful topics of conversation.

Figure 4

The goal structure for nurse and patient

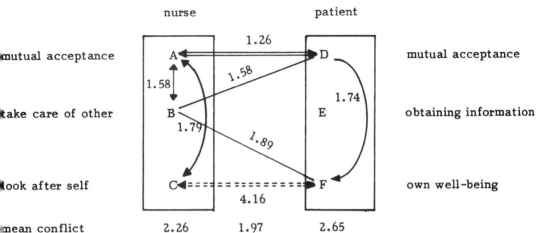

Special skills
Many social situations require special social skills, as in the case of various kinds of public speaking and interviewing, but also such everyday situations as dates and parties. A person with little experience of a particular situation may find that he lacks the special skills needed for it (cf. Argyle et al, in press).

Repertoire of elements
Every situation defines certain moves as relevant. For example, at a seminar it is relevant to show slides, make long speeches, draw on the blackboard, etc. If moves appropriate to a cricket match or a Scottish ball were made, they would be ignored or regarded as totally bizarre. We have found 65-90 main elements used in several situations, like going to the doctor. We have also found that the semiotic structure varies between situations: we found that questions about work and about private life were sharply contrasted in an office situation, but not on a date.

Roles
Every situation has a limited number of roles; for example, a classroom has the roles of teacher, pupil, janitor, and school inspector. These roles carry different degrees of power, and the occupant has goals peculiar to that role.

Cognitive structure
We found that the members of a research group classified each other in terms of the concepts 'extraverted' and 'enjoyable companion' for social occasions, but in terms of

'dominant', 'creative' and 'supportive' for seminars. There
are also concepts related to the task, such as 'amendment',
'straw vote' and 'nem con', for committee meetings.

Environmental setting and pieces
Most situations involve special environmental settings and
props. Cricket needs bat, ball, stumps, etc.; a seminar
requires blackboard, slide projector and lecture notes.

How do persons fit into situations, conceived in this
way? To begin with, there ARE certain pervasive aspects of
persons, corresponding to 20 per cent or so of person variance found in P x S studies. These consist of scores on
general dimensions like intelligence, extraversion, neuroticism and so on. In addition, persons have dispositions to
behave in certain ways in classes of situations; this cor-
responds to the 50 per cent or so of the P x S variance in
relation to dimensions of situations like formal-informal,
and friendly-hostile. Third, there are more specific reactions to particular situations: for example, behaviour in
social psychology seminars depends partly on knowledge of
social psychology and attitudes to different schools of
thought in it. Taken together these three factors may
predict performance in, and also avoidance of, certain
situations, because of lack of skill, anxiety, etc., and
this will be the main expectation in such cases.

Friendship and love

These are two of the most important social relationships;
failure in them is a source of great distress, and so this
is one of the main areas of social skills training. The
conditions under which people come to like or to love one
another have been the object of extensive research, and are
now well understood.

Friendship
There are several stages of friendship:

* coming into contact with the other through proximity at
  work or elsewhere;
* increasing attachment, as a result of reinforcement, and
  discovery of similarity;
* increasing self-disclosure and commitment;
* dissolution of the relationship.

Friendship is the dominant relationship for adolescents and
the unmarried; friends engage in characteristic activities,
such as talking, eating, drinking and joint leisure, but not
usually working.

Frequency of interaction
The more two people meet, the more polarized their attitude
to one another becomes, but usually they like one another
more. Frequent interaction can come about from living in
adjacent rooms or houses, working in the same office,

belonging to the same club, and so on. So interaction leads to liking, and liking leads to more interaction. Only certain kinds of interaction lead to liking. In particular, people should be of similar status. Belonging to a co-operative group, especially under crisis conditions, is particularly effective, as Sherif's 'Robbers' Cave' experiment (Sherif et al, 1961) and research on inter-racial attitudes have shown.

Reinforcement

The next general principle governing liking is the extent to which one person satisfies the needs of another. This was shown in a study by Jennings of 400 girls in a reformatory (1950). She found that the popular girls helped and protected others, encouraged, cheered them up, made them feel accepted and wanted, controlled their own moods so as not to inflict anxiety or depression on others, were able to establish rapport quickly, won the confidence of a wide variety of other personalities, and were concerned with the feelings and needs of others. The unpopular girls on the other hand were dominating, aggressive, boastful, demanded attention, and tried to get others to do things for them. This pattern has been generally interpreted in terms of the popular girls providing rewards and minimizing costs, while the unpopular girls tried to get rewards for themselves, and incurred costs for others. It is not necessary for the other person to be the actual source of rewards: Lott and Lott (1960) found that children who were given model cars by the experimenter liked the other children in the experiment more, and several studies have shown that people are liked more in a pleasant environmental setting.

Being liked is a powerful reward, so if A likes B, B will usually like A. This is particularly important for those who have a great need to be liked, such as individuals with low self-esteem. It is signalled, as we showed above, primarily by non-verbal signals.

Similarity

People like others who are similar to themselves in certain respects. They like those with similar attitudes, beliefs and values, who have a similar regional and social class background, who have similar jobs or leisure interests, but they need not have similar personalities. Again there is a cyclical process, since similarity leads to liking, and liking leads to similarity. The effects of similarity on liking have been shown experimentally; for example, Griffitt and Veitch (1974) paid 13 males to spend ten days in a fall-out shelter, and found that those with similar opinions liked each other most by the end of the ten days. Similarity in attitudes which are important to those concerned has most effect. Duck (1973) has produced evidence that similarity of cognitive constructs is important; that is, the categories used for describing other people. As far as other aspects of personality are concerned, it now seems that neither similarity nor complementarity have much effect on friendship.

Physical attractiveness
Physical attractiveness (p.a.) is an important source of both same sex and opposite sex liking, especially in the early stages. Walster et al (1966) arranged a 'computer dance' at which couples were paired at random; the best prediction of how much each person liked their partner was the latter's p.a. as rated by the experimenter. Part of the explanation lies in the 'p.a. stereotype'. Dion et al (1972) found that attractive people were believed to have desirable characteristics of many other kinds. However, people do not seek out the most attractive friends and mates, but compromise by seeking those similar to themselves in attractiveness.

Self-disclosure
Self-disclosure is a signal for intimacy, like bodily contact, because it indicates trust in the other. Self-disclosure can be measured on a scale (1-5) with items like:

> What are your favourite forms of erotic play and sexual lovemaking? (scale value 2.56)

> What are the circumstances under which you become depressed and when your feelings are hurt? (3.51)

> What are your hobbies, how do you best like to spend your spare time? (4.98) (Jourard, 1971).

As people get to know each other better, self-disclosure slowly increases, and is reciprocated, up to a limit.

Commitment
Commitment is a state of mind, an intention to stay in a relationship and abandon others. This involves a degree of dependence on the other person and trusting them not to leave the relationship. The least committed has the more power.

Social skills training
The most common complaint of those who seek social skills training is difficulty in making friends. Some of them say they have never had a friend in their lives. What advice can we offer, on the basis of research on friendship?

* As we showed earlier, social relations are negotiated mainly by non-verbal signals. Clients for social skills training who cannot make friends are usually found to be very inexpressive, in face and voice.
* Rewardingness is most important. The same clients usually appear to be very unrewarding, and are not really interested in other people.

* Frequent interaction with those of similar interests and attitudes can be found in clubs for professional or leisure activities, in political and religious groups, and so on.
* Physical attractiveness is easier to change than is social behaviour.
* Certain social skills may need to be acquired, such as inviting others to suitable social events, and engaging in self-disclosures at the right speed.

Love

Loving is not the same as liking, though it includes it. Love usually involves sexual attraction, is more intense than liking, shows a rapid build-up and later declines, rather than increasing slowly; there is a great need for the other and a caring for him or her, and a high level of intimacy and disclosure. Its presence can be measured by questionnaires like Rubin's (1973) with items such as:

I would do almost anything for ...
If I could never be with ... I would feel miserable.

The best available theory of love is a version of the two-factor theory of emotions (Schachter and Singer, 1962). To be in love is a combination of a high level of arousal and labelling or interpreting it as 'being in love' as defined by the culture (Berscheid and Walster, 1974). Several experiments show that heightened arousal of various kinds leads to love.

The nature of the love relationship varies between different cultures and historical periods; young people learn how they are supposed to feel and behave. Traditionally there are two public rituals - engagement and marriage - which proclaim the stages in the relationship, and result in others treating the couple in a new way. The effect of cognitive labelling is shown in a study by Rubin (1973), who found that couples who accepted the love mythology fell more rapidly in love than those who did not. He also found that married couples had a more realistic view of love.

A number of experiments have tried to find out what makes people fall in love. Physical attractiveness is most important, particularly in the early stages. Parental interference tends to strengthen attraction; this is the 'Romeo and Juliet' effect. Playing hard to get does not work very well, but those who seem to be hard for others to get are found attractive. People high in internal control are less likely to fall in love. And the variables discussed for friendship also affect love: similar attitudes, being liked, and so on.

Love goes through a number of stages. As we have seen, sexual attraction is signalled by non-verbal cues - facial expression, gaze, etc. - as for friendship, but also including touch and pupil dilation. The process of falling in love is probably due to massive reinforcements, and a sudden upward surge of interaction and liking. This makes increased demands for synchronizing and mutual adjustment, and inevitably the scope for conflict and disagreement is greatly increased, while each partner is also very dependent on the other for rewards received. This has the properties of an approach-avoidance conflict and would be expected to lead to an oscillation of intimacy-withdrawal, until smoother synchronizing is attained. The periods of the engagement and honeymoon appear to be designed to help this process to happen. It is interesting that in the USA honeymoons are often found stressful, and that honeymoon couples often seek out the company of other such couples and return home earlier than planned (Rapoport and Rapoport, 1964).

Assertiveness and social influence

'How to make friends and influence people' are two classic social problems, and we now come to the second. Assertiveness is taken to include a number of somewhat different but, it is believed, related patterns of social behaviour. Assertiveness is now taken to include:

* the ability to say no;
* the ability to ask for favours or make requests;
* the ability to express positive and negative feelings;
* the ability to initiate, continue and terminate general conversations (Lazarus, 1973).

It is also often taken to include an individual's ability to stand up for his rights, and to act in his own best interests. Typical instances of assertiveness are dealing with laundries who lose shirts and with other students who borrow notes and fail to return them.

It was originally believed that assertiveness was a general trait; however, a number of studies have shown that assertiveness consists of a number of different factors, corresponding to different situations, and different modes of response (e.g. Eisler et al, 1975). The most valid measure of assertiveness asks for self-reports for a number of specific assertiveness situations.

It is believed in some quarters that assertiveness is the whole of social skills. However, research in social psychology has repeatedly shown that there are two main dimensions of social performance: control (or assertiveness) and warmth (or concern with social relationships). Making friends, of either sex, is not a matter of bullying others to be friendly, but requires quite different skills.

Various practical schemes for helping people to be assertive have been put forward. Bower and Bower (1976) proposed 'DESC Scripts':

* Describe: what unwarranted behaviour has the other person been displaying?
* Express: how can I tell him the way I feel about his behaviour?
* Specify: what behavioural changes might I contract for? Also what will I need to change in my own behaviour?

* Consequences: what rewarding consequences can I provide to him for sticking to the contract?

Verbal requests

Verbal requests usually lie at the heart of social influence: if you want someone to do something, you have to ask them. There is considerable skill in choosing the right words, the ones which will be acceptable and successful. Not 'Post this letter', but 'Would you mind posting this letter, if you are passing a pillar box?', or whatever is the local form of words for a polite request. Social influence is usually achieved by a combination of assertive and rewarding behaviour, and the combination generates a special style of social behaviour. One of the keys to successful leadership is consultation; it is found that people act with more enthusiasm if they have been consulted and have helped to make a decision. This principle applies to all face-to-face social influence, and means that the other person has to be persuaded and agree with what he is to do.

Persuasion

The design of persuasive messages has been studied most in connection with the mass media, but some of the principles apply in face-to-face situations. It is necessary to appeal to the needs, values or interests of the other in some way, and then show that what you want him to him to do will satisfy one of those needs: 'Come and do the washing-up while I change, then we will be able to go out to the pub earlier'; 'If you do some work during the holidays, you'll get better A levels and be more likely to get to university.' This may require some initial exploration of what the other does want, as when a salesman tries to find out the customer's needs. The objections to the behaviour being requested may be neutralized by appealing to higher loyalties, by denying that injury will result, or by other ways of changing the act or the situation that is perceived (Sykes and Matza, 1957): 'It's nothing, just a matter of taking a small present to a friend of mine in Amsterdam.' Moral exhortation, on the other hand, is no good if the exhorter is seen not to be behaving in this way himself (Bryan and Walbek, 1970). The very words used can create certain assumptions or ways of defining the problem: politicians may manage to make the public think primarily in terms of unemployment and the problems of social inequality, or alternatively of national prosperity and the creation of collective wealth. Similarly, face-to-face persuasion may be achieved by using the right rhetoric, making the other think in terms of your concepts.

Non-verbal signals

Requests need to be made in a sufficiently assertive manner. We discussed these non-verbal cues earlier: talking loudly and most of the time in a confident tone of voice, interrupting others, adopting an attentive but unsmiling facial expression, and an erect posture with the head tilted back, shoulders squared and hands on hips. For most situations rather small amounts of these signals will be enough, and again these social techniques must be combined with sufficient warmth and rewardingness to keep the other in the situation. There is a clear difference between assertive and aggressive behaviour: aggressive behaviour may or may not produce the desired influence, but it also damages the relationship.

Reinforcement

It is possible to influence another's behaviour in the immediate situation by systematic rewarding of the desired behaviour immediately it takes place, and non-reward or punishment of other behaviour. Rewards based on the need for affiliation include smiling, looking, agreement, head-nodding, etc. Punishment could consist of frowning, looking away, looking bored, looking at watch, disagreeing, etc. It may be easier to influence another person in this way if he is of higher status, and direct influence might be inappropriate. Members of groups often conform because they want to be accepted rather than rejected. Endler (1965) found that conformity could be increased if the experimenter reinforced it, and reduced if the experimenter reinforced nonconformity.

1. USING THE PERSONAL RELATIONSHIP: it is easier to influence another person if they like you, because they do not want to lose your approval or damage the relationship. This is the basis of ingratiation.

2. RECIPROCATION OF FAVOURS is similar: if A does something for B first, B is more likely to do what A asks. Regan (1971) found that subjects bought twice as many raffle tickets from a confederate who had previously bought them a Coke, compared with other confederates. This kind of reciprocity or exchange of gifts plays an even more important part in African countries, where officials often have to be bribed (as we call it) before they will be helpful.

3. POWER: persuasion is more effective if the source of it is regarded as an expert: on university entrance, to take an example. There are other kinds of power, such as the power to reward and punish, possessed by most formal leaders. This makes influence easier, particularly if the influencer is thought to be a legitimate source of directions, in view of his ability, experience, or his sheer rank in a hierarchy. In the experiments by Milgram (1974) it was found that 65 per cent of subjects gave what they thought were 450-volt shocks to what they thought were other subjects, who gave signs of intense suffering and apparent collapse, because the experimenter ordered them to do so as part of a learning experiment. The most likely interpretation is that subjects assumed that the experimenter was in charge and knew what he was doing, therefore it was all right to do what he said.

The experiment shows the very high degree of obedience which can be commanded by a legitimate leader, with no power to reward or punish.

4. PERSUASIVE STRATEGIES: by a 'strategy', we mean a planned sequence of at least two moves. These may be conscious and deliberate, as in some sales techniques, but they may also be acquired and used with little conscious awareness of what is being done. Interviewers commonly ask questions in a carefully prepared order; the more intimate ones come last, the most harmless ones first. A salesman may offer the most expensive objects first, and then produce cheaper ones, depending on the customer's reaction. This is similar to starting negotiations with exaggerated claims, with the intention of making concessions and extracting reciprocal concessions from the other party; this does not work if the initial demands are seen as bluffing. The foot-in-the-door technique consists of making a small request which is followed by a larger one. Freedman and Fraser (1966) found that if housewives had been asked to answer a few questions earlier, 53 per cent agreed to allow a survey team into their houses for two hours, compared with 22 per cent who had not been asked those questions.

Handling social groups

Before describing the skills of handling social groups the main group phenomena are described briefly.

* Formation: work-groups, committees, groups of friends, families and other groups come together in different ways. However, there are usually two basic motivations: task needs and various interpersonal needs.
* Conformity: groups form norms on many matters, especially those related to the group task. Members conform partly in order to avoid rejection, partly because they think the other members are better informed.
* Leadership hierarchy: a hierarchy of influence develops, with one or more informal leaders, and often a 'socio-emotional leader' who keeps the group together. There may be other informal roles, such as the 'leader of the opposition' in a jury, and there may be a formally appointed leader.
* Groups versus individuals: groups are usually better at making decisions than individuals. People are more aroused, work harder and have complementary skills and knowledge. On the other hand, groups can take risky decisions, and members can lose their heads and behave antisocially.
* Cohesion: group members become attracted to one another and value group members highly; cohesive groups are more satisfied, co-operative and work better together, but can become hostile to members of other groups.

Supervision of working groups

1. It is essential that the supervisor should really supervise:

* planning and scheduling the work to be done, and making sure supplies are available;
* instructing and training subordinates in how to do their work;
* checking and correcting the work that has been done;
* giving subordinates feedback on how well they are doing;
* motivating them to work effectively.

If he fails to do these things, it is likely that the group or some of its members will take over these functions. On the other hand, the supervisor (S) should do all this with a light hand, since people do not like him breathing down their necks and constantly interfering. He should see them frequently, showing interest, giving help where it is needed, but giving as little direction and criticism as possible.

2. Ss are more effective when they look after the needs, interests and welfare of their workers. This is particularly true when they are powerful enough really to be able to do something for them. In matters of discipline they should be persuasive rather than punitive, and try to find out the causes of the offending behaviour. It is interesting that foremen who are more concerned with the welfare of the men than with production usually succeed in getting higher rates of production. On the other hand, a number of studies show that S should be somewhat detached and independent: he should do his own job rather than theirs, and not be afraid of exerting influence over them.

3. Democratic leaders are usually more effective than autocratic ones. A democratic leader does not just rely on his formal powers, but on:

* motivating people by explanation and persuasion, rather than just giving orders;
* allowing subordinate to participate in decisions that affect them;
* using techniques of group discussion and group decision.

By these skills the supervisor succeeds in getting the group to set high targets, and to internalize the motivation to reach them, without exerting pressure himself. There are, of course, limits to what the group can decide. It can usually decide about details of administration: who shall work where, how training or holiday schemes shall be implemented. The group can also make suggestions on more far-reaching matters which S can relay to his superiors. He exerts real direction and influence but in a way that does not arouse resentment and antagonism. Autocratic leaders make more use of their formal powers, and give orders without explanation or opportunity for discussion (Likert, 1961).

So far, we have considered social techniques that are generally effective. Now we turn to those that are needed in particular circumstances. The good supervisor should be able to adjust his style through the operation of 'translation' processes. It has been found by Fiedler (1964) and others that the style described above is not always the most effective. It may be necessary to use different techniques at different times with the same group: a research group in the planning stage needs permissive handling so that all ideas can come forward, but once the design has been decided a stricter style is better. Similarly, there are advantages in a more autocratic style when the group is large, or when the members are themselves authoritarian in personality and accustomed to a strict pattern of leadership.

Another range of problems arises in connection with difficult group members. Sometimes such people are more amenable to group influence than to leaders, for example those who are hostile to authority; they should be left to the other group members to control. Another type is more responsive to people in authority; they should be dealt with by the leader privately. The most difficult to deal with are the psychopaths, who care neither for leaders nor groups. The only solution is to isolate them as far as possible from the main group activities, to prevent them disrupting the group. Ss also have to deal with interpersonal problems in the group. They will be better able to do so if they understand something of the dynamics of social groups. Sometimes the solution may be to rearrange the workflow system, to change the membership of sub-groups, to conduct a group discussion, or to interview separately those concerned and work out some solution.

Committee chairmanship

The task of committees and other discussion groups is to solve problems and take decisions in a way that is acceptable to those present, and to those they represent. In some cases the emphasis is on problem-solving and creativity, in others the emphasis is on obtaining consensus. The main value of taking decisions in committee is to find widely acceptable decisions; those present will then be committed to carrying them out. Groups are better than individuals at solving problems if individuals with different skills and knowledge can be combined. Thus they produce more 'brain power' than any one person. There is also interaction between members, so that one suggests new thoughts to another, and one member's bright ideas are criticized and evaluated by others. These groups usually have a chairman, unless there are only three or four people present. The chairman has a generally accepted social role of controlling discussion and helping the group make decisions. His position is often more temporary than that of other group leaders, and the chairmanship may be rotated so that other committee members take it in turns. Being chairman carries a certain amount of power, but it has to be used with skill. A chairman should see that all members are able to express their views, and that the decisions arrived at are agreeable to as many of them as possible. He should be able to keep control with a light touch, and keep people in order without upsetting them.

A certain amount of research has been done by Maier and Solem (1952) and Hoffman (1965) into which skills of chairmanship produce the best effects. They found, for example, that better and more widely accepted solutions are obtained if minority views can be expressed. Sometimes groups arrive at a solution rather quickly; if the chairman asks them to think of an alternative solution, this is often preferred in the end. The chairman can help the group by focussing on disagreements and searching for a creative solution.

The chairman should study the agenda carefully beforehand, and prepare his introduction to the different items. He should be able to anticipate the items which may cause difficulty; he may speak to some members beforehand if he wants to call on their expertise, or needs their support.

At the beginning of the meeting the chairman should create the right atmosphere, by the use of appropriate non-verbal signals. There are several phases to the discussion of each item on the agenda. First, the chairman introduces the item by outlining the problem to be discussed, summarizing briefly the main background factors, the arguments on each side, and so on. Then the committee is invited to discuss the problem; enough time should be allowed for different views to be expressed, and the chairman should try to keep the discussion orderly, so that different points are dealt with in turn. Now the chairman can help the group to come to a decision, by focussing on disagreements among members and trying to arrive at a creative solution, evaluating different solutions in relation to criteria if these can be agreed, considering sub-problems in turn, or asking the committee to consider two possible solutions. Finally, an attempt is made to secure the group's support for a particular solution. If this is impossible it may be necessary to take a vote; this is unsatisfactory, since it means that some members are not happy about the decision, and will not support it very enthusiastically.

A chairman should be aware of the main processes of behaviour in groups, and be able to prevent these processes interfering with the effective working of the committee. The formation of a status hierarchy will inhibit low-status members from contributing: they should be encouraged to speak. The reason that groups often take riskier decisions than individuals is that, in most situations, risky behaviour is valued in the culture, and it is flattering to the self-image to believe that one is riskier than the other members of the group. As a result, those who discover that they have been making less risky decisions than others shift in the risky direction after the group discussion.

The meaning and assessment of social competence

By social competence we mean the ability, the possession of the necessary skills, to produce the desired effects on other people in social situations. These desired effects may be to persuade the others to buy, to learn, to recover from neurosis, to like or admire the actor, and so on. These results are not necessarily in the public interest: skills may be used for social or antisocial purposes. And there is no evidence that social competence is a general factor; a person may be better at one task than another, such as interviewing rather than lecturing, or in one situation than another, perhaps parties or committees. Social skills training (SST) for students and other more or less normal populations has been directed to the skills of dating, making friends and being assertive. SST for mental patients has been aimed at correcting failures of social competence, and also at relieving subjective distress, such as social anxiety.

To find out who needs training, and in what areas, a detailed descriptive assessment is needed. We want to know, for example, which situations a trainee finds difficult: formal situations, conflicts, meeting strangers, etc., and which situations he is inadequate in, even though he does not report them as difficult. And we want to find out what he is doing wrong: failure to produce the right non-verbal signals, low rewardingness, lack of certain social skills, etc.

Social competence is easier to define and agree upon in the case of professional social skills: an effective therapist cures more patients, an effective teacher teaches better, an effective saleswoman sells more, an effective performer of effective skill is one who gets better results of the kind relevant to the task. Having said that, when we look more closely, it is not quite so simple: examination marks may be one index of a teacher's effectiveness, but usually more is meant than just this. A saleswoman should not simply sell a lot of goods, she should make the customer feel she would like to go to that shop again. So a combination of effective skills is required and the overall assessment of effectiveness may involve the combination of a number of different measures or ratings. The range of competence is quite large: the best salesmen and saleswomen regularly sell four times as much as some others behind the same counter; some supervisors of working groups produce twice as much output as others, or have 20-25 per cent of the labour turnover and absenteeism rates (Argyle, 1972).

For everyday social skills it is more difficult to give the criteria of success; lack of competence is easier to spot, such as failure to make friends, or opposite sex friends, quarrelling and failing to sustain co-operative relationships, finding a number of situations difficult or a source of anxiety, and so on.

Self-report methods of assessment

The assessment of social competence is based at least in part on some kind of interview or questionnaire. It is generally recognized, however, that self-report measures are far from satisfactory in this field, and need to be used with caution. Behavioural measures are better, but much more difficult to obtain.

1. INTERVIEW: clients for SST are usually assessed by a kind of clinical interview. A neurotic patient with inter-personal problems will probably speak first about his own depression or anxiety, or about the difficult behaviour of others. He can be asked to describe in detail the behaviour which occurs in his main social encounters and relation-ships, especially the ones which he finds difficult. The interviewer tries to obtain as detailed an account as possible of what happens in these difficult situations, in particular what the patient himself does or fails to do. This can be supplemented by the use of rating scales, on which he reports which situations are most difficult.

2. RATING SCALES AND QUESTIONNAIRES: there are several questionnaires which assess general assertiveness, such as the Rathus Assertive Schedule (Rathus, 1973). However, since the discovery that individual assertiveness varies greatly between situations, scales have been devised which ask about assertiveness in specific situations. Such scales have been found to correlate 0.6-0.8 with ratings of assertive behaviour. Other scales have been constructed for measuring social anxiety, and a number of separate factors have been found. Trower, Bryant and Argyle (1978) devised a list of 30 situations, on which subjects rate five levels of difficulty, the fifth point being 'avoidance if possi-ble'. Another scale presents a series of difficult situ-ations, and the open-ended responses are then rated or classified by judges (see Hersen and Bellack, 1976).

3. SELF-MONITORING: this has been developed in connec-tion with behavioural self-control techniques of therapy. The trainee reports systematically on selected aspects of his behaviour and keeps a record of some kind; the behaviour recorded is itself the target of therapy, and this method leads to direct attempts to change the behaviour; in addi-tion, the very act of recording is 'reactive'; that is, it changes the level of smoking, eating, or whatever is being recorded. Social behaviour has rarely been recorded in this way, apart from frequency of dating, and may be more diffi-cult to record accurately. Eisler (1976) suggests that trainees be trained during role-playing to record the re-quired aspects of their behaviour. However, self-reports do not always correlate highly with behavioural measures, or with physiological measures of anxiety. It has been found that self-reports correlate better with behavioural measures if the self-report inventory describes in detail the situation in which behaviour was observed.

Observation of social performance

Samples of an individual's performance may be obtained and analysed from role-playing, or from real life.

1. ROLE-PLAYING: the subject may be presented with a number of assertiveness situations (e.g. laundry loses shirt), dating situations, or other situations like those in his real environment. In view of the extent of situational variability, it is desirable to sample a number of different kinds of assertiveness situations on whatever dimension of behaviour is being assessed. We have used a social inter-action test based on different phases of a getting-acquainted encounter, with two partners, one male, one female; there are periods of interruption, of non-response, and of assertiveness by others. The role-playing is video-taped and scored, in terms of the use of elements of verbal behaviour (use of questions, etc.), and non-verbal beha-viour (use of facial expression, etc.) and also in terms of general dimensions of behaviour (e.g. assertiveness, warmth, etc.). Raters are found to have a reasonable degree of agreement on such ratings of behaviour, and indeed on over-all judgements of social competence (Trower et al, 1978). While some of these ratings are based on carefully defined criteria, others are deliberately 'subjective', leaving the observer to decide how far the trainee's behaviour is 'warm', 'rewarding', 'socially competent', etc. (Eisler, 1976).
    Some doubt has been cast on the validity of role-playing by a number of studies in which role-played performance was compared with performance in staged real-life situations involving assertiveness. Bellack et al (1979) found rather low correlations for male subjects and on certain measures, such as questions and amount of speech. All that can be said is that the validity of role-playing will be greater if a sample of situations is used which are similar to the criterion situation.

2. STAGED EVENTS: if a person knows that his assertiveness, for example, is being assessed, his behaviour changes a lot, thereby making the measure invalid. To avoid this happening, in some follow-up studies of assertiveness training staged events have been created in which, for example, a trainee encounters a person in a waiting room, who looks like another trainee, and who makes a series of unreasonable demands for a loan of books, notes, etc., the whole enc un-ter being recorded (Rich and Schroeder, 1976). This is possibly an unethical procedure, but does provide a valid measure of assertiveness.

3. OBSERVATION IN REAL-LIFE SETTINGS: several investi-gators have made use of ratings by colleagues, relations or friends. For example, in some studies of marital therapy each partner has recorded the other's rewarding and

unrewarding behaviour for a two-week period. King et al (1977), in a multiple baseline study with psychotic patients, assessed progress by a therapist unobtrusively accompanying the patient into three situations: a shop, a petrol station and a restaurant. In each situation the patient was asked to make ten requests, and a score was kept of how many he carried out.

Physiological measures

These have been used for example in training to reduce public speaking anxiety (Paul, 1966). However, physiological measures of anxiety have not been found to correlate at all well with self-reported discomfort, or behavioural measures. This is probably because the same state of physiological arousal may sometimes be labelled as euphoria or excitement, and sometimes as anxiety. Some people can perform very effectively while in a state of high physiological arousal, as in the case of many entertainers (Eisler, 1976).

Methods of social skills training

Role-playing with coaching

This is now the most widely used method of SST. There are four stages:

* instruction;
* role-playing with other trainees or other role partners, for 5-8 minutes;
* feedback and coaching, in the form of oral comments from the trainer;
* repeated role-playing.

A typical laboratory set-up is shown in figure 5. This also shows the use of an ear microphone, for instruction while role-playing is taking place. In the case of patients, mere practice does no good: there must be coaching as well.

For an individual or group of patients or other trainees, a series of topics, skills or situations is chosen, and introduced by means of short scenarios. Role partners are used who can be briefed to present carefully graded degrees of difficulty.

It is usual for trainers to be generally encouraging, and also rewarding for specific aspects of behaviour, though there is little experimental evidence for the value of such reinforcement. It is common to combine role-playing with modelling and video playback, both of which are discussed below. Follow-up studies have found that role-playing combined with coaching is successful with many kinds of mental patients, and that it is one of the most successful forms of SST for these groups.

1. MODELLING: this can consist of demonstrations by one of the therapists, or showing films or videotapes. It is used when it is difficult to teach the patient by verbal description alone. This applies to complex skills for

Figure 5

A social skills training laboratory

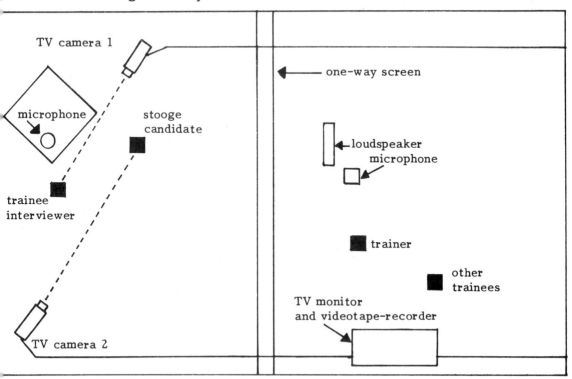

neurotic or volunteer clients, and to simpler skills for
more disturbed patients and children. It is generally used
in conjunction with role-playing, between role-play
sessions, and is accompanied by verbal instructions; that
is, coaching.

2.   VIDEO PLAYBACK: this is used in conjunction with role-
playing. Bailey and Sowder (1970) and Griffiths (1974) have
reviewed some of the studies comparing the effectiveness of
role-playing with and without video, and come to the conclusion that there is little evidence for its usefulness. In
fact, nearly all the studies cited showed that patients did
better when video playback was used. A later carefully
designed study by Maxwell (1976), on people who replied to
an advertisement for SST, obtained clearly better results
with video; the criterion measure consisted of blind ratings
of role-playing. Most people find it mildly disturbing at
first, and that it increases self-consciousness; however,
this wears off by the second or third session. The author
has found it particularly useful in training non-verbal
behaviour.

3.   HOMEWORK: how do trainees apply what they have
learned in the training setting to real life situations? The

main solution so far has been via 'homework'. Trainees are asked to try out the skills which they have just learnt several times before the next weekly session, and to report back on any difficulties. They may be given written notes on the exercises to be carried out, and the steps involved in each, and they may be asked to keep notes of what happened. Falloon et al (1977) found that out patients who were given structured homework assignments did better on nearly all outcome measures.

4. INDIVIDUAL versus GROUP METHODS: most trainers take patients in groups of 6-12, since groups have the advantage of providing a ready-made social situation, a series of role partners, and make more economical use of therapist time, while patients feel more at ease in the company of other similar people. On the other hand, groups of patients contain bad models, so there should be more than one therapist present, and it is difficult to concentrate on individual problems. One solution is to start patients in groups, but also to give them some individual sessions for particular problems. Very disturbed or regressed patients should be taken individually (Trower et al, 1978).

5. TRAINING SIGNIFICANT OTHERS: Goldsmith et al (1978) trained staff members, peer group leaders, and other inmates of an institution to observe, coach, prompt and reward competent skill performance by trainees. It is recognized that SST for disturbed children should be accompanied by the co-operation of teachers and parents (Van Hasselt et al, 1979). This principle could be extended to SST with any kind of trainees.

Special training methods
Some forms of SST have drawn heavily on the results of research in social psychology, and this is particularly the case with the Oxford form of SST. Here are some examples, related to the processes described earlier.

1. EXPRESSION OF NVC (non-verbal communication): people who are unable to express emotions and interpersonal attitudes can be given training in the use of the face and voice. Facial expression can be taught with the help of a mirror, and then a videotape-recorder; vocal expression training needs an audio tape-recorder.

2. PLANNING AND INITIATING: patients who fail to pursue persistent goals, and who react passively to others, can be given special exercises. Simple interviewing is useful; the trainee makes notes beforehand, and directs the encounter; an ear microphone can be used to coach him during the role-playing.

3. TAKING THE ROLE OF THE OTHER: Chandler (1973) succeeded in improving ability to see others' points of view

(and reducing delinquency) by means of exercises in which groups of five young delinquents developed and made video-recordings of skits about relevant real-life situations, in which each member of the group played a part.

4.   SELF-PRESENTATION: in addition to the usual role-playing exercises, trainees can be given advice over clothes, hair, and other aspects of appearance. Their voices can be trained to produce a more appropriate accent or tone of voice.

5.   SITUATIONAL ANALYSIS: for clients who have difficulty with particular situations, situational analysis is useful. The goals, rules, repertoire, roles, and other features of the situation are established, the difficulties located, and the best solutions are discussed and practised.

6.   ANALYSIS OF CONVERSATIONAL SEQUENCES: many patients cannot sustain a simple conversation. Study of their social performance in role-playing sessions makes it possible to discover exactly what it is they are doing wrong: for example, failure to reciprocate or hand over conversation, failure of non-verbal accompaniments, etc. Coaching is then directed towards these deficits.

Other methods of training
1.   TRAINING ON THE JOB: this is a widely used traditional method. Some people improve through experience but others do not, and some learn the wrong things. The situation can be improved if there is a trainer who regularly sees the trainee in action, and is able to hold feedback sessions at which errors are pointed out and better skills suggested. In practice this method does not appear to work very well: for example, with trainee teachers (see Argyle, 1969).

2.   GROUP METHODS: these, especially T-groups (T meaning training), are intended to enhance sensitivity and social skills. Follow-up studies have consistently found that 30-40 per cent of trainees are improved by group methods, but up to 10 per cent are made worse, sometimes needing psychological assistance (e.g. Lieberman et al, 1973). It has been argued that group methods are useful for those who are resistant to being trained.

3.   EDUCATIONAL METHODS: methods such as lectures and films can increase knowledge, but to master social skills it is necessary to try them out, as is the case with motor skills. Educational methods can be a useful supplement to role-playing methods.

Areas of application of SST

Neurotic patients
Role-playing and more specialized methods described above

have been found to be slightly more effective than psychotherapy, desensitization, or other alternative treatments,
but not much (Trower et al, 1978). Only one study so far
has found really substantial differences, and that is
Maxwell (1976). In a study of adults in New Zealand reporting social difficulties and seeking treatment for them, she
insisted on homework between training sessions. However,
SST does produce more improvement in social skills and reduction of social anxiety. A few patients can be cured by
SST alone, but most have other problems as well, and may
require other forms of treatment in addition.

Psychotic patients

These have been treated in the USA by assertiveness training
and other forms of role-playing. Follow-up studies have
shown greater improvement in social behaviour than from
alternative treatments. The most striking results have been
obtained with intensive clinical studies of 1-4 patients,
using a 'multiple baseline' design; one symptom is worked on
at a time over a total of 20-30 sessions. It is not clear
from these follow-up studies to what extent the general
condition of patients has been improved, or how well they
have been able to function outside the hospital (Hersen and
Bellack, 1976). It has been argued by one practitioner that
SST is more suitable than psychotherapy for working-class
patients in view of their poor verbal skills (Goldstein,
1973).

Other therapeutic uses of SST

Alcoholics have been given SST to improve their assertiveness, for example in refusing drinks, and to enable them to
deal better with situations which they find stressful and
make them drink. Similar treatment has been given to drug
addicts. In both cases treatment has been fairly successful,
though the effects have not always been long lasting; SST is
often included in more comprehensive packages.

Delinquents and prisoners have often been given SST with
some success, especially in the case of aggressive and sex
offenders. SST can also increase their degree of internal
control. Modelling and coaching are the main methods used,
and it is common to obtain the collaboration of teachers and
parents.

Teachers, managers, doctors, etc.

SST is increasingly being included in the training of those
whose work involves dealing with people. The most extensive
application so far has been in the training of teachers by
'micro teaching'. The pupil teacher is instructed in one of
the component skills of teaching, such as the use of different kinds of question, explanation or the use of examples;
he then teaches five or six children for 10-15 minutes, followed by a feedback session and 're-teaching'. Follow-up
studies show that this is far more effective than a similar
amount of teaching practice, and it is much more effective

in eradicating bad habits (Brown, 1975). In addition to role-playing, more elaborate forms of simulation are used, for example to train people for administrative positions. Training on the job is a valuable addition or alternative, provided that the trainer really does his job.

Normal adults
Students have received a certain amount of SST, especially in North American universities, and follow-up studies have shown that they can be successfully trained in assertiveness (Rich and Schroeder, 1976), dating behaviour (Curran, 1977), and to reduce anxiety at performing in public (Paul, 1966). Although many normal adults apart from students have social behaviour difficulties, very little training is available unless they seek psychiatric help. It would be very desirable for SST to be more widely available, for example in community centres.

Schoolchildren
A number of attempts have been made to introduce SST into schools, though there are no follow-up studies on its effectiveness. However, there have been a number of successful follow-up studies of training schemes for children who are withdrawn and unpopular or aggressive, using the usual role-playing methods (Rinn and Markle, 1979).

Conclusion

In this chapter we have tried to give an account of those aspects of social psychology which are most relevant to the work of teachers, social workers and others, both in understanding the behaviour of their clients and also in helping them with their own performance. We have used various models of social behaviour such as the social skills model and the model of social behaviour as a game. Some of the phenomena described cannot be fully accounted for in terms of these models: for example, the design of sequences of interaction. A number of practical implications are described; in particular, discussion of the skills which have been demonstrated to be the most effective in a number of situations, and the methods of social skills training which have been found to have most impact. It should be emphasized that much of this research is quite new and it is expected that a great deal more will be found out on these topics in the years to come.

References

Argyle, M. (1972)
The Social Psychology of Work. London: Allen Lane and Penguin Books.
Argyle, M. (1975)
Bodily Communication. London: Methuen.
Argyle, M. (1969)
Social Interaction. London: Methuen.
Argyle, M. and Cook, M. (1976)

Gaze and Mutual Gaze. London: Cambridge University Press.

Argyle, M., Furnham, A. and Graham, J.A. (in press)
Social Situations. London: Cambridge University Press.

Argyle, M. and Kendon, A. (1967)
The experimental analysis of social performance. Advances in Experimental Social Psychology, 3, 55-98.

Argyle, M., Salter, V., Nicholson, H., Williams, M. and Burgess, P. (1970)
The communication of inferior and superior attitudes by verbal and non-verbal signals. British Journal of Social and Clinical Psychology, 9, 221-231.

Bailey, K.G. and Sowder, W.T. (1970)
Audiotape and videotape self-confrontation in psychotherapy. Psychological Bulletin, 74, 127-137.

Bales, R.F. (1950)
Interaction Process Analysis. Cambridge, Mass.: Addison-Wesley.

Bellack, A.S., Hersen, M. and Lamparski, D. (1979)
Role play tests for assessing social skills: are they valid? Are they useful? Journal of Consulting and Clinical Psychology, 47, 335-342.

Bersheid, E. and Walster, E. (1974)
Physical attractiveness. Advances in Experimental Social Psychology, 7, 158-215.

Bower, S.A. and Bower, G.H. (1976)
Asserting Yourself. Reading, Mass.: Addison-Wesley.

Brown, G.A. (1975)
Microteaching. London: Methuen.

Bryan, J.H. and Walbek, N.H. (1970)
Preaching and practising generosity: children's actions and reactions. Child Development, 41, 329-353.

Chandler, M.J. (1973)
Egocentrism and anti-social behaviour: the assessment and training of social perspective-training skills. Developmental Psychology, 9, 326-332.

Curran, J.P. (1977)
Skills training as an approach to the treatment of heterosexual-social anxiety. Psychological Bulletin, 84, 140-157.

Davitz, J.R. (1964)
The Communication of Emotional Meaning. New York: McGraw-Hill.

Dion, K., Berscheid, E. and Walster, E. (1972)
What is beautiful is good. Journal of Personality and Social Psychology, 24, 285-290.

Duck, S.W. (1973)
Personal Relationships and Personal Constructs. Chichester: Wiley.

Duval, S. and Wicklund, R.A. (1972)
A Theory of Objective Self Awareness. New York: Academic Press.

Eisler, R.M. (1976)
The behavioral assessment of social skills. In M. Hersen

and A.S. Bellack (eds), Behavioral Assessment: A
practical handbook. New York: Pergamon.

**Eisler, R.M., Hersen, M., Miller, P.M. and Blanchard,
E.B.** (1975)
Situational determinants of assertive behavior. Journal
of Consulting and Clinical Psychology, 43, 330-340.

Ekman, P., Friesen, W.V. and Ellsworth, P. (1972)
Emotions in the Human Face. New York: Pergamon.

Endler, N.S. (1965)
The effects of verbal reinforcement on conformity and
deviant behaviour. Journal of Social Psychology, 66, 147-
154.

**Falloon, I.R.H., Lindley, P., McDonald, R. and Marks,
I.M.** (1977)
Social skills training of out-patient groups: a
controlled study of rehearsal and homework. British
Journal of Psychiatry, 131, 599-609.

Fiedler, F.E. (1964)
A contingency model of leadership effectiveness.
Advances in Experimental Social Psychology, 1, 150-191.

Flanders, N.A. (1970)
Analyzing Teaching Behavior. Reading, Mass.: Addison-
Wesley.

Flavell, J.H. (1968)
The Development of Role-taking and Communication Skills
in Children. New York: Wiley.

Freedman, J.L. and Fraser, S.C. (1966)
Compliance without pressure: the foot-in-the-door
technique. Journal of Personality and Social Psychology,
4, 195-202.

Giles, H. and Powesland, P.F. (1975)
Speech Style and Social Evaluation. London: Academic
Press.

Goffman, E. (1956)
The Presentation of Self in Everyday Life. Edinburgh
University Press.

Goldstein, A.J. (1973)
Structured Learning Therapy: Toward a psychotherapy for
the poor. New York: Academic Press.

Goldstein, A.P. et al (1978)
Training aggressive delinquents in prosocial
behaviour. Journal of Youth and Adolescence, 7, 73-92.

Griffiths, R.D.P. (1974)
Videotape feedback as a therapeutic technique:
retrospect and prospect. Behaviour Research and Therapy,
12, 1-8.

Griffitt, W. and Veitch, R. (1974)
Ten days in a fall-out shelter. Sociometry, 37, 63-173.

Harre, R. and Secord, P. (1972)
The Explanation of Social Behaviour. Oxford: Blackwell.

Hersen, M. and Bellack, A.S. (1976)
Social skills training for chronic psychiatric patients:

rationale, research findings, and future directions.
Comprehensive Psychiatry, 17, 559-580.

Hoffman, L.R. (1965)
Group problem-solving. Advances in Experimental Social
Psychology, 2, 99-132.

Jennings, H.H. (1950)
Leadership and Isolation. New York: Longmans Green.

Jones, E.E. (1964)
Ingratiation: A social psychological analysis. New York:
Appleton-Century-Crofts.

Jones, E.E. and Nisbett, R.E. (1972)
The actor and the observer: divergent perceptions of
the causes of behavior. In E.E. Jones et al (eds),
Attribution: Perceiving the causes of behavior.
Morristown, NJ: General Learning Press.

Jourard, S.M. (1971)
Self Disclosure. New York: Wiley-Interscience.

**King, L.W., Liberman, R.P., Roberts, J. and Bryan,
E.** (1977)
Personal affectiveness: a structured therapy for
improving social and emotional skills. European Journal
of Behaviour Analysis and Modification, 2, 82-89.

Lazarus, A.A. (1973)
On assertive behavior: a brief note. Behavior Therapy,
4, 697-699.

Lieberman, M.A., Yalom, I.D. and Miles, M.R. (1973)
Encounter Groups: First facts. New York: Basic Books.

Likert, R. (1961)
New Patterns of Management. New York: McGraw-Hill.

Lott, A.J. and Lott, B.E. (1960)
The formation of positive attitudes towards group
members. Journal of Abnormal and Social Psychology, 61,
297-300.

Maier, N.R.F. and Solem, A.R. (1952)
The contribution of a discussion leader to the quality
of group thinking: the effective use of minority
opinion. Human Relations, 5, 277-288.

Maxwell, G.M. (1976)
An evaluation of social skills training. (Unpublished,
University of Otago, Dunedin, New Zealand.)

Mehrabian, A. (1972)
Nonverbal Communication. New York: Aldine-Atherton.

Meldman, M.J. (1967)
Verbal behavior analysis of self-hyperattentionism.
Diseases of the Nervous System, 28, 469-473.

Milgram, S. (1974)
Obedience to Authority. New York: Harper & Row.

Mischel, W. (1968)
Personality and Assessment. New York: Wiley.

Paul, G.L. (1966)
Insight v. Desensitization in Psychotherapy. Stanford,
Ca: Stanford University Press.

Rapoport, R. and Rapoport, R.H. (1964)

New light on the honeymoon. Human Relations, 17, 33-56.

Rathus, S.A. (1973)
A 30-item schedule for assessing assertive behavior. Behavior Therapy, 4, 398-406.

Regan, D.T. (1971)
Effects of a favor and liking on compliance. Journal of Experimental Social Psychology, 7, 627-639.

Rich, A.R. and Schroeder, H.E. (1976)
Research issues in assertiveness training. Psychological Bulletin, 83, 1081-1096.

Rinn, R.C. and Markle, A. (1979)
Modification of social skill deficits in children. In A.S. Bellack and M. Hersen (eds), Research and Practice in Social Skills Training. New York and London: Plenum.

Rubin, Z. (1973)
Liking and Loving. New York: Holt, Rinehart & Winston.

Rommetveit, R. and Blakar, R.N. (1979)
Studies of Language, Thought and Communication. London: Academic Press.

Schachter, S. and Singer, J.E. (1962)
Cognitive, social, and physiological determinants of emotional state. Psychological Review, 69, 379-399.

Sherif, M., Harvey, O.J., White, B.J., Hood, W.R. and Sherif, C. (1961)
Intergroup Conflict and Cooperation: The Robbers' Cave experiment. Norman, Oklahoma: The University of Oklahoma Book Exchange.

Sykes, G.M. and Matza, D. (1957)
Techniques of neutralization: a theory of delinquency. American Sociological Review, 2, 667-689.

Tagiuri, R. (1958)
Social preference and its perception. In R. Tagiuri, and L. Petrullo, Person Perception and Interpersonal Behaviour. Stanford, Ca: Stanford University Press.

Trower, P., Bryant, B. and Argyle, M. (1978)
Social Skills and Mental Health. London: Methuen.

Van Hasselt, V.B., Hersen, M., Whitehill, M.B. and Bellack, A.S. (1979)
Social skill assessment and training for children: and evaluation review. Behaviour Research and Therapy, 17, 413-437.

Walster, E., Aronson, V., Abrahams, D. and Rottmann, L. (1966)
Importance of physical attractiveness in dating behavior. Journal of Personality and Social Psychology, 5, 508-516.

Wish, M. and Kaplan, S.J. (1977)
Toward an implicit theory of interpersonal communication. Sociometry, 40, 234-246.

Questions

1. Is it useful to look at social behaviour as a kind of skill?

2. What do bad conversationalists do wrong?
3. What information is conveyed by non-verbal communication?
4. In what ways do non-verbal signals supplement verbal ones?
5. How is the perception of other people different from the perception of other physical objects?
6. When and why do individuals engage in self-presentation?
7. What information about a social situation would a newcomer to it need to know?
8. Is social behaviour due more to persons or to situations?
9. Do we like other people primarily because they are rewarding?
10. Why do some people have difficulty in making friends?
11. Is assertiveness a matter of persuasion or self-presentation?
12. What kind of arguments are most persuasive?
13. What is the most effective style of leadership? When are different styles required?
14. Can social competence be measured?
15. How can the effectiveness of social skills training be assessed?
16. Is social skills training successful with mental patients?
17. If someone has inadequate social behaviour, what else may he require in addition to SST?
18. What criticisms have been made of experiments in social psychology? What other methods are available?
19. Does social behaviour take the same form in other cultures?
20. Are there fundamental differences between social behaviour in families, work-groups and groups of friends?

Annotated reading

Argyle, M. (1978) The Psychology of Interpersonal Behaviour (3rd edn). Harmondsworth: Penguin.
   Covers the field of the chapter, and related topics at 'Penguin' level.

Argyle, M. and Trower, P. (1979). Person to Person. London: Harper & Row.
   A more popular account of the area covered by the chapter, with numerous coloured illustrations.

Argyle, M. (1975). Bodily Communication. London: Methuen.
   Covers the field of non-verbal communication in more detail, with some illustrations.

Berscheid, E. and Walster, E.H. (1978). Interpersonal Attraction (2nd edn). Reading, Mass.: Addison-Wesley.
   A very readable account of research in this area.

Bower, S.A. and Bower, G.H. (1976). Asserting Yourself. Reading, Mass.: Addison-Wesley.
> An interesting and practical book about assertiveness, with examples and exercises.

Cook, M. (1979). Perceiving Others. London: Methuen.
> A clear account of basic processes in person perception.

Goffman, E. (1956). The Presentation of Self in Everyday Life. Edinburgh: Edinburgh University Press.
> A famous and highly entertaining account of self-presentation.

Trower, P., Bryant, B. and Argyle, M. (1978). Social Skills and Mental Health. London: Methuen.
> An account of social skills training with neurotics, with full details of procedures.

Relevance to the teacher
DAVID FONTANA

From our comments in the introduction to Part IV it can be inferred that the study of social behaviour in the classroom helps the teacher do the following things:

* to understand the precise nature of the interaction between himself and the child, and the meaning this interaction has for the latter;
* to understand the interaction between the children themselves and the interaction between the various sub-groups within the class;
* to develop strategies for encouraging those forms of interaction most likely to assist learning.

We can now take each of these in turn and discuss it in the light of the information in Argyle's section.

Social interaction between teacher and child

Argyle stresses that every item of social interaction is a two-way process. When the teacher talks to the child he receives a response which helps determine what he himself says next. The response may be verbal but may just as easily be non-verbal. We mean by a non-verbal response that the child may, by his expression, by the direction of his gaze, by the shuffling of his feet, or by other similar means, convey to the teacher the nature of his thoughts and feelings. These may involve comprehension or incomprehension, interest, boredom, anxiety, hostility, amusement, or a host of other similar things, each of which influences the teacher's own thoughts and feelings in turn.

It is one thing to know that this is happening, of course, and quite another to be able to analyse it in detail and decide where and how to change one's own behaviour in order to help change that of the child. In his section, Argyle shows that social interaction can be categorized in terms of 'two-step sequences', 'social skills sequences', and 'episode sequences' respectively, and stresses that socially inadequate people are usually very bad conversationalists, probably because they fail to master some of these sequences. If the reader studies what Argyle has to say about these three sequential categories in detail, he will be able to see how a knowledge of what takes place within each one can assist the teacher in extending and developing verbal and non-verbal exchanges with the class. For example, we see that a proactive two-step sequence, by combining for instance an answer with a question of one's own ('I did such and such; what did you do?') allows the conversational sequence to continue into a further cycle, whereas failure to make a proactive move (as happens when one simply provides an answer to a question and leaves it at that) can bring it to a stop. Similarly, with a social skills sequence we can see that perseverance by the teacher can be rewarded eventually by the desired response from the child. The teacher's first conversational move (A1) produces an unsatisfactory response from the child (B2); the teacher then modifies his own conversational move and produces A2, which now prompts the child to produce the desired B2. Note that if the teacher had persisted with A1 (e.g. repeated a question or an instruction in the same form), then the child might well have gone on replying with B1, leading to mounting frustration and anxiety all round.

The lesson as an episode sequence
Episode sequences, which Argyle suggests consist usually of five main episodes or phases, may appear at first sight to have less relevance to the classroom than two-step or social skill sequences because they contain longer and more complex units of interaction than are usually contained in the relatively brief verbal encounters that the teacher has with each child. Yet if we look more closely, we see that the typical classroom lesson takes the form of an extended episode sequence, with the teacher first of all greeting the class ('Good morning, children', 'Hello everyone', or - less desirably - 'Er, well now'). This greeting leads on to (and inevitably influences) the second phase, which consists of establishing a relationship. The teacher tells the class to listen carefully, or to look at the board, or to get out certain books, or to hand in their homework or simply to pay attention and stop looking round. The better the teacher knows and understands the class, and the more acceptable he is to them, the shorter this second phase is likely to be. The lesson then moves on to the central task, which obviously consists of the material to be studied and the exercises to be carried out, and which will include several subtasks. When this is complete (or time runs out), the fourth phase of re-establishing the relationship comes round, and the teacher will again address the whole class and tell them what he thought of their work and what he expects from them in the future, and then he will dismiss them (pleasantly,

gratefully or wearily as the case may be) and the fifth phase will be complete and the sequence terminated.

The reader may wonder why, apart from purely descriptive purposes, we need to view the lesson in terms of a five-episode sequence. The answer is that it helps us appreciate the extent to which each phase interacts with and influences the next. The way in which the teacher greets the class influences their response to his attempt to establish a relationship, which in turn influences the success with which the central task is tackled, which in turn influences the attempt to re-establish a relationship, and which in turn influences the parting. This completed cycle then influences the way in which teacher and class think about each other during the interval before the next lesson, which influences the way in which they greet each other when this lesson begins, which inevitably influences the whole of the next cycle. Thinking about the lesson in terms of this five-episode sequence also helps us to appreciate what is really going on in terms of teacher-child interaction and not merely what seems to be going on. The teacher might, for example, snap at the class to come in quietly as they enter the room, seeing this as nothing more than a routine rebuke whereas, for better or worse, the children see this as his greeting to them.

A greeting is not simply something that we decide to call 'a greeting' whenever it happens; it is the first interchange that takes place between people when they meet, and the studies of Argyle and other social psychologists show that this interchange is of great importance in determining the nature of the relationship that follows. If the greeting is not a welcoming one, then we may have to work very hard in the following episodes to repair the damage. Similarly, the next phase - that of establishing a relationship - is not just a convenient label that Argyle has decided to use. Research shows that after the greeting (and, as we have said, influenced by it) there is a definite stage in which the individuals concerned weigh each other up, make deductions on each other's intentions and so on. Thus, although the teacher may think that he is simply giving the class the results of a test or handing back homework, what is actually happening is that he is moving into this second phase and providing the class with clues which help them in this weighing-up process. They decide whether he is pleased or disappointed with them today, whether he is going to make more demands on them over the 40 minutes of the lesson than he usually does, whether he is going to arouse anxieties or not, whether he has positive or negative concepts of them and their abilities, and even whether he is in the same mood as he was last time they met. These decisions help determine their own responses - enthusiastic, wary, friendly, hostile, co-operative, aggrieved and so on - which in turn influence the teacher's own behaviour and the way in which the whole class settles to the central task of the lesson.

The nature of communications

Having categorized the social interaction itself, Argyle
then goes on to categorize the nature of the communications
that it contains. So far we have been using such general
terms as 'welcoming', 'friendly', 'co-operative' and so on,
but there are in fact much more precise categories that help
us formalize our thinking in the matter. Argyle tells us
that communication can be egocentric (directed to the self)
or, if socially directed, can consist of orders, questions,
information, informal speech, expressed emotions, 'performative' utterances, social routines or latent messages. By
studying the definition provided by Argyle for each of these
categories, and by then applying them to his own characteristic behaviour with children, the teacher can gain
valuable insights into his professional skills. Do the
majority of his social interchanges with children take, for
example, the form of orders and information rather than of
questions? If so, does this mean that he is directing his
class too frequently instead of prompting them to think and
examine and deduce? Does he use informal speech where
appropriate to encourage a relaxed and friendly atmosphere?
If not, then is he creating unnecessary barriers between
himself and the class which inhibit children from asking his
help and guidance? On the other hand, does he perhaps overdo
informal speech so that the children find it hard to recognize his authority when he wishes to re-assert it? Does he
encourage the expression of emotion where this is helpful to
the child and to his learning (this means not just encouraging expressions of humour and pleasure but prompting the
articulation of anxieties and disappointments: for instance,
'I can see you're upset about it; what's the trouble?'). Or
does he dismiss emotions as inappropriate (e.g. 'Pull yourself together'; 'Don't be so silly')? Does he frequently
express latent messages in his utterances, and are these
often of the negative kind (e.g. 'I'm too busy for that
now' might imply 'I'm just not interested in your
problem')?

   This task of analysing his communications is helped if
the teacher looks at one of the many systems now available
for coding and classifying classroom interaction. Normally
these systems are used by an observer, who sits at the back
of the class and watches closely what happens each time the
teacher communicates with the class or with individual
members of it. Because of the demands made upon the observer, particularly in a busy classroom where several things
seem to be happening at once, the categories employed in
these systems tend to be a simplification of the full range
provided by Argyle. The best-known of these systems is that
of Flanders (1970), which is set out below. When using the
Flanders system, the observer marks one of the ten categories every three seconds (which is about the top speed at
which he can operate), and analysis of the data after the
lesson gives the teacher a clear indication of the percentage of time taken up by each of the ten behaviours, and

also the extent to which he talked compared with the extent to which the children were stimulated into so doing.

Flanders' categories for interaction analysis

From Flanders, N.A., ©1970, Analyzing Teaching Behaviour, Addison-Wesley Publishing Co. Inc., chapter 2, p. 34, table 2.1, 'Flanders Interaction Analysis Categories (FIAC)', and is reprinted with permission.

TEACHER TALK

Response

1. Accepts feelings: accepts and clarifies the feeling tone of the students in a non-threatening manner; feelings may be positive or negative, predicting or recalling feelings are included.
2. Praises or encourages: praises or encourages student action or behaviour; jokes that release tension (not at the expense of another individual), nodding head or saying 'um hm?' or 'go on' are included.
3. Accepts or uses ideas of student: clarifies, builds, or develops ideas suggested by a student. (As a teacher brings more of his ideas into play, shift to category 5.)
4. Asks questions: asks a question using own ideas about content or procedure with the intent that a student should answer.

Initiation

5. Lectures: gives facts or opinions about content or procedure; expresses own ideas, asks rhetorical questions.
6. Gives directions: gives directions, commands, or orders with which a student is expected to comply.
7. Criticizes or justifies authority: makes statements intended to change student behaviour from non-acceptable to acceptable pattern; bawls someone out; states why the teacher is doing what he is doing; refers very often to self.

STUDENT TALK

Response

8. Response: makes a predictable reponse to teacher; teacher initiates the contract or solicits student statement and sets limits to what the student says.

Initiation

9. Initiation: initiates talk; makes unpredictable statements in response to teacher (as student introduces own ideas, shift from category 8 to 9).

10. Silence or confusion; pauses, short periods of silence and periods of confusion in which communication cannot be understood by the observer.

Over 100 of these interaction analysis systems are now in existence. Some are what is known as low-inferential, in that like the above they simply allow the observer to record what happened. Others are high-inferential or evaluative in that they allow the observer to record whether in his opinion the teacher was, for example, 'warm', 'enthusiastic' or 'stimulating'. In some systems the observer is able in addition to note the type of student with whom the teacher is interacting (e.g. 'high achiever', 'low achiever'). The choice as to which system to use depends to a large measure upon the kind of information required. If the aim is merely to record the percentage of time spent on the various categories of teacher and of student talk respectively, then an instrument of the Flanders type is ideal. If, on the other hand, we want to know whether the teacher, say, behaves differently towards boys than towards girls, or whether he uses non-verbal signals such as tone of voice or facial expression, then a more complex system with inferential categories would have to be employed.

If, as a third possibility, we wished to study a specific teacher skill, such as questioning, then we could use a system that concentrates on this aspect alone. Such an instrument would look at the type of question asked (seeking facts, seeking opinions, seeking emotional reactions), at the manner in which it is delivered (challenging, threatening, neutral, encouraging), and at the individual to whom the question is directed (boy or girl, high, medium or low-achiever). In its simplest form, such a specialist system is constructed as a matrix, with the type of question asked down the left-hand side and one other variable (e.g. manner in which delivered) across the top. Yet another possibility is for the observer to try and ascertain what the teacher expected to come out of a particular item of interaction between him and a particular child and what the child himself thought the teacher expected. This involves video-taping examples of classroom interaction, and then showing the tape as soon as possible afterwards independently to both teacher and child and asking them a number of appropriate questions (e.g. the teacher will be asked what he wanted from the child and whether or not he considered it was forthcoming, while the child will be asked for his version of events). Results sometimes indicate that teacher and child have quite different ideas about what was going on. The child may, for example, have thought the teacher was requesting opinion when in reality he was demanding fact, or that the teacher was being serious when in reality he was trying to be humorous, or that he was offering censure when in reality he was offering help. Similarly, if we reverse the procedure, the teacher might interpret child behaviour as being impertinent when it was not intended by the child as such, or as providing incorrect reponses to a

question when in fact the child was trying to convey
something quite different and much nearer the truth.

Analysing the results of interaction analysis

Whatever the system used, a teacher can often be surprised
to see how much of the lesson he spent lecturing (talking at
the class), or how infrequently he offered praise or encouragement, or how often children had to seek direction
from him on points that he should have made clear to them
at the start. Alternatively, he may be heartened to see how
often he asked questions or accepted feelings or stimulated
the class to initiate their own ideas. Where a videotape has
been used to keep a visual record of the interaction, then
the teacher may be surprised to notice not only the number
of times he censured the class, but the ferocity of his
expression as he did so or the number of mannerisms he
appeared to have developed. (Or, again, he may be charmed
at what a debonair and handsome picture he cut, but such
a discovery is not, in itself, without dangers!) If the
teacher is analysing the results of a system designed to
look at just one aspect of his work, such as motivation, he
might be disturbed to see how often he employed the use of
threats (e.g. 'Work quietly if you want to get out to play
on time'; 'Pay attention if you want to get through the
examination'; 'Work hard or else'). On the other hand, he
might be pleased to realize how often he motivated through
positive encouragement ('I know you'll be able to do this
because you've been working so well'; 'I'm sure you'll find
this fun').

In the light of the complexity of social behaviour, as
suggested by Argyle, it is only to be expected that no
system for measuring classroom interaction is going to be
completely comprehensive. There are all kinds of subtle
interactions that in any case we cannot yet score, and two
identical score sheets for two different teachers (or even
for the same teacher with two different classes) may cloak
numerous important variations in social behaviour. And of
course, children will respond to the teacher not just on the
strength of what he says or does in the present lesson but
(as we pointed out when discussing episode sequences above)
on their memories of the social interactions that took place
on the previous occasions they were being taught by him.
('When old Jones looks like that it means he's in a bad
mood'; 'Miss Wombat won't shout at you if you get it wrong';
'We've never once had a good laugh in Griefee's lesson').
Nevertheless, interaction analysis systems provide one of
the best practical ways for helping a teacher to study his
own professional strengths and weaknesses (to say nothing of
the behaviour of children), and it is unfortunate that in
Britain at least more use is not made of them both in
initial training and in in-service work.

Social interaction between child and child

In his discussion of friendship Argyle tells us much about
the forces that operate within the social group. Friendship

appears to depend to a considerable extent upon frequency of interaction (e.g. two or more children sit near each other, are often paired off in games lessons because of similarities in height, live near each other and walk home together and so on), upon mutual satisfaction of needs (the children help each other in their work, provide companionship in the face of some outside threat), upon similarity (they come from the same socio-economic background, share the same hobbies or anxieties, have the same kind of ability levels), and upon physical attractiveness (the children like the look of each other). Where these conditions are met, bonds seem to be formed between the children concerned, and they may become still closer if they develop new interests together.

Some children, however, seem to be generally popular with the whole class, even though they may appear to have little in common with some of its members. Such individuals, Argyle suggests, appear to have other additional important qualities. They seem to show a concern for others as well as for themselves, to inspire confidence in some way, and to satisfy group needs. For example, they may be able to offer encouragement or support, or to 'liven things up' in dull lessons, to offer instances of expertise in certain prized areas (e.g. sport, musical skills), to stand up for classmates when threatened, or to set some kind of desirable standard (perhaps in matters of dress or life style). Such children often develop into unofficial group leaders, either for the whole class or for a particular sub-group within the class. Research shows that people likely to become leaders tend also to be able to define the group in some way: that is, to give it identity, to recognize and emphasize those things about it that other group members feel (consciously or unconsciously) to be important. In addition they seem to have some social quality (charisma, prestige) which enables those in receipt of their friendship or attention to feel they are having status conferred upon them. To complete the picture, they generally appear to be a little above the average intelligence of the group, to show a problem-solving orientation, and to be able to initiate problem-solving behaviour.

Sociometry

One way of identifying the leaders in a class of children is simply to ask people to vote on who they are. A widely used technique for doing this, known as 'sociometry', involves asking each child to write down the name of the classmate they would most like to see in charge of a group in which they are working. We can be more specific if we wish and specify the kind of group concerned (academic, social, sporting). Alternatively, we could ask the children who they would least like as their leader, and thus get some idea of those with low leadership qualities (though we must always have reservations about inviting children to make negative comments about each other). Such children would not necessarily be unpopular, but might simply be regarded as too prone to act the fool, or perhaps too lacking in the skills required by the group.

Sociometry is not, of course, confined to studies attempting to identify group leaders. It can be employed in any study designed to pick out individuals with particular social skills, and has perhaps been most widely used in studies of friendship patterns. In these studies each child is asked who they would like to be friends with, and the children receiving the highest number of choices are labelled stars while those receiving the least are labelled isolates. Results are sometimes plotted in the form of a sociogram with each child's name entered on the gram with an arrow drawn pointing towards him from each child who has nominated him as a friend. The sociogram enables us to see at a glance not only who are the stars and who are the isolates within the class, but also what sub-groups exist, since these often show up as clusters of children who tend to choose only each other.

Once these patterns have been identified, we can then study the sets of circumstances that appear to mark children out as stars and isolates, or which go to help the formation of sub-groups. We have already discussed this within the context of friendship above, and much of the research to which we then made reference has emerged from work with sociograms, but there may be other factors which help determine whether a child is a star or an isolate in addition to simple matters of friendship. A star might perhaps bathe in the reflected glory of a popular brother or sister higher up the school, or of a parent or relative with local or national prestige. An isolate might simply be marked off from the rest of the class by widely differing academic ability or socio-economic status, or he could be socially aggressive in some way, or exceptionally timid and retiring, or have some other kind of personality problem which may need particular guidance and counselling (see chapter 14).

Note that stars are not necessarily class leaders (though they often are), and that they, along with isolates and sub-groups, are subect to fluctuating social fortunes. The class, like most other social groups, is a dynamic unit, subject to constant change and development, and this term's star may be less popular next (for any one of a variety of reasons), while today's isolate could be more generally acceptable at a later date. The sympathetic teacher, sensitive to the social relationships within the class, can do much to prevent the formation of undesirable sub-groups simply by remembering Argyle's assertion that friendship depends largely upon frequency of interaction. Thus by seeing to it that all children within the class have opportunities to interact with each other as often as possible (e.g. by the way in which group and project work is organized), the teacher can ensure that certain children are not thrown together unduly. Similarly, a great deal can be done to prevent vulnerable individuals from becoming isolates by

ensuring that children are not always left to choose their
own partners or to define their own social environments
within the class, though this must be done carefully so that
the children are not robbed of social choice or made to feel
that the teacher is trying consistently to force unwanted
work-partners upon them.

Social learning and role models

Every teacher is a teacher of social skills. We teach these
skills not only when we counsel children to have concern for
others and to show this concern in the way in which they
relate to them, but also when we encourage them to join in
more, to speak up for themselves, and to value themselves
at their true social worth. Such teaching will sometimes
take place as part of a formal lesson (e.g. in drama or in
any of the humanities subjects), but will occur more frequently as part of the day-to-day contact between teacher
and child, in science subjects as well as in arts, and in
extra-curricular activities as well as within timetabled
ones.

We have already indicated at a number of points throughout the book that this kind of teaching involves example as
well as precept. It is not only what the teacher tells his
children that is important, but the way in which he himself
behaves towards them. A formal lesson on the subject of
politeness, for example, is likely to be completely wasted
if at the end of it the teacher is seen to act with extreme
discourtesy towards a member of the class (or perhaps
towards a colleague). Using the correct technical term (to
which the reader was introduced earlier in the book) we say
that the teacher should 'model' for his children the kind of
behaviour that he wants them to acquire. Bandura, one of
the main exponents of what are called 'social learning
theories', argues that we have tended to under-estimate the
importance of modelling, particularly when it comes to the
learning of social skills. Thus although he agrees that
reinforcement (see chapter 8) is important in many learning
acts, he argues that it is not always essential. The child,
he claims, has an innate propensity for imitating the
behaviour of others, particularly when these others enjoy
prestige or status in his life. Such imitation is often
unconscious in the sense that the child is not deliberately
setting out to ape the model concerned. Where the imitation
is on a large scale and relates specifically to one of the
child's roles in life (e.g. to 'maleness' or 'femaleness')
then we refer to this model as a role model. The child's
earliest role models, as we said in Part I, are usually his
parents, but as he grows older teachers, elder brothers and
sisters, prestigious friends and, later still, national
figures such as sportsmen and women come to assume
increasing importance.

It can be seen, therefore, that Bandura's theories are
referred to as social learning theories not because they
explain how the child comes to learn many of his social

skills, but because they suggest that social contact in itself produces learning, whatever category of skills happens to be involved. Of particular relevance for present purposes, since obviously such expression is closely linked to social skills and social acceptability, Bandura has demonstrated (1973) that the expression of emotions seems to be strongly influenced by this social contact. He has made a particular study of aggression, and has demonstrated that children who witness adult aggression are subsequently much more likely to behave aggressively themselves. This is not, of course, because watching aggression in others makes them aggressive, but because seeing adults behave aggressively seems to sanction the expression of the aggressive feelings they already have. They take the adult as their role model, and appear to consider that if it is all right for him to behave in that way then it must be all right for them too. This is an important point to bear in mind when we are considering the influence of television and of the media generally upon children. Watching televised violence does not make the child act violently, but it may seem to sanction any violent inclinations he may already have and to suggest to him specific ways in which these inclinations can be put into practice. The more prestigious the person perpetrating the televised violence (whether fictional or factual), the more likely is this to happen. However, if the child already has a well-developed value system taken over from parents and teachers, then he will resist the temptation to adopt new role models that appear to contradict this system, and his behaviour will in consequence remain unchanged.

Variation in children's responses to the same role model is also indicated by the fact that dependent children appear to imitate prestige figures of all kinds more readily than do those who are more independent. Similar research shows that timid or anxious children copy fearful responses in others more readily than do secure and confident ones, while socially helpful children imitate helpful responses more readily than do those who are less socially inclined. This seems to indicate that, once a child's repertoire of social behaviours is beginning to show some consistency, he will imitate more readily those models who confirm him in what he is already doing than those who introduce him to less familiar behaviours. Research also shows that children who have learnt in the past to respond to particular role models (such as teachers) will be readier in the present to take them as models again than will individuals who have learnt to reject them. Thus a child in this latter category who would be perfectly ready to accept a certain adult as a role model on the strength of his personal qualities may nevertheless reject him if he discovers that he happens to be a schoolteacher in his professional life. Finally, research shows that children are less likely to imitate the behaviour of someone whom they have seen to be unsuccessful in the past, even though he now appears before them in a quite new role, than someone whom they have seen performing successfully.

Although social learning does not appear to depend upon reinforcement, it is nevertheless greatly strengthened by it. Thus a child who takes over courteous behaviour from a teacher will be more likely to persist in this behaviour if he finds it brings about desirable ends. For example, he may find that other people respond more thoughtfully to him in turn, that he becomes generally better liked, or that things which were denied him when he tried to take them by other means become available now that he knows how to ask for them in a socially acceptable way. On the other hand, if he comes from a background in which courtesy is undervalued and brings no extrinsic reinforcement then he may decide, however strong the role model in favour of courtesy may be, that after all it does not seem to pay and may as well be abandoned.

Strategies for encouraging social skills

In addition to learning social skills through listening to the teacher and through social learning, Argyle suggests that they can be taught through systematic training pro- grammes. Perhaps surprisingly, little such training is as yet done in schools. We have said that the child may learn social skills formally through drama lessons and through the humanities, but usually such learning is sporadic and the teacher may have only a limited idea of the precise skills that he hopes will emerge. Argyle has in mind something very much more specific, with the teacher drawing up clear con- cise objectives just as he would in any subject (see chapter 8). Inevitably, some of the examples Argyle offers may ap- pear less relevant to the teacher than others. Few teachers would, for example, see it as part of their task to hold lessons on falling in love (though why such an important and rewarding activity should not be seen as relevant to formal education is a topic of interest in itself), though most would agree that assertiveness and social influence training are very much their concern, and careful thought should be given to programmes designed to further such training.

Obviously one approach is simply to organize a class discussion, in which children are invited to explore all the relevant variables and relate them to their own experience. Another method would be to ask children to act out possible situations associated with these variables (job interviews, returning faulty goods to a shop, complaining to a neighbour over some domestic matter, speaking up for someone who is underprivileged, approaching strangers at a party, explain- ing to a teacher that he has marked work unfairly, talking about something one likes, etc.). One problem with work of this kind is that it sometimes appears highly artificial to all concerned, but this is primarily due either to the fact that we are placing too much emphasis upon dramatic skills, thus making children feel self-conscious and over-anxious to get it right, or to the fact that the situations we have

chosen lie too far outside the child's experience. Obviously, looking back at the examples we have just given, job
interviews would only be of direct relevance to children
about to leave school, while complaining to a neighbour
would only work if children came from an area in which there
was a great deal of friction between householders. The rule
is that if we are engaged in assertiveness training we are
not trying to teach children to be assertive at some indefi-
nable date in the future but to be assertive now, or if we
are engaged in social skills training we are not trying to
teach children how to relate to people at the sort of
mythical cocktail party dreamed up by television producers
but how to relate to people at the local youth club or
disco. Often this will mean that the teacher should have no
preconceived notions about the detailed behaviours that go
with such relationships, but should instead study his children carefully and see what problems these relationships present to THEM. Often the children's own comments, if offered
in the right spirit, will be of more help in guiding each
other in these behaviours than will anything that the
teacher can himself say.

It is important, however, that exercises of this kind
should be designed to teach general lessons, and not be
specific attempts to make child A more assertive or child B
less so, or child C more socially graceful and child D less
socially tongue-tied. By spotlighting individual problems in
front of the class the teacher may make life difficult for
the children concerned, if only because other children may
become over-curious about their 'problems', or may see them
as subjects of amusement. Individual social problems are
best dealt with (in the context of the school at least) on
an individual basis and in confidence. We look at some of
the ways in which this can be done in the next chapter.

References

Bandura, A. (1973)
   Aggression: A social learning analysis. Englewood
   Cliffs, NJ: Prentice-Hall.
Flanders, N.A. (1970)
   Analyzing Teacher Behaviour. Reading, Mass.:
   Addison-Wesley.

Additional reading

Chanan, G. and Delamont, S. (eds) (1975) Frontiers of
Classroom Research.
   Readers interested in learning more about interaction
   analysis and classroom based research generally will
   find this of great interest.

Flanders, N.A. (1970), Analyzing Teacher Behaviour.
Reading, Mass.: Addison-Wesley.
   Describes Flanders' own work.

Hook, C. and Rosenshine, B. (1979) Accuracy of teacher

reports of their classroom behaviour. Review of Educational Research, 49, 1-12.

The discrepancy between the teacher's ideas on what is going on in the classroom and the idea held by the children is brought out fully in the research reviewed here.

Simon, A. and Boyer, E. (1967, 1969, 1970) Mirrors for Behaviour: An anthology of classroom observation instructions. Philadelphia: Humanizing Learning Program, Research for Better Schools Inc.

A good review of over one hundred different instruments used to analyse teacher and child behaviours is given here.

Good, T. and Brophy, J. (1978) Looking in Classrooms (2nd edn). New York: Harper & Row.

Very highly recommended for its survey of the ways in which classroom data can be collected (as well as for its examination of all aspects of classroom management).

Aronson, E. (1976) The Social Animal (2nd edn). San Francisco: Freeman.

One of the best introductions to the whole field of social interaction.

Bany, M.A. and Johnson, L.V. (1975) Educational Social Psychology. New York: Macmillan.

Looks in detail at the practical problems of social psychology within the classroom.

Tajfel, H. and Fraser, C. (eds) (1978) Introducing Social Psychology. New York: Macmillan.

A comprehensive collection of papers covering the broader aspects of social psychology.

Shaw, M. (1976) Group Dynamics: The psychology of small group behaviour. New Delhi: McGraw-Hill.

A readable and very thorough survey of the whole field of small group behaviour.

Gahagan, J. (1975) Interpersonal and Group Behaviour. London: Methuen.

A useful short survey, which gives guidance on sociometry and allied techniques.

14

Educational Guidance and Counselling
David Fontana

The pattern of this chapter and of the two that follow
differs from the rest of this book in that, instead of
having the main part followed by a section drawing attention
to matters of specific relevance to the teacher, theory and
practice are linked together throughout. This is because the
three topics concerned, that is, educational guidance and
counselling, discipline and class control, and teacher
personality, draw much of their research evidence from work
done within the classroom, and we shall therefore find
ourselves discussing the role of the teacher right from the
outset.

Counselling in school

Our examination of the first of these topics must begin
by insisting that, just as in the last chapter it was
claimed that every teacher is a teacher of social skills,
every teacher is an educational counsellor. By this we mean
that part of his function is to help children deal with
personal problems and to make decisions about the course
that their lives should take. Since teachers are individuals
they will inevitably vary in the degree of importance they
attach to their counselling roles, and they will also vary
in the extent to which children seem prepared to consult
them about their difficulties. Some teachers tend to invite
confidences more readily than others, and to be more sympathetic and patient in their relationships with children.
Children feel they can talk to them, and can trust their
reactions. It is in fact these two qualities, sympathy and
trustworthiness, rather than any great familiarity with
counselling techniques, that children appear to look for
when deciding to whom they should turn when in need.

The second of these qualities, trustworthiness, sometimes seems to be compromised by the fact that the teacher
has a dual role. Primarily he represents the authority of
the school, and only secondly does he represent the dis-
interested confidentiality of the counsellor. Thus, if a
child wishes to discuss with him some problem related to
school, such as alleged unfair treatment by another member
of staff, or theft of school equipment, or cheating in a
school examination, he may feel unsure whether the teacher
will consider it proper to report matters to a higher

authority. Similarly, the teacher may himself feel the tug of divided loyalties and be worried as to where his professional duty lies, and this may be one strong reason why some teachers appear to discourage the kind of confidences that would put them in this invidious position.

One way of avoiding this problem is for the school to employ a member of staff whose duties extend only to counselling, and who does not carry a teaching or a disciplinary function at all. The reason why this practice is not more widespread is hard to say for sure, though some teachers express themselves to be a little uneasy at the presence of a specialist counsellor on the staff. They are concerned that they might be the subject of discussion between the counsellor and their children, that by his very presence in the school the counsellor is threatening their own pastoral roles, and that if there are secrets which the counsellor is not prepared to divulge even to the headteacher, then the latter's authority must to some extent be undermined within the school. It is probable that financial considerations also play some part. An extensive survey (Antonouris, 1974) indicates that only some seven per cent of local education authorities make counsellors extra to quota in secondary schools (i.e. allow schools to appoint counsellors over and above their normal staff entitlement), and although many of them claim that the decision on whether or not to have a specialist counsellor is left to individual headteachers, one is bound to conclude that few heads will choose to avail themselves of this facility if it means depriving themselves of a subject specialist in order to do so. The author of the survey would seem to be right when he suggests that local education authorities are generally in favour of counselling but not in favour of counsellors.

It seems, therefore, that however much we may be in favour of specialist counsellors, it is probable that the counselling role will still very much be left to the ordinary teacher for the foreseeable future. Thus it is important for him to have at least a limited knowledge of the major variables involved. Some schools give Heads of House or Heads of Year the responsibility for co-ordinating counselling activities and for advising new members of staff on what to do, while others appoint a Head of Pastoral Care, but few of those involved have attended more than short local education authority or Department of Education and Science courses on counselling, and fewer still have actual formal qualifications in the subject. This again is unfortunate, since one of the best ways of disseminating counselling skills is for someone on the staff with specialist training to become responsible for handing this information on to others. Thus the individual teacher can learn these skills within the practical context in which he has to apply them, and can seek a convenient source of expert advice whenever he feels unsure of himself.

The problem of confidentiality
To go back to the beginning, it has been stressed that

trustworthiness and sympathy are the basic gifts that the
good counsellor has to offer to the child. We have also
said, however, that a major problem arises when the child
brings to the counsellor's attention material that concerns
disobedience to important school rules, or that threatens
important values and standards. Should the counsellor maintain confidentiality, or should he betray the child's trust
and go to the headmaster or to another member of the school
hierarchy? Some writers suggest that the teacher should
always warn the child before he offers a confidence that he
may feel it necessary to break confidence, and this is good
policy as far as it goes. The problem is that it may deter
the child from seeking help, and he may keep silent on
matters that, in his own interest, should be brought out
into the open. There is, too, always the chance that con-
fidential material may come up during conversation when the
counsellor is unprepared for it and has not had a chance to
issue his formal warning. This is particularly true when it
is the ordinary teacher who is acting as counsellor, since
he does not have the benefit enjoyed by the specialist
counsellor of the semi-formal counselling interview at which
certain procedural guidelines can be agreed upon at the
start by counsellor and child. In a sense, therefore, each
counsellor must consult his own conscience on what to do
about confidentiality (though ideally he should be able to
do this within the context of an agreed school policy worked
out in consultation between headteacher and staff). The
two basic rules that must always apply, however, are that
(i) the child's permission should first be sought before any
confidence is broken or, at the very least, he should be
told in advance of any action the counsellor plans to take
in this direction, and (ii) consideration should only be
given to the breaking of confidence when it seems to be in
the child's long-term interests so to do. On no occasion
should a confidence be broken simply to get the child punished or to show the head what a zealous member of staff
one happens to be.

Sometimes, of course, the child may need a great deal of
persuasion before he agrees that the matter must be taken
further. Here the job of the counsellor should be to help
the child to see that even if there may be certain unpleasant immediate consequences, in the long term he will gain
both the respect and understanding of others and greater
self-esteem. Some counsellors argue that this is being too
directive (a term to which we return in due course below),
and that the child should always be allowed to come to his
own decision, but this seems to be placing undue responsibility upon young children who may genuinely want guidance
as to their best course of action. Where it is agreed that
confidentiality must be broken (and we are not using the
term 'broken' here in a pejorative sense: 'terminated' might
be a more appropriate word), the child must be assured of
the counsellor's continuing support, even to the extent of
accompanying the child to the head or possibly to parents or
whoever else is involved. Should the child refuse his

permission for confidentiality to be broken, once having asked for this permission, the counsellor must then abide by this. He may feel it necessary to indicate, however, that this limits the practical support and help he is enabled to give, since there may be no clear alternative desirable course of action for the child to take.

The only exception to the course of action outlined above would seem to be if the actions the child is reporting to the counsellor involve risk (or potential risk) to himself, other children or the community at large. This would apply, for example, if the confidences included information about drugs or involved threats of violence to another individual. The law in Britain rarely imposes a positive duty upon a person to reveal knowledge of a crime or a possible crime, provided that the person concerned is not himself involved in the crime in any way (though it could be difficult to prove lack of involvement if it is demonstrated subsequently that one possessed such knowledge), but the teacher's contract of employment often lays clear duties upon him in this direction, and he must of course abide by these. In any case, whether a duty exists or not, the teacher has a moral responsibility to prevent harm, and this means he may have no option but to inform the relevant authorities if he fears that his silence may allow such harm to take place. It is important also to remember that, even if a teacher is employed as a specialist counsellor, it is unlikely that his contract of employment will differ from that of the ordinary teacher, and therefore unlikely that it would be accepted that his responsibilities for the safety and well-being of the whole school community, whether these responsibilities be legal or moral, would differ in any way from those of the rest of the staff. This means that confidences imparted in what we might call the formal counselling interview are legally no more sacred than those imparted in normal conversations between the ordinary teacher and the child.

Certainly it is a painful business deciding that one must not under any circumstances keep silent, but once the decision is made it must be acted upon at once. The only proviso is that the child must, as we have indicated above, be informed first, and then given all the support the counsellor can offer. The counsellor's reasons for taking the course of action he proposes must also naturally be explained, and an attempt made to show how, in the long run, this course of action is likely to be in the child's own best interests as well.

The importance of sympathy

Turning now from trustworthiness to the other main quality demanded of the counsellor, namely sympathy, we find that fewer problems are raised. Sympathy means that the child must at all times be left in no doubt that the teacher understands his position and wants to help. In conveying this guarantee of sympathy, attention must be given not only to what the teacher says but to the non-verbal signs to which reference has already been made. A smile is a better non-verbal signal of sympathy than a frown, an encouraging nod better than a disapproving shake of the head, steady eye contact better than a remote gaze out of the window. And in verbal exchanges themselves it is much better to hear the child out, letting him put things in his own words, than to keep interrupting him or finishing his sentences off for him. At all points, the teacher should be conveying to the child interest and patience. He is interested enough to want to hear what the child has to say, and patient enough to be prepared to let him say it, however long this may take. Above all, perhaps, sympathy is conveyed through action. The teacher and the child together identify the latter's problems, and the teacher then shows himself ready to do something practical to help. This does not mean taking over responsibility for doing the things that the child ought really to do for himself. It means supplementing and supporting the child's actions by appropriate actions of his own in those areas where the child has little power (e.g. he may have to talk to other members of staff on the child's behalf, obtain information and perhaps supplementary learning materials for him, liaise with welfare authorities, see to it that the child is better integrated into the social life of the class, give parents guidance on how they can best help him with learning problems, take up his case with the headteacher and so on).

The counselling process

We have already suggested that the counsellor should be characterized by trustworthiness and sympathy, and that these qualities should be apparent in conversations and interviews between the counsellor and the child. There are other important considerations to be borne in mind when discussing the counselling process, however, which are now examined.

Categorizing the child's problem

The first of these is to find some way of categorizing the child's problem. One way of doing this is to regard it as either simple or complex. A simple problem is one that can be regarded as essentially self-contained. The child has got himself into difficulties with a certain member of staff, or has been blamed for something serious for which he is not responsible, or is having trouble with certain sections of his work that are beginning to worry him. Usually simple problems can be dealt with through a single course of action, agreed between teacher and child (though this action may inevitably take some time to implement fully). The job of the counsellor faced with a simple problem is to listen carefully to the child, question him on necessary points of detail, assure him that he has done the right thing to ask for help, and then turn to the constructive business of working out what is to be done. There is little virtue in

passing judgement on who is to blame for the child's pre-
dicament, or in spending time criticizing him for his actions. This will only deter him from asking for help in the
future. On the other hand, there may be occasions when the
teacher feels the child will benefit personally from thinking through how a situation came to be caused for himself,
and deciding how he might prevent it from arising again in
the future.

A complex problem, by contrast, is one that appears to
involve the wider issues of the child's own personality. He
may, for example, be excessively shy, or feel himself unduly
prone to victimization and bullying by other people. Or he
may be low in self-esteem, or be too impetuous, or too prone
to making violent responses to others. There might also be
long-standing problems at home, or difficulties with the
opposite sex, or extreme feelings of guilt or anxiety. Note
that sometimes a simple problem may cloak a complex one,
either because it arises directly from it, or because the
child comes to the teacher with a minor problem in the half
hope that while discussing it a more major one will be
allowed to come into the open. Note also that because a
child is aware of a problem this does not mean he is also
aware of its cause. His problem may be, for example, that
he finds himself generally unpopular with others, but is
unaware that the cause may lie with himself rather than with
the 'unfair' attitudes of his classmates.

The role of the counsellor
Where complex problems exist, the first job of the counsellor in the counselling process is simply to encourage the
child to talk, and to listen to him in the atmosphere of
trust and sympathy to which I have already made reference.
Indeed, if he does no more than this then he will still be
performing a valuable service. But most counsellors will
want to do more. Let me summarize now some of the other
major points that they should bear in mind.

* In general the counsellor should try not to be too
  directive. A great deal has been written in recent years
  about the relative merits of so-called directive and
  non-directive counselling respectively, with the emphasis in the former being upon telling the child what he
  ought to do and the emphasis in the latter being upon
  helping him find his own solutions, but the consensus
  now seems to be that, wherever feasible, the child
  should at least play some part in deciding what his
  future course of action should be. If the counsellor
  decides for him, then this is the counsellor's decision
  and not the child's. And for all the counsellor's concern, he does not know the situation as well as does the
  child since it is the child who lives with it and has to
  experience his own reactions to it. The counsellor's
  decision, though it may appear to contain a nice neat
  little solution, may just not be appropriate for the

child concerned. Clearly, if the problem involves moral issues, with obvious responsibilities towards others, then in the case of a child (particularly if he is a young child) the counsellor may wish to nudge him towards what seems to him to be the right decision, but even here the child's own moral and social background must be taken into account. To force him into taking a decision which is quite out of keeping with his background, and which does not therefore feel right to him, may be only to invite failure, and perhaps in future an even stronger rebellion against the views of others.

The immediate aim of counselling is to help the child set his problem within its proper context, and to recognize and understand the important variables associated with it. This will involve posing the child questions from time to time designed to prompt him to reflect upon what has been happening and upon the views of the various other people who may also be involved (e.g. 'What do you think your mother/father/friend thought about that?'; 'What do you think you might have done instead of what you actually did?'; 'How would you feel about it if someone said that to you?'; 'Why were you upset about that?'; 'Did you think it meant they didn't like you?'). It will also involve showing the child that the counsellor understands and accepts his feelings, thus encouraging him to put them into words for himself ('That made you feel fed up, did it?'; 'You felt pleased when that happened?'; 'So you went away and worried about it?'). By putting his problems into context and by reflecting upon the variables associated with them the child gains insights into them and, of equal importance, into himself, and generally gains confidence in his ability to be objective and resourceful.

* The counsellor should strive to maintain a generally non-judgemental approach. In other words, he should not give the child the impression that he is only waiting for the latter to stop talking before delivering a weighty opinion on his actions and upon his qualities as a person. Many children who need the help of a counsellor are already feeling inadequate, with perhaps low self-esteem and a dismal history of failure. The last thing they need is for the counsellor to start delivering his own vote of censure. If any judgement is required, far better that it should come from the child himself, and if the counsellor deems it to be too harsh he can then encourage the child to see himself in a more worthy and self-accepting light.

* At all times, the child should be helped to take increasing responsibility for his own behaviour. One day he will leave school and will gain the age of majority, and it will be up to him to decide what he wants to make of himself. In spite of some opinions to the contrary, it is not the job of the school to 'mould' the child's

personality (even were such a thing possible in a democratic society), but to place the child in a position where he can make wise and informed choices for himself. By observing the points we have already made above the counsellor will go some way towards encouraging this reponsibility, but he should in addition help the child to realize the nature of personal choice (i.e. he should help him to recognize what is involved in this choice, why it becomes necessary, and how the individual can best go about it). This again is better done by prompting the child to think for himself than by reading him lectures, however worthy and well-meant, on the subject.

* Next the counsellor should try always in his conversation with the child to keep the latter focussed upon his real problem once this has been identified. The tendency is sometimes to digress from this painful topic once things really get under way. Prompts such as 'but you were telling me that ...', or 'tell me more about ...' are usually all that is needed, but a useful technique is to ask for some kind of clarification. This has the added advantage of showing the child that the counsellor needs his assistance too, and that the problem is therefore something they are engaged on jointly. Wording such as 'if you could tell me more about ... that would help me understand', or 'I need some help over this; could you tell me about ...' usually proves to be suitable.

* Finally the counsellor should never intrude where he is not wanted. The child should be encouraged to be honest, but if after prompting he clearly does not wish to go into further details (for instance about his private life or the relationship between him and his parents) then he should not be pressed to do so. He may be worried by feelings of loyalty to the other people concerned, or by embarrassment of some kind. It is no good trying to get the child to accept responsibility and make decisions if we do not consider him competent to decide what aspects of his personal life he wishes to keep to himself. And the counsellor's very attempts to probe him too deeply may deter the child from giving the information voluntarily at a later date when his confidence in the counsellor has increased. They may even stop him from coming back for another chat altogether, since he may feel that such chats are dangerous because they make you reveal more about yourself than you should, or because they leave you feeling shy and embarrassed in the counsellor's presence.

Problems facing the counsellor

Readers wishing to know more about counselling are referred to the recommended reading at the end of the chapter, but one of the best strategies is to attend counselling workshops run by universities or colleges or local education authorities. There is no substitute for seeing techniques actually demonstrated, and for trying them out under guidance and in simulated circumstances where one's mistakes can cause no harm. Such workshops also offer the opportunity of learning about other kinds of counselling which have great relevance to education but which the teacher is not able actually to use himself, such as family therapy. Family therapy is a recognition of the fact (as pointed out in chapter 2) that when we have a child with a problem we also usually have a family with a problem. The latter problem does not necessarily arise out of the former (though it may be exacerbated by it), and in fact could itself actually be the root cause of it.

The family therapist, who is usually a trained psychologist or psychiatrist, meets the whole nuclear family together and prompts them to bring into the open the complexes and behaviours that have led to family tensions and perhaps to the child's difficulties. This is skilled, delicate work, and must be left to the expert, since the family members must each be protected from potentially harmful revelations until they appear to have gained the strength to deal with them and use them constructively. But knowing of the existence of family therapy is of great value to the teacher because it helps him reflect on the way in which family problems arise, and confirms yet again that the problem child does not exist in isolation but at the centre of an intricate web of shifting tensions and pressures, many of which are responsible for creating and sustaining his difficulties.

Social forces and conflicts

This last point was emphasized by Lewin as long ago as 1936 when he wrote that 'the behavior of a person or of a group is due to the distribution of social forces in the situation as a whole, rather than to intrinsic properties of individuals'. This means that, for example, the child with a particular kind of temperament or with a tendency towards aggression is not bound, ipso facto, to become a problem. He will only develop into one if he is placed in a particular kind of relationship with a particular kind of social environment. Elsewhere, Lewin argues also that many of the problems with which the counsellor is faced can only be fully understood if one views them within the context of this relationship. Briefly, he holds that the social space within which the individual functions can be divided into a number of areas or valences. In the case of the child these valences would be such things as home, school, youth club, scouts or guides, church, groups of friends and so on. Ideally, we should each be able to move from one valence in our lives to another (e.g. go from home to school or from school to youth club) without having to make undue changes in our social behaviour and in the standards and values that inform it. As Lewin puts it, the barriers between the valences should be low. Thus the individual is able to lead a relatively harmonious social life, without feeling he has to fragment his social personality in order to make himself acceptable to the people he meets in each of the valences. (The reader may care to speculate on how such fragmentation delays the growth of identity and personal maturity that we discussed in chapter 9.)

Where the barriers between valences are high, and the child is constantly being forced into changing his social behaviour if he is to make himself acceptable within each of them, this sets up conflict and self-doubt. The individual is unsure which of his various social 'selves' is the real one, and is prone to feelings of guilt at the way the behaviour of one self (e.g. the self when out with friends) contradicts the behaviour of another (e.g. the self when in church). Lewin considers that the conflicts faced by such individuals tend to fall into one or more of three major categories, namely:

* TYPE 1 CONFLICT (approach-approach conflict). This occurs when the child is faced with two valences of equal force (e.g. home and school) but with a high barrier between them. The conflict can only be resolved by either rejecting one of these valences altogether (e.g. rebelling against the home or ceasing to bother about school) or changing behaviour markedly as he moves from one valence to the other, thus creating the kind of self-doubt and guilt to which we have just made reference.

* TYPE 2 CONFLICT (avoid-avoid conflict). This kind of conflict happens when the child is faced by two valences which he desires equally to avoid. For example, he may know that if he works hard at a certain school subject he will be moved into a higher set but with a teacher he intensely dislikes. On the other hand, if he refuses to work hard he will stay where he is and be bored by the simplicity of the work and troubled by the thought of lost opportunities. The conflict can only be properly resolved by changing one of the valences into a positive one (e.g. getting to like the teacher in the top set after all) or by rejecting both of them (e.g. by dropping the school subject altogether).

* TYPE 3 CONFLICT (approach-avoid conflict). This conflict occurs when the child is faced by positive and negative valences of equal force. For example, he may wish to move into the positive valence of having passed an exam, but can only do this by accepting also the negative valence of having to lose his friends and take up a more solitary social life in order to study. Type 3 conflicts can only be resolved by making a decision on whether the advantages of the positive valence are worth the disadvantages of the negative one. If they are not, then the positive valence must be abandoned and replaced by one at a lower and less demanding level.

The examples we have advanced in connection with the above conflicts only cover, of course, a small part of the range of problems that can be associated with them. The reader might like to think of other important examples for himself. The point to emphasize is that by thinking in terms of these conflicts the counsellor cannot only help himself to understand the difficulties that may be facing the child, but can also help the child to identify and analyse these difficulties, and thus come to an informed and sensible solution on how they might best be resolved. The child can also be helped to see that his behaviour up to the present has perhaps been due to his inappropriate attempts to solve his conflicts for himself. School refusal (truancy), for example, could be an attempt at resolving the home-school conflict (it could also be an attempt to escape the experiences of failure and of low self-esteem which school can bring for the less able child). Stealing or bullying could be an attempt to resolve a Type 3 conflict, with the child having to adopt 'tough' behaviour in order to make himself acceptable within the positive valence of his friends, but at the expense of having to move into the negative valence of being regarded as antisocial by the school and by society in general.

It is important to stress that we are not pretending the child's behaviours are never 'wrong' and that direct action is never necessary to curb his truancy or stealing or whatever. But this direct action is the responsibility of the school acting in its authoritarian role. The role of the counsellor, on the other hand, is to help the child get at the reasons and the implications of his behaviour and to develop strategies to amend and alter it that actually mean something in terms of the way in which he himself views the situation. Ideally we want the child to change because he sees both the need and the possibility of change, and not simply to avoid punishment and censure. Change of this former kind is likely to be much more permanent than change of the latter kind, and is likely to lead to further opportunities for growth and development in the future.

Vocational guidance

We return to some of the above points in the next chapter when behaviour problems are discussed. For the moment we need to turn our attention to another kind of counselling, namely that associated with vocational guidance. In offering vocational guidance, the counsellor has two main questions to ask: first, what occupation appears most likely to appeal to the child; and, second, to which occupation does he appear to be most suited? Ideally the answer to both questions should be the same, but sadly children often have ambitions which appear quite clearly to be beyond them. While no teacher wishes to prevent a child from trying for something that really appeals to him (children often surprise us by what they can achieve when they really apply themselves), it is as well to remember that children go through various stages before they arrive at a final career choice, and some of these stages are characterized by a lack of realism in that the child knows neither what is actually involved in the job that appeals to him nor the qualifications and skills required by employers.

Developmental stages in career choice

Super (1957) has put forward a model, based on earlier work by Ginzberg, that attempts to define these stages. Note that this model, sometimes referred to rather misleadingly as a model of 'vocational development', suggests the period of childhood that goes respectively with each stage, but some individuals pass through these stages much later than others, and it is quite possible for someone even in adolescence to be still primarily in the 'fantasy' stage usually associated with early childhood. A summary of Super's model is given below.

STAGE 1. FANTASY STAGE (early childhood): during this stage, which persists usually at least into the lower junior school, the child imagines himself as being anything that appeals to the imagination. Little thought is given to the realities surrounding the jobs concerned.

STAGE 2. INTEREST STAGE (later childhood): by the time he reaches the later junior school years interest is beginning to take over from fantasy. The child is now drawn towards those jobs that seem to embody the things which he finds interesting. Thus whereas in the fantasy stage he might have wanted to be an astronaut, this ambition might now be rejected as the child finds he is not really interested in astronomy or in rocket propulsion.

STAGE 3. CAPACITY STAGE (middle teens): by the age of 14 or 15 or so capacity is becoming increasingly important to the child, and he develops a tendency to reject possible careers that appear to fall above or below his ability level.

STAGE 4. TENTATIVE CHOICE STAGE (later teens): the later teens see the child making a tentative choice as he begins the process of putting in the first job applications and finding out more about the realities of working life.

The above stages are the ones with which the teacher is primarily concerned, but Super's model does cover the whole of life. The early twenties are seen as the trial stage, in which the individual is trying things out and may frequently change jobs, while the period of middle age is seen as the specialization stage, with the individual now usually committed to a particular calling. To complete the picture, the years from 60 onwards are seen as the deceleration stage, with the individual no longer usually concerned about promotion and getting further ahead, and the years from 65 onwards as the retirement stage.

It should be kept in mind that Super's model was originally devised at a time when most women did not pursue careers outside the home (hence his retirement age begins at 65, and not at 60). Super was also writing at a time, back in the 1950s, when people did not change their jobs frequently in middle life, and it may be that the specialization stage is less applicable now than it was then. Nevertheless, his model still serves as a useful guide for the teacher when thinking about vocational guidance. The adolescent who, with little chance of even a single pass at the General Certificate of Education Ordinary Level, confidently sees himself as an airline pilot or as a medical doctor is obviously still primarily in the fantasy stage, while the more able child who sees himself one day as a waiter is still clearly in the interest stage, where hobbies or the enthusiasms of the moment are allowed to overrule all other more long-term considerations. (The choice of degree course by some university students, made without any thought to the eventual market value of the degree concerned, suggests that this interest stage may be much more persistent than Super supposed.)

The role of the counsellor in vocational guidance

Obviously, it is the job of the vocational counsellor to encourage children to think carefully about what occupation most appeals to them, and then to make available to them all possible information on the skills and qualifications demanded by that occupation, and the kind of long-term prospects and opportunities it is likely to offer. Obviously, no counsellor should ever try to tell the child what he ought to do (though of course he may want to suggest possibilities), but where an individual is genuinely unable to make up his mind there are several job categorization systems that might help to clarify his thinking. One such is proposed by Holland (1959), and involves dividing jobs up in terms of the occupational environments they provide. The system is exemplified below, together with instances of the kind of jobs that fall into each category.

Occupational environment	Job examples
Motoric	labourer, machine operator, truck driver, mechanic
Intellectual	technician, scientist, university lecturer
Supportive	social worker, teacher, vocational counsellor

(continued)

| Persuasive | salesman, politician, publicity officer |
| Aesthetic | musician, writer, poet, photographer |

When he comes to study this system a child who, for example, thinks he would perhaps like to work with people might decide that he is interested in working in a supportive or persuasive capacity, and would then go through the examples (plus others that the teacher might like to provide) until he finds one that appears to suit his particular inclinations. He would then be provided with details of the qualifications needed and the availability of jobs. In each of the categories there are, of course, jobs suited to various different levels of ability. Thus, for example, the child interested in an intellectual or scientific job could go from nuclear physicist at one end of the range to laboratory technician at the other.

Children must be cautioned, however, that some jobs at the lower end of the ability range that require little talent and few qualifications (e.g. stage hand, assistant groundsman and, dare one say it, pop star?) are nevertheless very hard to come by either because they are competed for by able people who see them as a stepping stone to something higher or because they carry with them an apparently desirable life style and some kind of glamour. The counsellor must also urge children to take into account a number of other factors which could affect his chances of obtaining the job of his choice, such as his readiness to move away from home, his ability to impress at an interview, his physical strength, his appearance, the quality of his voice, and his general conscientiousness and readiness to take responsibility.

There is obviously no virtue in pressing children to make up their minds too soon about their future careers, but it is essential that when children take subject options within the school curriculum, or when they unilaterally decide not to bother very much with certain subjects in order to do well at others, they be informed what career avenues they may be closing for themselves. Unless children are provided as a matter of top priority with this kind of information they may very well find themselves tragically without the necessary Ordinary Level pass in a certain essential subject when they eventually come to fill in a job application form, or apply for entry into some area of higher education (e.g. they might find themselves without mathematics when applying for teacher training, or without English Language when applying for a job in the media).

Vocational guidance tests

In addition to the kind of structures provided by Super and Holland there exist a number of vocational guidance tests which the teacher can use with older children. These tests are by no means infallible, and should only be used along with other forms of guidance, but they do help discover the child's inclinations and concerns and provide examples of the kind of jobs for which these inclinations and concerns suit him. The most widely used of these are of the self-report type, in which the individual answers a number of relevant questions about himself. On the strength of his answers, the Rosenberg Occupations and Values Test, for example, assigns him to the category of those interested in people, or to the category of those orientated towards extrinsic reward (money, status), or to those orientated towards intrinsic reward (creativity, self-expresssion). The Rothwell-Miller Interest Blank, an even more widely used test, assigns him to one of 12 general job categories such as outdoor, scientific, social service, mechanical, clerical, or medical, and then like the Holland system provides examples of a wide range of jobs which go under each category. Having found himself assigned to one particular category, and if he agrees it is appropriate, the child can often then be helped to focus upon one of these jobs and to find out more about it.

Local education authorities often provide a careers advice service that visits schools and interviews school leavers, but such a service is normally badly over-stretched and can do little for many children on the strength of one or perhaps two shor interviews. Far better for the school, which of course knows the child best, to provide him with detailed careers guidance that begins well before school leaving approaches, and that includes visits to the school by local employers, regular visits to local factories and places of work, and special help in obtaining necessary qualifications and interviewee skills. The sad fact is that without such help many children reach school-leaving age with only the haziest notion of what they want to do in life and of the qualifications they may require. Usually these children are at the lower end of the ability range, with no obvious avenues open to them in further and higher education. They badly need the assurance that the school really cares about their future, and is prepared to go to the trouble of providing all possible practical help. They should see the school as orientated towards what they may one day become, and not simply towards the way they are at present, and should see careers guidance as an integral part of their school life and not as a somewhat haphazard last-minute scramble carried out at a stage in their progress when many desirable avenues have already been closed to them.

References

Antonouris, G. (1974)
Subsequent careers of teachers trained as counsellors. British Journal of Guidance and Counselling, 2, 160-170.

Holland, J.L. (1959)
A theory of vocational choice. Journal of Counselling Psychology, 6, 35–43.

Lewin, K. (1936)
Principles of Topological Psychology. New York: McGraw-Hill.

Super, D.E. (1957)
Vocational Development: A framework for research. New York: Teachers College Press.

Questions

1. Discuss some of the problems that the dual role of teacher and counsellor can create.
2. What are the qualities a child is likely to look for in a counsellor?
3. Give the arguments for and against the presence of a specialist counsellor on the school staff.
4. What are the considerations the counsellor must bear in mind before terminating a confidence entrusted to him by a child?
5. How does the counsellor convey to the child that he sympathizes with his problem?
6. One broad way of classifying children's problems is into those that are 'simple' and those that are 'complex'. What is meant by these terms in this context?
7. What is meant by 'directive' and by 'non-directive' counselling respectively? Can you think of some of the advantages and disadvantages that may attach to each?
8. The que ions put by the counsellor to the child are of vital importance. What general form should these questions take, and what are they designed to do?
9. What is meant by a generally 'non-judgemental' approach on the part of the counsellor? Why is such an approach important?
10. Discuss ways of helping the child to stay focussed on his real problem or problems during the counselling interview.
11. Lewin suggests that the social space we each inhabit can be divided into a number of 'valences'. What does he mean by this term and why is it important to the counsellor?
12. What are the three major types of conflict Lewin feels the individual has to face in his social space?
13. What are the two main questions the vocational counsellor has to ask when offering guidance to school leavers?
14. What are the four stages Super (1933) suggests the child passes through on his way to the development of mature career orientations?
15. How can the kind of job categorization system advanced by Holland (1959) be used in helping the child make up his mind about his future career?

Annotated reading

Rogers, C. (1951) Client Centred Therapy. London: Constable.

> One of the most valuable and influential books on counselling to appear since the war; the book could be said to have ushered in a new era in counselling, with the emphasis upon the part played by the client himself in solving his problems. The reader interested in counselling will enjoy the book, not only for the practical guidance it provides but for the humanity and sympathy that characterize it throughout.

Wolff, S. (1973) Children Under Stress. Harmondsworth: Penguin.

Laufer, M. (1975) Adolescent Disturbance and Breakdown. Harmondsworth: Penguin.

Ryle, A. (1973) Adolescent Casualties. Harmondsworth: Penguin.

> The reader interested in the causes of personality problems in children and students will find these three to be of great value.

Murgatroyd, S. (ed.) (1980) Helping the Troubled Child: Inter-professional case studies. London: Harper & Row.

> Deals comprehensively with methods of treatment.

Rutter, M. (1975) Helping Troubled Children. Harmondsworth: Penguin.

> Also of interest in this context.

Fullmer, D.W. (1978) Counselling: Group theory and system (2nd edn). Cranston, RI: Carroll Press.

> Recommended for the more advanced students, anxious to know something of group counselling methods.

Fullmer, D.W. and H.W. Bernard (1977) Principles of Guidance (2nd edn). New York: T. Y. Crowell.

> Also of value as a general text.

Lewis, D.G. and Murgatroyd, S. (1976) The professionalisation of counselling in education and its legal implications. British Journal of Guidance and Counselling, 4, 2-15.

> Sets out the counsellor's legal position in England and Wales fully.

Jackson, R. and Juniper, D.F. (1971) A Manual of Educational Guidance. London: Holt, Rinehart & Winston.

Lytton, H. and Craft, M. (1969) Guidance and Counselling in British Schools. Leeds: Arnold.

> Both of these general texts provide useful practical information.

PFT - X

School Council Working Paper, 40 (1971) Careers Education in the 1970s. London: Evans/Methuen.

One of the most helpful books available on vocation and careers guidance.

Hopson, B. and Hayes, J. (1968) The Theory and Practice of Vocational Guidance. Oxford: Pergamon Press.

Kline, P. (1975) Psychology of Vocational Guidance. London: Batsford.

Both of these are also recommended.

Jersild, A.T. and Brook, D.W. (1978) The Psychology of Adolescence (3rd edn). London: Collier Macmillan.

Contains a lengthy and excellent treatment of vocational ideas and career orientation in adolescence.

The material produced by the Careers Education and Guidance Project mounted by the School Council (1971-1974) is also likely to give the teacher many useful practical ideas.

15

Class Control and Management
David Fontana

Of all the professional anxieties that assail the teacher, those associated with class control often loom the largest. Children, singly or in groups, can present problems that even the most experienced teacher may find hard to handle, and there is no denying the misgivings that working with children, control of whom is slipping away from one, can bring. To make matters worse, many teachers suggest that in the final analysis all the teacher's authority is based upon a kind of bluff. There are strict limits to the sanctions he can bring to bear upon his children, and if children test these limits and find themselves unimpressed by them, then his bluff is called and there is little further he can do.

As we shall see, this suggestion is somewhat over-pessimistic, but it does draw attention to the fact that a teacher who relies upon repeated threats in order to control his class may find in the end that children in effect dare him to carry out even the most extreme of these threats, knowing that if he remains within correct professional limits he cannot really harm them, while if he oversteps these limits he puts his career at risk. Besides rendering himself ineffectual in this way, the teacher who adopts a constantly threatening manner also needs to ask himself whether he really wants a relationship with children which depends upon attempted intimidation, and must inevitably lead to mutual dislike and lack of respect. There are better ways of working with children than this.

Defining problem behaviour
The question of class control is linked inextricably with that of problem behaviour. If children never exhibited problem behaviour then the need for class control would never arise. We can define problem behaviour as behaviour that proves unacceptable to the teacher. This definition, which might at first sight seem an over-simplification, is of value because it introduces us to the important fact that problem behaviour is only problem behaviour because it appears so to the teacher. And since teachers are all individuals, what may appear a problem to one teacher may not appear so to another. One teacher, for example, may be happy to tolerate a certain amount of conversation between

children while they are working, but another may demand complete silence. One teacher may put up with children calling out in class while another may insist they wait quietly with their hands up until asked. One teacher may be happy with a certain amount of familiarity in his relationship with children, and a certain amount of humour in class, while another may prefer formality and a serious approach. One teacher may allow a certain amount of day-dreaming in class while another may want attention always to be focussed upon work; and so on.

The point about these examples and the many more that we could offer is that they show that problem behaviour, like beauty, is in a sense in the eye of the beholder. So the first step in dealing with this behaviour is for the teacher to ask himself why he sees it as a problem in the first place. Is it a sign of his own insecurity that he regards a child's attempt at humour as a threat to his authority? Has he perhaps been over-reacting to the group who tend to chatter over their work? Has he been setting unrealistically high standards and then become frustrated and angry when they are not achieved? Does he vary sharply from his colleagues in what he expects, so that children become confused and resentful in his lessons? Has he perhaps forgotten what it was like to be a child, and to be cooped up in a classroom several hours a day? Does he see every transgression in his class as a deliberate threat to him personally, rather than perhaps as an attempt to liven things up or to amuse friends or to let off steam after a previous lesson? Questions of this kind indicate that the teacher needs to think carefully about his own behaviour, and to talk to colleagues to see how his expectations and experiences compare with theirs.

Having reviewed his own behaviour (and we shall have more to say about this review in a different context shortly), the teacher may well come to the conclusion that it is this behaviour that has been at the root of the problem or problems. By taking offence where none was intended, by tending to nag children, by being over-serious or apparently unfair, by being over-dignified and pompous, by expecting too much, by being inconsistent, he may well have aroused resentment or confusion (or mirth) in his class, which in turn has prompted them into further unacceptable behaviour to which he has again over-reacted, and so the process has gone on. The first move in bringing this process to a halt, therefore, is to change his own behaviour into a more appropriate pattern.

Behaviour modification techniques
Nevertheless, there will, of course, be occasions when the root cause of the problem does not appear to lie with the teacher himself. He may have a child (or a group of children) in class who cause problems throughout the school, with whatever teacher they happen to be working. There may be other children who consistently contravene perfectly

reasonable standards of behaviour, or who make it clear they
have decided not to like the subject or the teacher or the
ways things are organized even before the first lesson has
got properly under way. With such children a useful technique known as behaviour modification can be applied. Behaviour modification technique (or more correctly techniques,
since there is a range of them available) has been operated
successfully in special schools and in clinical psychology
and has obvious application to the normal classroom. While
by no means a panacea for all ills, in spite of the extra-
vagant claims sometimes made for it, behaviour modification
has the advantages of allowing the teacher to analyse the
child's behaviour carefully, to identify the various factors
that seem to be responsible for sustaining this behaviour,
to formulate strategies for changing it in desired directions, and to monitor these changes as they take place. It
warrants our attention in some detail.

Behaviour modification techniques are based essentially
upon the operant conditioning model of learning (see chapter
8). That is, they work on the assumption that behaviour
which is reinforced or rewarded is likely to be repeated,
while behaviour which is not reinforced will tend to disappear. At classroom level this means that the particular
items of problem behaviour identified by the teacher and
seen to operate persistently in his lessons are being
reinforced in some way by the environment. It is this reinforcement that accounts for their persistence. Without it,
they would gradually fade away. Conversely, the opposite
behaviours that the teacher would like to see replace the
problem ones may be receiving no positive reinforcement at
all, which may account for their failure to become
established.

When operating a behaviour modification technique the
teacher's first strategy is to compile a list of the items
of behaviour he considers to pose problems in a particular
child. Against each of these behaviours, which are known as
'target behaviours', the teacher writes down what his own
response (or sometimes the response of the rest of the
class) usually happens to be. The list may end up looking
something like this.

Target behaviour	Teacher response
Child comes in class noisily at start of lesson.	Teacher says 'I've told you before not to make that row.'
Child does not get out his books when class is told to do so.	Teacher says 'Why can't you do as you're asked like everyone else?'
Child yawns loudly and shows obvious boredom.	Teacher comments sarcastically that of course child can't be expected to be interested.

Child makes facetious remarks.	Teacher stops lesson and asks him where he left his brains.
Child calls out a silly answer to a general class question.	Teacher tells him to put his hand up first.
Child puts up his hand and again calls out the silly answer.	Teacher asks him to wait until he is asked before offering answer.
Child says 'But you never ask me'.	???

And so the list goes on. The important thing is that we put
down in the left-hand column each of the specific behaviours
to which we take objection. It is not enough simply to write
'disruptive behaviour' or 'insolence', we need to know
precisely what constitutes this disruptive behaviour and
this insolent behaviour. Of course, if the list is a long
one we need not put down the exact remarks made by teacher
and child, as in our example, since in any case these will
vary from lesson to lesson, but we would nevertheless have
to enter all the child's separate behaviours and against
each one the teacher's usual kind of response. The list may
stretch to 20 or 30 items, but it will not be endless, and
often the teacher will be surprised at how short it is, with
the child obviously going through the same small repertoire
of behaviours ad nauseam each lesson. We may be just as
frequently surprised, when looking at the right-hand column,
at how stereotyped the teacher's own responses appear to be.
Though the language may differ somewhat each time, these
responses may seem always to consist of interrupting the
lesson and administering a reprimand (to which the child may
usually reply with a grin or a guffaw or a glance round at
his friends).

The origins of undesirable target behaviours
Looked at in this way, it will probably become clear to the
teacher that, far from being a punishment, his own responses
are actually serving as reinforcement for the very behaviour
that he wishes to eliminate. What he has hitherto regarded
as a stern rebuke is seen by the child to be nothing of the
kind. To understand why this is the case, we need to think
a little about the child's possible background. He may come
from a home where he learnt at an early age, through operant
conditioning, that the only way to obtain any kind of attention from others was to make a nuisance of himself. Adult
attention seems necessary to a child not only because it is
through this attention that he obtains satisfaction for his
physical needs, but because this attention makes him feel he
counts for something as a person. It enables him to feel
significant, and to develop some kind of self-esteem (see

chapter 12). Thus although the attention he obtains through his disruptive behaviour may be angry attention, it is nevertheless more acceptable to him (and therefore more reinforcing) than being ignored altogether. Through such reinforcement, this disruptive behaviour then becomes an established part of his behavioural repertoire.

When the child starts school, he may find that an apparent lack of ability means that he tends to receive less teacher approval and praise than children from more favoured homes (teachers are after all only human, and it may take a lot to realize the desperate need that a difficult and awkward child may have for approval and acceptance), and may be further conditioned into believing that the only way he can get attention is by making life difficult for others. Note that this is not by any means necessarily a conscious process. Like all conditioning, it can take place without the individual concerned being actually aware of what is going on. The child's behaviour is therefore not necessarily a deliberate attempt to create problems for teachers and parents and other children, but a conditioned response associated with the need for their attention. We call such behaviour 'attention-seeking behaviour', and recognize it as one of the major causes of classroom problems.

The teacher may find, of course, that attention-seeking behaviour in some children takes a non-disruptive but nevertheless still troublesome form. A child may constantly come up to the teacher in class, or constantly ask for help when none is really needed, or bring the teacher little gifts, or wait at his desk each morning to recount some item of gossip, or stay behind consistently after school to offer to do jobs around the classroom, or ask to be allowed to walk home with the teacher, or send the teacher little (sometimes anonymous) notes, often containing intimate messages of affection and admiration. These activities are a sign that the child needs help, but often the teacher finds that by rewarding his demands with extra attention they become more and more insistent until finally they reach a point where they are distracting the teacher from his work with the rest of the class.

With other children the problem may take a different form again in that the attention they seek is that of other children rather than that of the teacher. They may have found themselves to be rather unpopular in class, and to have discovered, once more by operant conditioning, that the way to get a measure of acceptance is to raise a laugh at the teacher's expense, or to show themselves to be 'tough' or 'daring' by disobeying the teacher or by offering insolence.

Identifying discernible behaviours

With all these problems, the initial procedure in a behaviour modification programme remains the same, namely for the teacher to list the individual behaviours that go to make up the problem, together with his own usual responses to these behaviours. The next step is to draw up a second list, this time of all the behaviours in the child or children concerned which he would like to encourage, and again to enter beside each what his own response usually is on the odd occasions when these behaviours have occurred. We give an example of this second kind of list below. To simplify matters, we have assumed we are talking about the same child dealt with in our earlier example.

Behaviour	Teacher response
Child comes in room quietly at start of lesson.	Teacher breathes sigh of relief and turns to lesson notes in order to make a quick start.
Child gets books out with the rest of the class when asked.	Teacher starts lesson.
Child puts his hand up to answer question without calling out.	Teacher ignores him and asks someone else for the answer, afraid that child will give a silly response and spoil what is so far a good lesson.
Child works quietly.	Teacher continues thankfully to let sleeping dogs lie.

Looking at this list, we can see that the teacher response to each of these desirable behaviours involves taking no notice of the child of any kind. Thus instead of his 'good' behaviour producing reinforcement in the form of teacher attention (and better still of teacher attention in the form of praise of some kind), it receives the punishment of being ignored. Small wonder that the child starts playing up again next lesson, and that the whole wearisome cycle starts all over again.

We have said enough to show that we cannot understand the child's behaviour (and work efficiently to change it) unless we study the teacher's behaviour as well, which brings us back to the point we were making earlier in the chapter. Problem behaviour does not exist in a vacuum. It is the centre of a matrix of forces that work to create and sustain it. If we wish to change it, then we must first make a change in these forces. In the case of the class teacher this means, at its simplest, reversing what he has been doing up to now and applying the first set of reinforcers to the second set of behaviours and vice versa. In other words, attention is withdrawn from the child when he is producing the problem target behaviours, and is offered to him when he produces their desirable counterparts. This means (to use our own examples again) that the child is ignored when he comes in the classroom noisily but greeted in a friendly fashion when he comes in quietly; that the teacher takes no notice of him (and does not interrupt the lesson) when he makes facetious remarks or calls out in class but directs a question to him when he puts up his hand; that the teacher starts the lesson without him if he fails to get out his books, but takes some opportunity of directing an encouraging remark towards him when he co-operates; and so on.

Gradually, over a period of time, the child's behaviours may come to be turned round, with the desirable ones replacing the undesirable. There will, of course, be relapses, and sometimes the child will appear to come half way to meet the teacher and then spoil things. For example, if he puts up his hand and is asked for an answer he might give way to the temptation of producing a facetious one as before. In this case the teacher simply ignores him and goes on to the next child. On the other hand, if he gives a sensible answer, even if it is a wrong one, the teacher gives him a smile and a word of encouragement before seeking the right answer elsewhere.

Objections to behaviour modification techniques

Three practical objections are often raised to behaviour modification techniques as follows.

First, although we may well be able to identify the unwanted target behaviours and work to eliminate these, the child may show none of the opposite, desired behaviours, making it impossible for us to start reinforcing them. This is true, but the answer lies in what is called 'shaping'. Shaping means that we take the behaviour closest to that which we actually desire and reinforce that instead. Thus although, for example, the child may never come into the room quietly, he will nevertheless at times come in more quietly than at others, and it is these relatively quiet entries that we will watch for and reinforce. Research shows that gradually, through shaping, behaviours come to approximate more and more closely to those we specifically want.

Second, with the best will in the world there are some undesirable behaviours that we cannot just ignore, such as those behaviours which directly harm another child, or extreme insolence which might set a thoroughly bad example to other children. This is a valid and important point. The teacher has a duty to the rest of the class as well as to the problem child, and cannot let the latter's behaviour unduly affect everyone else. Nor does he want this child to become a role model for the more impressionable of his classmates. But the answer is that he will only become such a role model if his behaviour is seen to be effective. Thus, if the teacher shows himself to be frustrated or upset or made angry, the risks are far greater than if he is seen to carry serenely on with the work of the class, without apparently bothering in the least about the minor silliness of one isolated class member.

Should the teacher feel, however, that the latter's misdeeds are such that they cannot possibly be ignored, then the exponents of behaviour modification techniques suggest he employs what has come to be called 'time out from positive reinforcement'. Without using such a grand title, teachers have, of course, been resorting to this strategy from time immemorial by sending children out of the classroom. Once a child is removed from the room, all opportunities for receiving positive reinforcement in the form of attention from teacher or classmates disappear. Since, as we have seen, it is this very need for attention that has probably caused the problem in the first place, the child soon tires of being outside the room and wants to come back in, but is given to understand that he can only do so if he enters into a kind of contract to be of good behaviour (and this behaviour gives the teacher the very opportunity for which he has been waiting to apply positive reinforcement). If the child breaks his contract, out he has to go again.

In general, sending a child out of the room has been frowned on in schools for some time now, on the reasonable grounds that (i) the child is missing lessons, (ii) if the classroom has a glass door he will divert himself and the children within visual range by pulling faces through it, and (iii) he may simply just decamp and go home. Research indicates, however, that these objections can be overcome if the school has a special room (a so-called 'time-out room') to which the child is sent or taken, and where he must sit quietly under the eye of a member of staff. Even in a large school there would normally be no more than one or two children in the room at any one time, and there will always be a member of staff with a free period who can be posted there for supervision. Research suggests that the child need only remain in the room for a maximum of ten minutes before being returned to his class, thus missing only a short amount of lesson time. If he misbehaves again, he goes back to the time-out room.

It is sometimes objected that many children will find it vastly diverting to spend their day shuttling back and forth from classroom to time-out room, but this does not appear to be the case. After the initial novelty, children find the process both boring and unproductive in that, as we have said, it deprives them of most of their opportunities for attention. Of equal importance, the rest of the class usually find lessons to be more relaxed and interesting in their absence, and there are thus mounting pressures upon them from their classmates to behave sensibly when they return to the room. Naturally, if a time-out room is to be operated, this must be school policy supported by all members of staff and under the direct control of the headteacher or of his deputies.

The third objection to behaviour modification techniques is that there is something dehumanizing about them, with the child's behaviour being 'manipulated' by those in authority instead of being under his own conscious control. Most teachers would understandably much prefer to be able to reason with a child and get him to change his ways by convincing him that this behaviour is ultimately negative and self-defeating. The problem is, as we said when discussing attitude change in chapter 9, that even when we can change children's attitudes by talking to them there is no guarantee that their behaviour will necessarily change as well. Extreme exponents of behaviour modification techniques would in fact tell us we are wasting our time by making appeals to the child and by assuming that he has the freedom to change himself at will. Whether we like it or not, they argue, the child's behaviour results from the undesirable reinforcement schedules to which he has been subjected in his life up to now, and if he is to be changed then we must do so by changing these schedules for something more appropriate.

This argument is made clear by looking again at what we had to say about operant conditioning in chapter 8. Nevertheless, we can use this behaviour modification technique without accepting them to be correct. Most teachers would probably prefer not to be drawn into a detailed debate on the matter anyway. Given their usual concern and sympathy for their children, they would for the most part prefer to use reason and persuasion in the first instance, and resort to behaviour modification only if such reason and persuasion consistently fail to work. In most instances, of course, happily they do work. Behaviour modifiers will say that this is because most children come from satisfactory homes in which reinforcement schedules have been correctly applied, and which leave them seeking not teacher attention as such (since they already receive ample adult attention at home) but teacher approval.

The token economy
Behaviour modification techniques are the basis for the so-called 'token economy' that is employed to good effect in some special schools. Since it is usually only operated in closed communities, such as residential institutions and clinical units where the staff can exercise a measure of control over most of the inmates' lives, we need not spend too long discussing the token economy, but the teacher needs to have some knowledge of how it operates since it figures quite extensively in the educational literature and gives us some pointers for more limited strategies in normal schools. Under the token economy, the child is awarded tokens (which can be actual discs or marks entered in a book or any other suitable arrangement) each time he evidences the desired behaviours, and loses tokens each time he evidences the undesired. At the end of an agreed period he trades in his tokens for a treat of some kind (e.g. a certain number of tokens might win him extra television viewing time, twice that number might win him extra sports facilities or a trip into town, and so on). Thus the child has tangible evidence of the rewards his improved behaviour is bringing him, and

through operant conditioning this behaviour should become
an established part of his repertoire.

The token economy is essentially a form of 'performance
contract'. The child enters into a contract with his
teachers to produce certain kinds of behaviour in return for
certain kinds of reward. If he breaks his part of the contract, he loses the rewards. Thus he may contract not to be
aggressive towards others, and be given a token for, say,
each half day in which he refrains from offering an aggressive act. Each time he does assault another child he loses a
token. Performance contracts have also been shown to operate
satisfactorily in normal schools. The report card is an
example, where the child contracts to be of good behaviour
in each lesson, has the card signed by the teacher at the
end of the lesson, and is then able to exchange the card at
the end of the week for a clean bill of health. The main
problems with the report card are, first, that the reward at
the end of the week is not sufficiently impressive for some
children with severe behaviour problems, so that they seem
quite prepared to be put on report week after week and,
second, that it does not focus sufficiently on individual
items of behaviour. As we have seen, it is important that we
isolate each separate item of a child's difficult behaviour
and try to apply appropriate negative reinforcement to each
one. A card that simply covers the whole of a child's
behaviour during the whole of the lesson fails to do this.

Research indicates nevertheless that problem children
can be helped by the performance contract in the normal
school, particularly if we can enlist parents and the local
community in general as a source of rewards. This time,
instead of merely putting the child on report, we contract
with him that he will refrain from certain specific behaviours (e.g. failing to hand in work, insolence in class,
aggression towards another child). If he has shown a number
of these behaviours, then we concentrate on one at a time,
and eliminate that before going on to the next. After the
end of each lesson, if the child has fulfilled his part of
the contract, the teacher signs the record card. At the end
of the set period, the child exchanges his satisfactory
record (or more properly contract) card for the treat agreed
with him at the beginning of the contract. This could be an
outing or a favourite meal or a gift supplied by the parents
or a morning spent at the local garage or the local riding
stables, or some privilege conferred by the school itself.

The immediate objection to the performance contract in
the normal school is that one cannot go on with it indefi-
nitely, and the child may lapse when one day we have to
stop. The answer here is that while he is on the contract he
receives not only the agreed reward but all kinds of other
incidental (i.e. uncontrived) reinforcers. He will find that
teachers generally respond to him more favourably now he is
on better behaviour; that he begins to get higher marks now
that he is keeping up with the work; that his parents are
pleased with his improved progress; that other children

become more friendly towards him; that lessons are more interesting; that his self-esteem improves and so on. As his horizons broaden, it is these incidental reinforcers that will sustain his new behaviour after the contract has come to an end.

A second objection sometimes raised to the performance contract is that it is unfair on the law-abiding child, who sees trouble-makers getting reinforcers denied to him. It is sometimes even suggested that children will deliberately misbehave in order to be put on a contract. In the main, though, this objection is unfounded. The law-abiding child is usually already receiving the relevant reinforcers, because he comes from a home background and enjoys a relationship with the staff in school and together these factors ensure that these reinforcers are given as a matter of course. This is, indeed, the crux of the whole matter. To date, the problem child behaves as he does because he has learnt that for him this is the only way to get the things he wants. Our aim is to help him unlearn this lesson, and to discover instead that, as with the law-abiding child, socially acceptable behaviour can be a much better way of obtaining valued rewards.

General points on behaviour modification

Before we leave the general topic of behaviour modification techniques there are two further points to make. The first is that these techniques are not exclusively for use with disruptive children. The Underwood Report (1955) defines maladjustment as applying to the child who is 'developing in ways that have a bad effect on himself or his fellows', and this clearly covers the isolate child, the withdrawn child, just as much as it covers his more obtrusive classmate. In the case of the isolate child, behaviour modifiers suggest that we often unwittingly reinforce his isolation in the early school years, and thus help to make it an established part of his behaviour, by constantly approaching him and soliciting his participation in activities. As soon as we obtain this participation, we tend to move away to attend to other children who need help. Thus, unwittingly, what we are doing is positively reinforcing his isolate behaviour (by an approach response) and punishing his social behaviour (by withdrawing from him as soon as we have got him working with others). We should in fact seek to reward him with attention not when he is on his own, but when he makes a move in the direction of others. When he makes such a move we should draw him into activities, and stay with him as long as possible, thus rewarding him for his participation. True, we cannot always be with him once we have got him socially involved, but again incidental reinforcers should soon start to operate (e.g. access to the interesting activities that are going on at the tables where the other children are, the feeling of being part of a group, the friendship of other individuals), and these should serve to strengthen and sustain his social behaviour.

The second point we have to make is that extreme exponents of operant conditioning theories see behaviour modification as a kind of mechanical manipulation of the child, with the latter having no real power voluntarily to change his own behaviour. This harks back to the third of the three objections to behaviour modification that we discussed earlier. There is, however, no need for the teacher to accede to this view. He may prefer to see the child as being well aware of what the teacher is doing, and as making conscious decisions to go along with it as a way of getting what he wants from other people. This view sees the child as a free agent rather than simply as a unit acted upon by others. Such a view is perfectly legitimate, and need be no bar to the use of behaviour modification techniques. It does, however, presuppose a different and more optimistic (some would say nobler) concept of man, a concept which argues that he has free will and is not merely the victim of circumstances. This raises important philosophical issues that unfortunately we have not the space to pursue here. All we can say is that it is impossible to prove whether man has free will or not using the limited and precise methods of science. The German philosopher, Immanuel Kant, proposed some two centuries ago that the important consideration was therefore the demonstrable fact that man behaves 'as if' he has free will, and it is doubtful if even the strongest supporters of the mechanistic view advanced by operant conditioning theorists can dispute this. In any case, to most teachers, classroom problems seem to arise from a deal too much free will rather than from its absence!

Other aspects of class control and management

Often, of course, problems of class control and management stem not from individuals but from the class as a whole. Even the most conscientious and work-orientated class can be boisterous on occasions, or can be bent on testing out a new teacher and finding the limits to which he will allow them to go, or can become frustrated and angry with a particular teacher's methods. The best way of discussing these problems is to sketch out a number of general ground rules that have relevance in most classroom situations. These are given below, in no special order of importance, and are couched for convenience in the form of direct instructions to the teacher.

1. INTEREST THE CLASS: in general a class that is absorbed in its work will not want to cause problems. In addition, the class members will act disapprovingly towards any of their number who try to distract their attention.

2. AVOID PERSONAL MANNERISMS: we drew attention in our discussion of interaction analysis in chapter 12 to the fact that mannerisms of speech, dress or gesture on the part of the teacher can prove intensely irritating (or comic!) to children who have to sit and watch them, and may well lead to negative behaviour on the part of the class.

3. BE FAIR: real or imagined injustices can breed resentment and hostility in children. Fairness means ensuring that any loss of privileges, etc., is appropriate to the original misdeed (and is wherever possible related to it in some way, so that the child can see a causal link between the two); it means behaving towards children consistently so that they know what to expect, and it means keeping one's word.

4. BE HUMOROUS: this does not mean that the teacher tries to become some kind of knock-about comedian, but simply that he is prepared to laugh with his class (though not when the joke is on some unfortunate individual member of it), and to introduce humour into his teaching material where suitable. It also means that he is prepared to laugh at himself at times, both in class and in private. We all inadvertently do things on occasions that strike others as amusing, and the ability to join in the general laughter is a sign of security and a realistic sense of self-worth. The person who flies into a rage if others ever laugh at him suggests that he sees this laughter as a threat to an already depressed sense of self-esteem. And, of course, the teacher who is always standing on his dignity with children is in a sense challenging them to find ways of puncturing this dignity. It is sometimes said that all authority is faintly ridiculous, particularly where it verges on the pompous. A healthy sense of the realities of his position, helped along by memories of how he himself felt about members of staff when he was a child, is a great asset to any teacher.

5. AVOID UNNECESSARY THREATS: we have already drawn attention to the undesirability of relying upon threats to control children. But on the occasions when threats are felt to be unavoidable, they should always both be suited to the misdemeanour and realistic. Wild threats to, say, bring the class back on Saturday morning are simply an invitation to children to carry on with the prohibited behaviour for the sheer pleasure of seeing how the beleaguered teacher gets out of putting them into practice. And where threats are uttered they must be carried out. Constant offers of 'one last chance' soon weaken the teacher's standing in the eyes both of himself and of the class.

6. BE PUNCTUAL: a teacher who arrives late for a class not only sets the children a bad example but also may have to quell a riot before the lesson can begin. Punctuality at the end of the lesson is of equal importance. Children soon resent being constantly late out for break or last in the lunch queue or late for the next lesson.

7. AVOID ANGER: the teacher who loses his temper may say and do things in the heat of the moment that he comes to regret later. His loss of self-control will also be noted with interest by the class, and the experience committed to memory for general dissemination later through the school grapevine. Before long the teacher will find other classes,

with the true instinct of research scientists, trying out
various ways of getting him to mount a repeat performance.
Certainly all teachers on occasions will feel the need to
speak sharply to children, but this is quite different from
heated outbursts that do nothing either for the teacher's
standing in the school or for the state of his physical
health.

8. AVOID OVER-FAMILIARITY: the line between friendliness and over-familiarity can be a narrow one, but it is
better to start off rather formally with a class and become
more intimate as one gets to know them better; to behave,
indeed, much as one does when making any new friends.
Research shows that many weak teachers start off the other
way round, and then desperately try to tighten up when they
have already made an over-lax first impression. But too
much familiarity at any time is rather confusing to children, who know that the teacher is not really one of them
since he represents the authority of the school, and leads
inevitably to their feeling they have been deceived when the
time comes for him to try to assert this authority.

9. OFFER OPPORTUNITIES FOR RESPONSIBILITY: if all
responsibility rests with the teacher, then it is not
surprising that children behave irresponsibly when not under
his direct supervision. Offering children responsibility not
only shows them they have the teacher's confidence, it also
leads them to realize that what happens in the class is
their concern just as much as it is his.

10. FOCUS ATTENTION: general appeals for quiet or order
in a classroom are of much less value than calling out the
name of the child or children most directly involved, and
thus focussing the attention of the class. In the silence
that follows, the teacher can then issue his next instructions. One is much better able to focus attention in this
way if one quickly learns the names of all class members. A
seating plan is of help here (together with instructions
that children must occupy the same seats in the room until
told otherwise!). Getting to know children's names quickly
also demonstrates importantly one's interest in them as
individuals.

11. AVOID HUMILIATING CHILDREN: quite apart from the
potential psychological damage to the child or children
concerned, humiliation attacks a child's status in the eyes
of the rest of the class, and he may well use various
strategies, all aimed at the teacher's authority, in order
to re-establish it. Note here that children often find
sarcasm humiliating, and it has the added disadvantage of
inviting an equally flippant reply. The teacher who repri-
mands a child for looking out of the window by asking him
if he is watching for Little Bo Peep can hardly grumble if
the child answers that yes, he is, because he missed her on
her last visit.

12. BE ALERT: an important characteristic of the teacher with good class control is that he appears to know at all times exactly what is going on in his classroom. This impression that he has eyes in the back of his head comes from the fact that he not only has keen eyesight and good powers of concentration but is physically mobile. He moves frequently around the room, and insists children wait in their places until he arrives when they have difficulties with their work rather than allowing himself to become besieged, like an inexperienced general, by a determined detachment of hand-waving children who effectively isolate him from the main theatre of action.

13. USE POSITIVE LANGUAGE: the emphasis should always be upon what we want children to do rather than upon what they must refrain from doing. Thus we say 'Come in quietly' rather than 'Don't make so much noise', 'Look at your books' rather than 'Stop turning round', and so on. Negative language suggests activities to children that previously might not have entered their heads, and thus focusses the attention of even the law-abiding class members in the wrong direction.

14. BE CONFIDENT: the writer recalls that the only piece of advice he was given on class control when receiving post-graduate teacher training was that the teacher always gets what he expects from the class. He thought at the time that this advice was a little on the thin side, but in fact if one has to be restricted to only one useful tip this is perhaps as good as any. The teacher who goes into a class with a hesitant, tentative maner suggests to the children that he is expecting trouble and is probably accustomed to being disobeyed. Very well, the class think to themselves, he will not be disappointed. If, on the other hand, he is able to give the impression of a person who is used to getting on well with chidren, then once again the children will be inclined to take him at face value and offer co-operation. So even if the teacher is feeling inexperienced and apprehensive, the moral is not to show it.

15. BE WELL ORGANIZED: a well-organized lesson, with adequate material carefully prepared and with all equipment to hand and in good working order is far less likely to be disrupted by misbehaviour than one that even the teacher himself concedes bears a certain resemblance to a shambles. The shock to the teacher's own nervous system, when working with a potentially difficult class, of finding that the tape-recorder has the wrong mains plug, or that there are no pencils, or that a vital page is missing from his lesson notes, is in any case something to be avoided by all but the most masochistic amongst us! Good organization also means making clear to children exactly what is expected of them in the way of getting out or putting away apparatus and equipment before they start to do it, and while one has everybody's attention. It also means only releasing them in

carefully controlled groups to carry out these chores,
rather than letting them all rush at once and then
shouting vainly for order.

Good classroom organization also means that children
know where things are kept and that they each have clear
duties and responsibilities, both to deal with the normal
running of the classroom and the sudden emergencies when
things get spilt or broken. It also means planning lessons
carefully so that the practical activities are within the
scope and the competence of both teacher and class and never
threaten to get out of hand. Many practical activities which
seem such a good idea in prospect appear in retrospect
little short of disastrous. If in doubt try them out first
on a modest scale with a co-operative class. And finally it
means keeping the theoretical side of the lesson within
bounds too, and making sure it gives way to practical work
before it has gone on too long. A rough rule-of-thumb is
that the teacher should restrict the theory part of any
lesson to about a minute or a minute-and-a-half (depending
upon subject matter and the children's abilities) for each
year of the children's age. Thus 10-15 minutes is ample for
ten year olds, while with a sixth form one could go up to
25 minutes or so.

16. SHOW THAT ONE LIKES CHILDREN: many people, recalling their schooldays, have favourite stories of ogres of
whom they went in awe, and of kindly, well-meaning souls
whose lives they made a torment, but these stories are only
remembered because they are unusual. For the most part, the
teacher who relates satisfactorily to children has the gift
of conveying to them his sympathy and understanding and the
delight he gets from his job. He indicates to them that he
wants them to succeed at his subject not because this
demonstrates his own competence but because success is
important to them. Once they are convinced they have his
support, children will respond, as in any relationship, with
their own co-operation and esteem.

No excuse is offered if the above 16 points appear in format
(though not, let us hope, in substance) rather like the
hints and tips for teachers that used to appear in peda-
gogical manuals between the wars. It is often said nowadays
that inexperienced teachers should not be given guidance of
this kind, but should be allowed to develop their own teaching styles in response to the particular groups of children with whom they work. One does not hear it said, however,
by headteachers or by others faced with the problem of
helping a new member of staff over the first hurdles of his
professional life. Certainly we are not denying that the
teacher must be equipped to act as a researcher, able to ask
himself as we have indicated throughout this chapter why a
child behaves as he does and what strategies appear most
suited to his problems. But he should also be equipped with
the kind of generalizations, based upon psychological theory

and upon the results of classroom-based research studies in both Britain and USA, that we have tried to present above. As he grows in experience he will find there are others, and with experience he will be able to work out what is best for him and what seems most appropriate to his particular school and his particular children, but at the beginning he requires a knowledge of these generalizations if he is to make a sound start in the profession and provide effective learning opportunities for his class.

The application of punishment

While on the subject of class control we must make some reference to the use of punishment (perhaps sanctions would be a less emotive term) in the classroom. In general, any punishment carries with it certain risks of which the teacher should be aware, namely:

* the use of punishment of any kind may damage the relationship the child has with the teacher, perhaps permanently. This is particularly true if the punishment is seen as unfair (see point 3 above) or designed to humiliate (see point 11);
* the child may develop strategies, such as untruthfulness, to avoid punishment. This is not only potentially bad for the child's long-term personality development, but it also threatens the existence of any trust between teacher and child;
* punishment teaches the child the undesirable lesson that it is acceptable for the strong to impose penalties upon those weaker than themselves. This is particularly true of corporal punishment, and many local education authorities are now rightly banning its use in their schools.

Effective sanctions

Nevertheless, it would be unrealistic to pretend that sanctions of a limited kind are not seen as necessary by many teachers, and que ions are often asked as to what is effective and what is not. I have already indicated in the discussion of behaviour modification techniques that the careful use of positive reinforcement, together with some punishment, is often enough to produce the desired turn-around in behaviour by most children, but it would be incorrect to think that the teacher would class these techniques as punishment. By punishment, the teacher usually means some kind of imposition or some loss or privileges placed upon the child, usually as a deterrent to breaking school rules or as a prompt response to some particularly unacceptable piece of classroom behaviour.

The most frequently used item of punishment, and often the most effective with co-operative children, is the verbal rebuke. The teacher rebukes the child, the child accepts the rebuke, and the matter is finished with there and then. The reason why it is so effective is that children appear to have a need (Carl Rogers, 1951, regards it as an innate need) for adult approval. Granted that they are already receiving adequate adult attention, they now require it to be approving attention. This is probably linked in with their need for social acceptance (see our discussion of Maslow's work in chapter 9) and their need for self-esteem (see chapter 12). Thus the child feels uncomfortable and alienated from the social group if the teacher withholds approval from him, particularly if the teacher is liked and respected by the class. The child also, since such teachers are usually regarded by children as sound judges, suffers doubts as to his own worth, and is anxious to remove such doubts by producing the desired behaviour and quickly moving back on to good terms with the teacher.

Where stricter sanctions are thought necessary, a number of studies show that informing the parents of this lack of approval is very effective, since the child now feels that if he continues with his misbehaviour he will encounter increasing disapproval at home as well. One strategy operated with an apparently high rate of success is for the headmaster to prepare a letter for the parents, and then summon the child to his room and read it over to him. The child is then given the option of eliminating the unwanted behaviour or allowing the letter to be sent. Not surprisingly, he usually chooses the former alternative. The letter is then placed upon the file, and sent only if the child fails to keep his part in what is a form of performance contract. It is important that, as with behaviour modification techniques, the letter spells out in precise detail the form of behaviour to which the school takes objection, and the child is left in no doubt as to the way in which it must be remedied.

Schools use a variant of this strategy every year (or sometimes every term) when the school reports are sent out, and it is surprising that some teachers fail to recognize the impact that such reports can have upon a child's relationship with his parents. The problem with the school report, however, is that usually it is not specific enough in stating exactly where the child has gone wrong in his work or in his general conduct, and does not give clear directions on how these problems can be put right. Vague phrases such as 'could do better' (which doubtless applies to us all) or 'has done little work this term' (which may be as much the teacher's fault as the child's) succeed only in upsetting the parents and confusing the child. What is needed instead is practical guidance which the child can put into effect and of which he can be reminded from time to time by his parents. If the parents can also be enlisted into giving the child more specific help within the home, so much the better. Some teachers, for reasons that are not always clear or particularly defensible, are rather reluctant to draw parents into co-operating in their children's formal education. This is unfortunate because a few minutes of parental time every evening (e.g. spent hearing the child read or say spellings or tables, checking he does his homework and takes the right books to school, or testing him on revision exercises) bring enormous benefits to the child. Most parents are only too happy to co-operate, provided they know exactly what it is they are supposed to be doing and can speak to the teacher from time to time to make sure that all is going well.

Parents' evenings are also of great value here, though whether the knowledge that his teachers are going to report unfavourably on him orally, when the interchange may be softened by the natural sympathies created by face-to-face contact, carries quite the same impact upon the child as seeing things recorded in writing is not clear. One frequently voiced objection to both parents' evenings (see the comments in chapter 2) and to school reports is that the parents one most wants to reach do not seem to care. This objection is true, but only for a very limited number of cases. Most parents are deeply involved with their children, whether they normally show it or not. This is (ideally) because they love them, but there are other complex forces frequently at work too. They may want their children to be a credit to them, or to do as well as the children next door. Or they may feel that their children's failure, academically or socially, reflects back on them, or that there is a danger they will get into tr uble with the police or cause damage that will have to be paid for, or that they will be unemployable when they leave school and so on. Each of these reasons, for better or worse, helps to ensure that for the vast majority of parents the progress of their children is of a great deal more than passing interest.

The law of natural consequences

Another sanction often used effectively in schools is what Rousseau called 'the law of natural consequences'. Like behaviour modification this fits in with the operant conditioning model, but it differs from behaviour modification in that the consequences stem from the environment rather than from the teacher himself. Susan Isaacs, in her work at the Malting House School back in the 1930s, demonstrated the effectiveness of natural consequences, particularly with very young children. If a child carried on playing with a toy, for example, when he was called to lunch then he was allowed to remain where he was, but discovered when he did come to the table either that the food was cold or the second helpings had all gone. If a child was careless or destructive and broke something then he had to do without it for a certain interval of time. Obviously there are numerous occasions, particularly where physical safety is involved, when a child has to be protected from the natural consequences of his actions, but in general the law of natural consequences is of value because it allows children to see the causal link between their own actions and the undesirable results sometimes associated with them. In young children such an association is only likely to be set up if action and result occur close together in time (see our discussion of operant conditioning in chapter 8), but as the child grows older he becomes able to reason out the association for himself. Essentially, the law of natural consequences suggests that if a child commits some misdemeanour he will learn from it more rapidly if, instead of being punished by the imposition of some arbitrary penalty, he is allowed actually to experience the consequences of his misdemeanour. He then comes to understand the very good reasons why it is regarded as a misdemeanour, and thus grows in knowledge and in a sense of responsibility.

The only caution here (apart from the one of physical safety) is that children should not experience the natural consequences for too long. Thus if, as an act of thoughtlessness or vandalism, a piece of school equipment (say, a television set) is broken, the children are told clearly that they will be without it for a definite time (say two weeks), since members of staff are too busy to see to its repair straight away. If they are without it for much longer than this, then they will get used to the deprivation and, when they think about it at all, will by degrees come to see it as a deliberate act of revenge against them by the staff. Thus the impact of the lesson will be lost.

Discussion of the law of natural consequences leads us on to the point that missing breaktime or games or being in detention are not very effective in stopping specific problem behaviours because there is often a long interval of time between the behaviours and the penalties, and the two are in no way linked through natural consequences. Such penalties would work best if the children had brought them on themselves by, say, taking too long to clear up at the end of a previous lesson. Punishing a child by putting him into detention and stopping his games for offences which have no obvious link with these punishments will certainly make the games master or mistress apoplectic, but will do nothing to help the child learn why his offences are unacceptable.

roup behaviour
roblems

Sometimes problems of class control stem more from the behaviour of certain groups within the class than from the behaviour of individuals. Each of the children, on their own, may seem amenable and friendly enough, but put them in the group and they appear to become different people. When this happens, again the teacher's first task is to list the problem behaviours. As with individual behaviour modification programmes, it may well be the teacher's own responses that are sustaining these behaviours or perhaps creating the preconditions for them, for example by poor organization (see point 15 of our list on general aspects of class control), or by over-familiarity (point 8) or by unpunctuality (point 6) or by standing too much on dignity or losing self-control (points 4 and 7 respectively). If this does prove to be the case, then the remedy lies at least in part with a change in the teacher's own behaviour, as it does indeed if the children are simply bored (point 1 on our list) or are perhaps defending themselves against feelings of failure either in that specific lesson or in school generally (see our discussion of such matters at various points in Part III).

Whatever the causes of the group's behaviour, and whatever the methods the teacher uses to remedy it, there are some additional general strategies that prove helpful.

* As an early priority, identify the most influential member or members of the group. We discussed leaders and stars in chapter 13, and the points we made there will be relevant to this exercise. Once these individuals (the 'gatekeepers', as Lewin terms them) are picked out, the teacher is able to concentrate particularly upon them (using, for example, individual behaviour modification techniques) in the knowledge that once they are won over the rest of the group is likely to follow.
* Where possible, divide the group up as much as possible. This means directing them to sit apart from each other in class, involving them in different class and homework projects and so on. We have already stressed in chapter 13 the part played by frequency of interaction between children in establishing friendships; by reducing the proximity between group members the teacher tends to break up the cohesion within the group and to encourage group members to form friendships outside it. Ideally, of course, the children should not be made directly aware that this is the teacher's policy.
* Interact with the children as much as possible as individuals. Each child is therefore helped to form his own personal relationship with the teacher, which again serves to break up group cohesion in that it destroys the corporate image of the teacher that the group has hitherto maintained.
* See as much of the children as possible, again as individuals, outside the context of the classroom; for example, in out-of-school activities. This weakens their tendency to associate the teacher exclusively with the classroom.
* Where possible avoid direct conflict with a group member in front of the rest of the group. The need to maintain prestige and status in the eyes of the rest of the group will make him far more difficult to deal with than when he is on his own. This means doing one's best to defuse the situation at the time and to deal with it later. Assuming one is not using carefully formulated behaviour modification techniques with the child concerned one might, if he for example attempts insolence in class, tell him pleasantly that one can see he is upset about something and he can come and give the details after the lesson. Failure to do homework, which could be a simple ploy to 'see what the teacher will do about it', would

be met in the same way by an invitation to come and talk about it at the end of the lesson, together with the strong hint that the class has better things to do with its time than to listen to explanations now. Homework, after all, is done for the child's own benefit and not for that of the teacher (who has to spend many patient hours of his own time each week marking it), and the child should not be allowed to feel that he is somehow 'getting at' the teacher when he fails to produce it. If the teacher prefers not to be constantly heard inviting children to see him after the lesson (this can become a ritual, with class members vying with each other on the number of times they can be kept back afterwards!) he can simply call the child to one side as he leaves the room when the bell goes with the rest of the class.

Occasionally, the teacher may have to break up a physical confrontation between two children in the class. This raises special problems (particularly when the children are somewhat bigger than the teacher!) but the secret lies in quick, decisive physical action. With a confidence he may not feel the teacher strides across the room and parts the children, holding on firmly to the one who appears to be the aggressor. Verbal appeals for detente before making his intervention are usually little use, but once he has one of them under restraint he talks calmly to them both, using again the formula that he can see they are upset (or angry) about something, and he would like to hear about it when everyone has calmed down. Behaving in an angry manner himself is inappropriate. Unless he outscores both children in terms of muscle-power by a ratio of a least two to one his own anger is only likely to inflame matters further, and he may end up looking rather foolish as the children hurl him contemptuously to one side, the better to get on with their business. Calmness, and a hint of humour, are far more appropriate. Above all, no threats of dire punishments awaiting both protagonists should be voiced. Not unreasonably, they may feel that if they are to be punished anyway for fighting, then they might as well get the fight over and done with first. Once the teacher feels the tension relaxing, then he releases his grip on the child he is holding. And he keeps his promise to hear both sides of the story, sympathetically and patiently, either then or when the children have had time to calm down further.

hool refusal

One further important item of problem behaviour remains to be discussed, namely school refusal. The child who consistently absents himself from school for no good reason is signalling clearly that the consequences to himself of not going to school are outweighed by the consequences of going. Again, as with all the problems we have discussed so far, our first question each time must be why should this be the case? The answer usually takes the form of one or more of the following.

* The child may be the victim of bullying by other children.
* He may go in fear of a particular member of staff or of punishment of some kind.
* He may associate school so strongly with failure that school refusal is a way of protecting his self-esteem.
* There might be problems at home keeping him away. He might have to look after a younger brother or sister, or help in some kind of family business. Or he could be afraid of physical violence between his parents or that one or other of them might desert if he is not continually on hand.
* His parents may feel they are working off some kind of obscure grudge against society by preventing the child from attending school.
* He might, though this problem is still fairly rare, be taking alcohol or other drugs that leave him in no fit state to attend school (this is more likely to affect afternoon than morning classes).
* He might be involved in some sort of delinquent activity.
* He might just be plain bored, and be looking for something more exciting to do with his time.

Note that again, as we have said in connection with other problems, school refusal is therefore not exclusively the child's own difficulty. Other children, parents, teachers, school organization or delinquent peer groups can all be involved. And, of course, once a child starts staying away he falls further and further behind in his work (making school seem even less attractive), and becomes ever more enmeshed in a web of lies and deceit (making it difficult for him ever to confide in people and ask for help).

Once we have identified the probable cause of school refusal (often no easy task in view of these lies) then we can take appropriate remedial action. Usually punishing the child is unjustified, because as we have seen the problem is often not of his own making. Worse, punishment can be actually counter-productive in that the child comes to associate school even more closely with unpleasant experiences, thus making him more inclined to stay away than ever and to lie in order to cover his tracks. Getting the child to attend should not be seen as a battle between him and the school which the latter must win at all costs. Rather he should be helped to see that the school is there to understand and sympathize with the fears and the anxieties that he may be feeling over the problems in his own life, and is there to help him live with them. Even where a child appears to be staying away out of sheer boredom there is little to be gained by meeting him in head-on conflict. Usually, if the child is determined enough and cares nothing for the school or its sanctions, and has parents who care even less, then he will win in the end and just stay away for good. A more appropriate strategy is to try to work out with the child why school bores him to such an extent and seems so irrelevant to his needs. Schools that take the trouble to lay on special courses for their less able school leavers (and it is in this group that school refusal is most apparent) usually succeed in reducing the problem to relatively insignificant proportions.

It must be emphasized that school refusal is definitely not a candidate for treatment by the more obvious behaviour modification techniques. It might be tempting to believe that if we ignore a child's absence he will realize he has failed to draw attention to himself and will start attending again, but there is little evidence that this happens very often in practice! Occasionally, certainly, the child may stay away because he wants to be noticed, but usually even here there are other more important reasons (quite apart from the question of why should he have to go to these lengths to be noticed?), and the school must take vigorous and resourceful action, long before things get too bad, to find out what these are. Once these have been established and steps taken to deal with them, some form of performance contract can be entered into, of course, and this is often a useful additional strategy, particularly in very intractable cases. But perhaps the overriding consideration to keep in mind is that schools are there for the benefit of children, and if they choose not to avail themselves of this benefit we must look not only at the child himself but at the way in which this benefit is being packaged.

References

Isaacs, S. (1930)
Intellectual Growth in Young Children. London: Routledge & Kegan Paul.
Isaacs, S. (1933)
Social Development in Young Children. London: Routledge & Kegan Paul.
Rogers, C. (1951)
Client Centered Therapy. Boston: Houghton-Mifflin.
Underwood Report (1955)
Report of the Committee on Maladjusted Children. London: HMSO.

Questions

1. Why is it inadvisable to rely upon threats in order to keep class control?
2. Why is problem behaviour, in a sense, in the eye of the beholder?
3. Why should the teacher first examine his own behaviour when considering the causes of problem behaviour in children?
4. What is the reason suggested by operant conditioning theorists for the persistence of unwanted behaviour in children?
5. Describe the teacher's first strategy when compiling a behaviour modification programme.

6. What is 'attention-seeking behaviour' and why is an understanding of this behaviour important for the teacher?
7. What forms does attention-seeking behaviour take in the classroom?
8. What do we mean when we say the teacher should reverse his behaviour and withhold reinforcement from unwanted child behaviours and apply it to those that are wanted?
9. Define the term 'shaping' as applied to behaviour modification programmes.
10. Discuss the meaning of 'time out from positive reinforcement'.
11. What are the principles underlying the operation of the 'token economy' and the 'performance contract'?
12. What are 'incidental reinforcers' and why are they important in sustaining desirable changes in child behaviour?
13. Is the concept of the child as a free agent still tenable within the context of behaviour modification theory?
14. Suggest why a sense of humour appears to be an important quality in the teacher.
15. Why is it important to get to know the names of one's children as quickly as possible?
16. List the risks occasioned by the use of punishment with children.
17. Have school reports a value?
18. Give some of the reasons why parents are likely to be concerned about their children's progress and behaviour in school.
19. What is the 'law of natural consequences'?
20. Why is it important where possible to avoid direct conflict with group members in front of the group?
21. Give some of the considerations to be kept in mind when stopping physical conflict between children.
22. List some of the reasons for school refusal.
23. What do we mean when we say that school refusal 'is not exclusively the child's own problem'?
24. Why is punishment often counter-productive when dealing with school refusal?
25. Can performance contracts usefully be used in remedying school refusal?

Additional reading

Good, T.L. and Brophy, J.E. (1978) Looking in Classrooms (2nd edn). New York: Harper & Row.
An excellent book, dealing practically and sensibly with all aspects of classroom behaviour.

Clarizio, H. and McCoy, G. (1976) Behaviour Disorders in Children (2nd edn). New York: Crowell.

Williams. P. (ed.) (1974) Behaviour Problems in School. London: University of London Press.

Leach, D.J. and Raybould, E.C. (1977) Learning and Behaviour Difficulties in School. London: Open Books.
> These three books are more specifically concerned with the causes of behaviour problems in children, and are all strongly recommended. They also deal with the treatment of behaviour problems as well.

Poteet, J.A. (1973) Behaviour Modification: A practical guide for teachers. London: University of London Press.
> This is a more specific text in the area of behaviour problems, which forms a good introduction to behaviour modification techniques.

Gnagey, W.J. (1968) Psychology of Discipline in the Classroom. London: Macmillan.

Dollar, B. (1972) Humanizing Classroom Discipline. New York: Harper & Row.
> Two more useful books on discipline.

Rutter, M. et al (1979) Fifteen Thousand Hours: Secondary schools and their effects on children. London: Open Books.
> Geared more specifically towards the comprehensive school, it contains much useful information.

Upton, G. and Gobell, A. (eds) (1980) Behaviour Problems in the Comprehensive School. Cardiff: Faculty of Education, University College Cardiff.
> This has the advantage that many of the contributors are experienced practising teachers, able to discuss a number of strategies that have actually been demonstrated to work within their schools.

Duke, D. (ed.) (1979) Classroom Management (Seventy-eighth Yearbook of the National Society for the Study of Education, Part II). Chicago: University of Chicago Press.
> A good introduction to classroom management.

O'Leary, K. and O'Leary, S. (eds) (1977) Classroom Management: The successful use of behaviour modification. New York: Pergamon.
> Another recommended text, that also deals with behaviour modification techniques.

Brophy, J.E. and Good, T.L. (1974) Teacher Student Relationships: Causes and consequences. New York: Holt, Rinehart & Winston.
> This looks comprehensively at all aspects of social contact between the teacher and his class.

Walker, J.E. and Shea, T.M. (1980) Behaviour Modification: A practical approach for educators (2nd edn). St Louis, Mo: Mosby.
> Probably the best practical text on behaviour modification techniques for teachers.

16

Teacher Personality and Characteristics
David Fontana

A major emphasis throughout this book has been that, if we wish to understand child behaviour, we must consider not only the child himself but the various influences that are brought to bear upon him. Within the context of school, the most important of these is usually the teacher. Research into teacher personality, and by this we mean the whole range of personal characteristics that may affect the way in which the teacher goes about his task, has not been as systematic as research into child characteristics, but nevertheless there are a number of useful inferences that can be drawn.

Teacher effectiveness

Before we look at these, we should say that any discussion of teacher characteristics merges into a discussion on teacher effectiveness in general, which in turn raises the question of what we mean by the 'good' teacher. The present writer has pointed out elsewhere (Fontana, 1972) that even experienced teacher educators are by no means agreed amongst themselves on the answers to this question. Is a 'good' teacher a person who helps children's socio-emotional development, or who helps their cognitive development, or who teaches them subject knowledge or who gets them through examinations? And how, apart from the last named, do we measure whether a teacher is doing these things to our satisfaction or not? Just as we cannot understand the child's behaviour to the full without taking the teacher's behaviour into account, so we cannot understand the teacher's without taking into account that of the child. Some teachers may be very successful at, for example, fostering socio-emotional development with a particular group of children, but may be less good with another group where the problems, though no more extreme, are of a different kind. And the simple presence of one very disruptive child in a class may materially affect the teacher's performance with everyone else. So how and with what particular group of children do we attempt to assess teacher competence?

Teacher educators, faced with the difficult task of deciding who should enter the teaching profession and who should not, use the teaching practice as a formal examination, and attempt to assess students in a variety of teaching situations. A number of rating scales and systems have been devised to help them, and careful note is also taken of the recommendations of the headteacher and of the staff in the school in which the practice takes place. But even here there is a wide margin of error, and the correlation between final teaching practice grades and success and happiness in the profession five years later has been shown by a number of studies to be disappointingly low. It seems probable that interaction analysis (see chapter 13), with careful records kept over the years of precisely what teacher behaviour seems to go with what kind of responses in children, will do a great deal in the future to help us devise profiles of the successful teacher, but it must be pointed out that all teachers, and all children and all groups of children, exist as individuals, and we can never be certain that our generalizations about success will hold good in all instances. Thus it seems unlikely that, in spite of arguments to the contrary, we will ever have a precise 'science' of teaching, which allows us to predict accurately in all cases whether individuals will become good teachers or not.

Assessing teacher characteristics

With this caution in mind, we can now look at the evidence that is currently available and see what it appears to tell us. One of the most extensive investigations into teacher personality and its relationship to teacher effectiveness was carried out by Ryans (1960) in the USA. Ryans constructed a special Teacher Characteristics Rating Scale, and found that the successful teacher tends to be warm, understanding, friendly, responsible, systematic, imaginative and enthusiastic (a somewhat daunting catalogue of excellence), but that the importance of these qualities seems to decrease with the age of the children being taught. In other words, secondary school children seem able to accommodate better to teachers low in these qualities than do those in primary schools. This makes sense, because normally the older a child becomes, the better able is he to take responsibility for his own work, and the more resilient is he in his relationships with adults. These findings are of great importance when it comes to refuting the argument that it is 'easier' to teach young children than older ones, but we should remember in fairness that Ryans was not looking into the importance of specialist subject knowledge, which might play a larger part in overall teacher success with secondary school children than with those in the primary school (though primary teachers can reasonably counter that they have to know more about a wider range of subjects than their secondary colleagues).

In spite of the extensive nature of Ryans' research, correlations between the qualities indicated and teacher success were not very high, however. That means that even in primary school some teachers without high scores on these qualities nevertheless produced satisfactory results. This could be, to hark back to the points already made, because they had particularly well-motivated or particularly resilient children, or it could be (and this again indicates the difficulty of research in this area) that the adverse aspects of their influence upon children take time to show through, and that in consequence they are not apparent until these children have become the responsibility of another teacher. Or it could be that there are other qualities, not measured by Ryans, that tend to compensate in some cases for the absence of those which he did manage to identify. Research by Rosenshine (1970) and others into both parent-child and teacher-child relationships suggests that a reasonably uncritical approach to children's work may be one of them. We have said enough about self-esteem and about the devastating effects of constant failure upon children to indicate why this may be. A child who is frequently criticized by a teacher, especially if he is already inclined to be low in self-esteem, will lose confidence in his own ability and will tend in consequence to under-achieve. Thus a conscientious teacher who believes in pressurizing children to come up to a certain standard could conceivably do more long-term harm to the progress of particularly vulnerable children than a teacher who seems less conscientious and more inclined to let children find what he chooses to describe as 'their own level'.

Research also indicates (e.g. Bennett's discussion of teacher styles, 1976) that successful teachers are more likely to prepare their lessons well than are those who are less successful, to spend more time on out-of-school activities, and to show more interest in their children as individuals. Note, however, that this last quality does not mean that they become emotionally involved with their children. Teachers who rely upon their relationships with children to compensate for emotional deprivations in their personal out-of-school lives are being unfair both to themselves and to the children concerned. It makes it difficult for the former always to behave with professional objectivity, while the latter may feel they are having demands made upon them which embarrass and confuse. The teacher should certainly feel liking and affection towards his children, but this must go hand-in-hand with a professional detachment and sense of responsibility.

Emotional security in the teacher

What we are saying, in effect, is that another quality of the successful teacher is that he is himself emotionally mature. This means not only showing the behaviours advocated in the above paragraph, but also not being drawn into petty feuds and squabbles with children individually or in groups. Harder still, it means not being upset by the behaviour of children towards him even when, as sometimes happens, there appears to be reasonable cause for such upset. Children can at times be very thoughtless in their dealings with teachers, particularly teachers who are inexperienced or who have the reputation of being unable to keep order. Indeed 'thoughtless' might be considered by some as a euphemism, but it is doubtful if stronger language is really justified since children are not experienced enough to be able fully to empathize with what such teachers are going through. Anyway, be this as it may, the fact that a teacher shows himself to be upset only makes matters worse, with children now deliberately picking on him with a kind of awful glee. The teacher, on the other hand, who shows himself quite unmoved by even the most Machiavellian strategies mounted against him soon finds these strategies lose their appeal, and he is able to deal quickly and effectively with any subsequent sporadic fresh outbreaks.

Emotional security of this kind is linked to what in psychology is called 'ego-strength'. Ego-strength is a compound of realistically high levels of self-esteem and self-confidence, and an underlying composure that allows problems to be tackled calmly and objectively (see chapter 12). This applies, in the case of the teacher, not only to day-to-day classroom problems but to the many other challenges of professional life, such as relationships with parents and with colleagues, decisions on career and promotion matters, sudden crises (whether they be accidents in the playground or visits of advisers and inspectors), and dealings with the headteacher and with school governors. Further, ego-strength allows the teacher to rise above the failures and disappointments that, along with the achievements and the successes, are an inescapable part of school life. It allows him to analyse and learn from the former without torturing himself with feelings of guilt and inadequacy, and allows him to take delight in the latter without letting himself relinquish his sense of proportion.

Turning to standardized tests of personality, we find that there is no consistent evidence to show that successful teaching correlates with either significant levels of extraversion or significant levels of introversion. Common sense would suggest that the extreme introvert would not do well in the classroom, since he would find the social demands made upon him unacceptable, but it is doubtful if such a person would be attracted to teaching (at least to school teaching) in the first place. As we pointed out in chapter 9, however, the personalities of children must also be taken into account at this point, with extraverted children perhaps relating better to an extraverted teacher, and introverted children perhaps relating better to a teacher who tends towards introversion.

Teacher attitudes

In addition to the various aspects of teacher personality discussed above, there is some evidence that successful teachers have what are often referred to as 'desirable professional attitudes'. This means that they have positive attitudes towards responsibility and hard work, that they conceive of their role as extending beyond the business of simply teaching children subject matter and beyond the narrow hours of 9 a.m. to 4 p.m., and that they have a positive attitude towards the subjects in which they specialize and towards the place of the teacher in society.

A number of scales exist to measure the more obvious aspects of teacher attitudes, and in particular, of course, their attitudes towards children. One of the most widely used of these in Britain is that devised by Oliver and Butcher (1968), which scores teachers on three dimensions, namely naturalism, radicalism, and tender-mindedness. Student teachers interestingly tend to increase their scores on all three of these dimensions during the years of their training, and then to reduce their scores once they take up their first posts. This suggests that the realities of professional life serve to make teachers generally less child-centred, more conservative, and more tough-minded. This does not necessarily mean that teachers lose what we might call their idealism, but simply that they may find themselves working in less than ideal conditions, conditions in fact that at times may seem to render some form of compromise unavoidable. They may, for example, not only be battling against adverse environmental conditions (inadequate accommodation and facilities, over-large groups, problem children who really need specialist help), but may also find themselves working with colleagues whose philosophies and methods are somewhat different from their own.

This ability to compromise, however much we may regret its necessity, may be an important quality in the successful teacher. Cortis (1973), in a follow-up study of teachers during their early years in the profession, found that those who showed most career satisfaction and seemed to be making the best professional progress appeared able to put school before self and to submerge minor differences with colleagues in the interests of establishing within the school those coherent, consistent policies that enable children to feel secure and confident. By contrast, Cortis found unsuccessful teachers tended to be more self-orientated and to be more dominant, suspicious and aggressive.

Teacher styles

Another fruitful line of research is to look at teachers' preferred teaching techniques (i.e. at their 'teaching styles'). At a time when the debate about formal and informal teaching methods and their respective influences upon children's learning has not yet been resolved, such an exercise is particularly relevant. In the main, formal methods imply an emphasis upon the subject to be taught, with the teacher's task being to initiate children into those aspects of the subject deemed essential, while informal methods imply an emphasis upon the child, with the teacher's task being to identify his needs and to make available learning experiences appropriate to them. Formal methods usually involve a relatively high level of teacher talk and of individual work on the part of the children, while informal methods rely more upon project and group work, and give the child wider opportunities for choice and responsibility.

This kind of distinction is, of course, something of an over-simplification. Some teachers may employ a mixture of both approaches, while as Bruner (1976) points out, one can have formal lesson objectives, with the skills and techniques that one wishes the child to acquire clearly identified, but can work to achieve them by informal methods. This would involve, for example, providing the child with the necessary apparatus and equipment and setting him certain problems, whose discovery would lead him towards the kind of learning that one has carefully specified in advance. These and other related points are fully discussed in chapter 8, and we raise them here only to indicate that the terms 'formal' and 'informal' may, in fact, not be specific enough for our purposes. An alternative is to drop these terms altogether and to use instead the indirectness measures developed by Flanders in connection with his classroom interaction analysis instrument (see chapter 13). An 'indirect' teacher is described by Flanders as one who accepts children's feelings, uses praise and encouragement, and uses pupils' ideas. The 'direct' teacher, by contrast, is described as one who tends to lecture, to give directions, and to criticize pupils. A number of studies (Bennett, 1976, provides a good survey) show indirectness to be positively related to pupil achievement gains and to positive pupil attitudes, particularly in the case of more able pupils. Note, ho ever, that indirectness does not necessarily imply a low level of teacher talk (one of the supposed features of the informal classroom), and indeed some studies suggest that a higher frequency of teacher talk is related to enhanced growth of non-verbal creativity in children.

The value of teacher talk

This last finding is of some importance, since it indicates the extent to which some children are stimulated by listening to an adult. In recent years, particularly in the primary school, there has been a tendency to discourage teacher talk per se and to emphasize the importance of children's own activity. Teacher talk, as we indicated in chapter 15, should never go on for too long, but rather than classifying it as good or bad in itself we should place emphasis upon what the teacher actually says. A teacher who can talk interestingly and relevantly, and who can stimulate children's imagination and thinking, is a far better aid to learning than any amount of misguided and rather desultory project work. He also has the advantage, possessed by no other teaching aid, of being almost infinitely flexible. He can respond to questions, introduce a whole new topic because children show a sudden interest in it, express humour, excitement, encouragement, awe and any other human emotion. True, he can do this with individuals as he moves round the class and need not do it in the more formal 'teacher talk' situation with everyone listening, but this means that he can disseminate ideas only slowly, and cannot use the question posed by one child as a learning opportunity for the whole class.

Perhaps, therefore, we should add another attribute to the list of those already used in this chapter to describe the successful teacher: namely, that he should be a good talker. In the classroom context, being a good talker means being a disciplined thinker, with a mind that can concentrate creatively upon one group of relevant ideas and not keep darting off at a tangent. It means knowing when to provide an answer and when to leave the answer incomplete, so that the children are stimulated to make their own enquiries. It means using the voice expressively and fluently, and couching one's spoken thoughts in a form appropriate to the level of the children with whom one is working. And it means above all knowing when to stop, so that the children are directed to their practical work at a point when they would still like to hear more. Thus they never tire of teacher talk, but instead experience a pleasurable anticipation each time it is introduced into a lesson.

To be good at teacher talk may seem a tall order, since it is not the same thing at all as simply being a talker. The rather quiet teacher, who finds ideas do not come to him very fluently when he is on his feet, may even find this talk something of a strain, and may prefer to keep it to the absolute minimum. But if some teachers never acquire the art of good teacher talk there is no reason why they should not acquire the art of good listening. Every teacher must be able to encourage children to talk, and to hear them out with patience and interest, prompting only where necessary, and showing the child that he and his ideas are entitled to a hearing. Even when those children who would monopolize classroom debate, either through natural forcefulness or through a desire for attention, have to have their remarks brought to a close, the good teacher is able to do this in a way that protects the child's self-esteem and leaves him ready to make a contribution again next time.

Introducing variety into teaching methods

What we are saying, therefore, to go back to the debate about formal and informal teaching methods, is that a teacher can be non-directive, and a good talker and a good listener whatever methods he is using. There is also no reason why the teacher should not vary his methods depending upon the subject he is teaching. Bennett (1976) produces impressive evidence to show that, in the primary school at least, progress in reading, mathematics and English (the so-called basic subjects) seems in the main to be more rapid where formal methods are used, but Haddon and Lytton (1968, 1971) show that general creativity (at least as measured by divergent thinking tests, which are by no means infallible:

see chapter 7) tends to be more marked in informal than in formal primary schools, and that the differences are maintained even after transfer to secondary schools. This suggests that although work in the core curriculum of English and mathematics might benefit from being subject-centred, with the teacher offering children clear standards which they must attain before they can be said to be literate and numerate, in other subjects the work can be more open-ended and less judgemental, with the emphasis upon each child making a more personal, subjective response.

Note that we are not saying that such subjects as English and mathematics should cease to be enjoyable, while everything else on the curriculum should be seen as 'fun'. There is no reason at all why more formal methods, related carefully to the children's level of ability and understanding, and employing relevant and imaginatively used material, should not prove as acceptable as less structured methods. Interestingly, we have very little evidence of what teacher styles children themselves actually prefer in the long term. We do know, however, that they grow weary of situations in which they are unsure what is expected of them and in which their work is constantly being interrupted by the activities of others, and this can certainly happen more readily in an informal than in a formal environment.

Conclusion

The above arguments make clear that there is one final teacher quality to which we must draw attention, namely that of flexibility, the ability to suit one's methods to the subject and to the children one is teaching. If the teacher is too rigid, or has a doctrinaire belief that his methods are right and those of anyone who disagrees with him are wrong, then he will be depriving his children of a range of possible learning experiences, to their disadvantage and to his own. Most teachers never stop learning, and are always ready to consider new ideas and new techniques on their merits. If these new ideas often look suspiciously like the resurrection of old ones discarded years ago, then the teacher is still prepared to give them a fair hearing. In education, as in human psychology itself, no one has a monopoly of the truth, and the person who closes his ears to informed debate and to alternative views is the poorer for it.

References

Bennett, N. (1976)
  Teaching Styles and Pupil Progress. London: Open Books.
Bruner, J.S. (1976)
  The styles of teaching. New Society, April.
Cortis, G.A. (1973)
  The assessment of a group of teachers in relation to earlier career experience. Educational Review, 25, 112-123.

Fontana, D. (1972)

What do we mean by a good teacher? In G. Chanan (ed.) Research Forum on Teacher Education. London: NFER.

Haddon, F.H. and Lytton, H. (1968)

Teaching approach and the development of divergent thinking abilities in primary school children. British Journal of Educational Psychology, 38, 171-180.

Haddon, F.H. and Lytton, H. (1971)

Primary education and divergent thinking abilities - four years on. British Journal of Educational Psychology, 41, 136-147.

Oliver, R.A. and Butcher, H.J. (1968)

Teachers' attitudes to education. British Journal of Educational Psychology, 38, 38-44.

Rosenshine, B. (1970)

Evaluation of classroom instruction. Review of Educational Research, 40, 279-300.

Ryans, D.G. (1960)

Characteristics of Teachers. Washington, DC: American Council on Education.

Questions

1. Why is it difficult to define and assess the 'good' teacher?
2. List some of the qualities of the 'good' teacher identified by research.
3. What does 'emotional maturity' mean in the teacher, and why is it an important characteristic?
4. Give examples of what you take to be desirable professional attitudes.
5. How would you distinguish between so-called 'formal' and 'informal' teaching styles?
6. Is 'teacher talk' a good or a bad thing?
7. What are the qualities of a good listener?
8. Why is it important that the teacher should be able to show flexibility in his professional life?

Further reading

Brophy, J.E. and Good, T.L. (1974) Teacher-Student Relationships: Causes and consequences. New York: Holt, Rinehart & Winston.

Recommended reading for the last chapter, and is relevant here again.

Fontana, D. (1977) Personality and Education. London: Open Books.

This has also been recommended earlier in this book.

Solomon, D. and Kendall, A. (1979) Children in Classrooms: An investigation of person-environment interaction. New York: Praeger.

This is more specifically focussed on the topic in hand.

Bennett, N. (1976) Teaching Styles and Pupil Progress.
London: Open Books.
   This book also contains much relevant information.

Simon, B. and Galton, M. (1980) Progress and Performance
in the Primary Classroom. London: Routledge & Kegan Paul.
   A recent study which bears out some of the points made
   in the chapter on the effective teacher. Of particular
   relevance is their research-based finding that it is the
   teachers who spend most time on class teaching who ask
   the most open-ended, thought-provoking questions, and
   whose pupils make best progress in mathematics, reading
   and language. Their book, which contains the main
   findings to date of the long-term study of primary
   schools currently being carried out at the University of
   Leicester, makes interesting reading for all teachers.

Index